DESTRUCTIVE ENGAG T

Southern Africa at War

Editors Phyllis Johnson and David Martin

Foreword by Julius K. Nyerere

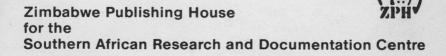

Zimbabwe Publishing House
for the
Southern African Research and Documentation Centre

Zimbabwe Publishing House
P.O. Box BW-350
Harare, Zimbabwe

© chapters by individual authors
this collection, SARDC 1986

First published by ZPH/SARDC 1986

ISBN 0 949225 31 2

Front cover photo of railroad in southern
    Angola sabotaged by South African action,
    courtesy of the DIP/MPLA-PT
Back cover photo of graves in Lesotho for
    victims of South African raid on Maseru,
    courtesy of WP
Cover design: David Martin, Phyllis Johnson,
    Tracy Dunn
Maps: Marjorie Wallace
Paste-up: Tony Namate, Aaron Bore
Imposition: Victor Kazembe

Typeset by Colorset
Printed in Zimbabwe by Zimpak

Contents

Acknowledgements

The escalating violence within South Africa now features almost every day in the media throughout the world. But very little space is devoted to the economic and social impact on neighbouring states. This is an attempt to redress that. We have sought to do so as factually as possible. Even as we go to press, new evidence is emerging of South Africa's behaviour in the region and the *apartheid* regime has recently staged fresh attacks on its neighbours.

The attacks on a housing estate in Gaborone, an office block and a suburban bungalow in Harare and a United Nations refugee camp in Lusaka were portrayed in a London evening newspaper as an offensive against 'terror bases'. In a region where it is *apartheid* which is conducting the acts of international terrorism, the headline could have more accurately read, 'Terrorists attack Commonwealth capitals'. The eloquent Foreword to this book puts regional terrorism into its international focus and context.

During the course of this study, many people in the region have given hours of their time to enhance our understanding. We hope they will regard it as time well spent. We have received considerable moral support from the governments of Mozambique, Tanzania, Zimbabwe and Angola, and from their officials.

There are some specific people we must mention. The first are our co-authors. For their knowledge, their commitment and their patience, we are grateful, and we believe that we have together contributed in some small way to a broader understanding of the circumstance of southern Africa.

We are grateful to Diana Cammack for coordinating our research and documentation, to Masimba Tafirenyika and Joanne Ambridge who brought order to our mounting archive, to Joan Thompson for typing and organizing our workload, and to Kephas Kuipa for his efficiency as social convener. Again, to the patience and speed of Batsirai Munyaradzi and Thokozile Muchena in typesetting, the staff at Colorset, Ross Photo and particularly the printers at Zimpak commanded by Colonel Ivey (Retd). To the staff of ZPH, enough cannot be said of their talents and their camaraderie.

Finally, this book would not exist without the material support of the Swedish International Development Agency (SIDA), and the moral support of two Swedish friends, Dag Ehrenpreis and Anders Bjurner, whose determination and faith made possible the study of *Destructive Engagement: Southern Africa at War*.

The Editors

Authors

ROK AJULU is currently a research student at the Institute of Development Studies (IDS), University of Sussex. Born in Kenya, he lived and worked in Lesotho for over seven years. During that period he was a part-time lecturer in the Departments of History, Politics, and the Institute of Labour Studies at the National University of Lesotho for four years. He is also a freelance journalist who has covered Lesotho and southern Africa for many years.

DIANA CAMMACK has been research co-ordinator for this three-year study of *Destructive Engagement*. She did her doctoral thesis at the University of California in 1983 on early twentieth century labour and political history in South Africa, entitled 'Class, Politics and War'. More recently she has been studying contemporary regional politics and is currently engaged in research on Mozambique's 'displaced persons'. In April 1986 she presented several papers on this aspect of the 'human face of destabilization'.

REGINALD HERBOLD GREEN is Professorial Fellow at the Institute of Development Studies (IDS), University of Sussex. He has been active in teaching and research consultancy in Africa since 1960, and is an advisor to SWAPO, UNICEF, World Council of Churches, CIIR and the International Centre for Law in Development. He is a member of SADCC's Liaison Committee and an advisor to SADCC, as well as to several of its member states.

MARGA HOLNESS has worked with the People's Movement for the Liberation of Angola (MPLA) since the 1960s and on the staff of both Angolan presidents. She headed the Angola Information Office in London and is now working with ANGOP, the Angolan news agency. She is the author of numerous articles and translator of several books.

PHYLLIS JOHNSON is a long-time student of southern African affairs. As correspondent of the Canadian Broadcasting Corporation (CBC) from 1973 to 1980, she travelled widely in eastern and southern Africa. She has since written several articles, produced a television documentary and co-authored two books, *The Struggle for Zimbabwe: The Chimurenga War* and *The Chitepo Assassination*. She is a director of Zimbabwe Publishing House.

PETER MANNING was a full-time functionary of the South West Africa People's Organization (SWAPO) in Namibia between 1976 and 1978. Since 1978 he has been based in the London office of SWAPO as Information Officer.

DAVID MARTIN has written about southern Africa for over 20 years, as Africa correspondent for the London Sunday newspaper, The Observer, as correspondent for several other organizations including The Guardian and the BBC, and as assistant editor of the Daily News, Tanzania. He has written several books including *General Amin, The Struggle for Zimbabwe: The Chimurenga War,* and *The Chitepo Assassination.* He is a director of Zimbabwe Publishing House.

WILLIAM MINTER is a writer and contributing editor of *Africa News.* He has taught in Tanzania and Mozambique, and now lives in Washington DC. He has just completed a book on Western policies toward southern Africa, *King Solomon's Mines Revisited: Western Interests, Images and Policies in Southern Africa* (forthcoming). He has written numerous papers and articles, two monographs and an earlier book, *Portuguese Africa and the West.*

ABDUL SAMAD MINTY is a South African who went to Britain in 1958 and, together with others, founded the Anti-Apartheid Movement (AAM) of which he has been Honorary Secretary for over 20 years. He has been active in international anti-apartheid campaigns, participated in numerous UN and other conferences, lobbied governments and organizations on behalf of the AAM and addressed the UN Security Council. Since 1979 he has been involved in the World Campaign against Military and Nuclear Collaboration with South Africa, which was initiated by the AAM at the suggestion of the UN Special Commission against Apartheid and whose founder patrons include the leaders of the Frontline States.

VELLA PILLAY is an international economist. He is economic adviser to a major international bank, director of the Greater London Enterprise Board, and vice-chairman of the British Anti-Apartheid Movement. He is the author of *Apartheid Gold* (United Nations) as well as numerous papers and studies on international economic and monetary relations, and on the South African economy.

CAROL B. THOMPSON is Associate Professor of Political Science at the University of Southern California. She worked in Tanzania 1977 to 1979 and in Zimbabwe 1984 to 1986. Her writing includes many articles on the Southern African Development Coordination Conference (SADCC) as well as the book, *Challenge to Imperialism: The Frontline States in the Liberation of Zimbabwe.*

The views expressed in this book are those of the authors and not of governments, organizations or institutions whom some of them represent.

Foreword

When is war not a war? Apparently when it is waged by the stronger against the weaker as a 'pre-emptive strike'. When is terrorism not terrorism? Apparently when it is committed by a more powerful government against those at home and abroad who are weaker than itself and whom it regards as a potential threat or even as insufficiently supportive of its own objectives.

Those are the only conclusions one can draw in the light of the current widespread condemnation of aggression and terrorism, side by side with the ability of certain nations to attack others with impunity, and to organise murder, kidnapping and massive destruction with the support of some permanent members of the United Nations Security Council. South Africa is such a country.

The people of South Africa have been fighting against racial oppression for most of this century. Their petitions, peaceful processions and demonstrations, and even their campaigns of civil disobedience, have been met with ever increasing repression and violence. But their humanity will not be denied. While the organised nationalist movements have in recent years succeeded — at tremendous human cost to themselves — in carrying out some sabotage of military targets, the mass of the people are spontaneously rejecting the laws and instruments of *apartheid* by the sheer force of their will and their numbers. The daily death toll does not stop them. Nor does the torture from which they suffer when detained or imprisoned. They are challenging the guns of *apartheid* with their own blood and with stones picked up from the streets.

At the same time, the people of Namibia are also fighting for freedom from domination by the *apartheid* government of South Africa. In legal terms they at least have won the whole world to their side. But their nation continues to be occupied illegally, and the most powerful states of the world prevent any serious external action from being taken against the occupier – or even side with the oppressor. South Namibian people's freedom struggle, and the armed struggle, continue under the leadership of SWAPO.

The intensification of the freedom struggle within South Africa during recent years does owe something to the advance of African liberation to the borders of that country. For Mozambique, Angola and Zimbabwe had to win political freedom by an armed struggle against racist administrations; their success renewed the hope and self-confidence of the South African people. Tied to South Africa by inherited economic and communication links as these countries were – and are – they are a beacon of freedom clearly visible from the towns of the *apartheid* state, and even from the Bantustans to which millions of South Africans have been banished.

It is that beacon of freedom which the *apartheid* state seeks to put out by its direct aggression, or by organising, arming and unleashing dissidents and mercenaries, and by using its undoubted strength to exert economic pressures on its neighbours. Its objective in all cases is so to destabilise those young nations that their leaders are forced to become puppets of the South African government, and to act on its behalf in the suppression of the African liberation movement. And in the process of trying to achieve this, South Africa is happy if it is able to cause such misery and suffering among the people of the free states that their governments get a reputation of incompetence and incapacity which dims the clear light of freedom shining across their borders.

All the neighbouring states – and some further away – have fallen victim to this aggressive South African policy. Botswana, Lesotho and Swaziland have not been exempted because of their geographically determined inability to do more than speak against *apartheid* and give a first haven for refugees from South Africa. Zambia has not been left alone on the grounds that it does not have a border with the *apartheid* state. Zimbabwe, which has from the beginning of its independence declared its inability to allow the South African liberation movements to operate from its territory, has still been subjected to South African sabotage of its economic and military facilities and to systematic murder campaigns against its citizens – both white and black. Mozambique and Angola, however, have been the foci of very special and sustained attack. They have been subjected to all the miseries of continuing aggressive war since the moment of their birth as independent states – or in the case of Angola, before that. Their declared philosophy of Marxism-Leninism, and their border on the Atlantic or Indian Ocean, caused them to be of special interest both to South Africa itself and to those who believe they have a right to control those oceans.

This book, *Destructive Engagement*, indicates something of the nature and the meaning of the aggression to which the victim states have been subjected. It provides in each case what I believe to be incontrovertible evidence of South African responsibility for the forms of this attack. And thirdly, it shows the involvement of the United States of America, both in the aggression against Angola, and in support of what President Reagan once described as 'our ally', South Africa.

The cost to the Front Line States has been immense. In financial terms, one estimate is 10 billion US dollars worth of damage done to the infrastructure and the economies of SADCC members. All are poor countries whose resources are in any case inadequate to provide the minimum of essential services to their people and to invest in future development.

Further, this estimate takes no account of the peoples of the border states. The total number killed is not known; the larger number who have been wounded in South African-inspired attack is uncounted – especially as many of these have no ready access to medical facilities despite the efforts of their governments. The people who have lost their homes, who have been terrorised against working in their fields, who have been bereaved or left to care for disabled family members, whose food has been destroyed – all this suffering is uncounted. And when widespread drought was added to the problems of the Mozambique government, the food convoys were attacked so that relief could not get through although sufficient food had been mobilised. Very many thousands of people died as a result.

The victim countries have received no compensation or special assistance in the light of these attacks. They have been left to carry the burden virtually unassisted. Sometimes even verbal support is denied them, as the United States of America and some European powers respond to a direct South African attack by mealy-mouthed condemnation of violence 'on both sides'. And when the victims of aggression seek military assistance from the only countries which will supply it – Cuba and the USSR and its allies – they are accused of falling into the 'Soviet sphere of influence'.

Despite all this, the beacon of freedom is kept alight in southern Africa. The struggle goes on. The condemnation of *apartheid* continues

to be expressed with commitment by the free nations bordering South
Africa even as they bury their dead from the latest raid.

Of course there have been set-backs in the struggle. The Nkomati
Accord was forced on the government of Mozambique by the
overwhelming pressure of innumerable murderous attacks from
South African forces and the South African surrogates, combined
with 'mediation' and 'assurances' from American and British
diplomats and conditional promises from the South Africans. So the
ceremony took place, the Mozambicans breathed a sigh of relief in the
expectation of an end to the attacks on them, and P.W. Botha went off
on a tour of Europe as 'a reasonable man'.

But the South African support for MNR continued unabated. The
attacks on the people of Mozambique intensified and spread more
widely; so did the attacks on SADCC communications facilities within
Mozambique. And those Western countries which urged the need for
peace on Mozambique – which had never wanted war – have done
nothing and said nothing. During this month of April 1986, a bomb in a
night club in Berlin has led to intense intelligence and diplomatic
activity, culminating in US air raids on Tripoli and Benghazi on the
grounds that whoever did it Libya was ultimately responsible. A car
bomb outside civilian residences in Maputo, where South Africa's
responsibility is undisputable, is met by silence from the same powers
which call upon the Third World to condemn terrorism.

Mozambique is non-aligned, poor, weak, and after 22 years of war is
held together only by the commitment and will-power of its government and people; for the West, South Africa is 'our ally'. So terrorism
stops being terrorism; aggression stops being aggression; solemn and
signed commitments undertaken by the strong and 'mediated' by the
stronger, stop being international commitments.

Lesotho, too, can with impunity be economically strangled to death
by South Africa until its defiant prime minister is overthrown and a
new military government accedes to South Africa's political demands.
The Western world does nothing and says nothing. Even after that, a
South African refugee, qualified in Lesotho and working in the legal
system of Lesotho, is subjected to 15 minutes armed attack on his
house and property (which he and his wife fortunately survived).
Nothing will be said by the great campaigners against terrorism; the
government from which the attacks emanate will not even be
subjected to an orchestrated media campaign of abuse.

And on Swaziland what can be said? At a time of great national
trauma arising from the death of King Sobhuza it was in the way of

South African ambitions. But there are still people, including some in prominent positions, who struggle to make a reality of Swaziland's independence.

Yet despite all this suffering, and some set-backs, the struggle against *apartheid* continues. For it is pre-eminently an internal struggle, supported morally, politically and diplomatically by South Africa's neighbours to the utmost of their capacity – severally and jointly. But these countries are incapable of supporting a military attack against their southern neighbour even if they wished to do so – as South Africa knows.

The greatest upsurge of internal opposition to *apartheid* began *after* Nkomati. It finds expression in all the major urban areas of South Africa and even in the Bantustans; incidents of sabotage take place as far south as Cape Town. Yet there are no guerrilla invasions across the borders of South Africa. The few freedom fighters who do return home sneak across the long borders despite all the attempts of the South African guards to patrol thousands of miles of bush land: and if the highly equipped South Africans cannot stop these valiant people how could their poorer and weaker neighbours be expected to do so? Those naturally concentrate such limited border defence power as they possess on trying to stop incursions from South Africa – and even on that the record shows little success.

The real offence of Angola, Botswana, Lesotho, Mozambique, Swaziland, Zambia and Zimbabwe – and any other countries within reach of South African power – is their existence as proudly independent African states. As such they have the temerity to back up the demand of the Organisation of African Unity for an end to *apartheid*. They dare to demand world action against the cancer of *apartheid* and to succour those who flee from its persecutions. Through SADCC they try to loosen the economic and communications bonds which tie them to South Africa, and to increase their self-reliance through regional co-operation.

In addition, these countries proclaim that, being no longer colonies of Western Bloc nations, they intend to follow a policy of Non-Alignment. In so doing they compound the offence of their existence. For the West is accustomed to regarding Africa as its 'sphere of influence', and regards with suspicion any African country which looks at the world and determines its policies without the prism of western-slanted spectacles.

An American diplomat once urged upon me the threat to African independence constituted by Cuban troops in Angola. When I asked why Cuban troops were more of a danger to Africa's freedom than French troops elsewhere in the continent, he replied, 'France is a Western country and we are the leaders of the Western world'. South Africa too is regarded as part of the 'Western world'.

So genuine non-alignment (in the case of Angola even the prospect of it), and especially the acceptance of help against South African attacks, condemns South Africa's external victims to being just that – victims. And on occasion, particularly in the case of Angola, there is irrefutable evidence – some of it quoted in this book – of active US involvement in the attacks on independent African nations. Instead of being restrained by those whom they regard as their friends and who themselves claim to be upholders of the integrity of nations, the South African aggressors are encouraged, or even joined in making the attacks.

In the light of so much hypocrisy, so much duplicity, and so much indifference to the sufferings of southern Africa, why write and publish this book?

There are those who are ignorant because they are wilfully blind, and those who are ignorant because they have lacked an opportunity to know. It surely is not possible that the administration of the United States of America, and the governments of major European powers, do not know the facts and the effects of the economic and military attacks against the free states which share a border with South Africa or Namibia. Apart from everything else, the Great Powers have satellites covering the whole of southern Africa. In some instances our infrastructure is so poor that it is likely that these external powers know about the event and the problem before the home government. Nor is it possible for the Superpowers to be unaware that South Africa is the instigator, the organiser, the financier and supplier for virtually all the attacks which purport to be made by rebels – apart, that is, from the ones initiated by South Africa directly or by the US itself. The major Western powers are there, in South Africa, and they have a privileged position in that racist state.

Yet perhaps we do an injustice to presidents and prime ministers; for they cannot know everything which is done, or not done, in their name. Perhaps the evidence does need to be set out so that those who know the real sincerity of these leaders' opposition to terrorism and to aggression can draw to their attention what is happening in southern Africa? If so, this book should help.

But in any case it is quite certain that millions of people, including many in leading or responsible positions in democratic Western countries, are unaware of what has been happening – and what is still happening – in southern Africa. Some of them may genuinely not know that the *apartheid* regime they abhor is threatening the very existence of the states whose independence they welcomed so short a time ago. Some may not realise that the identification of South Africa with anti-communism is the most powerful propaganda for communism which exists in southern Africa. They may not understand the pressures in favour of an anti-Western alignment which are being exerted on the non-aligned states by the attacks from the West's friend and ally, albeit one which is acknowledged to have an unpleasant racist domestic philosophy. And other genuine people may have come to believe that the South African president's talk of 'reform' really means a change of heart on the part of *apartheid's* leaders.

For such people this book is intended. The evidence is collected and summarised; the major themes are extensively documented. The reality behind the 'nationalist' and 'democratic' claims of UNITA and MNR is made clear. So are the facts about the sequence of events in Angola which has led to Cuban troops serving in that African country for more than 10 years. And so on. The economic aspects of the struggle are not forgotten, and the argument about sanctions is re-examined.

This book will be equally valuable and is equally intended for all those who, in numerous official and unofficial fora, have tried for years to draw attention to the dangers to world peace which exist in southern Africa. Its approach is openly and unapologetically political; it states the case for those independent nations and people under attack because of their opposition to *apartheid*. But the book is factual; it can therefore be an instrument for freedom. For Knowledge is Power; in particular it can be power for those who fight for justice, for human dignity and for human equality.

I congratulate all those who have contributed to this book. But most of all I offer, with great humility, my congratulations and my good wishes to all the people and governments of the victim states. They have kept the beacon of freedom alight by their endurance, their courage, and their absolute commitment to Africa's liberation. I salute them.

Julius K. Nyerere
26 April 1986

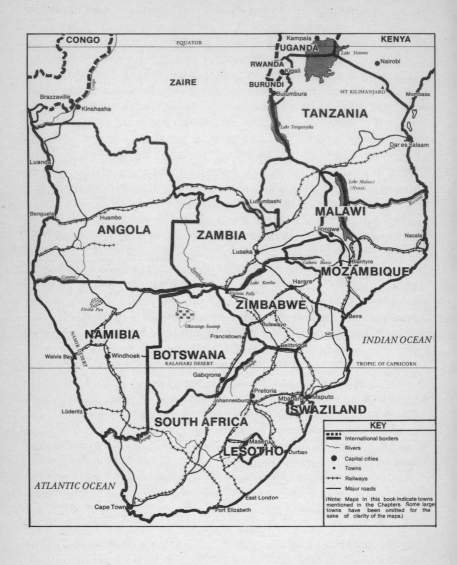

Introduction

South Africa, at war with its own people, is waging an undeclared war against its neighbours – the independent black-ruled states which have the geographical misfortune to share its borders. This war is part of South Africa's 'total strategy' policy which involves the mobilization of all forces — political, economic, diplomatic and military. The regional objective is to create and maintain a dependence that will be economically lucrative and politically submissive – and act as a bulwark against the imposition of international sanctions against *apartheid*.

The combination of tactics used against neighbouring countries has varied from state to state depending on its political, economic and military vulnerabilities. Some countries have been subjected to direct attack, or even occupation, by the South African Defence Force (SADF). Surrogates are trained and armed by the SADF to enter some countries to murder, maim, rape and destroy on their behalf. These military tactics mask economic and political goals, and the primary targets are invariably economic. 'Total strategy' uses destructive methods or 'disincentives', and it also uses 'incentives' toward more 'formative' action. At the heart of the 'total strategy' policy is the regional system of transportation and communcations which has been regularly sabotaged to ensure that all trade flows south through South Africa.

Government officials in Pretoria have threatened retaliatory sanctions against the independent states of the region in the event that international sanctions are imposed against South Africa. A 'sanction' is defined in the Oxford Dictionary as 'a penalty for disobeying a law or reward for obeying it, consideration helping to enforce obedience to any rule of conduct, economic or military action to coerce a State to conform'. What has emerged clearly from our study is that, through all of these methods, Pretoria is already imposing sanctions against the other states in southern Africa.

It is now more than a quarter of a century since Britain's foreign secretary, Harold Macmillan, spoke in Cape Town about the 'wind of change' gusting through Africa, his way of describing the movement for national independence. That was in January 1960 and only eight African nations were independent. The early and mid-1960s saw the birth of many more independent African states and then the 'wind of change' seemed to blow itself out at the Congo, the Ruvuma and the Zambezi rivers.

South Africa had sought the direct incorporation of the High Commission territories of Botswana, Lesotho and Swaziland (BLS). But when Britain refused to allow this, the South African prime minister at that time, Hendrik Verwoerd, proposed the establishment of a 'common market' or 'commonwealth' in southern Africa in which economic links would provide the basis for a regional political institution. This failed to materialize in its totality but the independent BLS states were incorporated into a South African-dominated customs union and into the rand monetary zone. These formal economic links gave Pretoria enormous leverage over the affairs of the BLS, which it continues to use to great effect.

Pretoria's regional policy until the mid-1970s concerned itself with attempts to thwart activities by liberation movements which were growing in strength in neighbouring countries as well as at home. It was shielded in this by a ring of 'buffer' states that included the Portuguese colonies of Mozambique and Angola as well as the British rebel colony of Southern Rhodesia, and by its own occupation of Namibia. Regional policy was directed toward reinforcing this barrier of states through various economic, political and military alliances.

With this regional base apparently secure, John Vorster, the next South African prime minister, launched his 'outward-looking' policy of 'dialogue' in the late 1960s, seeking allies within the newly-formed grouping of independent states, the Organization of African Unity (OAU). There were a few initial successes. The most spectacular of these was the establishment of diplomatic relations with Malawi and an exchange of state visits. Although this 'dialogue' initiative was finally condemned and blocked by the OAU in 1971, Malawi has remained one of *apartheid's* most consistent allies.

After the dictatorship of Marcelo Caetano collapsed in Portugal in 1974, the face of southern Africa altered almost overnight, with the independence of Mozambique and Angola the following year, and then in 1980, of Zimbabwe. This was not achieved without considerable bloodshed, and many of the defeated colonizers retreated into *apartheid's* laager.

Of great importance in the context of *Destructive Engagement* is that, during these liberation wars, the Portuguese and the Rhodesians created or co-opted groups to use as surrogates against the nationalist parties. In the case of Angola, there were three of these groups of which only one remains relevant today. That is the National Union for the Total Independence of Angola (UNITA) led by Jonas Savimbi. Letters and documents which have been published elsewhere reveal that when Unita was supposedly fighting against Portuguese colonialism, it was in reality an adjunct of the Portuguese armed forces. These documents have been dismissed by Savimbi as forgeries. However, during the course of our study we visited Portugal on three occasions to interview the commanders of the Portuguese army who were in Angola in the early 1970s.

None of them could be described as radicals seeking to belittle Unita. On the contrary, they harbour a nostalgic warmth for Savimbi and the role he played in support of the war they were fighting. But they confirm that the documents are authentic. They say that there was a 'gentleman's agreement' to provide arms, ammunition and medical assistance to Unita, a movement which purported to be anti-Portuguese when presenting itself to international forums. One of the main tactics of Unita, which continues to this day, was the disruption of the Benguela Railroad, a main artery not only for the Angolan interior but for trade from Zambia and Zaire.

On the other side of the continent is the Mozambique National Resistance (MNR), which is fighting against the government of President Samora Machel

— and disrupting the main trade routes to the sea for the land-locked Africa hinterland. The MNR was created by the Rhodesian Central Intelligence Organization, in Rhodesia, in 1976. We have spent many hours interviewing the men who trained, armed, administered and paid the MNR on behalf of Rhodesia.

We have stressed the origins of the MNR and Unita for, after the fall of the Portuguese empire and then Rhodesia, they were inherited by South Africa. They are now used as proxies, not only in the 'destabilization' of the region but in the sanctions that South Africa is imposing on its neighbours.

The collapse of Portuguese colonialism gave rise to a hasty reformulation of South Africa's regional strategy. Military capacity was expanded, while Vorster launched his diplomatic *détente* initiative, vaguely defined as a 'constellation' of independent states presenting a united front against common enemies. This was coupled with minor internal changes such as the removal of some forms of 'petty apartheid'. However, the *détente* initiative began to crumble with the invasion of Angola in 1975 and the eventual expulsion of South African forces by Angolan and Cuban troops in March 1976. Some impetus to maintain dialogue was dashed with the brutal repression of the Soweto uprising a few months later. African leaders could not be associated with a regime which murdered unarmed schoolchidren in the streets.

By the end of 1976, South Africa's regional policy had collapsed and the regime faced a growing internal crisis. Top military strategists, including the defence minister, P.W. Botha, began to flesh out the 'total strategy' which they had proposed as early as 1973, with its economic, political and military implications. This was laid out in the 1977 Defence White Paper which identified the need to 'maintain a solid military balance relative to neighbouring states,' while advocating economic and other 'action in relation to transport services, distribution and telecommunications' with the purpose of promoting 'political and economic collaboration' in the region.

After P.W. Botha became prime minister in 1978 he adopted 'total strategy' as the official policy. He reorganized the security structures, reflecting a desire for long term planning to replace the kind of *ad hoc* decision-making that had caused the embarrassing withdrawal from Angola in 1976, and a reaction to the kind of power wielded by individuals in the Vorster administration. Botha also resurrected the proposal for a 'constellation of southern African states' dominated by South Africa. Rhodesia, commanding access to the regional hinterland, would be a vital component if a maleable government could be put in power when it became Zimbabwe.

Pretoria's hopes for implementation of this plan were shattered by two related events in the space of 27 days in early 1980. The first event was the 4 March announcement of the results of the Zimbabwe independence election in which Robert Mugabe's party won an outright majority. The second event occurred on 1 April when leaders from nine countries in the region – including Malawi but excluding South Africa – formed the Southern African Development Coordination Conference (SADCC) with the stated aim of reducing the region's dependence on the *apartheid* regime.

Central to the creation of SADCC was the development of the regional transportation system to reduce dependence on South Africa. It was this new option for the contiguous states that Pretoria set out to destroy. The savagery of the attacks unleashed on Mozambique, Zimbabwe, Botswana and Lesotho, and escalation of the war against Angola and Namibia, using military, economic and political weapons, are documented in the first half of this book.

Another new circumstance that influenced the re-evaluation of South Africa's 'foreign policy' was the change in the US administration when Ronald Reagan took office in 1981. South Africa has sought to divert attention from the root cause of the growing conflagration of *apartheid* by presenting it as a 'total onslaught' organized by the Soviet Union and coming from outside the country, and by representing itself as the last line of defence in protecting Western interests in the region. This argument, used previously by Rhodesia and Portugal in defence of the indefensible, has been used to justify violation of neighbouring territories as 'hot pursuit' against 'terrorists' of the African National Congress (ANC). The Reagan administration's inability to distinguish between its hostility toward the Soviet Union and the real issue in southern Africa firmly allies it with *apartheid* and admirably suits Pretoria's intentions.

Historically, southern Africa is a British sphere of influence, not an American or Soviet one. Most of South Africa's neighbours are Commonwealth members and have good relations with Britain. The 'red' peril is a red herring. But created in whose interests?

The hypocrisy of the US position is best illustrated in the case of the Angolan government which it denies diplomatic recognition; yet the biggest investors in Angola are US transnationals and the US is Angola's largest export market. In Washington it is convenient to ignore the well-documented fact that South Africa invaded Angola in August 1975 from Namibia – which it occupies illegally. In contrast, the Cuban presence in Angola – which came in response to that invasion at the request of a sovereign government – is legal in international law. Angola (a State Department official candidly admitted) offers Washington an opportunity to give the Soviets a 'bloody nose'. To this end the US actively encourages, or certainly does not discourage, further South African invasions and has resumed arming its African 'contras' to try to overthrow the Angolan government.

South Africa probably has a more direct national interest at stake, in that the capture and control of Angola's oilfields would give Pretoria fuel security in the event of effective imposition of the international oil embargo.Secondly, it may not be long before sophisticated US military equipment given to Unita finds its way into the arsenal that South Africa uses against the Frontline states.

Increasingly, US policy allies Washington firmly with *apartheid*, a system it supposedly opposes. In the Zimbabwean capital, Harare, in January 1986, the vice-president of Botswana, Peter Mmusi, expressed the collective 'dismay and disbelief' of the African governments of the region at the Reagan administration's decision to resume arming its surrogates in Angola. 'This now places the United States clearly in league with South Africa in aggressing and fomenting instability in this region,' he said.

The US response during the massive destruction of the region has been a policy called 'constructive engagement' which seeks, through an unending shuttle by State Department negotiators, to give the appearance of positive motion where there is none and, in reality, while playing for time. The US engagement in southern Africa has been anything but 'constructive'. Its linkage policy stands in the way of Namibian independence (which senior officials admit has never been on the agenda); it is now directly involved in trying to overthrow the Angolan government; its 'mediation' in Mozambique has done nothing to decrease the level of that war; and it has introduced the spectre of superpower conflict and nuclear war into a region which craves nothing more than peace and development.Its sole success has been in allying itself with Pretoria against the region.

Analysis of South Africa's military and nuclear power, the state of its economy and that of the region, and the role of the Reagan administration's 'destructive engagement', form the second half of this study.

As the protective colonial *laager* on South Africa's borders was collapsing from 1974 through 1980, a new set of Afrikaner administrators with military experience was taking power in Pretoria. They believe themselves to be victims of the same colonial domination as the rest of the subcontinent, having 'liberated' their government from English-speaking control almost 40 years ago. They have a paranoic fear of socialism and the Soviet Union, which they believe is favoured by their neighbours and by citizens of their own country who fight for freedom.

Using the new array of circumstances which have appeared since 1980, they have begun to construct a different kind of *laager* that has grown out of the dynamics of conflict within different sectors of their administration. The new *laager* is based, like the old one, on regional economic co-operation, mutual security and a resistance to pressure from outsiders. But it uses military might beyond its borders – as far afield as Zambia and the Seychelles – to achieve political and economic ends.

Since that time different sectors of the leadership have drawn conflicting lessons from their experiences of international and regional contacts. Diplomats involved in negotiations in Europe, America and closer to home have learned that South Africa cannot rely totally on any Western governments for support – and perhaps does not need to because of its own economic and military strength in the region. They have a better understanding of economic pressures used by and against South Africa, and more knowledge about their immediate neighbours. Military leaders have learned form their regional campaigns and acts of sabotage that, although they are the military power in the region, the enemy hits back and South African financial and human losses may be heavier than expected. There is also a hardline security sector which, reinforced by its experience in Namibia, still believes that suppression of black opposition remains the most effective tactic on South Africa's borders as well as at home, and that preparation must be made for a conventional military attack from the north.

South African policy in the region is an amalgam of these points of view. Although still evolving, it is based on the belief that, in the long term, economic control is cheaper and more effective than military domination, but the latter must be used in the short term to achieve the former. The former SADF chief, General Viljoen, spoke of the security forces' role in gaining time for the country to solve its political problems, and predicted that this dependency on the efficiency of the security forces would last for the 'next few years, maybe even the next decade.'

The weakness of this integrated approach to conflict management is that 'failure' – in the Namibia war, in regional diplomacy, in the South African economy, in coping with urban black unrest – might bring perceptible basic divergencies among the system's power-brokers. 'Failures', therefore, must be balanced by 'successes' and these are most easily achieved through high profile cross-border attacks. Thus, in May 1986, when news leaked out of possible South African concessions to the initiative of the Commonwealth 'Eminent Persons Group', the predictable response was the attack on three Commonwealth capitals in the region, which received plenty of media attention in South Africa but did relatively little damage.

Another pillar of regional policy is that economic and security co-operation with neighbouring states will rebuild the lost colonial 'buffer' in a neocolonial form. Third, the South African government would wish to destroy any belief in socialist ideology as a development strategy for the continent and show that free enterprise capitalism is the logical course. So much the better if, when it buries socialism, it can also persuade its own population that chaos is the result of majority rule.

Another major goal is to limit the role and political influence of outside powers – including the West – in the region. In Namibia, for example they have tried with some success to minimize UN involvement and limit the US role as broker, while creating infrastructure for long term military and economic control.

Throughout their history, the Afrikaners have shown a strong instinct for survival. The last two years have brought home to their leaders the fragile nature of their own economic dependencies: internationally, on overseas financial markets for the price of gold and the exchange rate of the US dollar to the rand; regionally, on their neighbours for mutually lucrative business arrangments in preference to the high cost in money and lives of military intervention; internally, on the majority of their population to whom they have denied basic human rights, whom they have forced to live in appalling social conditions, and on whom they are ultimately most dependent for their prosperity and security. The reaction of political and financial leaders in Europe to P.W. Botha's tour in mid-1984 seeking investment and development assistance reinforced the point that destabilization is bad for business and that South Africa is an embarrassing ally for capitalism because in restricting the majority of its population on the basis of colour it cannot claim to have a 'free market' system.

The Afrikaners have also had the opportunity to scrutinize the power of their closest ally, the United States, as this power was used to support them and to pressure them. It is a power they would like to emulate – as a regional superpower. In late 1983, when Soviet officials summoned their South African counterparts at the UN to an unprecedented meeting to warn them that 'aggression cannot be left unpunished', South Africa took it as recognition of this role as regional superpower. Such status would ensure their survival through military and economic domination, and would enhance their future ability to resist pressure, even from their allies.

There are two spurious arguments which must finally be addressed. The first is that some elements in South Africa, particularly the military, are out of line with government policy. Given the authoritarian nature of the South African regime such an argument is, at the most charitable, ill-informed. At another level, it may be disinformation. While the politicians may not be aware of all details of military operations, the soldiers are certainly aware of the detail of government policy. They sit on the highest councils of state and formulate that policy. And, as occurred in the case of Mozambique in 1985, when they are caught in breach of publicly enunciated policy, they are not disciplined, they are promoted. Such promotion can only suggest that they followed official policy to the letter. Although there may be some disagreements over tactics to employ in specific situations, the policy of 'total strategy' – which emerged from the military – is accepted by all institutions of the regime.

The second misconception is that there must be political accommodation with surrogates to end the wars in the contiguous states. But political decision must be made by those who make policy – and peace must be negotiated with those who make war. None of the contiguous states have attacked South Africa, nor do any of them pose such a threat. It is South Africa which has attacked its neighbours and, in recognition that it is Pretoria – and not its surrogates – which makes both the policies and the wars, those states have talked to South Africa.

The international excuse that sanctions will harm South Africa's neighbours is rejected by all of them. The harsh reality is that destabilization and economic sanctions are already a fact of life in the region and will be as long as *apartheid* exists.

Phyllis Johnson, David Martin
25 May 1986

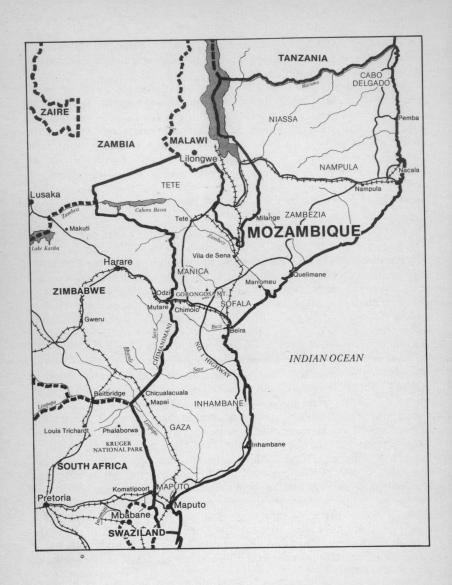

CHAPTER 1

Mozambique:
To Nkomati and Beyond

In the early evening of 24 April 1974, in an office on Rua António Maria Cardoso cushioned from the hubbub of Lisbon's traffic, two men sat talking quietly over a glass of port.

The office belonged to Major Silva Pais, head of Portugal's feared secret police, the General Security Directorate (DGS), more commonly referred to by its previous name, the International Police for the Defence of the State (PIDE).

Silva Pais, his visitor later recalled, seemed depressed and distracted as if preoccupied by a major problem. The visitor's mood was exactly the opposite. In the few days he had been in Lisbon he had concluded the details of an agreement he had been trying to reach for almost five years; an agreement which would profoundly affect events in southern Africa in the next decade and more.

The visitor left for Lisbon's Portela Airport to board a Portuguese Air Transport (TAP) Boeing 707 bound for the Rhodesian capital, Salisbury. It was the last flight allowed to take off from Lisbon that night.

During the transit stop in the Angolan capital, Luanda, he thought it a little odd that passengers were told to remain on board. The explanation for this – and for Silva Pais's preoccupation – came on his arrival at Salisbury Airport. There had been a military *coup d'état* in Lisbon during the night and the civilian government of Marcelo Caetano had been overthrown.

The following day a squad of Portuguese naval marines, led by Lieutenant-Commander Martins Cavalheiro, broke into Silva Pais's offices. The partially empty port bottle and two empty glasses on the ornate central table were of no significance to them. But they were to an organization several thousand miles away. On 4 May a photograph of the room showing the bottle and glasses appeared in the Portuguese magazine, *O Seculo Ilustrado.*[1]

The visitor's deputy had the picture rephotographed from the magazine and drew a bold arrow pointing to one of the glasses, adding a new caption in English: ' "X" MARKS EXHIBIT "A" – PORT GLASSES WITH K.F.'s FINGERPRINTS!'

The visitor, K.F., was Ken Flower, director-general of Rhodesia's Central Intelligence Organization (CIO).[2] The deal Flower had put together had its origins in the war which began on 25 September 1964 in Portugal's African colony of Mozambique which had an 800-kilometre border with eastern Rhodesia.

Rhodesia was concerned about the ability of the largely conscript Portuguese army to contain the guerrillas of the Mozambique Liberation Front (FRELIMO). The Rhodesians watched the unfolding struggle in Mozambique apprehensively. Their anxiety quickened in 1968 when Frelimo opened a new front in the Tete province on Rhodesia's north-eastern border; it increased again in 1970 when Frelimo guerrillas crossed the Zambezi and began operating south of the river down to the Rhodesian border.

The Rhodesians reasoned, correctly, that the successes of Frelimo guerrillas in Tete were likely to lead to a corridor being opened through the province for the infiltration of Zimbabwean nationalist guerrillas and their armaments.

Two steps were taken at this point by the Rhodesians. The first was that Rhodesian troops began to operate in Tete with the Portuguese in an attempt to hold the line and prevent infiltration into Rhodesia. Flower pursued his own plans with the second initiative, which was to take five years before an agreement was finalized in Lisbon in the days before the *coup d'état.* He was convinced that it was necessary to operate a clandestine movement inside Mozambique as his forward intelligence 'eyes and ears' against infiltration by Zimbabwean nationalist guerrillas.

In September 1971, Flower travelled to Lisbon to meet Caetano. He was under instructions from his own prime minister, Ian Smith, to 'represent our apprehension over the deteriorating security situation in Mozambique and to try to persuade them to allow us to further develop cross-border operations in Tete'. In August 1972 he travelled again to Lisbon to meet Caetano to discuss 'co-operation in dissident sponsorship. We offered to develop an internal resistance movement

in Mozambique along the lines of the *Flechas* [Arrows] in Angola. We
felt we could do it better than the DGS '[3]

Caetano gave qualified approval. The qualification was that Flower
must clear the plan with the Portuguese governor-general and the
heads of the armed forces and DGS in Mozambique. Flower's
relations with the head of the DGS in Mozambique, António Vaz, were
less than warm and Flower considered this a hopeless task. There the
matter rested for a further 16 months.

The assessment of the dangers by the CIO proved well founded. On
21 December 1972, guerrillas of the Zimbabwe African National
Liberation Army (ZANLA), the military wing of the Zimbabwe
African National Union (ZANU), attacked a white-owned farm in
north-eastern Rhodesia. They had infiltrated through Tete and had
spent many months mobilizing the local population. It was the first
attack in a phase of protracted armed struggle which was to last for
exactly seven years.[4]

Earlier, after Rhodesian troops had begun operating in Tete
against Frelimo, the movement's leader, Samora Machel, met Zanu
political and military leaders in the Zambian capital, Lusaka. During
the meeting he told them: 'Some of us, when we look at the situation in
Mozambique, realize if we liberate Mozambique tomorrow that will
not be the end. The liberation of Mozambique without the liberation
of Zimbabwe is meaningless.'[5]

The breakthrough Flower had been hoping for came in March 1974,
little more than a month before the Portuguese *coup d'état*. Silva Pais
convened a meeting in the Mozambique capital, Lourenço Marques
(now Maputo). In attendance were Vaz, his counterpart as head of the
DGS in Angola, São José Lopes, and Flower. It was agreed to start a
clandestine movement directed jointly by the CIO and DGS to operate
against Frelimo and Zanla. 'They virtually begged us to get cracking,'
Flower recalled later. Flower wanted the new movement to be
modelled on the special forces, *Flechas*, in Angola, which came under the
control of the DGS. In late April he travelled to Lisbon to finalize the
logistical details with Silva Pais and the Portuguese military
commanders.

Flower's initial reaction to the *coup d'état* in Lisbon, and the ensuing
confusion, was that his plan would not get off the ground. But on the
contrary, these events were to play into his hands.

On 2 June what Flower described as 'the entire control and

command of the resistance came across the border and offered their services to us.' This is an overstatement for there had not been time to set up any structures after Flower's last meeting with Silva Pais six weeks earlier. But the group which crossed the border, numbering about 40, did provide the CIO with a nucleus to begin operations against Frelimo and Zanla. They were almost all members of the DGS or Special Groups, some black and some white. Their commander was Major Oscar Cardoso, an officer who had been with the Angolan *Flechas*.

Of the many individuals and groups crossing into Rhodesia in this period the Cardoso group was regarded as the most promising. They were largely ex-servicemen with combat experience and they were taken to an old military camp in the northern part of Rhodesia. 'We located them at Makuti because the Rhodesian government was pretend- ing friendship with the Frelimo [transitional] government and we wanted Frelimo opponents well out of the public eye,' a senior CIO officer said.[6] The Cardoso group went operational against Zanla twice inside Rhodesia with the Rhodesian Light Infantry (RLI).[7] But they were never deployed inside Mozambique. When the Alvor Agreement, which was supposed to pave the way to a peaceful transition to independence in Angola, collapsed in March 1975, Cardoso and most of his men left for Zaire. They joined Holden Roberto's National Front for the Liberation of Angola (FNLA).[8] The FNLA, backed by plentiful funds from the American Central Intelligence Agency (CIA), could afford to pay mercenaries better wages than the CIO.

Of the several false starts in this period one other is worth mentioning. It was led by a Brazilian jet-fighter pilot who had served in the Portuguese air force in Mozambique. His group numbered about 15, including one coloured and three Africans. They were taken for training to an abandoned white-owned farm in Rhodesia's Chimanimani mountains bordering on Mozambique.

They claimed they could return to Mozambique to recruit and supply information about Zanla activities. They were sent to undertake reconnaissance in the Vila Pery area (now Chimoio). Their mission was a disaster. 'They didn't get 20 kilometres from the border.' They were involved in a 'contact' in which the coloured member of the group, Rui Manuel Nunes da Silva, was shot in the leg, abandoned and captured.[9]

Reference is made to this incident in the book, *Comandos Espeçiais Contra os Cubanos,* written by two former Portuguese commandos. In the book, Nunes da Silva is described as a hunter/guide with a special commando group infiltrated from Rhodesia. His leg was almost cut off by two bullets and the group's commander abandoned him. He reasoned that the wounded man would get medical treatment quicker if taken prisoner and the rest of the group, said to number eight, would be able to get away safely. Nunes da Silva did get medical treatment. But he was executed in Mozambique some years later on 31 March 1979, eight days after a Rhodesian Special Air Service (SAS) sabotage unit, landed from a South African submarine, blew up oil storage tanks at Beira.[10]

After these early failures the CIO decided to stop trying to use white opponents of Frelimo and to concentrate on recruiting Africans. Their search for suitable recruits was made in collaboration with the police Special Branch (SB) who were screening arrivals from Mozambique.

Former CIO officers say the turning point came with the arrival of André Matade Matsangaiza in about June 1976. Matsangaiza had served in the Frelimo forces from 1972 to 1974 without distinction. He was acknowledged as a brave fighter but never attained a command position as subsequently claimed. After Mozambique's independence in June 1975 he had worked in the quartermaster's stores at Dondo, north-west of Beira. This was a particularly difficult phase for Frelimo. The Portuguese *coup d'état* had come as a complete surprise. The pace of events thereafter left Frelimo with little time to prepare itself and its army for the challenges and temptations which lay ahead. Matsangaiza's case is a symptom of this period. Among the victorious Frelimo he was not alone in believing that he was entitled to share the spoils. He was brought before a military tribunal for the theft of a Mercedes car and items from the quartermaster's stores; he was convicted and sent to Sacuze 're-education centre' in Sofala province.[11] From there he escaped to Rhodesia to become the first leader of what was to become known as the Mozambique National Resistance (MNR) or RENAMO.[12]

In 1976, after Matsangaiza's arrival, the CIO decided to establish a permanent training camp. The site chosen was a tobacco farm just outside the small farming settlement of Odzi in eastern Rhodesia near the city of Umtali (now Mutare). The farmer was paid a rent for the use of the manager's house and the tobacco barns, which were converted into barracks to which rough lean-to structures were added. The trainees came under the control of the CIO operations desk headed by Eric 'Ricky' May. The CIO seconded a senior instructor and three others, former members of the SAS, to train the MNR at Odzi. All were from the operations desk, as was the last member of the team, the paymaster/administrator, who had been in the Rhodesian police before joining the CIO.[13]

The senior instructor subsequently described their strategy in this period. 'To start off with it was sabotage, to disrupt the population and disrupt the economy which really comes under sabotage, to come back with decent recruits at that stage and hit any Frelimo bases they came across. And if they came across Zanla they were to take them on.' They were equipped with captured weapons originating from Eastern bloc countries and China, initially dressed in blue boiler-suits like the police reserve and later in olive-green uniforms. All of their basic requirements, such as food, were taken care of by the CIO and Matsangaiza was paid $75 per month. His deputy, Afonso Dhlakama, who had served in the Portuguese colonial army fighting against Frelimo, was paid $65; and the ordinary recruits received $20.

Neither the Rhodesians nor, more surprisingly, Evo Fernandes, who became the voice of the MNR in Europe and later secretary-general, make any secret about who was in charge or what the objectives were.

'The way I ran them was I always consulted André [Matsangaiza] on everything,' the senior instructor said. 'I didn't always agree with him and if I didn't agree with him I'd say "No, we don't do that." ' Flower said, 'The objectives of the MNR were essentially to provide the opportunity for Rhodesia to deal with Zanla in Mozambique without doing so directly, and to perpetuate or create instability in areas of Mozambique.' Another of the CIO officers involved said, 'The MNR gave a cover for Rhodesian operations and, from initial intelligence-gathering operations, moved on to getting recruits and then on to the offensive, disrupting road and rail links and making it harder for Frelimo to support Zanu.'[14]

Such a cover was provided for the SAS attack on the Beira oil tanks in March 1979, which was claimed as an MNR operation but which Flower and the CIO instructors confirm had nothing to do with the MNR. It is noteworthy that they can recall only one incident of significance in that period which the MNR were involved in. That was the blowing up of a generator at the Sher power station on the Revue river (now Rebvuwe) which supplies electricity to Beira. But even this operation was commanded by SAS men – and it did not halt Beira's supply.

Fernandes said that in Matsangaiza the Rhodesians felt they at

last had a tool they could use. 'He went back and recruited his family.
But mostly the Rhodesians wanted information. It was an organization
without a name. It was a fifth column among Rhodesian forces. They
asked André to bring back information about Zanu bases. It was not
our war but a civil war in Rhodesia.'[15]

One problem about unravelling the history of the MNR in this
period is the role, if any, of various whites, both Mozambican and
Portuguese. Flower insists they had no role and the CIO instructors all
confirm this. The only one who was definitely involved, but on the
propaganda side and not with operations or training, was Orlando
Cristina, a former DGS officer who had been the liaison in Tete with
the CIO in the late 1960s. 'The Portuguese, in Lisbon, and these other
whites, once the MNR were producing some successes, started
shouting they were doing things and they wanted to take over. They all
wanted to climb in on the act. And the MNR said as a man, when the
Portuguese come in command here we won't operate. They would
have nothing to do with the white Portuguese and they did not like
Cristina,' the senior instructor said.

Fernandes, a Portuguese national, admits that the MNR were no
more than a Rhodesian fifth column but, not surprisingly, tries to paint
a different picture. He claims that six people met at Cristina's suburban
Salisbury home on 1 May 1977 and were responsible for giving the
MNR its name. He said the six were Cristina, Matsangaiza, Dhlakama,
Armando Khembo dos Santos, Leo Milas and himself. The CIO
instructors insist that Matsangaiza and Dhlakama could not have been
present without their knowledge because they were at that time at the
Odzi camp. But, they concede, it is possible that the other four
attended a meeting where the name MNR was proposed.

The backgrounds of these four provide a further insight into those
who came together in the MNR, if not in the CIO phase then certainly
after March 1980. Cristina, like Fernandes, had worked for Jorge
Jardim, who had extensive business interests in Mozambique, where
he was Malawi's consul-general in Beira, and who was a godson of the
Portuguese fascist dictator, António Salazár. After the Portuguese
coup d'état, Cristina moved to Malawi where he was detained for
about a month, apparently at Jardim's personal request, for stealing
confidential documents which he was said to have sold to a French
magazine. Once released, he left for Rhodesia, working behind the
scenes on the CIO/MNR radio station, *Voz da Africa Livre* (Voice of

Free Africa), which was opened near the central Rhodesian town of
Gwelo (now Gweru) on 5 July 1976 to beam into Mozambique.
Because of his past links with Jardim, whom the CIO officers insist
had nothing to do with the movement they founded and ran, Cristina
was distrusted by Flower. But he was the only one of the Portuguese
group who had contacts with the CIO/MNR in this period.

Fernandes, of Goan parentage and a lawyer by training, had worked
for the Portuguese judicial police in Beira during the colonial era.
Frelimo insists (though Fernandes denies this) that, like Cristina, he
worked for the DGS. He became administrator of Jardim's
newspaper, *Notícias de Beira*, before being ousted by the journalists
some months after the Portuguese *coup d'état*. He fled to Portugal on 23
September 1976 after, he says, receiving a warning from Cristina 'that
some military action may start and it would be safer to get away'. In
Lisbon he briefly joined the Mozambique United Front (FUMO) led
by Domingos Arouca, a Mozambican lawyer who had been detained in
the Portuguese colonial period and who formed Fumo after independence when Frelimo refused to offer him a major post. 'In the
beginning our idea was to have a political wing led by Arouca and a
military wing led by André,' Fernandes said. 'But we soon realized
that it was not possible to work with Arouca and we had to start our
own organization without Fumo.' Arouca tells the story differently.
Cristina and Fernandes, he says, tried to use his name, well known in
Mozambique, to gain political respectability. 'I declined, saying it was
not really a movement for independence. They only wanted me to be a
puppet outside to gain international acceptance. I decided not to be
used.'[16]

Armando Khembo dos Santos is the least known of the group that
Fernandes claims met at Cristina's house. He was briefly a member of
Frelimo, around the time of the organization's formation in 1962,
before disappearing for a lengthy period and resurfacing in Fumo.
Fernandes claims dos Santos is now the MNR representative for
Africa based in the Kenyan capital, Nairobi.

The final member of the group that Fernandes said attended the
meeting is the most intriguing. Variously known as Leo Clinton
Aldridge Jr, Leo-Aldridge Milas and Leo Milas, he had been elected
secretary of information at the formation of Frelimo in 1962. When the
movement's first leader, Eduardo Mondlane, had to return to the
United States for some months in this period, Milas was effectively
head of Frelimo. He expelled a number of senior officials and became
the secretary of defence and security. Milas excused the fact that he

spoke no Mozambican national language and poor Portuguese by saying he had left the country as a child and had been educated in the United States. This was not uncommon and he came into the first Frelimo central committee from the Mozambique National Democratic Union (UDENAMO), one of the three movements to form Frelimo. He had been introduced to Udenamo by Sikota Wina, a Zambian, who was later to become that country's minister of information.

When Mondlane was told that Milas was not a Mozambican at all but a black American, he went to the United States to investigate personally and he met Milas's parents. He learned that the name Milas was using in Frelimo was an amalgum of his father's name, Leo Clinton Aldridge Sr, and his mother's maiden name, Catherine Bell Miles; and that young Leo was born in Pittsburg, a small town in northeast Texas. His parents now lived in San Pedro, the port of Los Angeles, where his father was a dockworker. The Frelimo central committee expelled Milas on 25 August 1964. Apart from the falsification of his identity, one of the grounds given was collaboration with known agents of Portuguese colonialism. Milas, it transpired, was linked to Cristina, who, at least twice in this period, visited Dar es Salaam where Frelimo had its headquarters. Who Milas really worked for remains uncertain. But the link between a known DGS agent and a black American who had infiltrated Frelimo under a false identity suggests its own answer.[17]

A further element in the historical jigsaw puzzle which is difficult to unravel is the Malawi connection during the period when the CIO ran the MNR. A group known as *Africa Livre* operated out of Malawi. Because the propaganda station *Voz da Africa Livre* was operating from Rhodesia, and because of Cristina's links to Jardim, it was assumed the two groups were connected. But Rhodesian CIO officers insist they had no connection with the Malawi group. The most likely explanation is that Jardim, having been frozen out of the Rhodesian operation, set up his own, using minor groups opposed to Frelimo.[18]

The *Voz da Africa Livre*, although set up by the CIO, came under the Rhodesian Ministry of Information and was run by the Directorate of Psychological Warfare. Listeners in Mozambique, and it seems improbable there were many, given the level of the propaganda, could hardly have been fooled. Its address was given as P.O. Box HG 444, Salisbury, Rhodesia, the same address as the Rhodesia Broadcasting Corporation. On 12 July 1976, a week after the station opened, such listeners were told, 'Rhodesia has a government that works, and which carries out policies to improve the lives and happiness of millions of Rhodesians.' After 500 years of Portuguese colonialism, and given the fact that young blacks were leaving Rhodesia at the rate of 1 000 a week at this point to join Zanla, listeners could have been forgiven for question this claim. Later the station tried a new tack, one which continued after it was moved to South Africa and until it was closed down in March 1984. It spoke of two Frelimos. The first, led by Mondlane, was described as 'good', 'real' and 'nationalist'. The other, led by Machel, was 'evil' and 'totalitarian'.[19] Even that was far from subtle.

In 1978, with the MNR numbering about 500 and the Rhodesians confronted by Zanla infiltration along the entire 800-kilometre border with Mozambique, the CIO decided to increase the pressure. They set up an MNR base inside Mozambique on the top of Gorongosa mountain, 100 kilometres north-west of Beira. The senior instructor explained the reason for the decision: 'Well, it was because we had to get in and not waste time coming from Rhodesia and going so far and coming back again. What we wanted was a base somewhere in the middle of the country and Gorongosa was ideal. The other reason for this was that my new plan was to form a big base at Gorongosa and then start shifting out bases with the objective of cutting off Beira, Maputo and Tete. Just cutting them off from all communications, isolating them, and then seeing what would happen to the rest of the country, which would have been fairly fatal if we could have done that. And that was my next plan.'[20] About 400 MNR were moved in from Rhodesia to open the new base. They were commanded by Matsangaiza. A member of the SAS, an ex-British paratrooper, went in with them and Rhodesian SAS personnel were regularly at the base during the next two years to continue training and to direct operations.

'We were just breaking out of Gorongosa when peace was declared,' the senior instructor said, a reference to the Lancaster House agreement. 'I'd put Luke [Lucas Mhlanga] in charge of a base on the Sitatonga range and I was bringing one group down to take the area of the Buzi river and then the Save river further south. They were to cross the first river and to head for the second on a three-pronged drive, one east, one west and one in the middle. Another group were to go from Gorongosa to cut off Beira, and the remainder were to cut off Maputo. And then we had another team operational up north towards Tete, but they had not got into the Tete area by then.' Thus, the strategy was to cut Mozambique into three parts.

The activities of the MNR, particularly when compared to the massive assaults by the Rhodesian army and air force, were still conducted on a small scale; and in the last quarter of 1979 they suffered two serious blows.

The first setback came on 17 October 1979 when Matsangaiza, much admired by the CIO training team, was killed in a foolhardy attack on a well-fortified Mozambican army position at Vila Paiva de Andrade (now Vila de Gorongosa). The radio message received at the Odzi base from Gorongosa was, 'Your Sunray got it'. 'Sunray' is the code-name for 'commander'. The senior instructor went by helicopter to Gorongosa to evacuate the seriously wounded. He learned that Matsangaiza, infuriated that an earlier attack had been repulsed by the Mozambique People's Liberation Forces (FPLM), had been killed leading a suicidal attack across open ground against the FPLM position. His body and the bodies of about 20 others had been abandoned where they fell as the survivors fled in disarray.[21]

About 12 seriously wounded were airlifted back to Rhodesia in two helicopters, one of which was hit by FPLM ground-fire and made a forced landing near Chimoio. The occupants were quickly transferred to the other helicopter and Rhodesian bombers came in the next day to destroy the helicopter left on the ground.

The transfer of command from Matsangaiza to Dhlakama was immediate, although accounts of the latter's whereabouts at the time of his leader's death vary enormously. Although Dhlakama was deputy to Matsangaiza, the CIO instructors had little respect for him and would have preferred that Mhlanga took command. 'I thought he [Dhlakama] was a weak character,' the senior instructor said. 'I don't think he liked going across. He was a chap who on "ops" I wouldn't trust, someone who would come back and say he had done things he hadn't done. It was automatic that he should take over. But all the men realized he was by no means the same calibre as André. He had not got leadership qualities really.' Dhlakama, the CIO instructors say, was at Odzi when Matsangaiza was killed. He was flown to Gorongosa base to take command on the night of 18 October in a Rhodesian helicopter.

Fernandes says, 'Everyone accepted him as president. There was no election, everyone just accepted him as president and he went to the Gorongosa base. He was about 100 kilometres south at the time, and he just went there.' Even by Dhlakama's own subsequent admission he was far from accepted. He admits as much in documents captured when FPLM forces overran the MNR Garagua base in December 1981. At one point, he is recorded as saying, 'Some of you get and make available drugs to assassinate me in order to take my place.' Elsewhere in the Garagua documents, he says in a report given on 9 November 1980, 'Many fighters died this year, including commanders and other heads, and others were maimed and crippled – all because of a power struggle.'[22] But most of the killings appear to have been of leaders like Mhlanga who threatened Dhlakama's position. And there are several unexplained assassinations, such as that of Cristina in South Africa in April 1983, and the subsequent disappearances of prominent leaders such as the Bomba brothers.[23]

The second, and potentially most damaging, blow to the MNR came on 21 December 1979. At Lancaster House in London the Zimbabwean nationalists and the Rhodesian rebels were forced to accept a constitution and a cease-fire paving the way to elections and Zimbabwe's independence on 18 April 1980. The CIO were convinced that Zanu could not win a majority of the 80 African seats at stake in the election and so, on 4 March, when it was announced that Robert Mugabe was to form the government, it came as a major shock to white Rhodesia and thus to the MNR.

'We [the MNR] were given 72 hours to get out of the country,' the senior instructor recalled. 'As soon as everything was turning the wrong way, as they say, I was told to get as many blokes across the border into Mozambique as I could. So I shoved across everybody except for about 250. I must have put across 300 to 400, bringing the total inside to about 2 000.' At the same time the Rhodesians were frantically destroying documentation; as a result, it is impossible to verify these figures which appear to be too high. Flower puts the MNR numbers at this point at between 500 and 1 000, and two of the other CIO instructors at Odzi felt the figure was 'getting up to 1 800'. Whichever of these figures is true, the MNR was then comparatively small and, stripped of its Rhodesian rear base and support, should have been relatively easy for the FPLM to eliminate.

Certainly that was Frelimo's view. A few days after the Lancaster House signing, Machel handed the British a memorandum. He demanded an end to broadcasts from Rhodesia by the *Voz da Africa Livre*, protested at continuing Rhodesian violation of Mozambique air space, and insisted that MNR personnel still in Rhodesia were not refugees but mercenaries recruited and trained to fight against Mozambique.[24]

Soon after Zanu's victory was announced, Flower began to put into operation long-time contingency plans. Because of his own budget limitations he had been trying since 1976 to persuade the South African government to support the MNR. His overtures had been through General Hendrick van den Bergh, the head of the Bureau of State Security (BOSS), to South Africa's prime minister, John Vorster. But Vorster had refused to support the MNR. To do so, he argued, would be contrary to his policy of '*détente*' with the independent black-ruled states of Africa.

However, late in 1978, first van den Bergh and then Vorster fell from office in the wake of the 'Muldergate' information scandal. Vorster was replaced as prime minister by the minister of defence, P.W. Botha, and the army commander, General Magnus Malan, became minister of defence. The power of Boss was dramatically undermined; and the vacuum was filled to a large extent by the Military Intelligence Directorate (MID), headed by General Pieter van der Westhuizen. In his move from defence minister to prime minister, Botha had taken the military men with him into key positions of civilian power. In effect, there had been a constitutional military *coup d'état*.

Flower pressed the new South African government to support the MNR. The response was immediate and positive, although initially limited. The South Africans began to supply some weapons and vehicles. A Colonel Charles van Niekerk, whose name becomes much more prominent later in the MNR story, became the MID liaison officer to the MNR and visited the Odzi base on a number of occasions during 1979. According to the senior instructor, the South African government had committed one million rand (then worth more than US$ 1 million) in 1980.[25]

So the South African connection had been firmly established in the 12 months or so preceeding Zimbabwe's independence. And, with the Rhodesian military openly admitting they could not defeat the Zimbabwean nationalist guerrillas, Malan and his Rhodesian counterpart, General Peter Walls, had reached an agreement. In the event of the collapse of 'white' Rhodesia, 'compromised' units and individuals, such as the Selous Scouts and the MNR, whom the Rhodesians feared could be subject to reprisals for the atrocities they had committed, would be transferred to South Africa. This was the contingency plan now implemented for the remnants of the MNR still in Rhodesia.

Dealing through Malan, van der Westhuizen and van Niekerk, Flower arranged the transfer of the MNR, their equipment and vehicles, and the personnel of *Voz da Africa Livre*, to South Africa. Van den Bergh, he said, had told him that the South African Defence Force (SADF)

'might be stupid enough' to take over the MNR. The transfer was
'solely my responsibility', Flower said later.[26] But, in fact, Flower was
not solely responsible. When the transfer occurred, Rhodesia had
reverted from its former illegal status to that of a legal British colony,
with a British governor supposedly in charge. Furthermore, the
hand-over occurred at a historic watershed in relations between Britain
and Mozambique. Machel had played the most significant role of any
outsider in the Lancaster House agreement the previous December.
He had pressured Zanu's leadership into accepting the agreement
despite their strong opposition to certain obnoxious clauses, threatening
that if they did not they might lose their rear base in Mozambique.
The British prime minister, Margaret Thatcher, had acknowledged
her considerable debt to Machel and relations between the two
governments had reached an unprecedented high.

In the period between the Lancaster agreement and the announcement of election results, Mozambique had pressed Britain to
stop the activities of the MNR. Flower said that Sir Antony Duff –
deputy to the governor, Lord Soames, and later head of British internal
intelligence, MI5 – raised the issue with him on a number of occasions.
Flower says that after he made arrangements for the transfer of the MNR
to South Africa, he informed Duff or another of Lord Soames's staff,
Robin Renwick, then head of the Rhodesia desk in the Foreign Office.[27]
Thus the British knew about the impending transfer of the MNR to
South Africa and acquiesced. Had Flower not informed them, they
would have known anyway. Members of the Commonwealth military
monitoring force, which came under Soames's command, were
present at all main Rhodesian army and air force bases. Their task was
to monitor and report to the governor's office. They could not have
missed the shuttle of South African air force C130s landing at a
Rhodesian base to airlift the MNR personnel.

It would appear that Britain's repayment of its debt to Machel was
churlish in the extreme. But, debts notwithstanding, there are other
considerations to bear in mind. In the first place, as one of Soames's
staff frankly put it, 'we had responsibility without power'. Although
Soames was nominally in charge, the reality of power in the dangerous
weeks of the transition lay with the old Rhodesian structures: the
army, air force, police, civil service and so on. A wrong move – such as
trying to detain the MNR personnel and, as Mozambique wanted,
handing them over – could have ignited a very unstable powder-keg.
Furthermore, given the daily crisis management involved in guiding
the country to elections, the MNR was 'a very minor issue meriting

only passing attention,' according to one of Soames' staff who said he had known of the transfer. Finally, it was a problem that the British authorities were glad to leave to someone else to resolve. If the MNR were handed over to Mozambique the British were uncertain of their fate; and if they remained in Zimbabwe after independence the Mugabe government would certainly hand them over. Flower's formula offered the best solution to a potentially thorny problem — and at this point no one foresaw the consequences.

The transfer to South Africa was carried out in three phases. The first group to be moved were the staff of *Voz da Africa Livre* who, unconvincingly, announced they would be off the air for some time while they transferred their 'mobile transmitter to a new location in Mozambique'. A South African air force C130 landed at Fylde air base in central Rhodesia to fly them out with their equipment, including one car. They were accompanied by the CIO paymaster/administrator, and Cristina also went out on this flight. They landed at Waterkloof military base on the outskirts of Pretoria.

The CIO officer who had accompanied them returned to Rhodesia to take charge of the next stage of the transfer. This consisted of a team of SAS personnel driving the seven MNR vehicles from the Odzi base to the Voortrekkerhoogte military barracks in Pretoria.[28]

Phase three of the transfer was the largest and most important. Over a period of one day and one night a shuttle of South African air force C130s landed at Grand Reef air base in eastern Rhodesia near Odzi. They airlifted out about 250 MNR personnel and their armaments. Two of the CIO officers, the senior instructor and Des Robertson, went with them. They landed at Phalaborwa in the eastern Transvaal where they were met by a naval group headed by a lieutenant-commander. From there they were moved in a convoy of trucks to the edge of the Lutabo river, about one kilometre from the Kruger National Park. On the way to what was to become their new base, they passed through a large camp under construction for the 5th Reconnaissance Regiment, a new SADF 'special forces' unit initially set up for former SAS, Selous Scouts and members of other Rhodesian units who had fled south.

The new MNR base on the banks of the Lutabo was a crude affair in comparison. It had been a hunting camp and consisted of only a few broken-down huts. About 10 days later the South Africans began supplying equipment, ammunition, mortars and webbing; and it was immediately apparent that Pretoria intended to continue using the MNR. Next, the senior instructor was called to a meeting at the SADF headquarters in Pretoria and asked to outline his plans for future operations. He told them there were only two ways to get into Mozambique, by foot through the Kruger or by air. Infiltration through the Kruger was ruled out on the grounds that people in uniform were not allowed in the park. Flights into Mozambique, at this juncture, were adjudged too risky. The South Africans said infiltration must be through Mapai and the bottom of Kruger near Komatipoort. 'They wanted me to carry on reinforcing the MNR and take out certain targets, opportunity targets. Basically we were to proceed with my plan of cutting Mozambique in three,' the senior instructor said.

The MNR were to come under three South African intelligence services from the army, the navy and special forces, a command situation which the senior instructor felt was unworkable and he protested. But it was clear, he said, that van Niekerk was really in charge of the operation. After about a month, dissatisfied with conditions and having learned that there was little likelihood of their being victimized by the Mugabe government for their role in the MNR, the CIO instructors returned to Zimbabwe.[29]

Mozambican officials now frankly admit that Zimbabwe's independence and the victory of Zanu, whom they had supported, brought two distinct responses in the Frelimo leadership. There was a heady feeling of victory, that they could take on and defeat anyone. It was this, in part, which led them into their disastrous third war with South Africa, directly and through the inherited surrogates, the MNR. Frelimo, normally a movement which carefully considers all major matters of policy and strategy, neglected on this occasion to discuss and decide a most obviously fundamental issue: what support, if any, it could afford to give the African National Congress (ANC) of South Africa. In the event it took no decision and did not assess the reality of its own position. What it did was to turn a blind eye to the activities of the ANC infiltrating through Mozambique into South Africa. In the circumstance of Mozambique in 1980 it was ill-considered, after the price it had paid in supporting the Zimbabwean struggle, and given the circumstance of the South African struggle at that point and the changes which had taken place in Pretoria bringing the militarists to power. If criticism is to be made of Frelimo's behaviour then it must begin over the failure to weigh the inherent risks of indecision at that point rather than the ugly decisions it was subsequently forced to make.

The second point to be borne in mind about Mozambique's response to Zimbabwe's independence is economic. In the colonial period the Portuguese had developed Mozambique as a service country for the land-locked African hinterland and for the northern Transvaal of South Africa. The Mozambique government's decision, on 3 March 1976, to close its border with Rhodesia had deprived it of about one-third of its foreign currency revenue earned through rail and port charges. Mozambique had been subjected to continual Rhodesian attacks and many of the targets had been economic, not military. South Africa had reduced its usage of Maputo port, stopped the agreement under which a percentage of mineworkers' salaries was paid in gold at preferential rates, and reduced the number of Mozambican migrant workers in the country. The total cost to Mozambique in the four years preceeding Zimbabwe's independence is put at US$ 556 million but the price was certainly much higher.[30] Mozambique's reality in April 1980 was that it was on the verge of bankruptcy and could not afford to take anyone on.

The headiness of this period was exacerbated by the dramatic upturn in the Mozambique economy in 1980 and 1981. After two wars, comprising its own national liberation struggle from 1964 to 1974 and then Zimbabwe's until 1980, Frelimo at last felt in a position to offer its people the rewards of sacrifice and struggle. The 1980 and 1981 economic statistics show the first signs of Mozambique's recovery following the devastation of the Rhodesian war. Production figures for some of Mozambique's most important exports reveal what occurred in this period. Cashew nut production in 1981 was 90 100 tons, the highest figure since 1977. By 1984 it had fallen to 25 300 tons. Cotton production in 1981 was 73 700 tons, the highest figure since independence in 1975. In 1984, production was only 19 700 tons. Sugar production fell from 177 200 tons to 39 300 tons in the same period, coking coal from 167 000 tons to 23 500 tons. In 1981, exports reached almost 10 billion meticais (US$ 250 million), the highest level since independence. In 1984 exports were down by 60 per cent to just over four billion meticais (US$ 100 million).[31]

Two other developments in the region in this period had an important bearing on the actions the South Africans began to take. The first was the creation of the Southern African Development Co-ordination Conference (SADCC) on 1 April 1980. This brought together nine countries in a loose regional economic grouping: Angola, Botswana, Lesotho, Malawi, Mozambique, Swaziland, Tanzania, Zambia and Zimbabwe.

The second development arose from the efforts of the Mugabe

government to reduce dependence on South Africa by resuming use of
traditional trade routes through Mozambique. Zimbabwe's trade
through these routes was virtually non-existent at independence in
1980 because the border had been closed for four years. But by 1983
trade through Mozambique had increased to 53.9 per cent of
Zimbabwe's total traffic.[32]

P.W. Botha, in one of his first speeches after becoming South
Africa's prime minister, had emphasized his wish to see the creation
of a southern African 'constellation of states', which would obviously
be dominated by Pretoria. SADCC was such a grouping without
Pretoria, although its leaders emphasized that the creation of their
organization was not a declaration of war on South Africa. It was
simply an attempt to co-ordinate their development and make
themselves less dependent on their powerful neighbour. That was
exactly what the South African government did not want. The
reopening of the Mozambique trade routes to Zaire, Zambia and
Zimbabwe meant those countries could become increasingly independent of South Africa.

Thus, while the activities of the ANC infiltrating across the border
from Mozambique gave South Africa's militarists the excuse to pull
the trigger, this was not the sole reason for what followed. As important,
if not more important, was Pretoria's determination to enforce
continued dependence, and this factor is borne out by the strategic
economic havoc they now began to wreak in Mozambique.

The military situation in 1980 began on a positive note for Frelimo.
Not only had the Rhodesian raids been ended by the Lancaster
agreement but the FPLM went on a successful offensive against the
MNR who, certainly in the first few months of the year, must have
been demoralized at losing their mentor and rear base. In late
February the FPLM re-established control in the Gorongosa area.
Sitatonga became the temporary MNR stronghold until it was also
overrun, in Operation Leopard, at the end of June 1980. Evidence
that the South Africans were already supplying the MNR was found at
Sitatonga in the form of ammunition boxes, equipment and
parachutes.

An officer in Zimbabwe military intelligence reported that strong
South African backing for the MNR began in June 1980. Until mid-
1979, he said, the MNR 'had little other than nuisance value'. In a
report dated 26 June 1981, Captain Arthur Eastwood said, 'By

December 1980 MNR had between 6 000 and 7 000 fully armed men with an estimated 2 000 recruits in the pipeline. Trained rein-forcements were airlifted in from South Africa and by February 1981 total strength was in the region of 10 000.'[33] It was in this period that farmers in south-eastern Zimbabwe reported seeing what they described as 'an armada of helicopters passing overhead' from South Africa heading into Mozambique. One airlift alone, it was estimated, could have ferried as many as 1 000 MNR and their equipment. On the night of 21/22 October 1980 eight helicopters heading into Mozambique were seen between Mabalauta and the Save/Runde confluence in south-eastern Zimbabwe, and an official protest was made to Pretoria about the violation of Zimbabwe's air space.

On 5 December 1981, when FPLM forces overran the large MNR base at Garagua in Manica province, important documents were captured which revealed South Africa's strategy.[34] One aspect was the considerable difference in the way they planned to use the MNR.

Whereas the CIO had used the MNR as a clandestine movement with a low profile, Pretoria planned a very much more public profile. At a meeting between the South Africans and the MNR, apparently in September or October 1980, it was decided to send Dhlakama on a European tour. The objectives were to make him and the MNR internationally known and to establish contacts with would-be supporters among right-wing European governments, political parties and business circles. He left South Africa, referred to in the documents as 'Africa External', on 18 November 1980 to visit Portugal, the Federal Republic of Germany (FRG) and France. In Portugal he met Catholic churchmen, business people and journalists, and a delegation from the Social Democratic Party. In the FRG, according to the Garagua documents, he met delegations from the two opposition parties, the Christian Democratic Union and Christian Social Union, the latter led by Franz Josef Strauss. In France, on 27 November, he met an advisor of President Valery Giscard d'Estaing. Soon thereafter the MNR had offices in Portugal and the FRG, and some support followed.

The second part of South Africa's strategy was to expand the war. On 25 October 1980 Dhlakama had had a meeting at the main MNR training camp in South Africa at the time, Zoabostad, with a South African delegation led by van Niekerk, the MID liaison officer to the CIO/MNR in Rhodesia in 1979. Van Niekerk said they had now concluded training the MNR recruits evacuated from Rhodesia in March 1980. He stressed the need to open new fronts in

Mozambique's southern provinces of Gaza and Inhambane. In the case of Gaza, the objective was to create a destabilized buffer zone to curb ANC infiltration into South Africa. In the case of Inhambane, it was so South Africa could use the cheaper method of landing supplies for the MNR by sea, as airdrops were proving too expensive and 'each parachute costs around R500'. They were also instructed to open an offensive in Maputo province and to conduct urban terrorism in Beira and Maputo. Finally, at a time when Zaire, Zambia and Zimbabwe were reverting to use of their traditional trade routes through Mozambique and becoming less dependent on South Africa, the MNR were instructed to sabotage these routes.[35]

This is the pattern which now emerged. On 12 April 1981 Dhlakama addressed a meeting at Regu Kraal in the Gogoi area of Manica province near the Zimbabwe border. He predicted the overthrow of Machel by 1985 and promised there would be no further food shortages because adequate supplies would come from South Africa. And, he added, the oil pipeline from Beira to Feruka refinery in the eastern Zimbabwe city of Mutare would be destroyed.[36] A series of sabotages of the pipeline followed. The most serious was on the night of 10/11 October 1982 when a large MNR group attacked and destroyed a pumping station at Maforga and kidnapped three Portuguese technicians, their wives and a five-year-old child. From the Garagua documents it appears that the South Africans were counting on the low-level destabilization in Zimbabwe's south-western Matabeleland to ensure that the Mugabe government would not commit troops to Mozambique. But the Maforga attack had exactly the opposite effect and for the first time members of the Zimbabwe National Army (ZNA) were deployed to Mozambique to protect the railway, road and pipeline from the port of Beira to the Zimbabwe border.[37]

Elsewhere, also acting on South African orders, the MNR drastically escalated their activities and the scale of atrocities against the civilian population. Large groups were observed heading south from Manica province, crossing the Save river into Gaza. Later, other groups were seen crossing the Limpopo river, bringing them right down to the South African border and thereby establishing a link for northbound supplies. The railway to Zimbabwe was blown up in three places on 16 December 1981 and thereafter was regularly sabotaged. Communal villages – one with 709 houses, stores and schools – were destroyed. Overflights by planes from South Africa were heard regularly.

By 30 December 1981, intelligence sources were reporting the presence of a large MNR base in Inhambane 'to facilitate resupply of the movement by sea'. Captured MNR members said one of their targets was National Highway No. 1, the road linking Maputo to Beira. Soon it became unsafe to travel on much of this road, except in armed convoys. Towns and FPLM bases were attacked. On 10 May an intelligence report said that the MNR were 'receiving war materials regularly via the sea routes on beaches located between Galhina and Marromeu'. Communal villages were burned and ambushes on the roads became frequent.

In the northern Niassa province, a 1 July 1981 intelligence report stated that 'large numbers of MNR are entering Mozambique via Dobwe along the border with Malawi. It is as yet uncertain whether these elements are trained in Malawi, or whether that country is just a holding area.' In Zambezia province, which provided about 50 per cent of Mozambique's export earnings, MNR attacks also began in 1981. Next the fighting spread to neighbouring Nampula province and it was clear that Malawi, officially or unofficially, at South Africa's behest, was providing a rear base or transit routes for the MNR into the three provinces it adjoins, Niassa, Tete and Zambezia. In this phase only Cabo Delgado, in the extreme north-east, remained unscathed.

The Mozambican government and the FPLM had not expected South Africa to unleash such an offensive against them. 'After independence, when we took off our guns, and exchanged our uniforms for suits and ties, we made a mistake,' Machel told a mass rally in Maputo on 23 June 1982. 'We looked elegant, but the bourgeoisie had the guns. Now we're putting our guns on once more, and we won't make the same mistake this time.'[38] Thirteen months later opening the SADCC summit in Maputo on 11 July 1983, he said, 'We are aware that the fundamental aim of the actions of destabilization against our countries is to render SADCC non-viable. Our land, sea and air frontiers are regularly violated by the Pretoria regime. Destabilization through gangs of bandits is complemented by the operations of special units designed to destroy selected targets that are vital for regional co-operation. Our ports and railways, fuel depots and pipelines, bridges and roads, communications systems and other economic development projects are the targets for this kind of aggression.'[39] This was entirely true as the Garagua documents prove, but Frelimo had become aware of the danger too late and in some areas of the country the FPLM were outnumbered and poorly equipped.

In addition to training, arming and directing their MNR surrogates, the SADF has frequently been involved in direct actions in Mozambique. South African troops invaded the country in January 1981, killing 13 members of the ANC in the capital, Maputo. In May 1983 they rocketed a suburb of Maputo killing six people, only one of whom had ANC connections. The principal damage was to a jam factory. And in October 1983 a SADF commando group bombed the ANC office in Maputo, wounding five people. Such acts, when purportedly directed against the ANC, were not denied by the South African government.

It is, however, the third area of military action, in between surrogate support and admitted direct action, which is the most difficult to detail. Former Rhodesian CIO officers admit South African participation in their attack on Beira's oil storage tanks in early 1979 and there can be no doubt that the early 1982 Beira attack was also South African. But they have been involved directly in other acts of sabotage inside Mozambique and the story of Alan Gingles dramatically illustrates this.

In late October 1981 the SADF headquarters in Pretoria announced that one Lieutenant Alan Gingles, 27, had been killed 'in action against terrorists on October 15' in the 'operational area', a euphemism for the Namibia/Angola frontier area. At about the same time, Mozambique announced that unidentified 'Boer soldiers' had been killed in a sabotage attempt on Zimbabwe's communication route from Beira. Four men had been blown to pieces by their own explosives when attacked by an FPLM patrol. Pretoria dismissed the claim as 'lying propaganda'.

There the matter rested until a London Sunday newspaper, *The Observer,* unearthed the truth. The crucial pieces of evidence at the scene of the intended sabotage were fragments of a hand-written novel. A 'Larne Grammer School' and a girl called 'Antrim' were mentioned in the novel. The search took the newspaper to the town of Larne in the Irish county of Antrim where they learned a memorial service had been held in a local church for Gingles. He had attended Sandhurst, served in the British army and gone to fight for Rhodesia in the later stages of that war in the Selous Scouts. When Zimbabwe became independent, Gingles, like many other embittered white servicemen, moved to South Africa becoming a lieutenant in the SADF. He had been based at Phalaborwa, a camp in the eastern Transvaal where the MNR were being trained. He had not died in the Namibia/Angola 'operational area' but 1 700 kilometres away on a sabotage mission in Mozambique on 14 October 1981.[40]

There is one further important development to consider in this period. The MNR, which the South Africans inherited from Rhodesia, and the *Africa Livre* movement operating from Malawi, which may have taken its name from the Rhodesian propaganda station, were not linked in early 1980. But at some point thereafter they came together under the aegis of Pretoria. Given the fact that Malawi is a land-locked country dependent upon Mozambique for its trade routes (prior to 1983 about 60 per cent of Malawi's trade transitted Mozambique), the decision to support the MNR against Frelimo seems suicidal. Yet there is no doubt that to this day the MNR are receiving support from Malawi. Frequent representations have been made by the Mozambican government to the Malawi authorities who have denied that the government, as such, is supporting the MNR. However, workers at a large Mozambican state farm, the Agro-Industrial Complex of Angonia, which is right on the border with Malawi in Tete province, said that even in 1985 they could hear planes passing overhead nearly every night resupplying the MNR. In 1984 a total of 55 workers on the farm were killed by the MNR and the complex's headquarters was attacked twice in 1985 by large MNR groups who were repulsed and who retreated back into Malawi. In one of these attacks a wounded worker on the farm was taken to hospital in Malawi and found himself in the same ward as wounded MNR personnel.[41]

At first sight Malawi's involvement with MNR is inexplicable. Since October 1983 its major route to the sea through Beira has been cut as a result of MNR sabotage and attacks. For much of 1984–85 its alternate route to the port of Nacala was severed. And through much of 1984–85 its road route through Tete to Zimbabwe was also cut and many trucks were destroyed in ambushes. It was forced to export its tea and tobacco crops by air in 1985 and Malawian officials said the freight bill was five times the previous levels as a result of re-routing and air-freighting.

Malawi's aging president, Kamuzu Banda, who is the only African leader to have formal diplomatic ties with Pretoria, may not be directly involved in support for the MNR, some senior Mozambican officials believe. Instead, they argue, members of his security forces, at Pretoria's behest, give support to the MNR. But, given Banda's authoritarian rule during the past two decades, this explanation seems implausible. Furthermore, it must be remembered that Banda has

traditionally laid claim to much of northern Mozambique. In the early
1960s he visited Dar es Salaam taking with him an old atlas. He
sought to convince President Julius Nyerere that northern
Mozambique was historically part of Tanzania and Malawi, and he
urged the Tanzanian leader to accompany him to a number of African
countries including Ghana, and to Portugal, to put this case. Nyerere
refused. Later (see note 18) Banda gave support to the African
National Union of Rombezia created by Jardim who sought to have
the area from the Ruvuma river, bordering on Tanzania and
demarcating the northern border of Mozambique, to the Zambezi
river further south, annexed to form a greater Malawi. The
probability, we believe, is that Banda still harbours these territorial
ambitions and that, irrespective of who is directly involved in the
support for and contacts with the MNR, Banda must know about it.

South Africa was undoubtedly encouraged in the policies it pursued in
this period by the election of Ronald Reagan in late 1980. When
Reagan took office early the following year his anti-communist
rhetoric, and statements like 'South Africa is an ally of Western
interests in Africa', could have left Pretoria's policy planners in little
doubt as to where they stood. So while the United States pursued
Reagan's policy, enunciated as 'constructive engagement', Pretoria
pursued its own policy of a 'total national strategy'. But the latter was
to backfire against its instigators when the escalating spiral of violence
began to threaten Western interests.
    When the American assistant secretary of state for African affairs,
Chester Crocker, visited Mozambique in January 1983, he explained
the US perspective this way:
    1. that the conflict between Mozambique and South Africa was
increasing instability throughout southern Africa, adversely affecting
countries dependent upon Mozambique ports and affecting
investment in SADCC;
    2. that the conflict threatened American relations with African
countries and it could lead to other countries in the region, who did not
have military ties with the Soviet Union, seeking military aid from
Moscow and other socialist countries;
    3. that Mozambique may call for direct military intervention by the
Soviet Union – without the United States being able to intervene –
thereby provoking reactions of solidarity by other African states with
Mozambique;

4. that the United States was conscious of the impact Mozambique support for the ANC could have on the region;

5. that the United States thought it necessary for South Africa to reduce its destabilization of the region and raised the possibility of diplomatic and economic measures if it did not;

6. that the United States administration accepted there was a link between regional instability and *apartheid* and felt it necessary for South Africa to begin a process that clearly indicated the system of racial discrimination would be reformed.[42]

After Mozambique's noisy expulsion of four alleged agents of the CIA in 1981 and given its Marxist-Leninist policies, close ties with the Soviet Union and strong positions diametrically opposed to those of the United States on issues like Afghanistan, East Timor, Saharawi and so on, the Crocker visit was an important milestone. The American concerns were clear. The escalating level of violence, if left unchecked, could force greater Soviet presence into the region. Mozambique's support for the ANC threatened Washington's major ally in the region, South Africa. And Washington's support for Pretoria was threatening its relations with independent African states.

In June the American under secretary for political affairs, Laurence Eagleburger, announced that the Reagan administration now had what he called a coherent strategy for southern Africa.[43] The Mozambique government interpreted this to mean that South Africa was no longer the principal axis of Washington's relations with the region.

Crocker's visit to Maputo had come a month after the first ministerial-level talks between Mozambique and South Africa in December 1982 at the border town of Komatipoort. The two sides met again in May 1983. Such was the level of distrust that nothing substantial emerged from these meetings.

But they met again in December 1983 in the Swaziland capital, Mbabane. Mozambican officials say this meeting was 'as a result of efforts' of Frank Wisner, then Crocker's deputy in the State Department's Africa Bureau.[44] Despite a subsequent reference to 'fiery' exchanges, the Mozambicans felt there was a new atmosphere in which South Africa accepted Mozambique's 'sovereignty, its territorial integrity, and its chosen path for development'. Why then, when South Africa and its surrogates were moving towards destroying the economic and social fabric of Mozambique, did some of Pretoria's policy-makers decide to include negotiation in the ruthless 'total strategy' agenda they had been pursuing?

Pressure from the United States, against the background of their regional imperatives spelt out by Crocker, played an important part. So did pressure from European nations. But a critical factor lay in the very nature of the MNR for they remained without alternative policies and alternative leaders. If Pretoria intended to remove the Frelimo government, and this remains a debatable point, then the MNR alone could not do it. This had been proven by the fact that despite the massive South African/MNR offensive of 1981–83 they were no nearer to removing Machel and the Mozambique government. South Africa would have to play a public role and this was a price Pretoria could not afford, politically or economically. It was a price that Washington feared would increase Soviet presence in a region where Moscow had shown only limited interest and would alienate the United States from many African countries.

At the Mbabane meeting the two delegations outlined the principles upon which an agreement must be based. They met again in Pretoria on 16 January 1984. Mozambique laid out a seven-point basis for an agreement which included respect for sovereignty and territorial integrity, respect of borders, non-aggression, neither party to resort to the threat of force against the other, respective territories not to be used for aggression against the other, no bases in their respective countries for hostile forces, and no broadcasting facilities for such forces.[45]

At this meeting, as during others in this phase, the South African preoccupation was the total removal of the ANC from Mozambique. Machel's statement after the Mbabane meeting that Mozambique would continue to give the ANC political, moral and diplomatic support particularly troubled the South African government. That he was no longer including the word 'material' was too fine a distinction for them and their constituency. A further point which seemed to elude the South Africans was that no comparison could be made between the ANC and the MNR. The ANC had been formed inside South Africa in 1912, long before either Frelimo or the National Party. The MNR had been formed in Rhodesia in 1976.

On 20 February a South African delegation, led by Foreign Minister Roelof 'Pik' Botha and including Malan, flew to Maputo. For the first time Machel entered directly into the talks when he met the South African ministers to receive a message from P.W. Botha.[46] At the Maputo meeting the South Africans continued to press for total elimination of the ANC from Mozambique. The draft agreement they proposed 'went so far that it would have meant we could not even have Miriam Makeba in Mozambique to give a concert,' a Frelimo official said.

The final significant meeting in the sequence occurred in Cape Town on 2–3 March 1984 when the amended Mozambican draft was accepted with minimal change. Frelimo won its argument to prevent the total removal of all ANC personnel from Mozambique and to allow the liberation movement to retain an office in Maputo with a staff limited to 10 people. In addition, ANC members with full-time jobs in various sectors in Mozambique would not be affected.

On 16 March, Machel and P.W. Botha signed the 'Agreement on Non-Aggression and Good Neighbourliness' amidst much pomp and ceremony on their common border. The agreement, it had been decided at the Cape Town meeting, would be known as the 'Accord of Nkomati'. (The full text of the accord is included as Appendix 1.) Apart from the principles laid out by Mozambique, the main addition was the establishment of a Joint Security Commission (JSC) to consider alleged infringements of the agreement.

The same day, before the contents of the accord were made public the ANC National Executive Committee issued a bitter statement following a meeting in Lusaka. In recent weeks, it said, South Africa had been involved in a frantic 'diplomatic, political and propaganda counter-offensive' in southern Africa. The objectives were:
  – to isolate the ANC throughout Southern Africa and to compel the independent countries of our region to act as Pretoria's agents in emasculating the ANC, the vanguard movement of the South African struggle for national emancipation;
  – to liquidate the armed struggle for the liberation of South Africa;
  – to gain new bridgeheads for the Pretoria regime in its efforts to undermine the unity of the frontline states, destroy the SADCC and replace it with a so-called constellation of states and thus to transform the independent countries of Southern Africa into its client states and;
  – to use the prestige of the frontline states in the campaign of the white minority regime to reduce the international isolation of *apartheid* South Africa and to lend legitimacy to itself and its colonial and fascist state.'
The statement went on to say that in pursuit of these goals South

Africa 'sought to reduce the independent countries of our region to the level of its Bantustan creations.'[47]

The ANC's bitterness was understandable. Mozambique had been the only country bordering on South Africa to give them virtually unfettered access for infiltration to conduct military operations. Now that had been stopped and even if South Africa had not obtained the total elimination of the ANC in Mozambique it had blocked their military operations through Mozambique. It is true that the ANC were not consulted on the agreement; Mozambique is a sovereign country. But ANC President Oliver Tambo did receive two briefings, one from Machel and the other by Mozambique's security minister, Mariano Matsinhe, in late February. Machel outlined to him the reality of Mozambique's situation, adding that if he could see some timetable for the end of *apartheid* resulting from ANC activities then Mozambique might have been prepared to continue to endure the onslaught. But he could not – and he said he could no longer ask the Mozambican people to pay the price they were paying.[48]

Tambo, at a press conference in London, appeared to strike a conciliatory note. It was not for him to decide Mozambique policy, he said. 'They pursue what they think is necessary. I'm not sure that in their position I'd have gone quite so far, but it must be accepted that the South African regime had decided to destroy Mozambique, to kill it as a state, and the leadership was forced to decide between life and death. So if it meant hugging the hyena, they had to do it. The rest of us, we must accept that position, but we also had to defend our position.' Later he added that if Mozambique had been supported adequately, politically and materially, they would not have had to do what they hated doing.[49]

In January 1984, two months before Nkomati and with the objective of getting its US$ 1.4 billion foreign debt rescheduled, the government of Mozambique had issued an economic report compiled by its National Planning Commission. Table A, showing South African imports and exports through Maputo for a decade from 1973, starkly illustrates the vulnerability of Mozambique's captive economy.[50]

From Table A it is possible to see how South Africa progressively reduced its traffic through Maputo after the Portuguese *coup d'état,* deliberately undermining Mozambique's economy. By 1983 South Africa had reduced this traffic to 16.1 per cent of its 1973 level. Similar direct actions of economic sabotage occurred elsewhere in this period. High-tariff cargoes were no longer sent through Maputo or were severely

Table A

South African imports and exports through the port of Maputo

Year	Traffic/thousand tons	Percentage relative to 1973
1973	6823.5	100
1974	5665.1	83
1975	5638.5	82.6
1976	4974.4	72.9
1977	4248.2	62.3
1978	4064.8	59.6
1979	4155.2	60.9
1980	3428.0	50.2
1981	3023.9	44.3
1982	2216.8	32.5
1983*	1100.0	16.1

*denotes estimate

cut back. Low-tariff cargo was retained at similar levels or dramatically increased – as in the case of coal from 1980 to 1982. All of this reduced Mozambique's foreign exchange earnings. Losses from movement of cargo, including a theoretical growth of seven per cent per annum which had been normal in the colonial period,meant an accumulated loss to Mozambique from 1974 to 1982 of US$ 535 million.[51]

A similar trend occurred in the case of migrant workers between 1975 and 1983 when South Africa reduced their numbers from 118 030 to 45 491. That alone led to a loss of US$ 568 million in income remitted home by the miners. The figures go on indefinitely with the total cost, including withholding cargo from Maputo and direct or surrogate actions, estimated at almost US$ four billion. The cost of direct and indirect destabilization in this period is unbelievable for a country which at independence in 1975 was considered one of the world's poorest with a per capita income of $177 a year ; where only three per cent of the population were literate; and which at independence had inherited from Portugal only US$ one million in foreign exchange and gold reserves.[52]

What the economic report did not cover, or only skimmed over, was the social cost. Hard-nosed bankers attending a debt-rescheduling meeting are not expected to pay attention to such details as human suffering. But again, the statistics are of an unbelievable magnitude as the table of educational statistics (Table B) reveals; and the social impact in years to come cannot be measured. The figures inside brackets are those for 14 November 1983, four months before Nkomati. Those outside brackets are for 15 April 1985, revealing how the situation has deteriorated *since* Nkomati as a result of South African/MNR activities.[53]

Table B
Disruption to education system before and after Nkomati showing schools closed, pupils and teachers displaced.

Province	Schools closed	Pupils displaced	Teachers displaced
Cabo Delgado*	29(0)	5 713 (0)	91(0)
Gaza	98(98)	12 288 (13 374)	202(219)
Inhambane	247(233)	55 775 (56 131)	807(752)
Manica	98(49)	18 328 (9 653)	257(145)
Maputo Prov.	123(36)	15 061 (3 532)	258(82)
Nampula	230(43)	36 273 (5 454)	608(95)
Niassa*	193(0)	19 330 (0)	354(0)
Sofala	228(186)	39 197 (31 539)	597(495)
Tete	164(18)	22 092 (2 239)	434(39)
Zambezia	453(177)	89 709 (30 766)	1 384(569)
TOTALS	1 863 (840)	313 766 (152 688)	4 992(2 396)

* In the case of Cabo Delgado and Niassa provinces no statistics appear in the 14 November 1983 report. Bandit activity had not begun in Cabo Delgado; there were bandits in Niassa but it is unclear whether that province did not make returns or whether no schools were affected at that point.

One of the most basic requirements for a largely rural population is a good network of rural stores selling basic commodities and other consumer goods. But since 1971 the population-per-store ratio has dramatically decreased. There have been three main reasons for this: the flight of the Portuguese settlers in 1974–75, population growth and bandit activity. In 1985, for example, MNR activity was responsible for the destruction of some 900 stores and the closure of an indeterminate number of others. To restore the population-per-store ratio to its 1971 level would require an additional 12 723 shops.[54] Health posts, health centres and rural hospitals have been destroyed on a large scale, 102 in 1982, 110 in 1985. Livestock are another basic need of most people in the rural areas. From 1980 to 1985 the Mozambique national herd, 50 per cent of which belonged to the peasants, was reduced from 1 500 000 cattle to 900 000. Of the remaining figure many are now running wild in the forests, not 'under control' as the Mozambicans say. No fibre of Mozambique society has remained untouched by South Africa's 'total strategy' and at least a quarter, if not half, of Mozambique's 13 million people are today 'displaced' in one way or another in their own country. The schools for their children, their access to medical care, their local store, their livestock, their access to markets, have been destroyed.

The above excludes the series of natural calamities which befell Mozambique in the same period. The massive floods of the Limpopo, Incomati and Zambezi rivers in 1977 and 1978 caused damage estimated at US$ 97 800 000.[55] In 1981–83 drought hit the south and centre of the country and, because of MNR ambushes and mined roads, relief supplies could not get through to many areas. Some estimate the number who died from the effects of the drought to be as high as 100 000. In 1979 Cyclone Justine struck the north of the country causing serious damage to agriculture and to the prawn harvest (one of Mozambique's most important exports), and paralysing industrial production at Nacala because of damage to the power station.

Nkomati was a high-risk gamble for Frelimo arising from their harsh, and what must have been painful, assessment of Mozambique's reality. Machel initially hailed it as a 'victory', a description many people found easier to understand in the context of South Africa than Mozambique. What he meant was that it reduced the dangerous isolation of his country, which, in the view of the United States, 'did not have the right to exist' (like Cuba and Nicaragua). In addition, the aggressor, South Africa, had been forced, on paper at least, to commit itself to non-aggression, thereby tacitly admitting in public that it had been the aggressor. These were somewhat convoluted arguments which, 18 months after Nkomati, a Frelimo official said might have been put differently. 'It might have been easier to present our case as being simply that we had not been supported enough by the world and therefore we had to take care of ourselves.' Certainly, against the background of Mozambique's economic and social plight, that was easier to understand.

The two immediate questions arising from Nkomati were whether South Africa would honour the agreement and whether it would bring a cease-fire in the debilitating war. Many people felt that Mozambique was being naive, desperate, or both. But the reality was that it had little to lose and everything to gain.

In the prelude to Nkomati and the months thereafter Frelimo was pursuing a strategy which had two principle prongs, military and diplomatic. Military tactics had been reassessed, the FPLM had gone more onto the offensive, and troops from the Zimbabwe army were protecting the important Beira road, rail and pipeline.

Machel's visit to six European countries in October 1983 was one of the opening moves in the diplomatic offensive. 'Pik' Botha followed a month later on a European tour which received a generally frosty welcome. The message he received was that destabilization was bad for business.

Within a month of Nkomati a steady shuttle of officials began to ply between Pretoria and Maputo. Frelimo's preoccupation was to bring an end to the violence, 'to liquidate banditry'. On 16 May 1984 in Cape Town, P.W. Botha assured a Mozambican envoy that South Africa had had nothing more to do with the MNR since Nkomati. But, as the disruptions continued and escalated, it was decided that a Mozambican envoy should meet Fernandes in Europe to try to ascertain what the MNR wanted. The meeting took place in a Frankfurt hotel on 29 May and the envoy gave Fernandes a Mozambique newspaper of the previous day containing his government's amnesty offer. Frelimo had already excluded political negotiations with the MNR, and Fernandes's demands for a government of national reconciliation, a multi-party system and Cabinet posts were rejected.[56]

On 30 June, Machel met 'Pik' Botha and van der Westhuizen in Maputo. He reiterated that there could be no question of power-sharing and he spoke of Portuguese ties to the MNR which he described as *saudosismo colonialista* (colonialist nostalgia). At this point many MNR recruits were still in South Africa, many having been press-ganged, and the possibility was discussed of temporarily employing 8 000 of them as mineworkers in South Africa while Mozambique reintegrated those inside the country who accepted the amnesty.

Eleven days later, van der Westhuizen was again in Mozambique proposing another meeting with Fernandes. Despite the reservations of the Mozambique government this took place in Pretoria three days later. Again it was unproductive. Fernandes rejected the amnesty and reintegration, and again demanded power-sharing. Increasingly, the question arose as to whether Fernandes was speaking on behalf of the

MNR inside Mozambique or on behalf of Portuguese political and business interests opposed to Frelimo. During the next month 'Pik' Botha and Malan met Fernandes. They fared little better. Fernandes's attitude was characterized as 'tough', 'hostile' and 'arrogant'. With the wisdom of hindsight it is now clear that Fernandes's confidence and obduracy stemmed from his knowledge that Nkomati had not ended South African support for the MNR.

Discussions continued in Pretoria, 27–29 September. The strategy now became one of persuading the MNR to accept Machel as president of Mozambique, and thereby his government, and to accept an unconditional end to violence. Increasingly in this phase the Mozambicans faced a danger they sought to avoid. The two earlier meetings with Fernandes had been 'unofficial', reflecting the Mozambique government's objective of trying not to give the MNR any official status and international credibility. On 1–3 October the Mozambique government delegation and Fernandes again assembled in Pretoria with 'Pik' Botha as the go-between. The meeting culminated in the 'Pretoria Declaration' which was a joint 'declaration on a cessation of armed activity and conflict'. For the first and only time Mozambique government officials appeared publicly with the MNR. The four points of declaration were:

1. Samora Moises Machel is acknowledged as the President of the People's Republic of Mozambique;
2. armed activity and conflict within Mozambique from whatever quarter or source must stop;
3. the South African government is requested to consider playing a role in the implementation of this declaration;
4. a commission will be established immediately to work towards an early implementation of this declaration.

The Mozambique government delegation had obtained the two most important points they sought: recognition by the MNR of Machel and therefore the government, and agreement in principle upon an unconditional cease-fire.

Two days later the South African deputy foreign minister, Louis Nel, flew to Maputo where he discussed the modalities and time-scale for implementing a cease-fire. But, the government learned, Fernandes had thrown another spanner in the works by demanding already rejected political conditions.

The Mozambique government delegation were under no il

when they returned to Pretoria on 8 October. Their obj
fix the date for a cease-fire and to refuse to be draw

discussion until there was a total cessation of violence. The meeting dragged on for four days, leaving the Mozambicans wondering whether Pretoria was unwilling to disentangle itself from the MNR in case it wanted to reactivate its surrogates. By the night of 11 October, agreement appeared imminent. A total cessation of violence was to occur 45 days after agreement in the JSC.

Then Fernandes asked for a one-week suspension of the meeting. This request came after he took a telephone call which he said came from Lisbon, from Carlos Mota Pinto, the deputy prime minister and minister of defence in the Soares coalition government in Portugal. Fernandes claimed that he had been told not to reach any agreement before going to Lisbon for discussions, and that the head of the Mozambique government delegation, the minister of state in the president's office for economic affairs, Jacinto Veloso, should accompany him.[57]

Whether that telephone call sabotaged possible agreement at the eleventh hour is difficult to determine. Although the Mozambican and South African governments appeared to think agreement was imminent, Fernandes's behaviour since his meeting in Frankfurt on 29 May with a Mozambican official suggests that he, or whoever was giving him instructions, had always intended to demand impossible concessions. However, the 'Portuguese connection' does need some explanation.

In the wake of the Portuguese *coup d'état,* Portuguese business interests in Mozambique were subject to a series of nationalizations, firstly by the soldiers who seized power in Lisbon and then, to a lesser extent, by Frelimo. Jardim had been one of those affected. Another was Manuel Bulhosa, a one-time business partner of Jardim and, until its nationalization, owner of the Maputo oil refinery, SONAREP. Bulhosa, reputedly Portugal's richest businessman, employed Fernandes ostensibly at his Lisbon publishing house, Livraria Bertrand.[58] He also employed Jorge Correia, who replaced Fernandes as representative in Europe when the latter became secretary-general. These Portuguese MNR representatives came and went at will in Lisbon, which became the MNR propaganda headquarters, Mozambique government protestations notwithstanding. It became clear early on that they had highly-placed contacts among Portuguese civilian and military leaders who refused to accept Frelimo and who had either personally lost property in Mozambique or represented constituents who had.

'Pik' Botha appeared to have been infuriated by what he regarded as Portuguese interference which had denied him and his government a diplomatic and political prize. He told the Mozambique delegation that he had decided to travel immediately to Portugal to meet Soares, who had agreed to a meeting. Botha claimed he was at Johannesburg's Jan Smuts Airport on 12 October, waiting to depart, when a message was received from Lisbon saying that his visit was 'inopportune'.

The Mozambique delegation returned to Maputo and Nel arrived there again on 16 October to 'revive' the process. By then it had been decided that the situation must be presented to the Mozambique Council of Ministers for analysis and decision. Thereafter, certainly until August 1985, the Mozambique government kept the diplomatic option open but did not meet or negotiate by proxy with the MNR. The main emphasis was on the military option but the slaughter and devastation continued.

In this period of intensive negotiations and thereafter, the government in Maputo frequently protested to South Africa about violations of Nkomati. In Cape Town in January 1984, they had raised the point that between the Lancaster House agreement and Zimbabwe's independence the Rhodesians had infiltrated many additional MNR. The South Africans had replied that they were not Rhodesians on the point of collapse and would not resort to such measures. But that was exactly what they did. Supplies were moved in by air and sea to cover MNR requirements for many months. A very large number of MNR were pushed across the border from South Africa into the southern Maputo province and attacks began to occur near the capital. Road travel in the area became hazardous and the situation deteriorated seriously. In the north, operations were dramatically escalated from Malawi leading to a worsening of the situation in Nampula, Niassa, Tete and Zambezia provinces.

In June 1985, Machel, Mugabe and Nyerere met in Harare. By this time the ZNA force guarding the Beira road, railway and pipeline had risen to about 2 000 troops. Mozambique was now in serious trouble and its two closest neighbours and allies increased their military support. Tanzania, under almost as great economic constraint as Mozambique, agreed to train Mozambican recruits to fight in the three northern provinces: Cabo Delgado, which was still comparatively unaffected by the war, Niassa and Nampula. The recruits would be trained at Nachingwea in southern Tanzania, once Frelimo's major training base and then Zanla's.

Zimbabwe, in the midst of a comparative economic boom and with a well-trained and well-equipped army, was able to make a greater commitment. ZNA troops, in addition to those guarding the communications routes, moved into the three central provinces of Manica, Sofala and Tete. These were the provinces Zanla had operated from during its own liberation struggle and which posed few linguistic difficulties between the Zimbabwean troops and the local population. In mid-July, Zimbabwe deployed three combat battalions numbering about 3 000 men, backed by a further 2 000 support troops. Mozambique's four other provinces were left to the FPLM: Gaza, Inhambane and Maputo in the south and Zambezia in the north.[59]

On 28 August in Sofala, the MNR headquarters at Gorongosa was attacked and overrun. Psychologically it was an important morale boost in the new joint offensive against the MNR and, although few bandits were killed, large quanties of arms, ammunition and supplies were captured. But most important were the documents, which revealed the extent of South Africa's duplicity before and after Nkomati.

At a news conference in Maputo on 30 September, Mozambique's minister of security, Colonel Sergio Vieira, made public a portion of the 'Gorongosa documents', as they came to be called. [60] Extracts from three diaries revealed massive and premeditated violations of Nkomati. They also revealed some of the principle names involved in the violations: Nel, General Constand Viljoen, chief of the SADF, Lieutenant-General André Liebenberg, head of SADF 'Special Forces', van der Westhuizen, van Niekerk and Brigadier van Tonder of MID.

As stated earlier, it had been agreed that in the period between the Mbabane meeting and Nkomati no men or equipment would be infiltrated. The South Africans had insisted they would not behave as the Rhodesians had. In the event they behaved far worse. In Pretoria on 23 February, three weeks before Nkomati, Dhlakama met senior members of MID. Van der Westhuizen is quoted as saying, 'We, the military, will continue to give them [the MNR] support without the consent of our politicians in a massive way so that they can win the war.' Machel, he added, would only fall by the destruction of his economy and communications. He went on to guarantee resupply to the MNR and he defined targets – railways, Cahora Bassa, foreign aid workers[61] and economic targets *such as those involving SADCC*. It was arranged to re-arm and supply the MNR before Nkomati to give them autonomy for a six-month period and one of the diaries records innumerable resupplies by plane and ship in this period. In addition, a South African team was sent to Zambezia province to train 100 MNR instructors and 200 recruits. The Phalaborwa training camp in South Africa was moved to Louis Trichardt. A new transmission network was set up between the SADF and the MNR inside Mozambique. So much for the 'gentlemen's agreement'.

Mozambican enquiries as to the whereabouts of large numbers of MNR in South Africa and the location of arms caches in Mozambique were met by a refusal to give information, Vieira said. South Africa replied that it 'had parted with the bandits on not-so-good terms and that it had severed all links with the bandits and was fulfilling the accord. They made the statement on several occasions.' Protests about the violations of Nkomati were countered by South Africa installing radar on the common border to detect overflights. The whole time it was violating Mozambique's air space and territorial waters to resupply the MNR.

In June 1984, with Dhlakama reporting they were running short of ammunition in the south and centre of Mozambique, van Niekerk instructed him to conserve ammunition. They should avoid clashes with the FPLM and should concentrate instead on the destruction of the economy and infrastructure and gaining control over the population. 'The MNR must survive until Machel comes to an agreement with the MNR, but never give Frelimo the impression that you no longer possess war material,' van Niekerk ordered.

Viljoen, in a meeting with the MNR on 6 September 1984, recommended that they did not accept the amnesty which his government had proposed in the first place to Mozambique officials. The general said he would facilitate contacts with foreign countries, especially in Africa, and told the MNR not to be deceived by 'Pik' Botha 'because he is treacherous'. [62] The diary records on 17 September that microphones were to be installed to bug 'Pik' Botha's meetings with Frelimo and it is clear that the foreign minister's meeting with senior Western ambassadors was also bugged. The FPLM communications were also monitored and all of this passed on to the MNR.

Dhlakama's message of 16 June 1984 to van Niekerk, who is continually referred to as 'friend Commander Charlie', indicates the growing desperation of the MNR and shows that the FPLM's large-scale post-Nkomati military offensive was paying off. 'As we are at the moment without any war material,' Dhlakama said in a radio message, 'the enemy is bound to recuperate, which will force us to shift our bases round from one place to another. They will go on chasing us all over the place, which will possibly lead to a bad situation for us, similar to the situation we experienced in 1980 when we suffered so much because Rhodesia abandoned us.' The South African response was to send in more armaments by air and sea.

On 16 September 1985, two weeks before Vieira's press conference revealing the contents of the Gorongosa documents, Machel summoned 'Pik' Botha to Maputo. The Mozambican leader presented him with extracts from the documents and, according to officials, Botha was 'visibly annoyed' to find himself described as 'treacherous' by Viljoen and to learn that meetings he thought were private had been bugged by the SADF. Botha said he had not been informed that his deputy, Nel, had flown to Gorongosa on 8 June 1985 to meet Dhlakama. At a news conference in Pretoria on 18 September, limited to South African journalists, the foreign minister tried to minimize the damage. He admitted there had been continued contacts between the South Africans and the MNR after Nkomati but described the breaches as 'technical'. The South African air force had also made supply drops but he characterized these as being 'mostly humanitarian aid'.[63]

On 9 October, Viljoen also admitted the diaries were essentially correct. 'Pik' Botha had not been informed about his deputy's visit to Gorongosa in June. Nor, Viljoen said, had he informed his own minister, Malan, or P.W. Botha. He criticized the handling of the negotiations by the Ministry of Foreign Affairs but claimed the SADF accepted the government's 'change of strategy' towards Mozambique.[64] The following day, P.W. Botha publicly gave Viljoen his total support. 'Whatever you say of him [Viljoen], you can surely say that he is an honourable and brave officer. I asked him in front of witnesses whether he was guilty of transgressing the Accord. He denied it and assured me that he kept to the government's decision. I believe General Viljoen and no communist attempt to discredit him or former deputy Foreign Minister Louis Nel will succeed.'[65]

None of these comments addressed the most serious charges arising from the Gorongosa documents and the apparent contradictions within the South African establishment. Why had Viljoen described 'Pik' Botha as 'treacherous'? Why had his meetings with Mozambique officials and Western ambassadors been bugged? No one commented on the large number of well-documented arms drops to the MNR. Nor did anyone comment on van der Westhuizen's remark that the military would continue to support the MNR irrespective of what the politicians decided to do. The breach of the 'gentlemen's agreement' preceeding Nkomati was ignored, as was the fact that the SADF were giving the MNR specific targets to destroy in Mozambique.

Whether or not there were contradictions between some politicians and some soldiers over Nkomati is not the point. In the final analysis, government must be held responsible for the actions of its army and in this case, finally, P.W. Botha as head of government. For many years before becoming prime minister, he had been a very aggressive defence minister, standing on the political right of the National Party. His career, in effect, had been made by the military and he had brought them to power with him. By 1984 he was increasingly losing the support of the right wing of the party over his reform programme. His main constituency at that point was the military.

In all probability, P.W. Botha never wanted Nkomati. But South Africa, like Mozambique, was confronted in 1983 by the American analysis that the two countries were principal ones responsible for the state of insecurity in the region. If there was to be peace in the region then they were the ones to establish it. While Mozambique was certainly willing to consider an agreement leading to peace, the probability of this looked very slim until the two sides met in Pretoria on 16 January 1984. Thereafter the real bargaining and details took exactly two months before Nkomati was signed.

P.W. Botha then faced considerable difficulty. He had publicly committed himself in a very high-profile manner at Nkomati. To renege on the agreement would undermine his political credibility internationally and in South Africa. But, the Gorongosa documents reveal, senior members of the SADF were unhappy about Nkomati from the beginning and had no intention of abiding by it. There can be little doubt that they were supported in this course of action by their senior political leaders, including ultimately the state president, as most of those named have been promoted. Van der Westhuizen was moved from MID to the powerful post of secretary to the State Security Council (SSC). Nel was removed as foreign affairs deputy to the new post of deputy minister in charge of the state president's information bureau (responsible, among the other things, for foreign media coverage). Liebenberg was promoted to army commander. Viljoen's retirement had been announced months earlier and its timing had more to do with Angola than Mozambique.

Nothing has been heard of disciplinary action against van Tonder or
van Niekerk.

The timing of the discovery of the Gorongosa documents could not
have been worse for South Africa. When Machel called 'Pik' Botha to
Maputo on 16 September the Mozambican leader was about to leave
for his first official visit to the United States. By the time Machel met
Reagan at the White House the American had already been briefed
about the documents. He expressed 'shock' at the breach of Nkomati
and asked if there was anything the United States could do. The
meeting finished up with the two leaders on first name terms and
Machel struck the right chord by briefing Reagan on the situation but
asking for nothing. A few days later in Britain, Thatcher expressed
similar concern, noting that it was a very serious matter when armies
did not follow the orders of their governments.[66] Gorongosa had given
the diplomatic initiative back to Mozambique, leaving South Africa in
the dock.

At a press conference in the United States, Machel was asked how
he now viewed Nkomati, in the light of the seriousness of South
Africa's violations. He replied that he had three choices: to abrogate,
to renegotiate, or to do nothing. In October he suspended meeting of
the JSC, which had obviously become a powerless watch-dog. The
South Africans responded by accusing Mozambique of breaches of
Nkomati. The annual Ruth First memorial lecture at Eduardo
Mondlane University in Maputo was described as a 'provocation'.[67] A
police orphanage outside Maputo was described as an ANC transit
camp. Recognizing that South Africa must cover its embarrassment
by some means, no one took the allegations very seriously.

In control of the diplomatic offensive, and with a further
200 kilograms of compromising Gorongosa documents still not
made public, Mozambique continued to pursue the second principal
prong of the strategy it had embarked upon in 1983. Military
operations were stepped up and there was a steady flow of reports
from Mozambique of major MNR bases being overrun and large
quantities of arms, ammunition and other supplies being captured.[68] In
some sectors of Mozambique there were indications by late 1985 that
the MNR were again running short of ammunition and explosives; and
some acts of sabotage were carried out without explosives or with
crude weapons. With Britain bringing pressure to bear on Malawi to
cease MNR operations from that country and with the United
States and other Western governments trying to persuade South Africa to

honour Nkomati, 1986 promised to be a critical year for Mozambique. Certainly, P.W. Botha could not afford another Gorongosa scandal. But could he curb his military? – and did he even want to? – remained the critical unanswered questions.

Beyond that there is one final question which must be addressed: is the solution military, political, or a blend of both? While the Mozambique government has rejected negotiations with the MNR, it has not rejected a political solution in favour of a military one. What it has done is to define who it should talk to at the political level and who it must deal with at the military level. This distinction was succinctly summed up by one government official who said, 'We talk to the organ-grinder, not the monkey.'

The 'organ-grinder' is South Africa, as the trainer, supplier and director of the MNR. Therefore it was necessary to talk to South Africa and that was what Mozambique did – before, during and after Nkomati. That South Africa acted in bad faith and breached the Nkomati agreement is now well documented. But this does not alter the validity of the fact that the political solution had to be sought with South Africa. Furthermore, with whom in the MNR would Mozambique negotiate a political solution, even if it were willing to do so?[69] There is very clear evidence, even articulated by MNR propagandists, of serious divisions between the MNR non-African group in Europe and the bandits within Mozambique. Within the latter group there are also serious divisions. If a cease-fire were to be agreed, Mozambique officials do not anticipate much more than 30 per cent of the bandits would accept it initially.

In the circumstance there is no choice but to pursue both the political and military options while recognizing that the solution lies in a blend of both. If South Africa – and Malawi – were to cease their support for the MNR then gradually, probably over two years or more, the fighting would decrease. If they do not, the war will continue unabated with the ever-growing possibility of further internationalization.

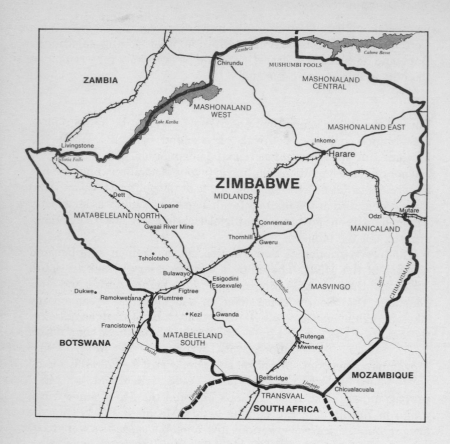

CHAPTER 2

Zimbabwe:
Apartheid's Dilemma

South Africa's destabilization of Zimbabwe can be subdivided into seven categories – direct military action including sabotage, clandestine support for banditry, assassination, espionage, economic sabotage, propaganda and disinformation. All of these have been used to varying degrees since Zimbabwe's independence on 18 April 1980. Yet Pretoria's policy planners face their greatest dilemma in just how far to go in destabilizing Zimbabwe.

The seeds of destabilization were sown in a 45-day period from 4 March 1980 to 18 April. At 9 am on 4 March, the Rhodesian registrar of elections, Eric Pope-Symonds, announced the results of Zimbabwe's pre-independence elections in a live radio broadcast to a hushed nation. The Zimbabwe African National Union-Patriotic Front (ZANU-PF) led by Robert Mugabe had won 57 seats, an outright majority in the 100-seat parliament. Only one of those seats was in Matabeleland bordering on Botswana and South Africa. The Patriotic Front-Zimbabwe African People's Union (PF-ZAPU) led by Joshua Nkomo had won 20 seats, 15 of them in Matabeleland. The United African National Council (UANC) led by Bishop Abel Muzorewa, prime minister of the short-lived and discredited Zimbabwe-Rhodesia government, had won only three.[1] The remaining 20 seats, reserved for whites on a separate roll, had already gone to the Rhodesian Front (RF), whose leader, Ian Smith, had rebelled 15 years earlier against the British crown to prevent black majority rule.

Mugabe and most Zanu leaders had assembled in Mugabe's temporary home at 3 Quorn Avenue in Salisbury's Mount Pleasant suburb to hear the results. As the results were announced, province by province, cheers reverberated through the house; and, as the victors celebrated, a convoy of Rhodesian armoured vehicles moved menacingly down the street outside. The faces of the white soldiers expressed their bitterness, and their guns were trained on Mugabe's house.

In most white Rhodesian homes there was stunned disbelief. Mugabe, the pariah, the man they had been told was the 'arch terrorist', had won. Some began packing their bags immediately, loading their cars and heading for South Africa. Thousands more made plans to follow. Among those who headed south in the exodus were members of 'compromised' Rhodesian units such as the all-white Rhodesian Light Infantry (RLI), the Special Air Service (SAS), and the Selous Scouts. They feared retribution for actions during the war. Others who fled included police officers, particularly from the Special Branch (SB), a handful of officers from the Central Intelligence Organization (CIO), members of the Guard Force, district security officers and members of Muzorewa's Security Force Auxiliaries. In all, some 5 000 'compromised' military and paramilitary went south. Some took with them invaluable intelligence and military knowledge; others took actual files.

They were gladly received by South Africa, which had pumped more than $2 million into a vain attempt to prevent a Zanu victory, subsidizing Muzorewa's campaign in particular.[2] Many of the Rhodesians went into the 5th Reconnaissance Regiment, a newly formed specialist unit which was to see action against independent African governments throughout the subcontinent, particularly in Angola. Others joined the Military Intelligence Directorate (MID) which was to have a key role in the destabilization of Mozambique and Zimbabwe. South Africa had inherited from Rhodesia a nucleus upon which to build its policy of destabilizing Zimbabwe.

The shock of the election result was equally acute among the losing black parties; six of them had failed to win a seat and in most cases had forfeited their deposits. Muzorewa's humiliation was total. In the stage-managed 'Zimbabwe-Rhodesia' elections of April 1979, in which neither Zanu nor Zapu participated, he had supposedly won a majority. Lord Chitnis, a British Liberal peer who observed that election, reported that it 'was nothing more than a gigantic confidence trick designed to foist on a cowed and indoctrinated black electorate a settlement and a constitution which were formulated without its consent and which are being implemented without its approval'.[3]

In that election Reverend Ndabaningi Sithole, deposed as leader of Zanu four years earlier, had been badly defeated by Muzorewa. Sithole still masqueraded as leader of Zanu but it was clear he had totally lost the confidence of the party rank-and-file, and he did not win a single seat in the 1980 election.[4]

Among all the contenders in 1980 the severest humiliation was reserved for Nkomo. He had been around nationalist politics for over 20 years and rejoiced in the titles of 'Father of Zimbabwe Nationalism' or 'Father Zimbabwe'. He had had himself declared 'President for Life' of Zapu; and defeat at the hands of Mugabe, whom he referred to as 'that young man', was unthinkable. Now the unthinkable had occurred. An embittered Nkomo argued that the result had been brought about by intimidation by Mugabe's supporters and that the election had been rigged by a bizarre coalition including China, Mozambique, Tanzania, Britain and the United States.

Mugabe was magnanimous in victory, advocating a policy of reconciliation, offering Nkomo the post of constitutional president and, when he refused, giving him the powerful post of minister of home affairs. But it was inherent in the success of the Lancaster House agreement leading to the elections that all parties should believe they would win, and Zanu's victory left a plethora of embittered parties and individuals in its wake.[5]

For the South Africans the outcome was a particularly bitter blow. They had invested US$ 300 million in the Rhodesian war against the nationalists and they had invested heavily in the election campaign against Zanu.[6] But, more importantly, they sought the creation of a Constellation of Southern African States (CONSAS) which they would economically and technologically dominate. Whereas some of the other election contenders might have been malleable, Mugabe certainly would not be despite his country's heavy economic and geographic dependence on South Africa. In the first place he advocated socialist policies based on Marxist-Leninist principles. Secondly, he was an outspoken critic of *apartheid*. Thirdly, he was determined to decrease Zimbabwe's dependence on South Africa and re-route his country's trade back to its traditional lines through Mozambique. On 1 April, 17 days before Zimbabwe became independent, Mugabe joined leaders from eight other independent states in the region to establish the Southern African Development Coordination Conference (SADCC). This loose grouping sought greater economic independence from South Africa, a policy diametrically opposed to the subcontinental hegemony Pretoria perceived as its role.

Thus, at the end of the 45 decisive days which embraced the period between the announcement of the election result and Zimbabwe's

independence, many of the pieces and players for the process of
destabilization had fallen into place. But Pretoria faced a dilemma in
the case of Zimbabwe. Dependence was not entirely one-sided.
Destroying the communications routes through Angola to the west
and Mozambique to the east ensured dependence upon South Africa
for trade routes for the land-locked countries of the regional hinterland. But Zimbabwe, located to the immediate north of South Africa,
commanded these access routes to Malawi, Zaire and Zambia. Of
necessity, the destabilization of Zimbabwe had to be on a less
devastating scale.

From the outset, it was bound to be an uneasy relationship but, as
Mozambique's President Machel has frequently observed: 'There are
two things you cannot choose, brothers and neighbours. We can't
move our country.' Yet the Mugabe government demonstrated early
on that it would not, and could not, allow Zimbabwe to be used as a
springboard for attacks on South Africa.

A large number of guerrillas of the African National Congress
(ANC) of South Africa had been infiltrated into Zimbabwe with
returning guerrillas of the Zimbabwe People's Revolutionary Army
(ZPRA), the military wing of Zapu. They had first gone into an
assembly point with ZPRA forces and then some had moved, going to
ground in houses in Bulawayo. When the government learned about
this they were quickly rounded up and returned to Zambia.[7] It was an
early and clear signal by the newly independent government on a
critical issue – an issue which the South African military would use as
an excuse to attack and destabilize Angola, Botswana, Lesotho,
Mozambique and Zambia. In theory, at least, the same excuse did not
prevail in the case of Zimbabwe. (However, when land-mines exploded in the northern Transvaal in late 1985, damaging vehicles and
killing several whites, the South Africans claimed the mines had been
carried through Zimbabwe and threatened to retaliate.)

In a broadcast to the nation on the night of his victory, Mugabe had
tried to allay South African fears. The Republic, he said, was a
'geographical and historical reality. And our reality is that we must
coexist with South -Africa.' Future relations, he said, would be
conducted on the 'basis of a mutual recognition of the differences
which exist between us'. Zimbabwe would not interfere in South
Africa's internal affairs and, similarly, it would expect South Africa to
respect Zimbabwe's sovereignty. Coexistence, however, did not mean

keeping silent about *apartheid*.[8] In May, a month after independence, he banned a visit by the British Lions rugby side who were touring South Africa, and in late June he announced the severing of diplomatic ties inherited from Rhodesia. 'We cannot have any political and diplomatic relations with South Africa until it puts its own political house in order and kills the repugnance and revulsion we have to *apartheid*,' he said. [9] Ten days later, the South African foreign minister, 'Pik' Botha, announcing the withdrawal of his diplomats from Harare, said South Africa would not interfere or do anything that might increase tension in Zimbabwe.[10] The diplomatic missions in the two countries were replaced by trade missions.

Mugabe and members of his government were already accusing South Africa of involvement in destabilizing Zimbabwe. Although no public evidence was immediately available to substantiate the charge, during the next 16 months a substantial dossier was to emerge of a sequence of events that began in August 1981.

The first incident occurred on 3 August 1981. Joe Gqabi, representative of the ANC in Zimbabwe, who had spent many years imprisoned on Robben Island, was assassinated outside his Harare house. Three weapons were found abandoned at the scene: a silenced pistol and two silenced, Israeli-manufactured, Uzi sub-machine-guns. All of them had been issued to the Selous Scouts prior to independence. But none was the murder weapon. They had been left, it would appear, to confuse the police investigators. The murder weapon was never found. Later it emerged that Gqabi had been targetted by the South Africans and eliminated by a squad sent into Zimbabwe to do the job.[11]

A small cell of strategically placed whites, at the time serving as members of the CIO, had supplied the vital intelligence for Gqabi's assassination. The cell was led by Geoffrey Price, an intelligence officer in Rhodesia who was retained as head of close security for Mugabe after independence. It included Colin Evans and Philip Hartlebury, who had been recruited by Price around the time of independence. Price escaped to South Africa via Britain after getting compassionate leave claiming 'his grandmother was dying'. His flight came some days after Evans and Hartlebury had been arrested. They were charged with espionage and illegal possession of arms. Both pleaded not guilty and a High Court judge, Mr Justice McNally, dismissed the cases against them after ruling their statements inadmissable. McNally's decision surprised the government and the two spies were detained under emergency powers legislation.

On 10 February 1982, the minister of state (security) in the prime minister's office, Emmerson Munangagwa, speaking from a brief prepared by a team of lawyers, made a lengthy statement to parliament challenging McNally's judgement and reading extracts from the statements made by Evans and Hartlebury.

'Immediately after their arrest,' the minister said, 'South Africa approached us through the mediation of their Trade Mission here in Harare, and admitted that the two spies were their men. Along with this admission came the request that we agree to release them and their families in exchange for 115 Angolan prisoners. We rejected that request. That was in January 1982. Towards the end of January or in early February the South Africans came again with a second proposal, this time offering one Russian spy and the 115 Angolan prisoners in exchange for the two spies at a venue of our choice. Again we rejected that offer.' A further approach was made through a third party. 'They, the third party, the Western regime, were willing to receive them and later pass them on to Pretoria. Incidentally, the two spies are British.' This latter comment appeared to indicate that the third party was Britain.

Both Evans and Hartlebury had admitted to being recruited by Price to spy for South Africa, according to extracts of their statements that the minister read to parliament. Both admitted to supplying information about Gqabi and said their contact, named as Erasmus, had said only three people knew the details of the assassination and 'it was best if it remained that way'. They believed the killers had come from South Africa. The public was left with the very definite impression that if McNally had not ruled the statements inadmissable, the court verdict would have been different.[12]

The next incident in the sequence occurred on 16 August 1981. A series of massive explosions ripped through the armoury at Inkomo Barracks near Harare destroying $36 million worth of armaments. A board of inquiry, including explosives experts from Britain and Yugoslavia, investigated three possible causes – enemy action, negligence and accident. They found the explosions were caused by 'deliberate enemy action against Zimbabwe'.[13]

Police investigations led to the arrest of Captain Frank Gericke, an explosives expert who had served in the Rhodesian security forces and stayed on in the Zimbabwe National Army (ZNA) as commander of the corps of engineers. He was in charge of the armoury at Inkomo, had an office in the compound and complete access to the bunkers containing the armaments.[14] Police investigations and the questioning of Gericke were continuing when the South Africans made a tacit admission that they were involved. Frederick Varkevisser, a detective inspector in the police, obtained Gericke's release 'ostensibly to undertake further enquiries', a Zimbabwe government statement said. That was the last the Zimbabweans saw of either of them. With the net closing in, the South Africans had opted for what is known in intelligence parlance as 'a hot extraction'. Gericke and Varkevisser are believed to have flown to South Africa in a light plane. Gericke is now serving in the South African Defence Force (SADF) and Varkevisser is working in Cape Town.[15]

On 18 December a ten-to-fifteen kilogram bomb exploded on the roof of the Zanu party headquarters at 88 Manica Road in central Harare. Six Christmas shoppers were killed and more than 100 injured. But investigating officers were sure that the real target was the Zanu leadership. The central committee was scheduled to hold a meeting on the third floor of the building at the time the bomb exploded. Fortunately, the meeting had been postponed. Subsequent information obtained by the investigators, and considered reliable, pointed to the operation having been carried out by former members of the Rhodesian SAS serving in the SADF.

There was another major sabotage attempt in this period that went unreported. Explosive devices were placed in the fuel tanks of about 30 tank transporters, tanks and armoured cars in KG VI Barracks, the ZNA headquarters in Harare. The charges had complex, electronically controlled timing mechanisms with a 33-day delay. But the fuses became saturated by diesel fuel and the two or three which detonated caused relatively minor damage. Had the whole lot gone off as planned, the bulk of the ZNA's armoured vehicles would have been destroyed.

Late July 1982 brought two more serious incidents. On 23 July six tourists – two Americans, two Australians and two Britons – were abducted by bandits on the road from Bulawayo to Victoria Falls. It was about two years before their bodies were found, and the publicity generated by the incident seriously undermined Zimbabwe's tourist industry.

Two days later, on 25 July, a quarter of Zimbabwe's air force planes were sabotaged on the ground at the Thornhill base near Gweru in the centre of the country. This virtually wiped out Zimbabwe's strike and jet interception capabilities. Incendiary devices detonated by a

clockwork timing mechanism were used. While investigators believed
that the saboteurs may have had help from inside the base, they were
convinced, from information they received and from the level of
expertise required, that this was another South African operation.[16]

The most damning evidence of South Africa's direct activities
against Zimbabwe came on 18 August 1982. The ZNA, acting on
information they had received, ambushed a group of South African
soldiers who had crossed the Limpopo river into Zimbabwe three days
earlier. The three white soldiers in the group were killed. The
remainder, believed to be Africans, escaped back to South Africa. The
South African government initially denied any knowledge of the
group. But, under pressure from the families to secure the return of
the bodies, the chief of the SADF, General Constand Viljoen, held a
press conference on 26 August. He identified the three dead men as
Staff Sergeant David Berry and Sergeants John Wessels and Robert
Beech. Berry had served in the Rhodesian SAS, Wessels and Beech in
the RLI. All three were believed to have been serving in the 5th
Reconnaissance Regiment of the SADF special forces, a unit made up
largely of former Rhodesian servicemen. Their base was at Phalaborwa in the northern Transvaal where dissidents to fight in Mozambique and Zimbabwe were trained. Viljoen claimed the group crossed
into Zimbabwe on an 'unauthorized raid' with the aim of freeing
political detainees. He was unable to explain why one of the dead men
was wearing an Angolan army uniform and another a T-shirt bearing
the slogan of Muzorewa's auxiliaries.[17]

This incident was acutely embarrassing for Pretoria. It was the last
known direct military operation in which the SADF, using former
white Rhodesian soldiers, were deployed inside Zimbabwe. Apart
from the attendant bad publicity, Africans were more expendable
than whites in the view of the South African military and an ample
supply of potential recruits existed. Not only had South Africa
inherited a considerable number of Africans from the Rhodesian
security forces and from among Muzorewa's auxiliaries, but it was also
able to utilize historical differences between Zanu and Zapu.

As the election result had demonstrated, Zanu's support lay primarily
among the majority Shona who make up about 80 per cent of the
country's population of seven million and Zapu's support was in the
south-west of the country among the minority Ndebele. A Zulu-
related people, the Ndebele had arrived in Zimbabwe in 1838 led by

their chief, Mzilikazi. They had settled in the south-west of Zimbabwe, linguistically and culturally assimilating the Shona people who lived in that area, who are now called Kalanga and who include Nkomo and most of his party's more influential leaders.

Historical differences were fanned by the creation of Zanu in 1963 by a group, including Mugabe, who broke away from Zapu because they were dissatisfied with Nkomo's leadership. These differences were exacerbated during the liberation struggle, partly because Zanu, based in Mozambique, attracted the vast majority of its recruits and support from the Shona in the eastern part of the country and Zapu, based in Zambia, from the Ndebele areas. Defeat in the 1980 independence elections and Nkomo's reaction left a bubbling cauldron of discontent.

Sporadic post-independence incidents between Zanla and ZPRA, the military forces of Zanu and Zapu respectively, spilled over into large-scale conflict in Bulawayo's eastern suburbs on 10 November 1980. A subsequent enquiry by a High Court judge failed to establish exactly what had triggered the fighting. However, the juxtaposition of the Bulawayo fighting and another incident, which occurred in the days immediately preceeding the fighting but which was not then publicly known, suggests an explanation.

Whereas the Zanla forces fought a classical guerrilla war relying heavily on politicizing and mobilizing the rural population, ZPRA, supported by the Soviet Union, had been prepared for more conventional conflict. In September 1979, as the Lancaster House negotiations began, Rhodesian intelligence estimated that 70 to 80 per cent of Zanla forces were inside Rhodesia. They also estimated that 70 to 80 per cent of ZPRA forces were in Zambia, and this was later confirmed by Zapu officials. In the last three months of that year ZPRA infiltration increased dramatically. Then, when the guerrillas moved into assembly points for the cease-fire, and right after independence, Zapu began infiltrating weapons.

Seven trucks which had carried maize north to Zambia, and which should have returned empty, came south with armaments. These were cached near Assembly Point Papa, close to Mushumbi Pools, which contained ZPRA guerrillas.[18] Although no announcement was ever made by the government, these were unearthed and there was a ruling that all armaments held outside the country must be surrendered to the new ZNA. Train-loads of Zanla armaments came in from Mozambique and these were escorted through to the main national armoury at Inkomo Barracks near Harare. But ZPRA were not willing

to surrender their weapons, and this may have been part of the trigger
for the Bulawayo fighting.

In the first few days of November, immediately prior to the
Bulawayo fighting, a number of trains laden with armaments crossed
the Victoria Falls bridge from Zambia into Zimbabwe. These should
have gone through to the armoury at Brady Barracks in Bulawayo. But
when the trains stopped at Dett siding, ZPRA guerrillas from the
nearby Gwaii River Mine assembly point were waiting. The
armaments were unloaded and taken to Gwaii. The shipments
included 571 tonnes of assorted ammunition for the standard AK 47
guerrilla weapon, 234 tonnes of rockets and grenades, 287 tonnes of
light weapons including pistols, 195 tonnes of heavy weapons from
mortars upwards, 22 tonnes of 7.62 ammunition, 39 tonnes of rockets
and rocket-launchers, 39 tonnes of various ammunition up to 1.45 mm
anti-aircraft, 234 tonnes of diesel fuel, two armoured vehicles and
ammunition, 273 tonnes of assorted ammunition and land-mines, 234
tonnes of small arms and six heavy guns from 5mm up to 105mm and
155mm. It was certainly more sophisticated weaponry than Zanla
possessed and quite enough to resume the war, this time against the
Mugabe government.[19]

It seems to be stretching coincidence too far not to connect the
arrival of 49 wagon loads of armaments at Gwaii and the outbreak of
fighting in Bulawayo a few days later. Mugabe said later that the
fighting started when ZPRA began shelling and firing on a Zanla camp
in the western Entumbane suburb of Bulawayo. This was borne out
by a report in *The Times* of London on 12 November by Nicholas
Ashford, one of the most reliable journalists covering southern Africa
at that time. 'Judging by the amount of damage done, Zanla had
suffered the most,' he wrote. 'Many of their huts were riddled with
bullet holes and some had been partially destroyed by mortar and
rocket fire. By contrast little apparent damage was done to the ZPRA
camp.'

Fighting broke out in Entumbane again on 8 February and on this
occasion, as Mugabe put it, it followed a more 'sinister pattern'. ZPRA
armoured columns from Essexvale camp, 40 kilometres to the south-
east of Bulawayo, and Gwaii, 230 kilometres to the north-west, began
advancing on Bulawayo. And at Connemara Barracks, 160 kilometres
to the north-east, ZPRA troops mutinied, breaking into the armoury
and killing some Zanla members of the integrated ZNA battalion in
the camp. Every major access road to Bulawayo was blocked and it
seemed clear that ZPRA intended to try to capture the capital of
Matabeleland.

Faced with this massive threat, Mugabe acted decisively. With three of his nine integrated army battalions in mutiny, he called in still-existing, former Rhodesian ground and air units to quell the uprising. Seven of the 12 armoured cars used by ZPRA to attack Zanla positions were destroyed, and the Gwaii column halted near the outskirts of Bulawayo after threats to bomb it were conveyed by airborne loudspeakers. Entumbane was a turning point. The mauling ZPRA received in their abortive bid to take Bulawayo, and Mugabe's decisiveness, had shown that they could not take control of even part of the country through conventional means.

Mass desertions of ZPRA troops followed from the integrated ZNA battalions and assembly points. Many took their arms with them. And the vast arms cache at Gwaii began to be distributed around the country. Nkomo and Zapu had spent some $20 million buying 52 properties, including farms, around the country in 1980–81, a number of them on strategic access routes around Harare.[20] The Mugabe government was to discover 10 months later that arms from Gwaii had been re-cached on some of these farms.

This was a strategic shift in tactics that had occurred after Entumbane. At Hampton Farm, 50 kilometres south-west of Gweru, the caches contained enough arms to equip two infantry battalions and enough medical equipment for two or three district hospitals. At another of the properties, the Castle Arms Motel in Bulawayo, communications equipment was found, capable of jamming or monitoring army and police communications within a range of 100 kilometres. Mugabe announced on 13 February 1982 that enough armaments to equip 20 000 men had been found. These included a total of 2 051 424 rounds of ammunition. The amount was 'astounding and stunning'. The intent, he said, had been to start another war. Turning his wrath on Nkomo, he described the Zapu leader as 'a cobra in the house. The only way to deal with a snake is to strike and destroy its head. How else can I describe a man we supposed was our friend and whom we invited to be part of the government when we could have been just our party?'[21]

Although some found Mugabe's language intemperate, there could be no doubting the justness of his anger. On 17 February he fired Nkomo and three of his colleagues from the government.[22]

Zanu's victory had left a cast of embittered, defeated politicians in Zimbabwe and embittered members of the Rhodesian army in South

Africa. Added to that were Zanu's declared socialist policies, its support for SADCC, and its critical geopolitical position which could determine whether trade from land-locked Africa flowed through Mozambique or South Africa. Entumbane added a new dimension. Some defeated ZPRA soldiers and politicians were determined to continue to try to overthrow the Mugabe government. But to do so, once existing supplies of arms and ammunition were exhausted, they needed a source of resupply and a rear base for training and sanctuary. Only South Africa could offer that.

The isolated acts of banditry which had begun after independence increased considerably in Matabeleland after Entumbane. But, initially, these do not appear to have been co-ordinated, falling largely into the category of 'robbery for personal gain'. In 1982, however, there was a dramatic increase in reported incidents. Between 1 March and 31 August a total of 1 136 incidents were reported in Matabeleland, Midlands, Masvingo and Mashonaland. Sixty-six people died in these six months, 41 of them civilians and 17 bandits. The others were members of the security forces. In the same period, official police figures show 175 bandits captured, 523 robberies involving bandits, 305 sightings of bandit groups, 46 contacts and 22 ambushes. Over two-thirds of the incidents, 847, occurred in Matabeleland. Midlands, which has a large Ndebele-speaking population, was the next worst hit with 141. In Matabeleland, bandit activity covered the entire six-month period, but it did not begin in Midlands and Masvingo until May, and in Mashonaland in June.[23]

Intelligence analysis in this period defined the strategic intentions of the bandits in three phases. The first phase was to recover cached weapons not yet located by the government, and to train and arm recruits. Phase two was to attack isolated economic targets such as white commercial farms, stores and so on. Phase three was to attack police stations, army posts and security force patrols with the objective of making Matabeleland ungovernable. Certainly, as the statistics in the previous paragraph reveal, phase two had been reached by late 1982. Resettlement and construction schemes, Zanu officials, white commercial farmers and communications routes all became targets in this phase.

In late 1982 definite proof was obtained showing that the bandits now had an external source of supply. On 1 December a group of seven bandits were involved in a series of contacts with Zimbabwean

security forces at Dorrington Ranch in the Mwenezi area to the north
of the South African border. Five members of the bandit group, a
member of the security forces and two civilians died. Two other bandits,
Benson Dube and Zwelibanza Nzima, were captured two days later.[24]

From this group the security forces recovered five AK 47 assault
rifles of Bulgarian manufacture and a Soviet RPG 7 rocket-launcher.
The original maker's numbers had been removed from the exterior
and breech blocks of the weapons with a centre punch; and new
numbers had been punched onto the AK barrels and engraved on the
RPG barrel with an electric Dremil-tool. The objective was obviously
to obscure the original numbers of the weapons which could have
traced them to South Africa or to a third party buying Eastern
European weapons on South Africa's behalf.

But what could not be obscured on live ammunition were the head-
stamps on the captured 7.62mm intermediate ammunition for the
AKs. The head-stamp, '22-80', was stamped on the base of cartridge
cases found at the scene. The captured arms, and live and expended
rounds, were given to police ballistics experts for analysis and their
findings confirmed conclusively that the bandits now had an external
source of supply. The first two digits of the head-stamp, '22',
indicated the country of manufacture, Romania; the next two digits
the year of manufacture, 1980. The RPG 7 had been manufactured in
1981. Further enquiries revealed that Zapu's last supply of arms had been
in September 1979. Thus this weaponry could not have been among
the armaments brought back by Zapu, and the Zimbabwe government had not received any armaments at this point from the Warsaw
Pact countries.

From captured bandits and other intelligence, the Zimbabwe
authorities were already certain that South Africa was arming and
training the bandits. But proving an external source of supply and
proving that the source was South Africa were different issues, even
when logic dictated that there was no other plausible explanation.

As soon as the significance of the weapons and ammunition
recovered at Dorrington Ranch was realized, instructions went out
that all weaponry recovered at the scene of bandit incidents must be
forwarded to the police armoury for analysis. During 1983 a total of
1 403 rounds of '22-80' ammunition were recovered in 49 incidents
with bandits. A total of 25 AK 47 rifles with their original numbers
erased were recovered from the same incidents.[25]

Ironically, the first person to die in 1983 in an incident where it was
known that '22-80' was used was an RF senator, Paul Savage. On 4

April, just before dusk, a group of about 20 bandits attacked the 70-year-old senator's Jahunda Farm in the Gwanda area about 230 kilometres south of Bulawayo, close to the South African border. The senator, his 20-year-old daughter, Colleen, and a visitor from Britain, Sandra Bennett, were killed. Mrs Betty Savage was seriusly wounded. Security forces recovered 26 '22-80' cartridges at the scene of the murders. On 11 June a farmer of Afrikaaner extraction, Mr H. Swaart, was ambushed at his farm in the Kezi area. Fourteen '22-80' cartridges were found at the scene. Three days later, a Figtree farmer, Ian Brebner, was killed by a group of eight bandits. Four '22-80' cartridges were found at the scene. On 13 July another RF senator, Max Rosenfels, and his son narrowly escaped death, and one of his employees died, when their vehicle was ambushed in the Figtree area. Six '22-80' cartridges were found at the scene.[26]

One further important development concerning '22-80' occurred in this period. The ZNA had gone into Mozambique in late 1982 to protect the pipeline, road and railway linking Zimbabwe to the Indian Ocean port of Beira. In clashes with Mozambique National Resistance (MNR) bandits inside Mozambique, '22-80' ammunition was also found, and weapons with their original numbers obliterated and false ones substituted. The source of external supplies for the Zimbabwe bandits and for the MNR was obviously the same. As the external supplier of the MNR was already known, another piece of circumstantial evidence was added to the mounting dossier.

Of the two bandits captured at Dorrington Ranch, one, Benson Dube, said he had been trained by the SADF in South Africa. Dube had been in the Rhodesian farm militia and had gone south after Zanu's election victory. He said he had been infiltrated back into Zimbabwe on a reconnaissance and sabotage mission on 20 October 1982.[27] Such statements were beginning to become increasingly common in this period and details of Dube's statements, which thoroughly compromised the South Africans, were given to Pretoria. They admitted he had joined the SADF and undergone basic training. But, they claimed, he had failed to meet the required standards and had been discharged. What had happened to him after that they claimed they did not know. That was a most unlikely claim coming from a regime which monitors Africans' movements so closely. But the Zimbabwean authorities did not expect the South Africans to admit that Dube had been on a mission for them. It was simply a case of letting Pretoria know that Zimbabwe knew what they were doing. Early in 1983 the Zimbabweans handed over a dossier of a further 15 cases. The South African rebuttal was again predictable.

By this time, resupply and other forms of support from the external source were causing division within the bandit ranks, and in 1983 they could be subdivided into three categories. There were those who were bandits purely and simply for personal gain. They had no ideology and did not pretend to act in the name of any leader or political party. Until some time in 1982, the remainder had been more or less homogeneous in that they said they supported Nkomo and Zapu and were committed to the overthrow of the Mugabe government.

The point of contention which emerged within the ranks of this latter group was not that there was an external source of supply, but the fact that it was South Africa. Fighting broke out among the bandits, the first recorded incident of which occurred in the Gwanda area on 4 September 1983. Another incident occurred on 29 September in the same area. At first it was unclear why the bandits were fighting among themselves. But from 'captures' the reason began to emerge, bringing with it further evidence of the South African connection.

One of the earliest detailed stories about conflict in the bandit ranks came from Judia Ncube alias George Thebe Dhliwayo. He had been deported to Zimbabwe by the Botswana authorities on 21 May 1983 after being arrested in Francistown a week earlier. Ncube had been a member of ZPRA from 1974 and had turned to banditry after being demobilized from the ZNA on 23 March 1982. In July he had crossed to Botswana going to the Dukwe refugee camp where he linked up with other dissidents. On 3 October, at the Marange Motel in Francistown Ncube and another dissident, Peter Ndebele alias Tafara, met three whites from South Africa. They were 'Mat' Callaway, a former member of the Rhodesian police special branch, another named Keith, and a third using an African name, Khumalo, whom it was suspected was a former Rhodesian police inspector, Allan Trousdale. The three said that South Africa would supply weapons. On 14 October a bandit group met the whites at the confluence of the Shashi and Limpopo rivers where the borders of Zimbabwe, Botswana and South Africa meet. A total of 20 AK 47 rifles with 80 magazines, 20 boxes, each containing 720 rounds of AK 7.62mm intermediate ammunition, 10 land-mines and detonators, two RPG 7s and 20 rockets were handed over.

A further meeting occurred in Francistown in December. This was followed by a hand-over of armaments at the Shashi-Limpopo confluence on 21 December. This shipment included 56 AK 47 rifles, 16 AK magazines and 20 boxes containing AK 47 ammunition. On 3

January 1983 a further 36 000 rounds of AK ammunition were handed over and, three days later, money to buy two vehicles, a Toyota registration number BA 1438 and a Datsun registration BA 3796. During March 1983, Ncube said, reports began to be received that bandits operating in the Lupane area were dissatisfied with their leaders including himself, Ndebele and Hillary Vincent Ndhlovu. The Lupane group said 'they had their own leaders in the operational area and that they did not like the idea of getting weapons from South Africa. Instead they preferred to be supplied by [the] USSR since it used to supply Zapu during the struggle. The bandits suspected South Africa to be using them to promote its own interests.'

Following this meeting, Ncube said, Ndebele sent Jabulani Moyo alias Mututuki to Pretoria to meet Callaway. He was 'tasked to find out from Callaway if the South Africans were using the group to further their own interests'. Callaway's response was to supply a further nine armed bandits who had been trained in South Africa. They were deployed in the Gwanda area, where Senator Savage was murdered the following month. During the same month the group operating from Botswana received a report that three bandits – including one supposed to have been involved in a July 1982 attack on Mugabe's Harare home – had been killed by the ZPRA group as suspected members of Super-Zapu, as the South Africa-aligned group was known. In April 1983, Ncube said, the South Africans handed over the biggest arms shipment to date. This included 60 AK 47s and 240 magazines, 60 light-green kit bags, 60 pairs of jeans, 60 pairs of boots, four bazookas, 12 bazooka shells, 30 boxes full of AK ammunition, three boxes of explosives and detonators, and six Russian Tokarev pistols. These were issued to the groups operating in Lupane and Tsholotsho on 2 May.[28]

The testimony of one captured bandit would not, in itself, be sufficient to identify the source of external supply. But the name of 'Mat' Callaway occurred in more and more statements from captured bandits as did details of dissent among the bandits over supplies from South Africa, training in South Africa, and the transfer of armaments at the confluence of the Shashi and Limpopo rivers.

The major breakthrough, positively identifying the external source, began to occur on 6 December 1983. On that date, and over the next two months, the Botswana government expelled 199 Zimbabweans in three groups. Why it did so is uncertain. But it is thought that the clashes between ZPRA and Super-Zapu bandits which had occurred inside Zimbabwe had spilled over into Botswana and that there had been fighting between the two groups at the Dukwe refugee camp. Among the 199, many were expelled for being in Botswana illegally without proper documentation. But they also included ZPRA deserters from the ZNA who had been involved in banditry and some of the top leaders of Super-Zapu.

The most important member of Super-Zapu to be expelled was Hillary Vincent Ndhlovu, mentioned seven months earlier in Ncube's statement. He was handed over by Botswana authorities at Plumtree on 9 December. Like many young Africans in Rhodesia, he had been forced to stop his secondary school education at Form 2 and, after a series of menial jobs, had left to join the guerrilla forces in December 1976. He had joined Zapu and gone for a series of training courses in Zambia. He had fought for almost two years in the Tsholotsho area prior to the cease-fire, gone to the Gwaii River Mine assembly point and thereafter been demobilized.

Frustrated and embittered, he linked up with other would-be dissidents in March 1982 'so that the revolution could continue'. After that he was involved in a series of acts of banditry with other former ZPRA members who had deserted the ZNA or who, like himself, had not been recruited into the new national army. In December 1982 he crossed into Botswana. In late December, in Francistown, he learned from other bandits that they had just met three whites, Callaway, Khumalo (a pseudonym) and Carpenter, at the confluence of the Shashi and Limpopo rivers. They had been supplied with armaments which included 56 AK 47s. This was their second supply. These details tallied exactly with Ncube's earlier statement.

But Ndhlovu, who had three other aliases, was not only to confirm independently what Ncube had already said; he provided a wealth of new information. Ndhlovu, by virtue of the fact that he had been a fighting ZPRA cadre for two years, had immediately been absorbed into the dissident group as a senior officer. During January 1983, Ndhlovu said, he and two other bandits met Callaway and Carpenter at the Marange Motel outside Francistown. A training programme in South Africa and resupply were discussed. The next meeting with Carpenter and another white, called Nick, occurred at the Holiday Inn in Gaborone towards the end of April.

Following complaints at this meeting that arms supplies were insufficient, the bandits received a new shipment which included six RPG7s, six RPKs, 88 AK 47 folding butt rifles with approximately 240 rounds per weapon plus four magazines per weapon and approximately 10 TM 57 land-mines. A further consignment followed in August. This included 10 RPKs, six RPG7s, 30 RPG 7 projectiles, six TM 57 land-mines, plastic explosives and more AK 47 ammunition.

Dissent about the external source of supply was mounting among the bandits inside Zimbabwe by this point, Ndhlovu said. They were demanding to know how their commanders had become involved in weapons resupply from South Africa, whether their cause was being manipulated by the South African government and whether payment was being made for the weaponry. The principal person involved in the contacts with South Africa was Tafara Ncube alias Kanka, another of the group believed to have been involved in the attack on Mugabe's home. Ncube, whose title was 'chief of operations', and Ndhlovu were delegated to go into Zimbabwe to explain the situation. In the Inseza forest in October, they met with about 100 bandits, who showed great hostility, particularly towards Ncube. At one point he was disarmed and beaten. The bandits allowed Ndhlovu to leave but insisted on holding Ncube. He escaped two days later, reporting that the bandits had become extremely hostile and were threatening to kill him. Ncube said he no longer wanted to work with the bandits and Ndhlovu replaced him as 'chief of operations' on the 'military high command'.

On 13 November they received another consignment of arms from South Africa. This included 100 AK 47 rifles, 10 RPKs, five belt-fed machine-guns, six RPG 7s, 24 RPG 7 projectiles and 30 land-mines. The weapons were cached inside Botswana not far from Plumtree in the early hours of 14 November. On 1 December, Ndhlovu led a group which attacked a train inside Zimbabwe near Figtree. He returned to Botswana on 8 December, was arrested the same day and handed over to the Zimbabwe authorities on 9 December. Ndhlovu and another bandit handed over at the same time, Kaiser Khumalo alias Mercenary, who was the 'deputy chief of operations', gave the Zimbabwean investigators the location of arms caches buried inside Botswana.[29]

Two buried caches of South Africa-supplied arms were dug up inside Botswana in the Ramokwebana Buthale area and at Selkirk Mine on 13 and 14 December respectively, as a result of Ndhlovu and Khumalo indicating their whereabouts. The caches included 67 AK 47s, 253 AK 47 magazines and 27 371 additional rounds of AK 47 ammunition. The caches also included a variety of mines, rocket-launchers and rockets, other types of weapons, 285 kilograms of plastic explosives and 20 446 rounds of ammunition for FN rifles of the type taken by deserters from the ZNA. More significantly, the

AK 47 ammunition included '22-80', proving beyond doubt that it could not have come from armaments brought back from Zambia by ZPRA and had to have come from an external source after Zimbabwe's independence. The statements of Ndhlovu and other Super-Zapu leaders handed over by Botswana left no doubt that the external source was South Africa.

On 3 February 1984, Munangagwa, the minister of state (security), announced in Bulawayo that 'some of the cream of dissident commanders' had been handed over by Botswana and were in custody.[30] His announcement came during a visit to meet representatives of the Matabeleland branch of the Commercial Farmers Union (CFU) led by its president, Mike Wood. The farmers had presented details of the deteriorating security situation as a result of bandit activities. Two white farmers had been killed by bandits in 1981; in 1983 the number had risen to 33. Some of the murders were directly traceable to bandits using '22-80' ammunition supplied by South Africa, and the possibility of the CFU making representations to the South African Commercial Farmers Union to ask them to exert pressure to halt the supplies to the bandits was discussed.

The Zimbabwe government had by now compiled a dossier of irrefutable evidence of South African involvement in supporting Super-Zapu. It contained details of Callaway's involvement, particularly with Ndhlovu, and his role in supplying arms to Super-Zapu, dates and places where armaments were handed over, the types and quantities of the armaments, vehicles used and where the armaments were taken. In addition, ballistics details about '22-80' proved that there was a post-Zimbabwe independence external source of supply and that that supplier was South Africa. Finally, details were supplied of incidents in which '22-80' had been used, with emphasis on the murders of whites such as Senator Savage.

Two days later, this dossier implicating South Africa in the destabilization of Matabeleland was given to Major-General H. Roux, of the South African Chief of Staff Intelligence (CSI). The unspoken question was obvious: was it really the policy of a regime committed to *apartheid* and white supremacy to arm bandits to slaughter the white population of Zimbabwe?

The South Africans were clearly embarrassed by the amount of detailed evidence accumulated by the Zimbabweans.[31] Callaway, the

South Africans admitted, had joined the SADF in 1982 on a one-year contract. His services had been terminated in July 1983 and thereafter they claimed they had no knowledge of his whereabouts. It was the same story they had used in the case of Dube, captured at Dorrington Ranch, and in the case of several people captured in Mozambique. Denials notwithstanding, the message seems to have got through. For the next 17 months there was no further evidence of infiltration of bandits or armaments from South Africa. Although there was concern over possible disruption of the mid-1985 national elections, infiltration did not resume until afterwards, in July. When the killing of white farmers in Matabeleland began again in November, after ZNA troops had gone on the offensive in Mozambique, the objective seemed to be to draw ZNA strength from Mozambique back to western Zimbabwe.

While, for obvious psychological reasons when dealing with the South Africans, emphasis had been placed on the number of whites killed, the catalogue of banditry grew on a scale that few realized. The police dossier from 1 February 1982 to 13 January 1986 listed a total of 7 313 bandit incidents. Many of these were reported sightings. But the list remained far from complete. A considerable number of people were given stiff prison sentences for failing to report the presence of bandits. But, faced with the atrocities being meted out by the bandits against those whom they described as 'sell-outs' (meaning collaborators with the government), many still chose to remain silent and risk prison sentences rather than be subjected to the sort of reprisals illustrated by the following list:

11 July 1983, Zabalingwani village, a group of bandits cut off the ears of 16 villagers;

12 October 1983, Nyamandhlovu, Mbembezi Forest Area, two armed bandits accused Moment Ncube of being a 'sell-out', an expression meaning he was a supporter of the Mugabe government. The bandits raped his two daughters in his presence and forced his son at gunpoint to chop off his father's head;

24 December 1983, Matopo Hills village in Kezi, two girls aged 13 and 16, returning from Christmas shopping in Bulawayo, were stopped by a group of five bandits. The girls were accused of being army informers and given a sharp knife and ordered to cut each other's ears and noses off. The 16-year-old later told the police, 'I was terrified, I only scratched my friend's ears and nose. The dissidents got angry with me and ordered my friend to chop off both my ears. They then cut off my nose too';

4 January 1984, Ruby Ranch, six armed bandits shot Hleki Nyathi and his wife accusing them of being 'sell-outs'. They put their bodies in their house, setting it on fire, and cut the ears off the couple's two sons;

21 February 1984, Mulelezi school, a group of five bandits accused the teachers of being 'sell-outs' for working for the government. Five teachers were mutilated. Benson Moyo and Timotia Chinamatira had both ears and their noses cut off. David Muhuku had both ears, his nose and upper lip cut off, Obort Masunda, both ears, and Musa Siwela was stabbed in the neck.

10 March 1984, two armed bandits accused Bhedu Dube of being a 'sell-out'. They chopped off his genitals and ordered his wife to cook and eat them.

2 April 1984, Matikiti village in Dete communal land, six bandits abducted Harold Masini, cutting off his eyebrows and burning his genitals before shooting him;

6 April 1984, Mbamba Dam, Gwaranyemba communal land, two brothers abducted and shot their grandmother, Moni Dube, accusing her of informing the security forces about their activities.

Zanu officials became a particular target:

5 September 1983, Lupane, the local Zanu chairman, Amos Mukwananzi, was set on fire, wrapped in plastic, and then hanged by a group of three bandits;

26 November 1983, Dimpanhiwa school, Mackenzie Mpofu, a member of the Zanu Youth Brigade, was killed by bandits who cut one ear off each of two of his friends;

12 June 1984, Zhombe, bandits shot dead the local Zanu vice-chairman, Celestine Jongwe.[32]

The similarity between the atrocities committed by the South African-supported bandits in Mozambique and Zimbabwe is inescapable.

Two other weapons, non-lethal but nevertheless destabilizing, which South Africa uses against Zimbabwe are propaganda and disinformation. Zimbabwean monitors first picked up a new station called Radio Truth on 15 March 1983, not long after the South Africans are known to have become involved with Super-Zapu. The new clandestine station broadcast initially in Ndebele and Shona at 7 am and 7.30 pm daily. Reception was poor and a change of frequency in June brought with it the introduction of broadcasts in English at 6.30 am and 7 pm. But reception remained poor. A further frequency change improved the quality of the reception of broadcasts in English but the reception in Ndebele and Shona remained of a poorer quality.

The South Africans, of course, claimed the station was based in Matabeleland, just as they said the *Voz da Africa Livre*, the propaganda programme supporting the MNR, was based in Mozambique. But Zimbabwean communications experts located the transmitter near Johannesburg at the Meyerton studios of the South African Broadcasting Corporation (SABC). The South Africans continued to deny they were responsible for the broadcasts. But then, on 25 November 1983, they broadcast evidence of their own involvement when the tapes were accidentally switched in the SABC studios. The 7 am vernacular broadcast of Radio Truth began with the introductory music of *Voz da Africa Livre*. And the *Voz da Africa Livre* programme began with the introductory music of Radio Truth. Within a minute the tapes were switched. But by then Zimbabwe had tape-recorded the evidence that the two stations were in the same place and not in Mozambique or Zimbabwe.

If the quality of reception left much to be desired, the quality of content was even more wanting. With almost 80 per cent of the electorate supporting Mugabe and Zanu, personalized attacks on the prime minister and his party were unlikely to have much impact with the vast majority of Zimbabweans. Nor were a people recently liberated from settler colonialism likely to be impressed by the innumerable broadcasts in defence of *apartheid*. This broadcast on 30 November 1983 illustrates the type of message Radio Truth was trying to get across. 'For the first time in 35 years, South Africa is taking steps towards redressing their racial problems. Surely they should be applauded for abandoning traditional attitudes and fears and for taking a giant leap forward towards a more equitable society. By this step the appelation *apartheid* falls away and socialist and Marxist Africa has lost one of its big sticks with which it could beat Pretoria.[33] Such claims from Radio Truth's all-white English language broadcasters hardly tallied with other news people were hearing.

Even for less sophisticated listeners, Radio Truth had a serious credibility gap. Heaping praise upon Pretoria's friends and denigrating its perceived enemies was a clear enough indication where the broadcasts were coming from. Communism generally and the Soviet Union and Cuba in particular were bad. The Radio Truth broadcasters clearly lacked any sophistication in propaganda. Even the unsophisticated audience in Matabeleland, the only likely listening group of consequence, knew that it was the Soviets in particular who had supported their party, Zapu, during the liberation war. And the former ZPRA guerrillas who had turned bandit were arguing for the continuation of Soviet support. The line Radio Truth was propagating was a measure of their lack of credulity for it would not even appeal to Ndebele supporters of Zapu who were opposed to the Mugabe government. Also in the bad group was the United Nations, a 'communist organization', which everyone in Zimbabwe knew by and large had supported their struggle. Another organization in this group was SADCC which, certainly the sophisticated listener knew, sought to reduce Zimbabwe's dependence on South Africa.

In contrast, the 'goodies' included 'our friends' Britain and the United States. Whitehall's large post-independence aid injections notwithstanding, the highly politicized Zimbabwean audience was well aware of Britain's role in their history in doing virtually nothing to prevent Smith's UDI, and the way in which successive British governments had shown greater affinity towards the white settlers than the nationalist leaders. Israel was in the same group. In a 3 January 1984 broadcast, Radio Truth said, 'Of all the countries, Israel has much to offer in the way of expertise and advice on how to successfully create a new nation'. Taiwan and South Korea were also mentioned positively. On 13 June 1984, some months before Zimbabwe's first post-independence election, listeners were told 'Remember when our Zanu-PF leaders use the word "socialism" they mean "communism". You will have a chance to vote against this foreign doctrine in 1985. Prepare now. Let us take a stand against communism and win a better life as did the people in South Korea.'

In the event, Zanu increased its number of seats in parliament from 57 to 63 and its share of the popular vote from 63 per cent to 77 per cent. Radio Truth had supported Nkomo, Muzorewa and Sithole during the campaign. The number of seats won by Nkomo was down from 20 to 15. Muzorewa lost the three he had held, thereafter belatedly retiring from politics. And a relative of Sithole picked up one seat in his home area due to the personal unpopularity of the Zanu candidate.

Apart from reflecting South Africa's policies, Radio Truth was to play one other important role in Pretoria's overall destabilization of the region. The *Voz da Africa Livre,* the propaganda station created by Rhodesia in support of the MNR, had gone off the air for some three months is early 1980 when it was transferred to South Africa. One of the terms of the Nkomati accord between Mozambique and South Africa was the termination of clandestine broadcasts. *Voz da Africa Livre* fell into that category and on the night of 15 March, the day before the accord was signed, it announced that it was to stop broadcasting for 'reorganization'.

The assumption was that South Africa had simply shut it down in line with Nkomati and that the MNR had been deprived of their propaganda station. On 7 July it became apparent that this was not the case. Radio Truth carried a lengthy item detailing the history of the MNR and arguing that it was not supported by South Africa. Thereafter, items clearly in support of the MNR became more frequent, and the South African and American line more apparent: only a complete break with communism would end the internal problems of Mozambique, free enterprise was vital, and the Mozambique government would have to negotiate with the MNR.

The South African campaign of disinformation against Zimbabwe has been affected in a number of ways, especially through unsolicited publications and circulars, a number of them mailed from Swiss Cottage in London, and attacks on individuals through anonymous letters. Some of them supplemented propaganda being broadcast by Radio Truth. The earliest case of disinformation was detected soon after independence when publications were distributed claiming the formation of a new party, Super-Zanu, in which members of the existing Zanu leadership were said to be prominent. There was no truth in this but it caused some confusion.

The disinformation campaign was stepped up in 1983 after the creation of Super-Zapu. Prominent politicians, diplomatic missions and individuals received a series of letters which purported to originate from a 'Joe Moyo', said to be a member of the ZPRA high command. One such letter was received by the manager of the Australian airline, Qantas. It raised doubts about the safety of an Australian cricket team due to begin a tour of Zimbabwe. The timing of the letter was significant; Qantas had just announced the cancellation of service from Australia to Johannesburg saying that they would be flying direct to Harare.

A more sinister anonymous letter was circulated, to the prime minister among others, following the assassination in Harare in March of the leader of the League of Socialists of Malawi (LESOMA), Attati Mpakati. It accused two white CIO officers of being implicated in the killing and the hope was obviously that the charge would be accepted at face value, causing suspicion within the CIO. But it was not. Investigations revealed that South Africa was the source of the disinformation and that Mpakati was murdered by agents from Malawi. After the discovery that South Africa was involved in that disinformation, a member of its trade mission in Harare was asked to leave Zimbabwe.

Zimbabwe's geographical and historical ties to South Africa, including the fact that it inherited Pretoria as its largest trading partner at independence, left it particularly vulnerable to economic destabilization. Joining the SADCC 17 days before independence was a recognition of this harsh reality. It was also a public statement that it wanted to do something about it. At the same time, from South Africa's standpoint, it was an unacceptable statement which, if left unchecked, threatened to reduce dependence on Pretoria in the future.

As Zimbabwe and other independent African countries sought to divert their trade to the Mozambican routes, all but one of the routes from Zimbabwe were systematically sabotaged. From December 1982, small arms, rockets, explosives and land-mines were used by the bandits in south-western Zimbabwe to disrupt the routes through Botswana. In Mozambique, the MNR damaged the routes to Beira and Maputo. In the six years after Zimbabwe's independence only one route to the south or east remained unscathed; this was the direct railway line through Rutenga and Beitbridge from Zimbabwe to South Africa. To the north of Harare the routes carrying South Africa's trade to Zambia and Zaire were also untouched. That was far more than coincidence. South Africa's surrogates were maintaining the need for direct dependence by ensuring that alternative routes were disrupted or completely blocked.

Much the cheapest route to the sea for Zimbabwe is through Chicualacuala, in the extreme south-east, to Maputo. This was subjected to continuous attack until the MNR closed it down completely on 20 August 1984. The implications of this for Zimbabwe are illustrated in Table C which shows the cost per tonne of comparative tariff charges.

Thus, through its surrogates and through direct action, Pretoria forced Zimbabwe and other land-locked countries to return to almost total dependence on South Africa's trade routes. But Zimbabwe's response in committing troops to secure the Beira route obviously surprised Pretoria. And in the second half of 1985, faced with the prospect of the Chicualacuala route reopening by mid-1986 if security improved along the line, South Africa introduced a new tactic. This was a two-tier tariff structure, offering lower contract rates than those

TABLE C

Comparative tariff charges showing rate per tonne over each route.

Commodity	Maputo via Chicualacuala	Maputo via Komatipoort	Durban via Beitbridge	Port Elizabeth via Plumtree
Steel	30.6	64.7	86.44	85.120
Sugar (ex Chiredzi	29.32	44.01	—	—
Tobacco (ex Harare, box rate)	806.00	1196.40	1366.80	1876.40
Jet A1	99.15	125.94	151.74	173.47

*All figures are in Zimbabwe dollars which at the end of 1985 were approximately Z$ 100 to US$ 60.

Source: National Railways of Zimbabwe.

published. The new contract rates undercut the previous Chicualacuala charges on four of Zimbabwe's main bulk exports – asbestos, tobacco, ferrochrome and steel. The message was obvious. Even if Chicualacuala was reopened it would be more costly to return to the traditional Mozambique routes than to use South Africa. Not only was this a way of further destabilizing Mozambique by denying it foreign currency earnings but it also exerted pressure on the Mugabe government. Given the competitiveness of world markets, and the fact that the bulk of Zimbabwe's commercial, industrial and mining sector is in private hands, the desire for greater independence from South Africa must be weighed against the greater cost of using the Mozambique routes. The South African government's decision to offer these contract rates, when its railway system was already losing money, and when the new rates were more favourable than those offered to its own producers, was obviously a political one. The response remains to be seen in Zimbabwe and elsewhere in the frontline if Chicualacuala reopens.

The vulnerability of Zimbabwe and other land-locked countries in the region was further demonstrated within a year of independence. First, South African Railways began to extend the turnaround time for railway wagons, claiming there was excessive demand for rail transport. Loadings per day, particularly of diesel tankers, were reduced. Then, in April 1981, South Africa withdrew 25 locomotives loaned to the previous government of Rhodesia. It did this on so little notice that the Zimbabwe transport network was under severe strain for some time, forcing the loss of orders and stockpiling of maize, steel and sugar for several weeks. Lost export earnings were estimated at Z$ 7 million a week.[34]

One of the ironies of Rhodesia's UDI in November 1965 was that, although it temporarily severed formal ties with Britain, it increasingly reduced the country to the status of a colony or province of South Africa. The UDI years consolidated South Africa's domination of Rhodesia in areas of finance, trade, investment, military and diplomatic relations. For the Mugabe government, disengagement in the military and diplomatic spheres could be effected relatively quickly but the other three areas posed far greater difficulties.

Insofar as finance is concerned, South Africa's investment in Zimbabwe is larger than in any other country in the region. Most new investment during the UDI years came from South Africa and during the 1970s the Rhodesian private sector provided up to US$ 40 million a year in credit loans from South African banks. In 1970 five out of the 10 largest manufacturing companies were wholly or partly South African-owned[35] and at independence about 75 per cent of the international debt was owed to South Africa.[36] The South Africanization of the Rhodesian economy was entrenched in sugar, citrus, timber, paper, food-processing, fertilizers, copper, chromium, nickel, coal, the press and financial institutions. The new government was able to sever diplomatic and sporting ties, and to end the relay of SABC broadcasts by the Zimbabwe Broadcasting Corporation (ZBC). South African shares in the main newspaper group were purchased by government, as were those in the country's largest bank which had been owned previously by the Netherlands Bank of South Africa. However, these and a few other actions barely scratched the surface of South Africa's economic stake in Zimbabwe. Severing the economic umbilical cord will take many years.

Furthermore, at independence in 1980, 19 per cent of Zimbabwe's total trade was with South Africa and 41 per cent of all Zimbabwean manufactured exports went to South Africa. Sixty per cent of these exports were sold under a preferential trading agreement signed between Rhodesia and South Africa in 1964. This agreement gave Zimbabwean exporters preferential tariffs without which they would have been priced out of the South African market with little likelihood of finding new markets elsewhere. Abrogation of that agreement would have caused an estimated annual loss of Z$ 50 million a year in foreign currency and a permanent loss of 6 500 jobs in the manufacturing sector.[37] In recognition of his country's reality, Mugabe said on the eve of independence, 'We must accept that South Africa is a geographical reality and, as such, we must have some minimum relationship with it.' Trade had to be included in that minimal relationship. 'We would hope that South Africa would reciprocate,' Mugabe went on to say, 'and not resort unduly to hostile acts against us. We are pledged to peaceful coexistence with it. We are opposed to the politics of South Africa, but we do not regard the people of South Africa as our enemies at all.'[38] He said later that while his government fully supported the international community in imposing sanctions against South Africa, Zimbabwe's geographical reality was such that it was 'not in a position to implement [them] to the full because of our present dependence on South Africa'.[39]

South Africa was already using its dominance in the transport sector to remind Zimbabwe of its economic vulnerability when a South African delegation arrived in Harare in March 1981. The Zimbabweans were under the impression they had come for the annual renewal negotiations for the preferential trade agreement. Instead the South Africans announced their intention to revoke the agreement. The following month the railway locomotives were withdrawn. They said that re-negotiation was possible in the 12 months before the agreement lapsed but they wanted a government minister to head the Zimbabwean negotiating team in Pretoria. Zimbabwe refused, arguing that this would constitute tacit diplomatic recognition of South Africa. Faced with Zimbabwe's determination, the South Africans finally backed off. A temporary continuation of the agreement was reached in March 1982. But it has never been formally signed because South Africa insists that this be done at ministerial level, and Zimbabwe refuses to do that. Thus, the threat of South Africa revoking the agreement continues to hang over Zimbabwe.

Fuel is another weapon South Africa has used to destabilize Zimbabwe. The rehabilitation of the Beira to Mutare oil pipeline, owned by the British transnational company Lonrho and closed during the UDI years, was a major post-independence priority. The reopening of the line was technically feasible by the end of 1981 but on 29 October the railway bridge over the Pungwe river, which also carries the pipeline, was damaged in a sabotage attack and the road bridge was totally destroyed.[40] The MNR claimed responsibility but it was generally believed to have been carried out by an SADF sabotage squad. Once again, the South Africans had demonstrated the vulnerability of Zimbabwe's hostage economy. In 1982, once fuel was again flowing through the pipeline, it became a frequent target, causing considerable financial losses to Zimbabwe because no insurance company was prepared to give cover for the lost fuel. The attack on the fuel storage tanks at Beira by an SADF squad, in March 1982, was clearly designed to check Zimbabwe's decreasing dependence on South Africa.

In December 1982 Zimbabwe suffered an acute fuel shortage which almost brought the country to a standstill and resulted in queues at petrol stations that stretched for many kilometres. With Zimbabwe once again entirely dependent upon South Africa for fuel supplies, the authorities there limited the fuel deliveries to Zimbabwe. At one point there was only one day's supply of petrol and two days of diesel in the country. The revelation that ZNA soldiers had been deployed to guard the pipeline should have come as no surprise. There were two more attacks on the pipeline in April 1983, four more attacks in 1984 and another in March 1985. But the presence of the ZNA ensured that one Zimbabwean route to the sea, independent of South Africa, remained open.

South Africa's destabilization in the first six years of independence cost Zimbabwe millions of dollars in additional import and export tariffs, lost orders, property destroyed by bandits, discouraged investment and tourism. Beyond that there was the cost of military operations against the bandits at home, the cost of guarding the Beira route and finally, in July 1985, the deployment of fighting units in Mozambique for a joint offensive against the MNR. The price cannot be fully quantified but a supplementary vote of Z$ 20 million was initially approved by parliament in the case of the latter and by the end of 1985 the army had requested a further Z$ 16 million for the operation. Members of Smith's RF party, by now the Conservative Alliance of Zimbabwe (CAZ), attacked the government in parliament for deploying troops in Mozambique and demanded to know where the money had come from to pay for the operation. That sort of negative attitude drew little popular support, for most people recognized Zimbabwe's historical debt to Mozambique for its support during the liberation struggle. Further, there was the matter of self-interest. Continued dependence upon South Africa not only left Zimbabwe vulnerable but also left Pretoria in a position to impose humiliating constraints and to hamper development policies.

By early 1986, unity talks between Zanu and Zapu appeared to be

72

Zimbabwe:

making some progress but it remained highly questionable what effect such unity would have on the bandit problem in the south-west of the country. In all likelihood it would cause further division among the ZPRA group with some supporting the Zapu political leadership and others refusing any link with the Mugabe government. If the latter continued to operate they would still provide a cover for the South Africans to step up operations through their surrogates, Super-Zapu. Even unity is unlikely, in the near future, to remove that problem. Nor will it remove South Africa's massive leverage on the Zimbabwe economy and sustained political and military attempts to keep it economically dependent upon South African trade routes.

Trying to control South Africa, one Western diplomat said, is like trying to house-train a fully grown grizzly bear. The indications in early 1986 were that the bear was running amok and that Zimbabwe and the rest of the frontline could expect more of the same.

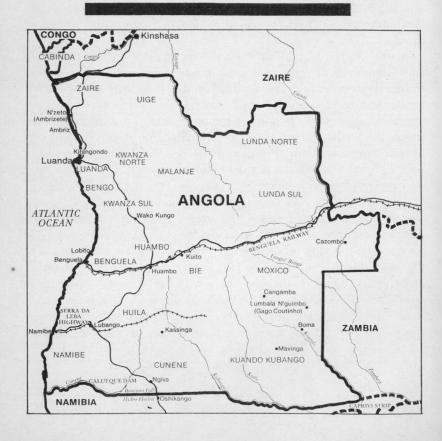

CHAPTER 3

Angola:
The Struggle Continues

Among all the independent countries in southern Africa included in South Africa's destabilization programme, Angola is in many respects a special case. Full-scale war at the time of independence, continued South African army attacks, invasions and occupations and, perhaps more significantly, the intense interest shown by Washington in Angola's destiny are factors now routinely ascribed by many in the West to the Cuban military presence in the country. Some historical background is needed to show that Western, and particularly US, involvement in Angola dates back to the start of the independence struggle in the early 1960s.

Angola is potentially one of the richest countries in southern Africa, with a vast array of minerals and substantial oil reserves. Geographically situated in both central and southern Africa, its Benguela Railway was, before independence, the main outlet for copper and other minerals from Zambia and from Zaire's Shaba province, the secessionist Katanga of the latter country's traumatic independence. It was indeed in former Belgian Congo (Zaire) that the United States for the first time deeply involved itself in the political life of a newly independent African country. After the assassination of Patrice Lumumba, on the subsequently acknowledged orders of the US Central Intelligence Agency (CIA), that country, bordering on Angola, became Washington's main ally in the region.

In the mid 1970s, however, when the focus of the decolonization process had shifted to southern Africa after the fall of fascism in Portugal, South Africa emerged as a far more powerful ally for the United States. Up to 1975, Washington's alternative to Portugal for leadership in Angola had been the president of the National Front for the Liberation of Angola (FNLA), Holden Roberto, who was brought up and based in Zaire. After the events of 1975, the firm favourite became Jonas Savimbi of the National Union for the Total Independence of Angola (UNITA), ever more openly allied with the *apartheid* regime.

The People's Movement for the Liberation of Angola (MPLA), formed in Luanda in 1956 from the fusion of several anti-colonialist organizations, stated from the outset that its goal was to unite all Angolan patriots – regardless of ethnic, regional or racial origin – to win independence. The MPLA put down deep roots in the main urban centres, the detribalized melting pots where patriotic resistance took on its most organized form (the same phenomenon is more than apparent in South Africa today); but when it went over to armed struggle in 1961 the bulk of its guerrilla forces were to come from the peasantry.

As a result of these beginnings, the MPLA retained clandestine networks in urban areas throughout the independence war. This was not true of the FNLA, formed among Angolan émigrés in Zaire around the ruling hierarchy of the former Kongo Kingdom. Nor was it true of Unita, also tribally based among Savimbi's Umbundu people, and created on the Zambian border in 1966. Indeed, the various trials of nationalists by the colonial authorities, particularly the renowned 1960 'Trial of the Fifty', were essentially of MPLA members.[1] And when the concentration camps and prisons were opened after the *coup d'état* in Portugal, the well-known personalities released were also from the MPLA.[2]

The armed struggle started in the area north of Luanda, in March 1961, after an abortive attempt by the MPLA, on 4 February that year, to storm Luanda prisons and police stations to release political prisoners. This was followed by ferocious repression and an estimated 20 000 people were slaughtered in the streets of the capital.[3] Many of the survivors fled north to the rural areas.[4]

It was in the Nambuangongo region north of the capital that the first inexperienced MPLA guerrillas started to organize armed struggle in what became their First Military Region. The Luanda events proved a catalyst, leading to uprisings, many of them unorganized, on settler plantations. Into that explosive situation came directives from the Union of the People of Angola (UPA, later renamed FNLA) based in the Zairean capital, Kinshasa, to kill all whites, all people of mixed parentage, all bearers of identity cards, so-called *assimilados* or educated Angolans, and all Umbundu migrant workers from central Angola employed as slave labour on coffee estates. The people were also told to await the arrival of 25 000 armed and trained UPA men, as well as American forces coming to their aid. None of these forces materialized.[5] The reference to American forces was not fortuitous. In 1959 Roberto worked at the Guinean mission to the United Nations (UN) in New York, and his CIA links are believed to date back to that time.

In October 1961, the MPLA established an office in Kinshasa, from where it tried to supply the guerrillas in its First Military Region. On 9 October, an MPLA column headed by Tomás Ferreira tried to cross the Zairean-Angolan border for this purpose. Captured by UPA elements, its members were put to death.[6]

Countless attempts were made by the MPLA, over the years, to reach agreements with UPA/FNLA, but these were always reneged on by Roberto. The first accord on united action was signed as early as January 1960 by Roberto and four representatives of an early grouping of liberation movements from the then Portuguese colonies, including Amilcar Cabral of the African Party for the Independence of Guinea Bissau and Cape Verde (PAIGC) and Lúcio Lara of the MPLA. The last such attempt was made in December 1972 when an agreement to establish an FNLA/MPLA joint high command again fell victim to FNLA separatism, reportedly encouraged by United States advisers. UPA's destructive and murderous activities led many of its leaders to switch their allegiance to the MPLA or to denounce their own movement.[7]

The United States consistently supported Portuguese colonialism against Angolan nationalism, both militarily and at the UN. However, as a result of African reaction to the assassination of Lumumba, strategists in the Kennedy administration realized that nationalism was a force to be reckoned with. The solution was to select African individuals who could be counted on to serve US interests.[8] Roberto, who had close ties with Cyrille Adoula, a US protégé who headed the first 'government of national unity' in Zaire, was the natural choice in Angola.

Following the FNLA's formation of a 'government of the Angolan republic in exile' (GRAE), in April 1962, life in Kinshasa became increasingly difficult for the MPLA. Their weapons were seized by the local *gendarmerie* who then fined them for possession of the weapons. Many of the leaders were arrested, refugee relief services were stopped and, in November 1962, the MPLA offices in Kinshasa were closed down and the movement was expelled from Zaire.

Angola's other borders were with Northern Rhodesia, a British colony later to become Zambia; Namibia, a South African colony; and

Congo (Brazzaville), from which only Cabinda was accessible to the
liberation movement, and this only after a change of regime when the
Abbey Youlou was overthrown. Cabinda, the northern enclave cut off
from the rest of Angola by a strip of Zairean territory, became the
Second Military Region. The armed struggle there provided
invaluable experience for many MPLA members who subsequently
fought on the Eastern Front, the MPLA's Third Military Region
bordering on Zambia. Zambia achieved independence in 1964; and in
1965 the MPLA set up an office in the capital, Lusaka, to start political
preparations for armed struggle. The Eastern Front, spreading from
Moxico province to Kuando Kubango in the south-east, Lunda in the
north-east and Bié in the Central Highlands, developed rapidly, with
the port of Dar es Salaam in Tanzania serving as the pipeline for
logistical support from abroad. This was then transported by truck by
the MPLA over approximately 3 000 kilometres to the Angolan-
Zambian border.

When war against colonialism was launched in the First Region, it
was UPA/FNLA that appeared as the foreign-backed force used to
obstruct it. In the Second Region, Cabinda, a separatist group called
the Front for the Liberation of the Cabinda Enclave (FLEC) played
the same role. One of the leaders was Alexandre Taty, former
'minister of war' in Roberto's GRAE and then an officer in the
Portuguese 'special forces' from which most FLEC members were
recruited. In the east, the group used to undermine the struggle was
Unita, formed in 1966 by Savimbi, also a former 'minister' in GRAE.

The Portuguese dictator, Marcelo Caetano, wrote in his memoirs that:
'The opening of the eastern front by the enemy was tremendously
worrying, and on assuming the responsibilities of defending Angola,
Costa Gomes [commander-in-chief of the armed forces in Angola]
faced the problem with intelligence and determination. Bettencourt-
Rodrigues was given the job of pacifying the region, with quite a lot of
autonomy and powers to coordinate all the authorities in the zone, and
this he achieved; it included coming to an understanding with the
Unita people, an insurgent group headed by Savimbi which was
operating there in disagreement with the MPLA.'[9]

A chameleon in Angolan politics, Savimbi's switches of allegiance
over the years do not reflect corresponding ideological change or
development, but appear to have been dictated by an overriding
ambition to rule Angola.[10] He likes to boast of his alleged friendship

with prestigious revolutionary leaders now dead and unable to set the record straight. These have included Che Guevara and Amilcar Cabral. In a letter to Basil Davidson, who has kindly allowed me to quote it, written in April 1972, Amilcar Cabral said, 'Yes, I knew Jonas Savimbi in Lisbon as a faithful servant of the Portuguese colonialists. In 1959 (I no longer remember the exact date) he even made a speech at the Geographical Society in favour of the Portuguese colonialists and their great work. Later he became a 'nationalist', a 'minister', 'leader of so-called Unita', etc., but in my opinion he is still serving the Portuguese colonialists. So the revelations of the German journalist do not surprise us. Jonas Savimbi is well aware of my opinion of him, because I told him in Lisbon as well as in Africa.'

Unita's claims about its 'anti-colonial struggle' in eastern Angola centre on acts of sabotage against the Benguela Railway. These were doubtless intended to cause friction between the Zambian authorities and the MPLA. Although it entailed sacrifices, because the line carried train-loads of Portuguese troops, the MPLA had given Zambia assurances that it would not touch the railway, which transported goods to and from the land-locked country then virtually surrounded by minority regimes. Neither Portuguese military bulletins nor foreign observers noted any military activity by Unita which, then as now, was given to dramatic communiqués reliant upon the credulity of uninformed outsiders.[11]

The true role of Unita in eastern Angola was revealed after the Portuguese *coup d'état* of 25 April 1974, when officers of the Movement of the Armed Forces (MFA) gained access to the secret files of the former fascist regime in Lisbon. These contained correspondence between Savimbi and high-ranking Portuguese military personnel in Angola. In a letter dated 26 September 1972 to General Luz Cunha, commander-in-chief in the colony, Savimbi recommended, as a way of ensuring peace in eastern Angola, 'weakening the MPLA forces inside Angola to the point of liquidating them', a task which could be fulfilled by the combined forces of the Portuguese 'military and para-military forces and Unita forces'. He further proposed 'liquidating the MPLA camps in the regions on the border between Angola and Zambia', pointing out that Unita's lack of political status made it easy to carry out such actions without being censured by any international body. Indeed, the Organization of African Unity (OAU) recognized Unita only after the *coup d'état* in Portugal.

On 4 November 1972, Lieutenant-Colonel Ramires de Oliveira of the Eastern Military Zone Command wrote to Savimbi, agreeing that Unita's clandestine activist cells in Zambia could be used 'to gather information on the MPLA's activities and on the political situation in Zambia and other African states' and 'to exert pressure on the Zambian government to make it change its policy towards Portugal'. He said that 'as far as UNITA is concerned, the main thing at this stage is to stay in the Upper Lunguê-Bungo region, far from the war, and secretly strengthen its cooperation with our troops.... At this stage, therefore,' he continued, 'the mass surrender of the population and guerrillas cannot be contemplated.'

Unita's contact with Portuguese military intelligence was maintained through settler timber merchants called Duarte and Oliveira, and also through a Portuguese Benedictine missionary, Padre António de Araújo Oliveira. Costa Gomes and Bettencourt-Rodrigues have since confirmed that there was a 'gentleman's agreement' with Unita in eastern Angola. This was, according to Costa Gomes, that 'we Portuguese do not fight Unita and Unita does not fight the Portuguese forces.' There were, he said, 'certain areas especially for Unita', i.e. 'Lunguê-Bungo... an area where we cannot go to fight, nor can the authorities collect taxes from the indigenous people'.[12]

When the files of the previous regime in Portugal were opened for the inspection of the international press in 1982, one British newspaper, *The Times*, headlined its article 'Secret files in Lisbon compromise Savimbi'. The report said: 'In one dusty file, a telegram from the DGS [new name of PIDE, the security police]... marked Top Secret and dated September 19, 1972, gave an account of a report by Dr Jonas Savimbi, who at the time was supposed to be fighting the Portuguese. According to the DGS, Dr Savimbi said his Unita guerrillas had successfully ambushed a 30-man force of the rival MPLA. He now wanted arms, ammunition, syringes, medicines and a safe passage for his men through Portuguese Army lines.'[13] Co ta Gomes estimated that Unita had no more than 600 men at the time. In June 1974 a Portuguese newspaper, *Diário de Lisboa*, put the figure at 'approximately 300 men under arms'.

Copies of these documents and others, including memos and minutes of meetings of the 'Timber Working Group' set up to co-ordinate 'Operation Timber', i.e. collaboration between the colonial authorities and Unita, are in the possession of the Angolan government. The 'Timber Working Group', chaired by Bettencourt-Rodrigues and including members of the military and military intelligence, met with the timber merchants Duarte and Oliveira, acting as intermediaries with Unita, and reported back to and received instructions from the colonial authorities in Luanda, who in turn maintained close contact with Lisbon over the operation.[14]

Little is known so far of the precise moment when Savimbi started his collaboration with the Portuguese military in eastern Angola. There are indications, however, that it dates back to well before November 1971, when the first meeting of the 'Timber Working Group' was held.[15]

By 1970, the MPLA had expanded the guerrilla areas to Bié, the Fifth Region in the centre of the country, and to the Fourth Region, Lunda. Costa Gomes admitted as much when interviewed in 1984; and countless foreign observers testified to the advance of the struggle from the liberated areas in Moxico province, where schools, medical care and elected local authorities were being established under MPLA leadership.

Unita's collaboration with the Portuguese in the eastern zones was not the only resistance encountered by the national liberation struggle in this period. In a document issued in January 1970, entitled 'Western countries are providing Portugal with arms to fight the Angolan patriots', the MPLA revealed a list of military aircraft supplied to Portugal by the countries of the North Atlantic Treaty Organization (NATO). The list included Thunderjets, Sabers and Lockheeds made available under the American Military Assistance Program, B-26 bombers provided by the CIA, and other equipment provided by Britain, Italy, the Federal Republic of Germany (FRG), France and Canada.

Another statement issued two months later announced the presence of South African troops in eastern Angola, consisting of 'four commando companies equipped with helicopters, artillery, automatics, bazookas and other types of weapon'. The statement said that the 'South African military interventionist corps' were 'quartered in their own private barracks' in Lumege district of Moxico, the Third Politico-Military Region. 'Two of these companies took part in many of the October–November 1969 enemy operations in the Lunda region. The remainder carried out criminal acts against population centres, crops and our people's fishing areas, even making incursions into Zambian territory.'[16]

The MPLA repeatedly denounced the use of napalm by the Portuguese forces, and also of herbicides and defoliants of the types

used by the Americans in Vietnam. Chemical warfare caused the
guerrilla struggle severe setbacks. The peasants – who received from
the MPLA such rare essentials as soap and salt, together with
schooling and medical care – were the main source of foodstuffs to
sustain the guerrillas. The destruction of their crops caused a massive
movement of peasants to the Zambian border, where the MPLA was
faced with having to provide relief for thousands of hungry peasants.
The guerrillas had not only to survive and fight, but to ensure the
survival of all these people.

This was one of the reasons why the April 1974 *coup d'état* in
Portugal found the MPLA in a militarily less favourable position than
in the first years of the decade, when it had been advancing from
strength to strength. Another factor was treachery within its own
ranks.

In late 1973 the MPLA revealed that it had foiled a plot to
assassinate the president, Dr Agostinho Neto, and other top leaders.
As in the case of the murder of Eduardo Mondlane, president of the
Mozambique Liberation Front (FRELIMO), in 1969 and of the
PAIGC leader, Amilcar Cabral, in 1973, traitors within the liberation
movement were instruments in the plot. In the MPLA this was Daniel
Chipenda, by no means a military leader as he is often described, but a
diabetic unfit for military activity. A member of the top leadership, he
used his post in logistics to devastating effect. Chipenda's tool was
tribalism and racism, the classic divisive tactic of reaction in Africa.
He himself was from Benguela.[17] Along one section of the Zambian
border, adjacent to what was known as the Southern Sub-Region,
MPLA camps were assaulted and overrun by those mobilized by
Chipenda's divisive slogans. That these fratricidal attacks did not
lead to ugly scenes of fighting was due to the restraint exercised by the
MPLA, mindful that the aim was to undermine relations between the
liberation movement and the Zambian authorities, as well as the
governments of other countries.[18]

Another faction, the so-called Active Revolt, opposed the MPLA
leadership after the *coup d'état* in Portugal. This was a small group of
no more than 70 people. The overwhelming majority of them were
intellectuals in exile who had failed to respond to Neto's appeals to all
Angolans to join the liberation struggle, regardless of class or
educational background, a policy which had resulted in the relatively
large number of university-educated people among MPLA field
commanders. That revolt had all the earmarks of a bid for power when
independence was already on the horizon. Most members of the group

subsequently acknowledged their error and hold responsible posts in Angola today.

These were all weakening factors in the crucial months leading up to the independence process. Yet they also resulted in the closing of ranks around the leadership of the MPLA, particularly behind Neto, whose single-minded determination, and refusal to accept the possibility of anything but victory, had provided a powerful incentive in overcoming obstacle after obstacle in the course of the struggle.

Fascism was overthrown in Portugal on 25 April 1974 but the 'Junta of National Salvation' headed by General António de Spínola did not recognize the right of the colonies to independence; and the new democratic freedoms of Portugal were not extended to the colonies, where the war continued. The MPLA issued a statement in Lusaka on 1 May condemning this and demanding that 'all Angolan prisoners be released, that Angolans be free to organise themselves politically and that Angolans be given the right to freedom of expression and assembly in our country'.

Then began a struggle in Portugal between the right wing of the new regime and those determined that the democratic aims of the MFA should not be betrayed. The conflicts were to influence events in Angola decisively, with Western powers, and particularly the United States, moving rapidly to promote their own interests. An MFA representative proposed that a referendum be held in Angola to decide on independence. Commenting on this in June 1974, General Costa Gomes said, 'I am convinced that Angola will decide to remain Portuguese. It should strengthen its relations with South Africa and Rhodesia.'[19]

That same month Unita signed a cease-fire with the Portuguese military authorities – before Portugal had even accepted the principle of independence for Angola. Padre Oliveira, the missionary who had already carried messages between Unita and the Portuguese military, acted as guide to the cease-fire talks in the bush. The Portuguese delegation to Operation Dove, as it was called, was led by Lieutenant-Colonel Fernando Passos Ramos of military intelligence, 'a man who already had Unita's full confidence', according to the padre.[20]

The Portuguese clearly attached no military significance to the cease-fire signed with Unita in June. In July the MPLA denounced the continued bombing of villages by the Portuguese air force and on 8 August 1974, the Junta of National Salvation issued a communiqué

which stated: 'Once a cease-fire agreement has been reached, the
Portuguese Government will set up a provisional government in which
all liberation movements will be represented, together with the ethnic
groups most representative of the state of Angola, which will obviously
include the white ethnic group.'[21] The MPLA condemned this as an
attempt to divide and rule by resorting to tribalism and racism, stating
its own position as: 'One nation, one people, and no minorities or
sectors of the people with special status.'

Conscious of the need for unity, especially at such a critical
historical juncture, the MPLA sought to iron out the problems with
Chipenda's Eastern Rebellion and the Active Revolt group. The
factions, however, refused all dialogue and lobbied for external
support, internationalizing what the fiercely independent MPLA
regarded as its internal affairs. The OAU and neighbouring countries
made themselves first intermediaries and then set up a 'good offices'
commission. Under external pressure and in the spirit of unity, the
MPLA agreed to take part in a congress held in Zambia in August
1974. An international press campaign, meanwhile, announced that
Chipenda was 'tipped for leadership'.

On 1 August, a week before the congress, 83 guerrilla commanders
signed the proclamation of the constitution of the People's Armed
Forces for the Liberation of Angola (FAPLA). This was unequivocal
support for the movement's leadership from the commanders fighting
in the field.[22]

The MPLA was obliged to attend the congress with the same
number of delegates as the Eastern Rebellion faction, 165, while all 70
members of the Active Revolt were delegates. During the checking of
credentials, 14 of Chipenda's delegates were found to be FNLA
members. These and other anomalies, including the droves of
journalists hovering around what was supposed to be a gathering held
in camera, caused the MPLA delegation, headed by Neto, to walk out
of the congress. Chipenda then proclaimed himself president of the
MPLA. Some months later he joined the FNLA.

In September, the MPLA held a conference inside Angola attended by
delegates from all the fighting fronts and from the clandestine
networks in urban areas. There the problems in the run-up to
independence were discussed. A multitude of political groups had
sprung up overnight in Angola, mainly among white settlers who were
massacring the people in the urban shanty towns. There were also
people advocating the killing of whites or of members of other tribes.
A statement issued at the MPLA conference denounced these

developments and stressed the need for unity to face 'the direct enemy, Portuguese colonialism'.

Added to the efforts to dilute Angola's independence, or even to exclude the MPLA from the process, were a number of schemes to carve up the country. There were reports in September 1974 of a meeting on the island of Sal, in Cape Verde, between President Spinola of Portugal and President Mobutu Sese Seko of Zaire, also attended by Roberto. The 28 September issue of *Horoya*, published in Guinea (Conakry), reproduced a letter to President Sékou Touré from a member of the Portuguese MFA who wished to remain anonymous. It said that during the Sal meeting on 14 September, it had been agreed that Portugal should support Roberto in an Angola shorn of oil-rich Cabinda province, which would be put under the Kinshasa-based FLEC separatist group. A Zaire-Angola-Cabinda federation was then to be formed with Mobutu as president, and possibly Roberto as vice-president. In exchange, the letter said, Zaire would help Portugal to obtain diplomatic respectability in Africa (the OAU had said it would not recognize the new regime until all the colonies were independent); to ensure that 'all Portuguese and multinational companies acting under cover of Portugal should, for a period of at least 20 years, dispose as they please of the vast natural resources of Angola, Cabinda and Zaire'; and to help Portugal 'to recuperate Mozambique and Guinea Bissau, either by provoking *coups d'état* or by undertaking assassinations by infiltrating mercenaries or corrupting certain cadres in the liberation movements'.

However, Spinola was forced to resign shortly thereafter. His successors in Portugal recognized the principle of independence for the colonies, and the MPLA was then able to sign a cease-fire in October. In November, the first official MPLA delegation arrived in Luanda to a tumultuous welcome.[23]

With a view to preventing further hostilities and further foreign intervention in Angola's affairs, the MPLA went to Mombasa, in Kenya, where an agreement was reached with FNLA and Unita delegations to co-operate in all fields and to start negotiations with the Portuguese government. In January 1975, at a meeting in Alvor, Portugal, an agreement was signed under which a quadripartite transitional government – made up of the MPLA, the FNLA, Unita and Portugal – would run the country until elections in October and independence on 11 November. That same month, when a tenuous platform for unity was being sought to avoid further bloodshed, the

CIA decided to give $300 000 of military assistance to its own Angolan protégés, the FNLA.[24]

Under the terms of the Alvor agreement, the various movements were to enter Angola legally and without arms. The MPLA respected this agreement, and Unita was too small a force at that time to matter; but the FNLA came in heavily armed. The United States supported them, both directly and through Zaire; and Zaire sent troops into Angola. The border between Zaire and Angola, in 1975, was uncontrolled, with troops pouring in, stolen Angolan coffee and other goods pouring out, and the Portuguese army – which was supposed to be controlling the situation – removed from that area.

Interviewed in Luanda the previous year, the MFA senior representative, naval officer José Martins e Silva, referred to an earlier FNLA plan to invade Angola with Zairean troops, a plan apparently postponed pending negotiations. He went on to say, 'We are not very worried about the guerrillas belonging to Unita, because they are not strong... Organisations like Unita and FNLA are unwilling to accept peace because they know they don't represent more than a small number of people in a small section of the country. The MPLA is different. It is the only one with sympathisers in all the urban centres of Angola. The greatest number of them were known before the revolution. We know that all the black intellectuals are MPLA.'[25]

In the capital, the FNLA was regarded as a foreign force, speaking mainly French and Lingala (the Kinshasa dialect), and, finding it had no political support there, tried to impose itself by military means. The big onslaught started in March. The MPLA instructed its army not to respond to provocations. Over the ensuing months, until July when the MPLA started its counter-offensive, Luanda became a charnel house, with the FNLA shelling the shanty towns, torturing and killing. The mortuaries were overflowing and MPLA members and leaders were hunted down, going into hiding as in colonial times.

Some insight into what the FNLA and Unita offered to the Angolan people in ideological terms is found in speeches made by their leaders in this period. In a radio broadcast in February 1975, Roberto, after dismissing direct democracy as 'utopian', said, 'We are a religious people and our faith is unshakeable. We are creating our true democracy based on that great faith, against atheistic materialism which crushes the individual, the group and the collective in its iron jaws.' Savimbi was more complex. In the Central Highland region of his birth, he sought to whip up tribal feelings, speaking in Umbundu of the need to kill whites and people from the north who, he claimed, wanted to take over the country. Speaking in Portuguese to the most reactionary sector of the settler population, which flocked to support him, he said that the Angolan people were not ready for independence. Unita was 'in favour of a period of preparation of the Angolan people to play the democratic game,' he said, according to a report in a Lisbon newspaper, *Diário de Notícias,* on 17 June 1974. 'After a period of educating the people', elections should be held for a legislative assembly out of which would come a government which would 'discuss what future relations between Portugal and Angola should be'.

The forces brought together under the Alvor Agreement to form a transitional government were therefore totally disparate, making the agreement impracticable from the outset. The United States, as shown by its aid to the FNLA, was determined that it should not work. The Soviet Union, in contrast, did not send any assistance to the MPLA throughout 1974 and the first eight months of 1975.[26] The Portuguese MFA, rent with internal contradictions and conflicting views, was unable to take a clear stand beyond defending what were regarded as Portugal's interests in Angola.

What actually sounded the death knell of the Alvor Agreement was when the FNLA tried to seize power by force. But, as a result of the MPLA's counter-offensive, the FNLA and Zairean troops were driven out of the capital in July 1975 and, with the massive support of the population, the MPLA finally brought peace to Luanda. Without troops to back them up, the FNLA leaders left Luanda, followed by the Unita officials. Government in Angola, only four months before the date set for independence, was left in the hands of the MPLA and the Portuguese, the latter due to leave the country in November. Contrary to propaganda claims, therefore, the MPLA was not put into power by Cuban or any other forces.

The United States reacted swiftly to the new situation and, also in July, the CIA and President Ford approved a further $14 million in covert support for anti-MPLA forces. It was now total war. Troops were pouring in from Zaire and settlers were openly demonstrating in favour of Unita. Having lost the capital, the FNLA and Unita sought to establish their own spheres of influence; the FNLA in the northern provinces of Uige and Zaire, Unita in Huambo and Bié in the Central Highlands.

By August the MPLA had established control over 12 of Angola's then 16 provinces. The CIA stepped up its interference. According to

John Stockwell, then chief of CIA operations for Angola, 'Paramilitary
and organizational specialists flew to Kinshasa, and the [CIA] task
force took form. The third C-141 flight was launched. And in long
working sessions of CIA paramilitary and logistics officers, the
composition of the shipload of arms was carefully formulated: twelve
M-113 tracked amphibious vehicles; sixty trucks, twenty trailers; five
thousand M-16 rifles; forty thousand rifles of different caliber;
millions of rounds of ammunition; rockets, mortars, recoilless rifles,
etc.... Strategic and tactical radio networks were devised for use by the
FNLA inside Angola. Mobutu's army and air force hauled enough
arms for two infantry battalions and nine Panhard armoured cars to
the FNLA base at Ambriz, seventy miles north of Luanda.'[27]

President Neto appealed to the people to resist and to ensure
national unity. The invasion from the north was followed by a far more
serious one from the south when a contingent of South African troops
entered Angola in August, allegedly to protect the Calueque
hydroelectric dam near the Namibian border. This was the prelude to
an invasion by motorized troops which resulted in the occupation of
the whole of the centre and south of Angola. The plan called for the
invading forces from the north and south to converge on the capital
and take it before independence on 11 November.

'During September and October, the CIA, with remarkable support
from diverse US government and military offices around the world,
mounted the economy-size war with single-minded ruthlessness,'
Stockwell later wrote. 'The lumbering USAF C-141 jet transports
continued to lift twenty-five-ton loads of obsolete US or untraceable
foreign weapons from Charleston, South Carolina, to Kinshasa, where
smaller planes took them into Angola. The USN *American Champion*
sailed from Charleston on August 30 with a cargo of arms and
equipment. Any 'snags' were handled by a phone call from the CIA to
the White House, Pentagon or State Department, and the problem
magically disappeared. CIA officers, eventually eighty-three
altogether, were dispatched to the field, where they beefed up the
Kinshasa, Luanda, Lusaka and Pretoria stations, and managed the air,
ground, maritime, and propaganda branches of the little war. An
additional $10.7 million, authorized by the president on August 20,
1975, for the purchase of more arms, ammunition, and advisors for
Angola, had brought our total budget to $24.7 million. The deadline
was November 11, 1975, when the Portuguese would relinquish
proprietorship of the colony to whichever movement controlled the
capital at that time.'

The entire operation was co-ordinated between Washington and Pretoria. A South African brigadier, Ben de Wet Rood, led the South African troops who manned the FNLA's artillery in northern Angola. In a 1984 interview, he said, 'I was called in to assist with the formulation of an attack on the capital by the FNLA, which was operating in the north of the country with the aid of the CIA, while South Africa and Unita were fighting in the south.' He went on to say that, 'After discussions with Roberto, I put in a request for some 5,5s [140mm] guns and in less than 48 hours they were flown in and ready for deployment. This shook Roberto to the core, because the SADF [South African Defence Force] had complied within hours to what the CIA could not do in weeks.' The brigadier described the battle at Kifangondo, some 20 kilometres north of Luanda, which took place on 10 November, the eve of Angola's independence. The FNLA was routed there, according to him, because of its total military incompetence. The brigadier and his 26-man SADF team then decided that discretion was the better part of valour and made their way to the port of Ambrizete, where the South African ship the *President Steyn,* secretly lying offshore, picked them up and carried them back to Walvis Bay in Namibia. The brigadier then flew north to act as chief-of-staff, and later of command, of the South African forces invading Angola from the south.[28]

Eyewitness reports that the white troops with Unita were South Africans found their way into the Western press, but the South African government continued to deny its involvement in what was supposed to be a secret war. In mid-December, however, the Angolan government announced the capture of four South African soldiers between Cela (now Wako Kungo) and Kibala, 750 kilometres north of the Namibian border. Only then was South African Defence Minister P.W. Botha forced to acknowledge that his army was deep inside Angola.

John Stockwell went into considerable detail about CIA co-operation with the South African Bureau of State Security (BOSS) in this phase. He described South African planes meeting US transport flights in Kinshasa to ferry arms into Angola, and South African planes and trucks turning up 'throughout Angola with just the gasoline or ammunition needed for an impending operation'.[29] South African Prime Minister John Vorster was later to admit implicitly that his government received a green light from the US administration for its invasion of Angola.[30]

On the eve of independence, there was also an invasion of the oil-rich Cabinda enclave by a Zairean force in support of FLEC. 'Seeing

his chance in October 1975 to annex the MPLA-held Cabinda,
Mobutu approached the CIA', Stockwell wrote. 'We promptly flew
in a one-thousand-man arms package for use in the invasion, and CIA
officers of the Kinshasa station began to visit the FLEC training
camps to coordinate.'[31] Fapla, however, continued to hold Cabinda,
with the help of a small group of recently arrived Cuban instructors.

The purpose of the Washington–Pretoria operation in support of
the FNLA and Unita was not, therefore, to avert an 'impending' Soviet
and Cuban take-over, as the propaganda made out, but to prevent the
MPLA from proclaiming independence. The first Cuban military
personnel arrived in Angola in October 1975: 480 instructors to help
train the vast numbers of young people flocking to join Fapla. The
experienced MPLA guerrillas were too busy on the various combat
fronts to handle training as well.[32]

The South African army, with armoured vehicles and heavy
artillery, took the towns of Lubango and Mocâmedes (now Namibe) on
27 October, and started to advance on Lobito and Benguela. South of
Benguela was a Fapla training camp where Cuban and Angolan
instructors, armed with nothing more powerful than a 75mm anti-tank
gun, fought the invaders and were defeated. Those were the first
Cubans to die on Angolan soil.

Independence took place as planned, to the sound of the boom of
artillery north of the capital. The celebrations were a moving event,
proud and festive. In the south, the South African advance was halted
about 200 kilometres from Luanda, mainly by blowing up bridges on
their route.

During the critical period before independence, the MPLA had
appealed to friendly countries for help. Cuba, Guinea Bissau and
Guinea (Conakry) offered to send troops. Having just come out of a
guerrilla war, Fapla had neither the numbers of men nor the
technology to defend the country against the conventional forces and
sophisticated equipment pouring across its borders. But neither could
the required numbers of friendly forces arrive before the 11
November independence date, as Portugal was still the administering
power in Angola. By this time Zaire was estimated to have 11 200
regular soldiers and officers in Angola. The South Africans numbered
about 6 000, a figure which doubled shortly after 11 November when
an army brigade moved across the southern border into Angola.
There were mercenaries of various nationalities with the forces in the

north, and also an organized group of Portuguese fascists who called themselves the Portuguese Liberation Army (ELP), and the FNLA and Unita.[33]

On 5 November, the Central Committee of the Communist Party of Cuba decided to send the first Cuban combat troops to Angola in response to MPLA requests. Operation Carlota was the code-name and it started with 650 Cubans aboard three, old, four-engine planes of Cubana Airlines.[34] The Soviet Union supplied arms and equipment to Fapla as did Yugoslavia, and Cuba continued to send men. With this assistance Fapla started to drive out the invading armies. On 14 November, according to Stockwell, the 40 Committee, which supervises the CIA and which had instructed them to 'prevent an easy victory by Soviet-backed forces in Angola', now asked the Agency to draw up a programme which would 'win the war'.[35] The South Africans were being pushed back, and in the north the invading forces had been reduced to a disorderly rabble, robbing, killing and raping as they retreated. When the FNLA chief-of-staff, former Portuguese colonial army colonel Santos e Castro, disappeared to South Africa, he was replaced by mercenary Costas Georgiou (the self-styled Colonel Tony Callan) as the CIA made a last-ditch effort to save the FNLA.[36] The story of the mercenaries captured and put on trial is well-known.

In the urban centres they occupied in the south of the country, the South Africans set up a Unita administration; and it was under a South African umbrella that the FNLA and Unita set up what they called a 'democratic republic of Angola' in Huambo, recognized by no government in the world. Fighting later broke out in Huambo between the FNLA and Unita, with Huambo radio broadcasting pleas for peace on 22 December 1975. By 23 December the fighting had spread to Benguela. When Huambo was liberated on 8 February, charnel-houses of bodies and mass graves were found. Special targets had been Umbundu officials of the MPLA. Wherever the FNLA and Unita had passed, banks, safes and vaults had been broken into and millions of escudos stolen from the country. Nowhere had they set up a viable administration.

Members of the US Congress, angered by revelations of clandestine operations in Angola and by the lying of CIA officials, introduced an amendment to the 1976 Arms Export Control Act, banning all military aid to anti-government forces in Angola without congressional approval. Known as the Clark Amendment, for the chairman of the Senate Foreign Relations Committee, Dick Clark, who proposed it, this became law on 9 February 1976.

Savimbi had already made his headquarters in Kinshasa, from where he had appealed for help. 'We do not need either American advisers or soldiers, but we do need arms. We ask for help from the United States and our friends in the West. It would be a pity if the US were not to help our cause. We know that the US was demoralised by its defeat in Vietnam, but it would be a pity if it did nothing to defend its interests in Angola. We are fighting for the interests of the West in Angola.'[37]

Stockwell recorded that Savimbi approached the CIA chief of station in Kinshasa in early February and asked what he should do next. 'When Washington finally answered, it encouraged Savimbi to continue fighting. On February 11 the CIA spokesman promised Savimbi another million dollars in arms and money. On February 18, 1976, Secretary of State, [Dr Henry] Kissinger sent the American chargé in Kinshasa a cable, instructing him to tell Unita leaders that the United States would continue to support Unita as long as it demonstrated the capacity for effective resistance to MPLA.'[38] This was after the Clark Amendment became law.

The South Africans were finally driven out of Angola on 27 March 1976. In their retreat, they blew up every bridge they crossed, plundering vehicles, machinery, pedigree cattle and everything they could transport into Namibia. The Angolan government estimated the quantifiable war damage at US\$ 6.7 billion.[39]

Military means having failed, the United States tried economic warfare against Angola. Stockwell recalls that 'CIA and State Department attorneys repeatedly discussed means of blocking Gulf [Oil]'s payments to the MPLA, and pressure was brought to bear... [but] Gulf could not be persuaded to deliver the money to Roberto or Savimbi unless they controlled Cabinda. On December 23 [1975] Gulf compromised and put \$125 million in an escrow bank account.'[40] The Angolan press reported that on 20 December the US technicians had abandoned Cabinda for Zaire after closing down all the oil wells.[41] Besides the money owing to Angola, no oil was pumped for three months, which meant loss of valuable revenue for both the Angolan government and the US company. Only in March 1976, when the invading forces had been defeated, did the US authorities permit Gulf Oil to resume operations in Angola.

In addition, at the time of the transitional government the Angolan airline had purchased two Boeing 737s from the United States. But, to quote Stockwell again, 'the CIA, the working group and Henry Kissinger were not about to permit the delivery of new American jet airliners to Luanda. Why provide the means for the MPLA to fly their delegations around the world, drumming up support? In November the State Department withdrew the export licences for the planes.'[42]

President Neto spoke about the Boeings in a speech on 26 December. 'You know that some planes we bought from the United States have not been delivered to us up to now, although we have paid for them. They are two big planes, Boeings, and the American state feels that it should not deliver the planes, which are ours. Obviously, this is pure and simple theft. Unless they want to keep the planes and return the money to us. But they have kept the money and also the planes.'

The US State Department asked George Wilson, president of Boeing, to deliver the following telex to the Angolan authorities:

THE UNITED STATES CANNOT STAND BY FOR A SOVIET POWER PLAY IN AFRICA.

IF THE MPLA IS WILLING TO WORK FOR A POLITICAL SOLUTION AND COMPROMISE WITH ITS RIVALS, THE UNITED STATES IS WILLING TO BACK A PEACEFUL SETTLEMENT.

THE MPLA WOULD DO WELL TO HEED OUR ADVICE THAT NO GOVERNMENT CAN PLAN THE RECONSTRUCTION IN POSTWAR ANGOLA WITHOUT UNITED STATES AND WESTERN HELP. NO GOVERNMENT CAN OBTAIN THE TECHNICAL AND FINANCIAL RESOURCES TO STIMULATE ECONOMIC DEVELOPMENT WITH-OUT AMERICAN CONSENT. IN FACT, THE UNITED STATES WOULD BE QUITE RESPONSIVE AND HELPFUL TO A COALITION GOVERNMENT THAT WAS NOT DEPENDENT ON THE SOVIET UNION.

THE UNITED STATES GOVERNMENT IS PREPARED TO THINK FURTHER ABOUT THE SUPPLY OF BOEING AIRCRAFT TO ANGOLA AND IS WILLING TO UNDERTAKE FURTHER DISCUS-SIONS DEPENDING ON THE COURSE OF EVENTS IN ANGOLA. THIS MESSAGE SHOULD BE GIVEN TO LUANDAN AUTHORITIES. AS THE MPLA IS AWARE, ACCESS TO SOPHISTICATED TECHNOLOGY IS A PRIVILEGE; THE PRESENT BOEING CASE IS JUST ONE, BUT A GOOD EXAMPLE OF THE ADVANTAGES OF HAVING ACCESS TO AMERICAN TECHNOLOGY.

However, as with Gulf Oil, the course of the war forced the State Department and CIA to back down over the Boeings. On 29 March, two days after the expulsion of the South African army, the Angolan

airline took out a full-page advertisement in the local press
announcing the arrival of the Boeings.

The United States, Stockwell records, 'launched a major political
effort to embroil and entrap as many countries as it could into
opposition of the MPLA. Secret agents were sent to third world
conferences', including the OAU summit in Addis Ababa in January
1976 and the summit of non-aligned leaders in Sri Lanka in August,
with a view to preventing Angola's membership. US officials based in
Africa used 'whatever leverage they could manage with their host
governments to prejudice them against the MPLA'.[43] However,
Angola became a full OAU member in February and the foreign
ministers of the non-aligned movement accepted Angola's admission
by acclamation even before the summit meeting. In June that year the
United States vetoed Angola's admission to the UN, and it was not
until after Republican Gerald Ford was defeated by Democrat Jimmy
Carter in November that the United States abstained from voting and
Angola became a UN member.

Intimations that the Carter administration would recognize Angola
proved illusory. Pursuing a vaccilating policy – depending on whether
the doves headed by UN Ambassador Andrew Young or the hawks
personified by Security Advisor Zbigniew Brzezinski were in the
ascendant – it posed as conditions for recognition of Angola the
withdrawal of the Cuban forces from the country and power-sharing with
Unita.

United States analysts were certainly not unaware that the Cubans
were in Angola as a result of South African invasion and that their
withdrawal would weaken the country militarily in the face of the
continued threat from Pretoria, although they chose to use this as their
excuse for continued US involvement in Angola. In April 1976, barely
a month after the expulsion of the South Africans, the Angolans and
Cubans agreed on a programmed reduction of Cuban forces and in
less than a year they were reduced by more than a third. Renewed
South African aggression, however, stopped the withdrawal. A further
decision by the two governments, in 1979, to reduce the number of
Cubans was followed by an escalation of SADF military operations
against southern Angola.[44]

On 25 July 1979, the Angolan government presented to the UN a
detailed account of South African acts of aggression against the

country during the period from 26 March 1976 to 11 June 1979. It described the types of operation, the damage caused and the estimated losses. The report (UN Document S/13473) listed 193 armed mine-laying operations, 21 border provocations, seven bombing raids and one large-scale operation in which both air and ground forces took part. Special mention was made of the 4 May massacre at Kassinga in Huíla province, when 200 SADF paratroopers, assisted by two C-130 troop transport planes, 14 Alouette SA-300 and Puma helicopters, nine Mirage III aircraft and a number of smaller planes launched a six-and-a-half hour attack on a Namibian refugee camp, indiscriminately slaughtering the occupants, mainly women and children. Paralysing gases were also used in the attack. The second-largest operation of this period was the bombing of a Patriotic Front training school at Boma, in Moxico province, on 26 February 1979, a combined operation of the South African and Rhodesian air forces.

Estimated human losses during this three-year period were at least 570 killed and 594 wounded among the Angolan population, 612 Namibians killed and 611 wounded, 198 Zimbabweans killed and 600 wounded, three South African refugees killed and eight wounded. Material losses were assessed to be almost US$ 300 million broken down under the categories of agriculture and livestock, construction, transport, machinery and equipment, fisheries, commerce, administration and public services.[45]

Unquantifiable losses in this and other periods have been those resulting from the forced exodus of people from war areas, interruption of schooling, unemployment caused by the destruction of economic targets, enforced deficiencies in social services, serious nutritional and material shortages. The non-completion of social and economic projects has resulted in repercussions on the economy as a whole. Even less quantifiable perhaps are the psychological traumas caused, particularly to those maimed, orphaned and subjected to relentless bombing.

During this period, in 1977, the five Western members of the Security Council – then the United States, Britain, Canada, the FRG and France – set themselves up as a 'contact group' to negotiate a Namibian settlement. Through shuttle diplomacy involving the Frontline states, the South-West Africa People's Organization (SWAPO) and South Africa, a Namibian independence plan was agreed upon by all the parties and its implementation demanded in Security Council resolution 435 of 1978.

The South African government, always stating publicly that it agreed to the plan 'in principle', invented pretext after pretext for not implementing it, while stepping up its undeclared war against Angola. This reached a new peak in 1979, affecting Huíla, Cunene and Kuando Kubango provinces, with ground attacks, the bombing and occupation of villages, and troops landed by helicopter. A major furniture factory was destroyed in Lubango, capital of Huila province, and so was a substantial part of the Serra da Leba highway in the same province.

South African military escalation continued through early 1980, culminating in June with Operation Smokeshell. Fapla put up fierce resistance and the SADF suffered many casualties, including the pilot of an Alouette helicopter shot down. Losses during the period from June 1979 to December 1980 were estimated as 400 Angolan civilians killed and 640 wounded, 85 soldiers killed and 95 wounded, and an unknown number of people kidnapped and missing. Precise figures were hard to obtain in semi-desert and thinly populated areas. Material damage during the same period was estimated to be US$ 230 996 805.[46]

The UN Geneva conference on Namibia, in January 1981, was the first attended by delegations from both Swapo and South Africa. UN sources expressed optimism that the independence process might start by March. But South Africa stalled again, intimating that it was waiting to see what US president-elect Reagan might do. Having 'haggled and delayed for nearly three years', one American newspaper said, Pretoria 'might well believe that a hardline Reagan administration will relax pressures for the cease-fire and elections' in Namibia.[47] South Africa stepped up its aggression against Angola during the conference.

After the Reagan administration took office, further progress on Namibia was effectively blocked and the 'Namibian problem' was transformed into the 'Angolan problem'. The United States, under Carter, had assumed the leading role in the 'contact group' which had arrived at the UN plan for Namibian independence through its shuttle diplomacy. Because the UN was responsible for Namibia under international law, after Pretoria's mandate was ended in 1966 and its occupation of the territory declared illegal in 1969, the 'contact group' had been presented as the then five Western members of the Security Council, with a UN mantle although no UN mandate. By introducing the 'linkage' issue, making Namibia's independence dependent upon the withdrawal of Cuban troops in Angola, the United States, under

Reagan, not only *de facto* scrapped the UN plan it had helped to draw up, but caused the demise of the 'contact group'. France withdrew from the group in protest over 'linkage' and the other members ceased to play any active role as the United States made itself sole negotiator. The effect of this was that pressure on South Africa to end its illegal occupation of Namibia was replaced by US pressure on Angola to accept 'linkage'. This diplomatic pressure was added to South Africa's military pressure on the young country, while the United States openly allied itself with Pretoria by supporting the South African-backed Unita group.

Reagan's only known statement on Africa during his election campaign was: 'Well, frankly I would provide Unita with weapons... I don't see anything wrong with someone who wants to free themselves from the rule of an outside power, which is Cubans and East Germans.'[48]

Referring to reports that the new US administration was actively studying the possibility of providing direct military aid to Unita, Zimbabwe's prime minister, Robert Mugabe, said, 'This would be a most hostile act – not only to Angola but certainly to the African states in this region. Africa would obviously condemn it. But I can't imagine that the Reagan regime would be that evil.' The *International Herald Tribune* commented on 9 March 1981: 'Covert aid to Unita... is under active consideration by the Reagan administration. Has the situation in Angola so changed that US intervention, a disaster six years ago, has become an attractive foreign policy option?'

At about this time it was disclosed that a report prepared 'for Washington' had recommended that the United States provide Unita with anti-tank and anti-aircraft missiles, as well as military advisers. US military experts were also reported to have made clandestine visits to Unita bases.[49] The State Department revealed at the same time that a US assistant secretary of state, Lannon Walker had met Savimbi secretly in Rabat, where the Unita chief has a villa. Speaking at a UN seminar in Paris on the arms embargo against South Africa, Angola's ambassador to France, Luis de Almeida, said, 'By sending military experts to the border of Namibia and Angola in order to assess the needs of the traitors and to study the situation on the ground, by official statements and secret meetings in Rabat with Jonas Savimbi, and in Washington between the Central Intelligence Agency and Unita representatives, the Reagan administration has shown its enemy face.'

The *Windhoek Observer*, commenting on these machinations on 4

April 1981, said, 'The American envoys who arrived under cover somewhere in the south of Angola but more or less all the time on South West African soil, are erroneously under the impression that they have dealt with Unita; these envoys are to advise Ronald Reagan on the great force Unita constitutes and they were given the full treatment so as to give an enthusiastic report.'

In May, US customs officials in Houston, Texas, seized a planeload of arms valued at US$ 1.2 million destined for South Africa. A customs official said at the time that 'the Unita forces in Angola are the obvious place for the final destination.'[50]

An increasing number of high-level meetings between US and South African officials indicated that new moves were probably afoot. Senior South African military intelligence officers, General van der Westhuizen and Admiral Duplessis, visited Washington secretly in March 1981, but left hastily when their identities were revealed. In April the US assistant secretary of state for African affairs, Dr Chester Crocker, had talks in Pretoria with the South African foreign minister, Roelof 'Pik' Botha, and the defence minister, Magnus Malan. Pik Botha visited Washington in May. It was during these latter meetings that the 'linkage' policy was formulated.

Documents on the US–South African talks, leaked to the *New York Times,* were given substantial press coverage in June 1981. Among them was a memorandum on Crocker's talks in Pretoria on 15 and 16 April which stated: 'SAG [South African Government] sees Savimbi as a buffer for Namibia. SAG believes Savimbi wants southern Angola. Having supported him this far, it would damage SAG honor if Savimbi is harmed.... Malan declared SAG view that Angola/Namibia situation is number one problem in southern Africa. Angola is one place where US can roll back Soviet/Cuban presence in Africa. Need to get rid of Cubans, and support Unita. Unita is going from strength to strength while Swapo grows militarily weaker.'[51]

The various pretexts used by Pretoria up to then for refusing to implement Resolution 435 – the composition of the proposed UN force (UNTAG), the alleged partiality of the UN, etc. – had never included the presence of Cuban troops in Angola. But this was henceforth made the obstacle to further progress, with the added advantage for Pretoria that it made it appear that it was the Angolans who were standing in the way of Namibian independence. Referring to the leaked documents, the *International Herald Tribune* of 2 June described the US–South African strategy as to 'Use the prospect of getting South African troops out of Namibia... as leverage on the Soviet-backed government of Angola. Demand from Angola both a withdrawal of Cuban forces from its territory and a sharing of power with Savimbi....The Angolans would be told that Moscow cannot help them economically, that Washington can, that they can get US diplomatic recognition only by acceding to the two conditions and that Washington would consider resuming military aid to Savimbi if necessary.'

Under Reagan, Carter's two conditions for recognizing Angola became conditions for Namibia's independence. Thus, the solution of the international problem of Namibia was made subordinate to Washington's policy on Angola. Although the US government presented itself as a mediator, an 'honest broker' in the negotiations, the joint Washington–Pretoria strategy laid down in 1981 has been followed to the letter.

A massive propaganda campaign was needed to gain acceptability for the strategy. The *apartheid* regime, internationally condemned as a crime against humanity and the only regime in the world at war with both its own people and all the peoples of its region, was to be dealt with through 'constructive engagement', a curious concept holding that only the racist minority itself can put an end to minority rule – and that it will do so only if not subjected to external pressure. Tension in the region, the reasoning followed, stemmed from an East–West conflict, a Soviet-Cuban threat. The Reagan administration, totally insensitive to African aspirations, echoed Pretoria's line that those who fought to win or defend their nationhood were mere pawns in an international power play. The victims of *apartheid* and aggression were thus made to appear the aggressors.

There can be no parallel between the illegal presence of South African troops in Namibia and the Cuban military presence to which Angola is fully entitled under Article 51 of the UN Charter which recognizes 'the inherent right of individual or collective self-defence' of a country under armed attack. No Cuban or Angolan soldier, for that matter, has crossed into or threatened any country in the region, whereas the SADF respects no borders and no country's sovereignty. Angola's repeated complaints to the Security Council have resulted in numerous resolutions condemning South African aggression. Despite its persistent claims about 'threats to security' in the region, Pretoria has not once lodged a formal complaint with the world body.

Indeed, the relatively new 'third world' majority at the UN has isolated Pretoria internationally and, increasingly, is isolating

Washington. Accordingly, the United States took the Namibian negotiations out of the ambit of the UN (to which the 'contact group', in its time, did report back), and chose the arena of secret bilateral talks. Angola, in participating in talks, repeatedly stated that it was prepared to do so if there were any chance of progress on Namibia's independence. It persistently rejected 'linkage' and ruled out talks with Unita.

The secret talks were accompanied by misleading leaks to the press, with US officials stating both in public and in private that Angola was about to accept 'linkage' and dismissing as 'rhetoric' official statements to the contrary. It was a way of creating a climate making the Cubans the main issue in the region, and a way of concentrating more pressure on Angola. In the same disinformation vein, there were said to be divisions among the Angolan leaders between 'pro-Western pragmatists' favouring US–South African strategy and 'pro-Soviet hardliners' blocking it. Anyone at all conversant with Angola's policy will know that a remarkable consistency was maintained when President José Eduardo dos Santos succeeded President Neto, and following all subsequent party and government reshuffles. Despite all the speculation, much of it involving libellous attacks on individuals and racist insinuations that their thinking is determined by their degree of pigmentation, the Angolan government is today no closer than it was five years ago to accepting that Namibia's independence depends upon Angola weakening its defences in the face of persistent South African aggression.

There was a marked increase in South African aggression against Angola after Reagan came to power, leading to the massive invasion and occupation of part of the south of the country in August 1981. The United States vetoed a Security Council resolution condemning South African aggression. The seeming contradiction of increasing military action against Angola while calling for a Cuban withdrawal indicated that insistence on 'linkage' was merely a way of easing pressure on South Africa to proceed with Namibian decolonization, and that the Cuban presence in Angola in fact suited both Washington and Pretoria. Without the Cubans to use as an issue the United States would find it much more difficult to present the conflict in the region in global East–West terms and to align itself so completely with the *apartheid* regime. Equally, the South African government would wish to retain the Cuban presence in Angola so they can be seen to be an active ally of the West against the Soviet Union.[52]

After a substantial increase in South African reconnaissance flights over Angola in the first half of 1981 and other armed operations, the Angolan authorities revealed in July that about 40 000 South African troops were massed on the southern border with Namibia.[53] Then, on 23 August, the SADF launched Operation Protea, a massive invasion of southern Angola. Operation Protea involved about 11 000 men, around 36 Centurion M-41 tanks and 70 AML-90 armoured cars, 200 armoured personnel carriers, artillery which included the G-5 155mm gun and 127mm Kentron surface-to-surface missiles, and about 90 planes and helicopters. After massive bombing raids on major urban centres in Cunene province and north into Huíla, three South African armoured columns entered the country and moved on the urban centres, where there was fierce fighting with Angolan forces. But South Africa's superiority in the air proved decisive.

The invasion resulted in the occupation for more than three years of about 50 000 square kilometres of Cunene province. It facilitated the infiltration of Unita forces further to the north of Angola while concentrating the attention of the Angolan armed forces on the permanent threat from South Africa's regular army. A full-scale propaganda campaign was now mounted in support of Unita. In November 1981, while the South Africans were bombing and killing Angolans from their bases in occupied Cunene and in Namibia – and at the very moment when South African commandos sabotaged the Luanda oil refinery – [54] Pretoria's protégé Jonas Savimbi arrived in the United States, where he was received by the secretary of state, Alexander Haig, as though he were the leader of a country.

More and more Western journalists visited Savimbi at his Jamba base on the Namibian border (a place not to be found on Angolan maps) and, sometimes after only a few hours in the bush, wrote enraptured articles in praise of Savimbi illustrated with maps showing vast swathes of Angola under Unita control. Normally sceptical newsmen, particularly where Africa is concerned, seemed prepared to believe anything Savimbi told them. The selling of the man as a 'freedom fighter' has been one of the biggest disinformation campaigns mounted in recent years.[55] Meanwhile, Angolan government and other reports on Unita's massacres and mutilations of defenceless peasants, particularly in the Central Highlands reputed to be its tribal support base, were largely ignored, as was

Savimbi's smuggling activity organized from his SADF-protected residence in the Caprivi Strip of Namibia.⁵⁶

Increased terrorist activity by Unita, particularly in areas further to the north where it had not previously operated, put a further strain on Angola's resources and social services, already hard stretched by massive loss of life and damage caused by the regular South African forces in the south.⁵⁷ In 1983, President dos Santos cited US$10 billion as the estimated total losses caused by South African aggression against the country, an astronomical figure which must certainly be higher by now in view of subsequent destruction, including whole towns razed.

The war, disrupting agriculture and transport, also led to increased foreign exchange expenditure on food imports. Another important factor affecting the economy of a young country seeking to rebuild is the cost of maintaining a modern and well-equipped army which keeps thousands of able-bodied young men out of productive activity. And because sophisticated equipment is needed to defend Angola against the SADF, Fapla needs skilled personnel who could otherwise be used in the economy. The country has been fortunate, until the sharp fall in oil prices in 1986, in having a thriving oil industry which not only ensures crucial fuel for defence but provides the bulk of foreign exchange earnings. Contrary to propaganda claims, however, oil revenue is not used to pay the Cuban troops, who for some years now have received from the Angolans only their local expenses in Angolan currency, kwanzas.

In the oil and other industries there are substantial numbers of foreign technicians from both East and West working in Angola. After South Africa's occupation of Cunene province, Unita started to make such technicians a special target. The foreigners it had killed or kidnapped up to then had been missionaries or farmers in remote areas. The spectacular kidnappings of foreign technicians, accompanied by threats from Unita representatives in Europe to all foreigners working in Angola, have been essentially publicity-seeking operations. They have also been a somewhat crude way of blackmailing the governments of those kidnapped to grant a kind of tacit recognition of Unita by negotiating the release of the hostages. This happened notably in the case of Czech technicians kidnapped in March 1983 at a paper plant in Alto Catumbela, Benguela province, and of British and other personnel taken hostage in the diamond-mining province of Lunda Norte in February 1984. Czech and British officials were obliged to go to Jamba to secure the release of their nationals. It is symptomatic of the propaganda that the taking of hostages – one of the Reagan administration's definitions of 'terrorism' – should elicit so much praise for Unita, even in major papers in the countries of those kidnapped. The United States raised not a murmur over an American killed when Unita destroyed a Transamerica plane in Lunda Norte.

Yet the military situation was substantially changing. The reorganized Fapla, better equipped and with newly trained commando troops to deal with guerrilla-type subversive action – an entirely different kind of war to facing up to the regular South African army – started an offensive to drive Unita out of the vantage points they had gained as a result of South African occupation. An outstanding victory in this new impetus was the battle of Cangamba in Moxico province, in the east, where an attempt by Unita to take the small town was prevented in August 1983, and an estimated 1 100 Unita men killed, many by crossing their own minefields. Only hours later, the South African air force flew in and razed the town, forcing the Angolan armed forces to withdraw. This was the first time that the South African military openly intervened to save Unita.

Fapla's anti-bandit operations had profound effects inside Unita, the deterioration in their military situation causing deep rifts and dissent. The *International Herald Tribune* of 26 January 1985 reported that, 'The Angolan rebel movement Unita appears to be overreaching its military capacity and is showing signs of internal dissent as it intensifies guerrilla and diplomatic activity to secure a significant role in negotiations toward a regional peace settlement.'

A number of once prominent Unita officials are no longer heard of. These include Jorge Sangumba, once the group's foreign affairs secretary, and former military chief Samuel Chiwale.[58] Other disappearances include António Vakulukuta, once Unita's secretary of the interior, a Kwanyama from southern Angola reportedly arrested by the South Africans at Unita's request amid tribal strife within Unita, with Umbundus from Savimbi's region killing members of other ethnic groups from the south.[59] Most recently, an unidentified group in Europe calling itself the 'true black cockerel movement' (Unita's flag bears a cockerel) has been circulating communiqués from Brussels, on Unita letterhead paper, denouncing killings within the ranks. Unita members in many parts of the country surrendered in response to the Angolan government's policy of clemency. Large numbers of the long militarily inactive FNLA, including some senior leaders, have also given themselves up.

The South African armed forces launched their biggest military operation to date in southern Angola in December 1983 and January 1984. Cloaked in the usual verbal disguise of a 'hot pursuit' operation against Swapo guerrillas, Operation Askari was designed to expand the occupied area. It failed, and even the South African generals were forced to concede that they had not expected such fierce resistance from Fapla,[60] making it the costliest SADF operation in Angola, in terms of their own losses, since the 1975–76 invasion. South Africa's air superiority had proved decisive in previous operations, with bombing and air strikes always preceding the advance of the infantry. This time Fapla were better prepared to withstand this 'softening up'. More than 10 South African aircraft were reported shot down, it being difficult to ascertain the exact number as many that are hit crash across the Namibian border. Once fighting was engaged on the ground – when the South African air force could no longer intervene – the Angolan army proved more than a match for the invaders, breaking through several attempted encirclements as the South Africans became increasingly over-extended. Even US business and intelligence sources have confirmed that Cuban troops were not only *not* involved in this fighting but had not fired on the South Africans since 1976. The Cubans are a reserve force, garrisoned well to the north of the area concerned.

The failure of Operation Askari, South Africa's economic crisis to which the war in Angola was adding an estimated cost of US$ 4 million a day,[61] and the Reagan administration's need for at least one foreign policy victory with presidential elections approaching, are thought to be the main reasons for the South Africans agreeing to go to Lusaka on 16 February 1984 and negotiate the withdrawal of troops from Angola. A break in offensive action while negotiations dragged on also offered the SADF time to re-equip. Another factor which cannot have passed unnoticed when Pretoria decided to use the language of peace, was a meeting in Moscow on 11 January, between Angolan, Cuban and Soviet delegations, at which it was agreed 'to help the People's Republic of Angola to strengthen its defence capability to safeguard its independence and territorial integrity'.

Before the talks in Lusaka, the Angolan government stated that the South African withdrawal should be followed by implementation of Security Council resolution 435 and the start of the Namibian independence process. It was agreed at Lusaka to set up a Joint Monitoring Commission (JMC), composed of Angolan and South African forces, to supervise the South African withdrawal from

Angola, which was to be completed within four weeks. US requests to be included in the monitoring activities on Angolan soil were rejected. An Angolan press comment at the time asked 'why are our enemies now so interested in monitoring the end of hostilities against us which they always encouraged and fuelled?' It was agreed that Angola would ensure that Swapo forces did not enter the areas vacated by the SADF during the period of withdrawal. Lieutenant-Colonel Alexandre Rodrigues 'Kito', leader of the Angolan delegation, stated at a press conference in Luanda on 21 February, 'we concurred, on condition that the restriction of Swapo activities in our country should lead to conditions being created for the implementation of 435... otherwise there would be no sense in Angola restricting Swapo'. Angola also made it clear that Swapo was consulted at every step of the negotiations and supported them. It stated that the next stage should be direct negotiations between Swapo and South Africa, the belligerent parties in the region. The Lusaka undertaking, therefore, was not a non-aggression pact, as the Western press presented it, and nor was there any *quid pro quo* arrangement on ending support for Swapo, on one side, and Unita on the other.

South Africa, however, neither withdrew its forces from Angola nor moved forward on the implementation of Security Council resolution 435. Angola continued to use diplomatic means to seek a peaceful solution in the region and further the Namibian independence process, showing remarkable flexibility in the face of South Africa's obvious decision not to end its aggression against Angola or its colonial occupation of Namibia. There were further meetings between Angolan and American and South African delegations. In early November a number of articles appeared in the South African press, especially, stating that Angola had accepted 'linkage' and put forward a detailed programme for the withdrawal of the Cubans. These reports were distorted versions of the continuing negotiations leaked by US and/or South African officials.

President dos Santos detailed Angola's proposals in a letter dated 17 November 1984 to UN secretary-general, Javier Pérez de Cuéllar, putting an end to all such speculations. The letter was published as a full page advertisement in *The Times* of London on 24 November (see Appendix 2). The proposals were a rejection of 'linkage', and made as a precondition for any withdrawal of Cuban troops from Angola that South Africa must start the implementation of resolution 435 and withdraw from Namibia all its troops barring the 1 500 stipulated in the UN plan (under which they were to be confined to bases in Namibia supervised by UN forces).

The letter detailed a subsequent proposed withdrawl of 20 000 Cuban troops over a three-year period, with the remainder staying in northern Angola, where South Africa could not claim they threatened its interests, let alone its borders. South Africa's response was to assail Angola for breaking the confidentiality of talks – despite the fact that the Angolan proposals, albeit distorted, had already been published in the South African and US press – [62] and to put forward counter-proposals. These were that all the Cubans must be out of Angola in 12 weeks, that the Angolans should provide detailed lists of Cuban personnel in the country, and that their withdrawal should be monitored by a commission to include South Africans who should be free to move anywhere inside Angola.

Here, most clearly, the 'Namibian problem' had been made the 'Angolan problem'. Far from contemplating the ending of its illegal occupation of Namibia, Pretoria was proposing further violation of Angolan sovereignty, with itself monitoring the withdrawal of Cubans legally in the country as a result of SADF aggression. The immediate US reaction was to state that there was no basic difference between the Angolan and South African positions and that the only problem was to 'bridge the gap between them'. There were, accordingly, press reports that the difference was a 'clash over time limit for pull out of Cuban troops'.[63] Angola's proposals, which had gone a long way towards addressing the purported concerns of its enemies, had come up against the brick wall of US and South African objectives.

All this diplomatic activity was withdrawing publicity from the other aspect of the Washington–Pretoria strategy: Unita. In early November 1984, a group of 45 journalists were flown in a Dakota aircraft from Pretoria to the Namibian border for a meeting with Savimbi at Jamba. There he announced, as he had in 1983, that he would take Luanda by Christmas. His aim was 'to make the inclusion of Unita in the negotiations a precondition for settling the Namibian issue'. He was, however, aware that his South African friends might not succeed in achieving this. 'Pieter Botha is my friend,' he told the journalists, 'but I know that he has to look after the interests of his country first.' A British newspaper, reporting the event under the headline 'Angolan peace summit soon', quoted diplomatic sources as saying that a meeting between President dos Santos and Savimbi was expected to follow the latter's threat to raid the capital.[64] Disinformation had become systematic.

In April 1985, more than a year after it had agreed to withdraw its troops from Angola, South Africa finally announced that it was doing so, although leaving two companies at hydroelectric schemes on the Cunene river, near the Namibian border. Western press reports presented South Africa as a 'peacemaker', although it was simply doing what it had failed to do many months earlier. At the same time, South Africa announced the installation of a puppet 'internal' government in Namibia, making it clear that it had no intention of ending its illegal occupation of Namibia.

A single event served to expose the true facts of the military, diplomatic and propaganda campaign against Angola. On 21 May 1985, a Fapla patrol foiled an attempt by a South African commando unit to sabotage the Cabinda Gulf Oil complex at Malongo, in Cabinda province, the most northern part of Angola separated from the rest of the country by a strip of Zairean territory. The commander of the unit, SADF captain Wynand du Toit, a member of 'special forces' based in Saldanha Bay in Cape province, was captured, two of his men were killed and six others escaped. At a press conference in Luanda on 28 May, du Toit said that his unit had come from Saldanha Bay in an Israeli-built South African destroyer, which lay off the Angolan coast about 150 kilometres while they landed at night in inflatable boats. Admitting that he had taken part in previous operations inside Angola, including the sabotage of the Giraul bridge in Namibe province, for which Unita claimed responsibility at the time, he said that in 'all or most of the operations that we usually do, we claim or Unita claims the responsibility'. Had the Cabinda attack succeeded, 'then it shows Unita is active also in the northern part, in the province of Cabinda'. In the substantial amount of material captured by Fapla was a tin of paint with which the commandos had intended to write 'Viva Unita' on the road. It was 'part of the deception', du Toit said. Although he claimed to have 'no political or personal contact with Unita', two Portuguese-speaking members of the unit are thought to have been from Unita. Perhaps he meant that he did not know Unita as a structure separate from his own SADF.

That one event shattered the credibility of 'constructive engagement', destroyed the peacemaking image the *apartheid* regime was trying to create for itself, and called into question all the Unita claims over the years. Had it not been for the action of that Fapla patrol, the Angolan economy would have been deprived of its main foreign exchange earner and of the fuel needed to keep everything going, including the armed forces. Headlines would have declared that Unita was in control of Cabinda province and about to make its long-anounced but continually postponed assault on the capital. One can only speculate as to what the reaction of foreign oil companies operating in Angola would have been, or the reactions of their governments.

South Africa had initially denied that its forces were in Cabinda, then later amended this by saying that they were engaged in intelligence-gathering activities against Swapo and the African National Congress of South Africa (ANC), but it no longer convinced even the most right-wing press. So radical was the turnabout that Unita, in a dispatch dated 31 May, accused the British press of 'racist sentiments' for questioning 'Unita's capability to carry out sophisticated sabotage missions'.

Meanwhile, the Fapla offensive against Unita was gaining momentum. Conservative elements in the US Congress moved to repeal the Clark Amendment banning open US military aid to anti-government forces in Angola. In the nine years that the amendment had been in force, Unita, despite South African backing, had failed to overthrow the Angolan government, and was suffering military and propaganda reverses. The State Department, still bent on making the United States appear an 'honest broker' in the region, gave assurances that the repeal did not mean that the United States would assist Unita, but events were soon to prove otherwise.

A beleaguered Unita pushed for rapid US support. On 23 August it announced that a Soviet infantry battalion was operating in Angola, a story to which no serious credence was given. In early September it claimed that Soviet officers were directing the Fapla offensive. South Africa said that the new and sophisticated military equipment used – Mig-23s and helicopter gunships – was piloted by Soviets, referring to intercepted cockpit talk in Russian. Just as Angolan civil aviation pilots use the internationally prevailing English terms, so did the military pilots refer to technical matters in the language of the country where they had learned the advanced technology. The capture of a 'Russian-speaking pilot' was subsequently announced with no mention that he was Angolan. It was this new military capability of Fapla, until then equipped for an essentially defensive war, which rang the alarm bells in Washington and Pretoria. The internal offensive to restore the Angolan government's sovereignty over its territory was presented as a 'red' threat to the entire region.

Johannesburg radio spoke of 'the gravity of Unita's position', as Fapla moved on Unita at Cazombo, in Moxico province, preparing to push on to Mavinga, in Kuando Kubango, and then Jamba, at the border.

During this period, Christoper Lehman, special assistant to Reagan on national security affairs, left his White House post to travel with his new employer, Paul Manafort of the public relations firm, Black, Manafort, Stone & Kelly, to meet Savimbi at Jamba. Savimbi reportedly took off time from a 'fierce battle' to discuss with the two, who returned to Washington a week later with a 'signed $600 000 contract' to sell Savimbi in Washington and organize a trip there for him.[65]

On 16 September, Pretoria announced that its forces had entered Angola, with air cover, in pursuit of Swapo. But just as Swapo is not to be found in Cabinda, it could not be expected to be found in Kuando Kubango, which the propaganda had always claimed to be wholly controlled by Unita. On 17 September, SADF chief Viljoen confirmed Angolan reports that a South African doctor had been killed in Moxico province. On 18 September, Unita was driven out of Cazombo in Moxico. South African intelligence sources were quoted as saying that 'SAAF [South African Air Force] aircraft flew Unita troops and equipment to Cazombo between September 2 and September 16'.[66]

Angola's Ministry of Defence announced that because of Unita's inability to resist the offensive, the SADF Buffalo Battalion, equipped with armoured cars, transport vehicles, artillery and grenade launchers, was advancing on Mavinga from the south and preparing to enter into combat with the Angolan army, after heavy bombing of Angolan troop positions the previous day. South African press reports confirmed this.[67]

On 20 September, South African Defence Minister Malan admitted in parliament that South Africa was helping Unita. In doing so, he said, 'we serve South Africa and Southern Africa and the West's interests'. That same day, Savimbi gave a press conference at Jamba at which he spoke of the possibility of his base being overrun by Fapla and appealed for US intervention.[68] Officials from the South African Foreign Affairs Department were sent to Washington to plead Unita's case.[69]

Malan again appealed for Western intervention. 'If these forces should wipe out Savimbi, then South Africa will be able to say that she did her bit to sustain this anti-Marxist force. The West will have to accept that it did not do its duty and that, as a result, a potent anti-communist force has been lost to us and to the West.'[70]

On 7 October, the UN Security Council voted unanimously to condemn South Africa for its 'latest premeditated and unprovoked aggression' against Angola. Explaining why his country had supported the resolution – rather than abstain or veto, as was its custom – US ambassador to the UN, Vernon Walters, said that the United States, in addition to condemning the raid, 'welcomes this resolution as an occasion to reiterate our call for an immediate withdrawal of South African troops from Angola'. Only two days later, a US State Department spokesman accused the Soviet Union of fanning violence in Angola. Meanwhile, bills were tabled in the US Congress to authorize aid for Unita totalling US$ 54 million, and there were reports that the Pentagon and Defence Department were pushing for assistance of up to US$ 300 million. A trade embargo against Angola was also proposed.

In New York in November, when he addressed the UN General Assembly, President dos Santos accused the Reagan administration of hypocrisy for trying to present the Unita terrorists as 'freedom fighters'. He pointed out that, despite forecasts by Ford and Kissinger that, under an MPLA government, bilateral economic relations would be impossible, Angola was Washington's fourth largest trading partner in Africa south of the Sahara and that financial relations with US banks in the first half of 1985 had amounted to more than US$ 100 million.

Also addressing the General Assembly, President Reagan announced a new 'initiative' on so-called regional conflicts, singling out Afghanistan, Kampuchea, Ethiopia, Angola and Nicaragua as wars caused by 'Soviet expansionism' which he would raise with Soviet leader Mikhail Gorbachev at their summit meeting in Geneva the following month. All these conflicts, he declared, were 'the consequence of an ideology imposed from without'.

Two months later, in January 1986, Savimbi made his much-heralded trip to Washington, where the red carpet was rolled out on every possible occasion. He was given all the protocol of a visiting head of state and received by Reagan, among other dignitaries. While anti-*apartheid* groups campaigned against the visit and the Congress Black Caucus refused to meet him, the State Department dropped any misgivings it had previously claimed over official support for Unita. Up to then it had preferred to use the proposed support as a threat to make Angola accede to US–South African demands. Now it was a *fait accompli*. Angola called it a 'declaration of war'.

In February, Crocker told the Senate Foreign Relations Committee that the United States had decided to provide military aid to Unita and that 'the process is in motion'. This means that it is covert aid, by-passing Congress and not requiring special legislation.

In a statement issued on 8 March, the Angolan government said, 'The direct involvement in the internal affairs of the People's Republic of Angola, confirmed on 18 February this year by the American administration's Assistant Secretary of State for African Affairs, jeopardised the future pursuit of talks to seek a peaceful solution in Southern Africa and put in question the seriousness and credibility of the US in the mediating role it was playing.... This position becomes even more grave in that any support given to Unita is support for racist South Africa and therefore undermines the Namibian independence process.' Reiterating the Angolan peace proposals contained in President dos Santos' letter to the UN secretary-general, the statement 'urges the United Nations Secretary-General to assume full responsibility for conducting negotiations leading to peace and guaranteeing the independence of Namibia and the security of states in the region'.

In the curious reasoning employed by US officials, Angola's efforts to defend its people against South African-backed terrorism and aggression are described as a 'military option', and US military interference in Angola as aimed at achieving 'peaceful negotiations'. It is worth noting what John Stockwell had to say about this earlier. 'Savimbi caused the United States a minor embarrassment in September [1975], when he sent feelers to the MPLA for a negotiated solution. The CIA learned of this move through an article in the world press, and a Kinshasa station officer promptly interrogated Savimbi. We wanted no "soft" allies in our war against the MPLA.'[71]

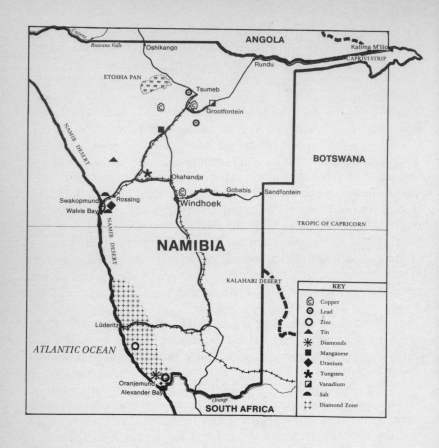

ANGOLA

Ruacana Falls
Cunene
Oshikango
Katima M'lilo
Rundu
CAPRIVI STRIP

ETOSHA PAN
Tsumeb
Grootfontein

NAMIB DESERT

BOTSWANA

Okahandja
Gobabis
Sandfontein

Swakopmund
Rossing
Windhoek
Walvis Bay

TROPIC OF CAPRICORN

NAMIBIA

KALAHARI DESERT

ATLANTIC OCEAN

Lüderitz

KEY

Ⓒ	Copper
⊙	Lead
○	Zinc
▲	Tin
✳	Diamonds
■	Manganese
◆	Uranium
✦	Tungsten
◪	Vanadium
▬	Salt
‡	Diamond Zone

Oranjemund
Alexander Bay
Orange
SOUTH AFRICA

CHAPTER 4

Namibia:
Preparations for Destabilization

Festus Thomas is an ordinary Namibian, one of the many whose story seldom comes through in the sterile atmosphere of United Nations debates and resolutions, international conferences, speeches and statements about Namibia.

Born in northern Namibia in 1942, he received precious little formal education. He married, had six children and in 1978 was a driver for the South West Africa People's Organization (SWAPO) in the Namibian capital, Windhoek.

He was arrested by the South African Security Police on 10 April 1978 after spending the Easter weekend with his wife and children at Ukwaluuthi in northern Namibia. That weekend, Clemens Kapuuo, a leading South African collaborator, had been assassinated in Windhoek. But Thomas, as the security police could have easily checked, was hundreds of miles away and could not possibly have been involved.

Nevertheless he was detained and what happened to him during the next 74 days – verified by doctors who treated his injuries after his release – reads like a horror story from the Nazi era.

The first 12 days of his detention were relatively 'normal', Thomas said later. He was given electric shocks on the genitals and anus, frequently beaten and hung off the ground with his hands manacled behind his back.

But, on Friday, 21 April, the torture took a new and horrifying twist. Four security police officers took him handcuffed from their headquarters in a blue Chevrolet car. First they stopped to buy beer and meat. Then, after they left town, Thomas was blindfolded and put in the boot of the car.

Some 30 kilometres out of town they stopped and, when the

blindfold was removed, Thomas found himself standing on a dried-up river bed. The police officers lit a fire and began cooking meat. Then Thomas was told to lie down and he realized he was being measured for a grave.

The officers ordered him to dig his own grave. Once he was told to lie in it, but the officers decided it was too shallow. When they were finally satisfied that it was deep enough, Thomas was told again to lie in it and given the choice as to whether his head pointed east or west. Stones were piled on top of him and a hole was left so he could breathe. After 30 minutes, the officers excavated him, ramming stones and shovels into his body. As they did so, they sang 'No more Festus', a sadistic play on a song then sung at nationalist rallies, 'No more Vorster'.

After a brief respite, Thomas was ordered to clean the grave and lie in it again. This time he was completely covered and lost consciousness. When he recovered he found that he had been dug out again and was lying on the side of the grave with water being poured on him. Some sort of grenade or fire-cracker exploded next to his body. Then Thomas was made to stand next to a rock while a Sergeant Botha fired a pistol at it, sending chippings into his leg. Finally, as he put out the fire, the officers stoned him.

Late on 22 April he was admitted to ward four at Katutura hospital in Windhoek's African township. Doctors and nurses said his body was covered with cuts and bruises consistent with his story. When Swapo learned where he was and instituted enquiries, Thomas was immediately transferred back to police custody. His medical records were removed from the hospital, and police officers said he had a fever.

Four days later, the security police took him out again, to a river on the Okahandja road. There he was severely beaten and his head held under water until he lost consciousness. His shoulder was dislocated and a tooth broken. When he was returned to his cell he was so weak that he could not stand. Finally, on 23 June, with his wounds healed but the scars very visible, Thomas was released. He made a sworn statement to lawyers about his treatment and they arranged that he should be medically examined. Three days after his release he told his story to the press.[1]

The brutality meted out to Festus Thomas is not unusual. For decades the torture of Namibians has been documented by lawyers, the churches and by SWAPO.[2] This is the common everyday experience of thousands of Namibians. Beatings, torture and 'dis-appearances' following arrest are regular means used by the Pretoria regime in an attempt to suppress SWAPO. The inevitable outcome of South Africa's continuing illegal occupation of Namibia goes well beyond the enormous suffering of the Namibian people. This chapter seeks to illustrate how Namibia features as part of South Africa's policy of regional destabilization.

In Namibia this policy takes a different form from that in Angola, Mozambique or other southern African states because Namibia is a South African colonial territory and has been for over 70 years. However, South Africa has abandoned its earlier goal of literal incorporation of Namibia as a fifth province so the strategy and tactics toward Namibia are increasingly an integral part of the regional – rather than the national – front of 'total strategy'.

Domination and exploitation remain the central themes but Pretoria's tactics have varied – partly as a consequence of deteriorating results in Namibia, partly because of international constraints, and partly because the failure of the Smith-Muzorewa regime in pre-independence Zimbabwe showed that initial plans for a neo-colonial solution for Namibia would not work. As a result the details, and even some of the main features, of the present South African design for preserving and consolidating domination and exploitation in Namibia are by no means clear, probably not even to decision-makers in Pretoria. Further, Angola and Namibia are clearly interlocking elements in South African regional strategy with policies in respect to each partly dependent upon, and partly determining, those in respect to the other.

The elements in South Africa's strategy for Namibia turn on:
a) Political developments in Namibia, domestic considerations in South Africa, and the international efforts being made to secure Namibia's independence.
b) Economics relating to the gains and costs of continued occupation and the burden of the war.
c) War and repression.

Since the late 1970s, South Africa has – with strategic foresight or as a consequence of tactical actions or both — created an ominous structure for the destabilization of an independent Namibia without major direct intervention by overtly South African troops. While not impregnable, that infrastructure for destabilization will require substantial diversion of resources and of policy attention by an independent Namibian government to limit its impact. Even then it will significantly reduce the room for manoeuvre open to Namibia at independence, assuming that this predates the liberation of South Africa.

The roots of the present South African position on Namibia go back to its 1915 military occupation of what was then known as German South West Africa. After the 1914–18 war in Europe, South Africa sought to annex this former German colony. At the Versailles peace conference in 1919, South Africa was granted a mandate over Namibia, but it was of the lowest category, class C. This bore the obligation 'to promote to the utmost the material and moral well-being of the inhabitants of the territory'.[3]

The South African view of this mandate was clear from the outset. Within two years, South Africa's prime minister, General Smuts, told a visiting German delegation that 'The mandate over South West Africa [Namibia] was nothing else but annexation.' In 1925 he told his parliament: 'I do not think it is necessary for us to annex South West Africa to the Union. The mandate for me is enough and it should be enough for the Union. It gives the Union such complete sovereignty, not only administrative but legislative, that we need not ask for anything more.'[4] The scene had been set for Namibia's protracted struggle to regain its independence.

Soon after the UN was set up in 1946, South Africa presented its case for the annexation of Namibia, which it had long regarded as a fifth province. Pretoria argued that the territory was a *de facto* part of South Africa. The UN Fourth Committee rejected the argument and the General Assembly, in a resolution on 14 December 1946, called upon South Africa to place Namibia under international trusteeship. South Africa rejected the demand in 1947 and on ten other occasions over the next eight years. Although it had appealed to the UN in the first instance to annex Namibia, South Africa now questioned the international organization's competence to take over from the defunct League of Nations.

The lengthy legal wrangle over Namibia began in 1949. The following year the International Court of Justice at the Hague, in an advisory opinion, found that South Africa still exercised the mandate over the territory and was obliged to submit reports to the UN on its administration of the territory.[5] South Africa refused; and its disregard for UN resolutions and the opinion of the International Court of Justice was further illustrated in the early 1960s with the establishment of the Odendaal Commission. In 1964 the Commission reported its recommendations for the bantustanization of Namibia.

Resolution after resolution followed from the UN. In 1966 it found that South Africa had 'disavowed the Mandate' as it had 'failed to fulfill its obligations in respect of the mandated territory'. Therefore, 'henceforth South West Africa comes under the direct responsibility of the United Nations.'[6]

Due to the attitude of Western powers, the Security Council had remained aloof from the debate. But in 1968 they joined the fray, demanding that South Africa stop the trial of 37 Namibians in Pretoria, release them and repatriate them to Namibia. Pretoria predictably ignored the demand and, in a display of contempt for the UN authority over Namibia, proceeded with a second trial and began implementing its 'bantustan' policy.[7]

On 20 March 1969 the Security Council declared that South Africa's continued occupation of Namibia was illegal and contrary to the principles and decisions of the UN. Five months later, it gave Pretoria until 4 October 1969 to withdraw its administration from Namibia. During that debate the British representative clearly spelled out the lack of will on the part of some member states that made the UN powerless to enforce its decisions over Namibia. The three Western permanent members of the Security Council (Britain, France and the United States) in practice have acted on the basis of his statement that Britain 'could not and would not contemplate an economic war with South Africa and sanctions against South Africa under Chapter VII of the Charter', which relates to a country found to be a threat to international peace and security.[8]

In 1971, the International Court of Justice delivered a second advisory opinion. The Court upheld the validity of the revocation of the mandate and, therefore, the illegality of South Africa's continued occupation of Namibia. This made it incumbent on all UN member states to 'refrain from any acts' and in particular 'any dealings with the Government of South Africa implying recognition of the legality of, or lending support or assistance to, such presence and administration.'[9] But all attempts to move South Africa, including a visit in 1972 by the UN secretary-general, Dr Kurt Waldheim, failed.

This visit initiated a technique that South Africa has since used of seeming to negotiate in good faith while simultaneously proceeding unduanted with their own programme no matter how inconsistent it is with what is supposedly being negotiated. In this instance South Africa declared that 'Ovamboland' and 'Eastern Caprivi' would be granted 'self-government' in the immediate future as the next step in advancing the bantustan division of the country. Later, Pretoria was to give the appearance of negotiating seriously regarding UN Security Council Resolution 435 (1978), while at the same time going ahead with its own long term programme designed to retain and consolidate control over Namibia.

The Africa Group at the UN, in an attempt to introduce more effective pressure, presented a draft resolution to the Security Council in June 1975 proposing an arms embargo against South Africa. It was blocked by vetoes cast by Britain, France and the United States. However, there was growing concern among the three Western members that Pretoria's refusal to consider any solution could lead to greater pressure on them to impose sanctions.

As a result, UN Security Council Resolution 385 was adopted with Western support on 30 January 1976. This demanded that South Africa withdraw its administration from Namibia and that elections be held, under the supervision and control of the UN, leading to independence for Namibia. In the wake of South Africa's invasion of Angola, the US secretary of state, Henry Kissinger, launched his much-publicized diplomatic shuttle in April 1976 in an effort to deflect mounting pressure on the West over developments in South Africa. Britain, France and the United States again used their vetoes in late 1976 to block a mandatory arms embargo resolution in the Security Council. As a result they found themselves to be in an increasingly untenable position as the veto tended to highlight their role as South Africa's protectors.

The five Western members of the Security Council at that time (Britain, France and the United States, plus rotating members, Canada and the Federal Republic of Germany), began a series of contacts in 1977. The five, who presented themselves as the 'contact group', and South Africa, continually tried to give an impression of forward momentum. In September 1977, Pretoria appointed a judge, Justice Marthinus Steyn, as administrator-general of Namibia. He initiated a review of Namibian laws, repealed some elements of *apartheid* legislation and streamlined so-called security legislation. But the exercise was more cosmetic than real and South Africa's determination to continue to wield power in Namibia, directly or through a surrogate group, remained undiminished.

However, in retrospect 1977 does represent a strategic shift. The mock constitution, produced by a gaggle of white and collaborationist parties, was a blueprint toward indirect South African rule of a nominally independent, confederal but white-dominated Namibian state. Both integration as a fifth provice or as a set of 'bantustans' like Transkei, and also permanent colonial rule, were tacitly dropped. At this point, destabilizing a potentially hostile government was not on the agenda because a neocolonial state was assumed.

In early January 1978, 'proximity talks' were held in New York with members of the 'contact group' shuttling between delegations from SWAPO and South Africa, who refused to talk directly with Swapo. Again, as had consistently been the case during the preceding months of negotiations, SWAPO was pressured to accommodate the demands which Pretoria continously made. The argument was that if SWAPO did not make the concessions, then the whole process would break down. The 'proximity talks' resumed in early February 1978, but lasted only three days because South Africa's foreign minister, 'Pik' Botha, suddenly left New York, warning that aspects of the proposals 'would be totally unacceptable and so dangerous that there is a serious danger of people in the territory being overrun and being governed by a Marxist terrorist organization'[10] by which he meant SWAPO. What became clear from this and other statements by Pretoria was that they would, under no circumstances, accept a SWAPO government in Windhoek. They sought to delay a solution and would only ultimately agree to a settlement which provided the Pretoria regime with what they perceived as a clear opportunity to install a puppet government with international approval.

After another flurry of 'contact group' activity, the South African government announced on 25 April 1978 that it accepted the group's proposals for a settlement in Namibia. Nine days later, in a savage attempt to dissuade Swapo from accepting the proposals, South African forces bombed a Swapo settlement at Kassinga in southern Angola. In one day, 4 May 1978, they massacred more than 600 Namibians, almost all of them non-combatants. The timing of this left little doubt that South Africa's true motive was to provoke their adversary into refusing the proposals, but Swapo accepted them on 12 July.

Towards the end of that month, the proposals were considered by the Security Council who instructed the secretary-general to appoint a special representative to take the matter further. He chose Martti

Ahtisaari, a Finnish career diplomat who was then UN commissioner
for Namibia. Within a week, accompanied by a 50-member UN team,
he was in Namibia.

   But events, it would seem, were moving too rapidly for Pretoria's
liking. No sooner had the secretary-general reported back to the
Security Council than South Africa raised objections. Foreign
Minister Botha objected to the size of the proposed military component – 7 500 men to be called the UN Transitional Assistance Group
(UNTAG) – and to the inclusion of a civilian police unit. And he
insisted that elections be held before the end of December.[11] This
latter point, Botha well knew, was impossible within the timetable of
the 'contact group' proposals and the secretary-general's report. In
contrast, on 9 September, Swapo offered to sign a cease-fire with
South Africa, an offer which was promptly rejected by Pretoria.

   Eleven days later, South Africa announced it would go ahead with
its own 'internal settlement' elections in December without the UN.[12]
The UN responded quickly, adopting Security Council Resolution
435 on 29 September. This formalized the acceptance of the
secretary-general's report and the action plan for Namibia's independence.

It is clear that Pretoria has never intended to allow genuine
independence for Namibia. But the evidence suggests that the
regime was at this point seriously considering the offer from the
'contact group'. They were, it seems, considering the possibility of
Resolution 435 eventually offering them a means of securing
continued domination of Namibia but with the UN out of the way and
SWAPO's struggle seriously undermined for years to come. To
achieve this Pretoria believed that more time was needed to build up
an alternative to SWAPO, and to establish an administration, army
and police which was ostensibly Namibian but loyal to the South
African regime. When independence came, a state apparatus would
be left in place, creating major difficulties for any incoming government opposed to the South African regime. Time was also needed to
experiment with literally buying out a population during an election
process.

   This last element took the form of the December 1978 'election' in
Namibia and the carbon copy of that election in March 1979 in Rhodesia.
Swapo boycotted the election as did the Patriotic Front in Rhodesia.

In both cases, lavish election rallies, with free food and drink, were funded by the South Africans. In both cases there were claims of high voter registration and voting. And in both cases it was claimed that internal parties secured an overwhelming majority. The DTA claimed it had won 41 of the 50 seats. Neither result was recognized by any government other than that which had manipulated it.

Judging from the inspired articles which appeared in the press in South Africa, Namibia and Zimbabwe at that time, Pretoria was working on the theory that the prestige of holding government office would enhance the puppets' chances of victory in any later election. Thus when the Lancaster House settlement was proposed, Pretoria put pressure on Smith and Muzorewa by threatening the withdrawal of supplies from South Africa. The South Africans had convinced themselves that the March 1979 Zimbabwe election results could be repeated in the independence elections. The outcome of Zimbabwe's independence elections left Pretoria stunned. The lesson was obvious: a similar fate awaited their puppets in Namibia.

Throughout 1979 and 1980, the South African government raised one objection after another to Resolution 435. It objected to the presence of Swapo bases in Namibia and demanded the monitoring of Swapo bases in neighbouring countries. It demanded that its internal surrogates be included in any negotiations and that its external surrogate, the National Union for the Total Independence of Angola (UNITA), also be included. UN 'partiality' was posed as another barrier to implementation of Resolution 435 and Pretoria demanded the cessation of UN funding to Swapo.

Pressure was again mounting on the 'contact group' over South Africa's intransigent position. To deflect this pressure and to give the appearance of forward momentum, a 'pre-implementation' meeting was held in Geneva, in January 1981, at the instigation of the group. When the meeting began, Swapo immediately agreed to co-operate in implementing Resolution 435 and to sign a cease-fire as the first essential step. South Africa refused and the meeting collapsed.

There is some considerable significance to the timing of this meeting and Pretoria's continuing obduracy. Ronald Reagan had just won the US election and was about to move to the White House. The South Africans, correctly, expected more sympathy from the new administration in Washington. Not long after his inauguration, Reagan confirmed Pretoria's analysis. In a television interview, he described South Africa as a 'friendly country' and then, taking up

Pretoria's favourite theme, went on to say that South Africa is 'a country that strategically is essential to the free world in its production of minerals that we all must have'.[13]

Five senior South African Defence Force (SADF) officers were permitted to visit the United States in March – the first known to have done so in some years – despite the mandatory arms embargo and Washington's accepted policy of not allowing such visits. The same month, a DTA delegation and Unita's leader, Jonas Savimbi, visited Washington, and conservative pressure began to mount for the repeal of the Clark Amendment which forbade support for anti-government groups in Angola. Pretoria had read the meaning of Reagan's election well. There would now be another change of direction in the campaign to buy more time for South Africa's occupation of Namibia.

In late May 1981, confidential State Department documents relating to the visit to Washington two weeks earlier by 'Pik' Botha and the South African defence minister, General Magnus Malan, were leaked to the American press. The documents provided an insight into the new approach to the Washington–Pretoria axis. The State Department appeared to accept South Africa's proposition that Angola and Namibia afforded the US the opportunity of 'rolling back Soviet influence in Africa'.[14] The approach fitted the 'Cold War' scenario that South Africa sought to project in the region and was obviously appealing to Reagan's own ideological idiosyncracies. Changes to Resolution 435 were mooted and South Africa's determination to prevent Swapo coming to power at any cost was clear.

A State Department briefing written for the designated assistant secretary of state for African affairs, Chester Crocker, referred to a 'semantical' problem, saying the alterations being sought should be referred to as 'attempts to complement rather than to change 435'.[15] In the event they referred to these attempts to undermine Resolution 435 as 'strengthening' the resolution.

The argument was put forward that if the South Africans were to be persuaded that Resolution 435 should be implemented, then their 'concerns' with the resolution and with 'regional security' would have to be met. There was no question of forcing an intransigent South Africa to agree to implementation. On the contrary, the whole direction was toward making the resolution acceptable to Pretoria, which meant altering it so that it would again be perceived as a means of retaining effective control of a nominally independent Namibia.

The logic of this approach was that all concessions would have to be made by SWAPO. Reopening negotiations would also provide a legitimized delay which South Africa needed to reshape circumstances within Namibia. Pretoria's objective was to make nonsense of fundamental aspects of Resolution 435 and lay the foundations for continued economic and political dominance or massive destablization of Namibia.

In June, the US deputy secretary of state, William Clark, accompanied by Crocker, visited South Africa. Their policy was being labelled in Washington as 'constructive engagement', a policy description which clearly inferred that all previous attempts to move South Africa had amounted to 'negative engagement'. The real motivation was revealed in a memorandum from Crocker to the secretary of state, General Alexander Haig, in which he proposed that in return for South Africa's co-operation in reaching a Namibia settlement, the US administration should work 'to end South Africa's polecat status in the world, and seek to restore its place as a legitimate and important regional factor with whom we can co-operate pragmatically'. It was during this visit that the Reagan administration made public their new condition to the implementation of Resolution 435: the withdrawal of Cuban troops from Angola, thereafter referred to as 'linkage'.[17] The South Africans were delighted by the American proposal which ensured a further substantial delay to Namibian independence.

The other four members of the 'contact group' acquiesced to this major obstacle as well as many points of detail that Washington and Pretoria now littered in the path of Resolution 435. In the Security Council, with the United States abstaining, Swapo and the southern African grouping of frontline states condemned 'linkage'.[18] But, by linking South Africa's illegal occupation of Namibia to the withdrawal of Cuban troops (legally in Angola at the request of that government in response to Pretoria's 1975 invasion), the Reagan administration had placed a seemingly insurmountable hurdle as a pre-condition to Namibian independence.

Pretoria still faced the problem of trying to create a viable alternative to Swapo and President Sam Nujoma. When the term of office of South Africa's DTA surrogates expired in September 1982, Pretoria was confronted by an untenable level of corruption and chaos – and an excessively expensive bureaucracy. Finally, at the beginning of 1983, South Africa was forced to return the governorship of Namibia to another administrator-general. This was followed by a proposed but stillborn State Council and, when this failed to materialize, by the Multi-Party Conference (MPC), a grouping of eight disparate political parties including the DTA and Afrikaner nationalist groupings. But by the end of 1983 two of these – the Damara Council and the Christian Democratic Party – had withdrawn, arguing that the MPC was no more than an anti-Swapo front, anonymously funded by South Africa through a West German source. Another member of the group, the South West African National Union (SWANU), withdrew on similar grounds in 1984.[19] Once again the attempt to create an alternative internal grouping to Swapo was in tatters.

Nevertheless, Pretoria continued to pursue the internal option. The administrator-general said in his New Year's message that South Africa was 'pinning its hopes' on the MPC.[20] Soon thereafter, P.W. Botha called the MPC to Cape Town to tell them they were to agree to a concrete alternative to the implementation of Resolution 435.[21]

By this time another strategic element had become coequal with the continued attempt to create a client administration. This was, and is, the creation of a set of military and political-economic structures to limit any Namibian government's ability to rule without South African approval of its policies – and to serve as land-mines to destabilize or destroy such a government if it attempts to do so.

The interminable, often bewildering and invariably Machiavellian, twists and turns of the Namibian saga now brought Zambia's President Kenneth Kaunda briefly to centre stage. Kaunda, it transpired, had written to P.W. Botha suggesting that if he were serious about finding a solution he should give Namibia its independence as a 'Christmas gift'. The South African prime minister had replied, indicating a willingess to arrange talks between SWAPO and the MPC, and had offered a guarantee of safety if SWAPO would send a delegation to Windhoek. Swapo's leaders declined to meet the MPC but reiterated their willingness to hold direct talks with the South African government.[22]

The illusion that something might at last be happening was to be maintained for several months. On 30 January 1984, a high-level delegation from SADF military intelligence flew to Lusaka for an unpublicized meeting with Swapo leaders. The delegation included the head of the Military Intelligence Directorate (MID), General Piet van der Westhuizen, Brigadier van Tonder, and Brigadier Hammon.

Swapo took the meeting seriously but found that nothing more than negotiation with Pretoria's Windhoek puppets was on offer.

The SADF delegation flew home the same day. In parliament, the following day, P.W. Botha gave further momentum to the illusion of progress. He announced that the SADF had begun its withdrawal from Angola as a first step towards a hoped-for cease-fire. He went on to say that the cost of retaining Namibia had become too high, and he urged political leaders to find an acceptable solution to bring the territory to independence. 'Our determination [to hold Namibia] has exacted a heavy price – in material, in international condemnation, and in the lives of our young men,' Botha added.[23]

The release, early in 1984, of Andimba Toivo Ja Toivo and a number of other Namibian political prisoners, one of the conditions of Resolution 435, served to maintain the illusion. On 11 March, P.W. Botha went a step further. South Africa was willing, he said, to take part in a peace conference involving all Namibian parties, without pre-conditions. Swapo had already indicated its willingness to meet the administrator-general if he were the designated representative of the South African government. Kaunda now invited Swapo to meet in Lusaka with a South African delegation led by the administrator-general. The meeting collapsed when it became clear that South Africa was trying to lure Swapo away from Resolution 435 and a seven-month transition to elections, and into protracted constitutional negotiations with the unrepresentative MPC. SWAPO would have to disarm while South Africa's military forces, police and administration would remain in place. It was thus being proposed that SWAPO become part of the client administration in Windhoek, thereby legitimizing South Africa's continued illegal occupation. So ended yet another Namibian illusion. South Africa remained as determined as ever to prevent Swapo from taking power and now it had the open support of Washington through its insistence on linking Namibia's independence to the presence of Cuban troops in Angola.

Swapo had started its armed struggle on 26 August 1966 directly as a result of Pretoria's violent suppression of SWAPO's political activity in Namibia, its obduracy and the determination of Western states with the greatest economic stake in southern Africa to protect the Pretoria regime from any form of effective international action through the United Nations. During the first years of the conflict, responsibility for attempting to contain Swapo guerrillas rested with

the South African police. The military began to take over in the early
1970s. In 1974, SADF strength in Namibia was 15 000 men. By
1976 it had risen to 45 000; by 1980 to 80 000; and by 1985 to between
100 000 and 110 000. These figures, especially in later years,
included mercenaries, members of UNITA and SWA territorials
which are in fact, if not necessarily in name, part of the South
African military command structure. Since taking control of
South Africa's military machine in Namibia in 1972, the military has
continued joint operations with the police, referring to both forces as the
'security forces'. This, in part, was the increasingly costly burden of
holding Namibia to which P.W. Botha referred.

Behind these cold statistics lurks a more sinister objective.
Inevitably, sooner or later, South Africa must relinquish its direct,
illegal rule of Namibia. It has tried, and failed, to create an alternative
to Swapo. It is still trying to do so; but Pretoria must be fully aware
that the likelihood of success is, at best, minimal. It can, through
'linkage', carry on buying time for a while, with the support of the
Reagan administration. But, one day, it must recognize the
probability of having to deal with a Swapo government in Windhoek.
Thus, while delaying that day and trying to find an alternative, it is also
building structures within Namibia to limit the options of an
independent country and a Swapo government.

Force has been the primary vehicle used by South Africa to retain
its domination of Namibia, so it is not surprising that the first neo-
colonial structures created were military. Within two years of the
SADF taking over military responsibilities from the police, they began
forming black 'ethnic' units. The first of these was a San unit, created
in 1974 and today known as 201 Battalion. Other 'ethnic' units
followed, recruited from among the 'Ovambo', 'Kavango', 'Rehoboth',
'Caprivian', 'Damara', 'Nama', 'Herero', 'Tswana' and 'coloured' groups.[24]
In essence what South Africa was doing was recruiting Namibian to fight
against Namibian in defence of Pretoria's illegal occupation of the
territory. And, in a country where so few people are in salaried
employment, recruitment is not such a difficult task. But it certainly
sows the seeds of disunity both now and, more importantly, in the
future. The 1980 establishment of the South West Africa Territory
Force (SWATF), bringing these units together with a number of SADF
units, was an attempt to create a potent force for the future destabilization of an independent Namibia.

It is important to note that the SWATF was created after the passage
of Resolution 435. This explicitly states that the SADF would be

withdrawn from Namibia during the transition, with the exception of
1 500 troops who would remain in two specified bases. 'Ethnic', or
tribal, units would be disbanded. By creating SWATF the South
Africans sought to create the impression that the 'ethnic' units no
longer existed and that there was now a 'legitimate' Namibian force
not covered by Resolution 435 which should remain intact and
continue to exist as the national army of an independant Namibia.

The SWATF has its own formal command structure although ranks
used are a little different from those in the SADF, and SWATF has
distinctive uniforms so as to give the appearance of separate force.
Military communiques in Windhoek are now always issued by the
SWATF and not the SADF. This, however, is an obfuscation of the
fact that the SWATF remains an integral part of South Africa's miliary
machine, with Pretoria remaining in overall command and retaining
control of its entire functioning.[25]

The SWATF has been set up as if it were a fully fledged 'SWA'
army, incorporating a command infrastructure, a permanent force
infantry component, a citizen force, a commando network comprising
26 area force units, a training wing, and an administrative and logistics
component. The 'air force' currently consists of a light aircraft
commando; the privately owned aircraft are flown by their owners on a
part-time basis.

In 1982 the then Officer Commanding SWATF, Major-General
Charles Lloyd, spelt out South Africa's view of the position of the
SWATF in the event of Resolution 435 being implemented. The
essence of what he said was that the SWATF would be partially
demobilized for a temporary period during implementation but not
fully dismantled. It would retain its command structure, bases,
weapons and capacity to be fully mobilized within hours. Pretoria
clearly hopes to make utter nonsense of the fundamental principal
in Resolution 435 that all South African forces in Namibia must be
withdrawn, bar the 1 500 who would remain confined to two bases
for the transitional period. The SWATF is an integral part of the
South African forces in Namibia. Pretoria's obvious intention is to
have a military force in Namibia which is ostensibly Namibian even if
it is commanded, equipped and supplied by Pretoria and owes
allegiance to its South African master. In the longer term, the
apartheid regime probably hopes the SWATF can be virtually totally
locally staffed, largely locally financed, and backed and run by South
Africa less overtly and ubiquitously than at present. The goal was,
and is, a neocolonial army for a neocolonial state.

Apart from the SWATF the Pretoria regime has developed a motley collection of 'special' unconventional units, some of which are used specifically in Namibia while others are used more widely. Although they operate in great secrecy, it is known that the same process of making them ostensibly Namibian is in progress.

Koevoet (crowbar) is the most notorious of these units, responsible for many brutal murders and the extensive use of torture. Recently officially 'disbanded', it has basically been transferred from the South African Police (SAP) to the 'South West African Police,' with a formal change of name although it seems that it will be unable to shake off the name *Koevoet* in practice.

Pretoria's 'Law and Order' Minister, Louis la Grange, announced in May 1985 that members of the SAP who are members of *Koevoet* or the 'security police' would be 'seconded or transferred to the South West African Police' and that the SWATF would expand its 'counter insurgency' function. This illustrates the method Pretoria is using to 'Namibianize' its name and further its identification as a Namibian unit.

While *Koevoet* is technically designated a police unit, it is in fact the cutting edge of the South African military in Namibia. It functions as a military unit and has never had anything other than a military function, operating in much the same way as the Selous Scouts did in pre-independence Zimbabwe. Pretoria's reasoning is obvious in technically designating it as a police unit. This is an attempt to circumvent a fundamental element of Resolution 435 which makes provision for the withdrawal of all SA forces from Namibia (bar the 1 500 who would be confined to two bases for the transition period) and the total disbanding of all 'ethnic' units. But it also provides for the existing police force to maintain law and order during the transitional period. Pretoria can be expected to argue that *Koevoet* units are 'police' units and should remain operational during the transition. This type of deception by Pretoria should be firmly dealt with by the UN. The SWA Special Task Force is also technically a police unit, presumably for the same reason as stated above. It too is a brutalized, professional military unit into which Pretoria is transferring members of *Koevoet*.

The so-called 'reconnaissance commandos', the 'recces' in South African military jargon, constitute another element of Pretoria's army of occupation in Namibia. There are known to be six such commandos based at secret locations in South Africa. They are highly trained troops and operate in great secrecy, mainly in destabilization operations in neighbouring states.

32 Battalion is a very large mercenary force made up of the remnants of UNITA and the National Front for the Liberation of Angola (FNLA), as well as black Mozambican ex-members of such Portuguese para-military units as the *Flechas* (Arrows). They are led by a white officer corps of South African permanent force members and mercenaries. It is widely held that they are '32 Battalion' while at rear bases or operating in Namibia and 'UNITA' while operating in Angola.[26] 44 Battalion has its origins in the recruitment by South Africa of members of the Rhodesian Light Infantry (RLI) when Zimbabwe became independent in 1980. It is primarily deployed in so-called 'follow-up operations'. The SWA Specialists undertake tracking using San trackers and dogs (including pack hounds). They make extensive use of scrambler motorcycles and horses in their operations. It can be expected that any of these units not yet falling under the SWATF will be transferred within the next couple of years. Clearly Pretoria's objective is to impose on Namibia military and police structures loyal to themselves as part of their programme to retain effective control of the country even after Resolution 435 has been implemented.

Although Namibia's economic history has been characterized by intensive and brutal exploitation of its natural resources and its people, it was not until the late 1940s that the country became relatively economically significant. From then until the late 1970s Namibia's economic importance – and its contribution to South Africa's coffers – increased dramatically. Throughout that period, and thereafter, Namibia remained a grossly exploited, unequal and racist society. The differential between per capita white income and that of African and coloured Namibians is in the range of 18 or 20 to one, as against a differential in South Africa itself of 12 or 15 to one and marginally less in former Rhodesia. [27] During the economic halcyon years, the foreign enterprises and the settlers prospered, and so did Pretoria. Then the bubble burst.

What had happened? The reasons are several and by no means related solely to the liberation struggle. They include the post-1975 slump in metal prices, reduced diamond output by De Beers to try to stabilize world prices, the collapse of the karakul wool industry, overfishing, and the semi-permanent drought since 1977 which has reduced agricultural output and livestock by up to 75 per cent.[28] Not all of these factors were unique to Namibia and several were shared by other countries in the region.

However some special factors affecting the Namibian economy do relate to the liberation struggle and to the response to it by other factors. These are:

1. Major enterprise employers raised real African wages and began to create a stratum of semi-skilled wage elite (partly to reduce costs, as white workers were much more expensive, and partly to secure an African group 'loyal' to employers).

2. A similar policy toward professional and semi-professional personnel (especially teachers, nurses) was combined with a strategy of creating a class of well-paid politicians, clerks and home guards, and extending some mobility – both economically and socially – to selected members of this group.

3. Massive recurrent and capital expenditure was incurred – on military camps, cleared border zones and roads – to slow the advance of the guerrilla war.

4. There was an increase in risks and costs associated with the war, for example: the need to move fuel by convoy, to use air passenger and freight transport in the north, to guard ranches and installations, to repair sabotage damage to transport and power links (as far south as the main Van Eck power station in Windhoek), and to build a new power line to the Cape to supplement the Ruacana Falls dam supply rendered uncertain by war.

5. This led to an increased exodus of ranchers and other whites, partly bought off by higher wages and subsidies.

6. It also led to a collapse of enterprise investment as the investors calculated the military and political risks of putting in new capital (even out of territorial profits) as too high until an independence settlement and peace emerged.

These factors account for the explosive rise in the recurrent budget deficit, met partly by South African transfer increases (largely for a portion of military and police spending) and partly by external commercial borrowing, almost all from South African financial institutions.

By the end of the 1982–83 financial year, South African government spending on Namibia had risen to about R900–950 million. Local revenue plus the analogue to customs and excise covered R420–450 million of that figure, South African transfers R215 million – of which R115 million was for 'territorial' army and police – and external borrowing (mostly from South Africa) over R300 million. Of the approximately R750 million in recurrent spending, R50 million was for debt service and R240 million for 'second tier', 'representative

authority' or, more bluntly bantustan administration. The latter transfers were to bodies which even the Pretoria-appointed Thirion
Commission found to be monumentally incompetent, wasteful and
corrupt.[29]

In 1984, P.W. Botha restated South Africa's old refrain that it
subsidizes Namibia, but this time he had three new angles. He warned
the territory's 'internal' leaders that South Africa had to look out for
its own people first, especially in times of recession and resource
scarcity; so Namibians could not expect much help. Secondly, he
made a plea to Western countries, especially the contact group, to
take over the financing of the Namibian deficit from South Africa (ie,
take over subsidizing South Africa's occupation). The intention was,
quite likely, to cause them to hesitate to take on the costs of a transition
to independence and economic rehabilitation. Thirdly, he gave a more
complete set of cost figures than had been presented before.

Botha asserted that in 1984–85 the cost to South Africa of holding
Namibia was R1 143 million (almost US$ 600 million at average 1985
rate of exchange). This broke down as R663 million for defence; R250
million for customs and excise transfer, R318 million in budgetary
grants; and R95 million for the South African Transport Service (SATS)
deficit. Some of these items are hardly what they purport to be.
Customs and excise represents a purchase of preferential market
access and may well be below what Namibia could get on an
independent customs/excise system, while the SATS figure appears
to combine capital and recurrent costs.

A more complex matrix of costs would be:

1. Defence expenditure in and on Namibia and Angola, which is
33 per cent of total South African military, police, security spending –
R1 500 million.

2. Budget grants plus external borrowing guaranteed by the South
African treasury and most unlikely to be accepted as valid by an
independent Namibia – R500 million.

3. SATS net cash flow loss (assuming that capital inclusion and
Walvis Bay exclusion cross cancel) – R90 million.[30]

That total of R2 100 million was about nine per cent of the South
African government's budget for 1984–85 or about R500 per white
South African. Even more striking, it is only slightly smaller than the
likely 1984 Gross Domestic Product of Namibia, which is R2 250
million when adjusted upward from official data to include Walvis Bay
and subsistence.

Admittedly, R2 100 million is not a net figure. Profit and wage remittances plus capital flight to South Africa (offsetting in part loans in the other direction) may come to R300–400 million, reducing the net cost to R1 700–1 800 million. South Africa still probably has a slim external balance gain from Namibia. But that surplus is now negligible.

Thus from a South African economic perspective, Namibia no longer pays.[31] Recession, drought, military spending and the costs of regrouping to create a broader base for the total strategy have achieved that turn around.

In the economic sphere, as in the military, South Africa has created the infrastructure for destabilizing Namibia – whether as a strategic pre-independence design or as a result of the tactics of regrouping. To ignore this, or assume it will not be used, would be exceedingly unwise, given South Africa's regional strategy of domination and history of destabilization. At least seven elements can be identified.[32]

First, South Africa has created for Namibia an 'external debt' which by the end of 1983 was of the order of R500 million, with interest and debt service of about R100–120 million a year and a rate of increase of perhaps R250–300 million a year. By mid-1986 it may well have been approaching R1 000 million principal (100 per cent of export earnings) and R200–250 million annual overall debt service (20–25 per cent).[33] In part this represents nominal transfers of railway, power and selected mining assets from South African entities to the occupation regime along with parallel debt liabilities to South Africa for their 'purchase'. This creates a slightly more plausible 'external debt' bill as well as raising its level. To accept that debt would cripple the economy of an independent Namibia. To repudiate it – despite the 1971 International Court of Justice opinion which clearly renders it legally void – might damage Namibia's external financial standing and access to credit.

Second, it has created a budgetary shambles both in terms of actual revenue and expenditure, and, even more, in the appearance of total, permanent insolvency. The attempt to cast Namibia as a fiscal 'basket case' not worth assisting is quite clear in some of P.W. Botha's statements on the cost of the territory to South Africa. So is the warning that instant cut-offs of South African funding before a new tax and expenditure system was in place could cause a breakdown of governmental ability to act.[34]

Third, in the multiple-tiered and racial administration, South Africa has created a bureaucratic monstrosity. It is not merely politically unacceptable as an entrenchment of racism; it is corrupt, wasteful and unable to operate competently for any purpose, as even the South Africans have admitted. While these functional weaknesses are a drawback to South Africa in occupation, at independence they will threaten the independent state with paralysis. South Africa can hope to enhance this paralysis by the sudden withdrawal of key technical, professional and administrative staff.

Fourth, the flirtation of large companies, and especially the occupation regime, with the creation of a stable and skilled black labour force will leave a potential time bomb. The professional and skilled/semi-skilled workers are not politically loyal to South Africa. However, their pay scales of R5 000–12 500 a year pose serious problems. It is economically impossible to generalize these income levels to all workers. Even if it were, the effect on rural–urban income inequality and on siphoning off resources otherwise available for rural development would be politically dangerous in the extreme. To limit these scales to certain posts would both entrench massive intra-African income inequality and make expansion of basic public services fiscally impossible. To sustain them for present African job-holders only, with new entrants on lower scales, would create great bitterness among returning liberation war veterans. To cut them – by direct scale changes or even by a freeze – would at best lead to loss of morale and resentment that gains 'won' from the South African occupiers were promptly eroded at independence.

The bantustan politician, clerk and home guard pose a different set of problems. Their 'services', unlike those of the professional and skilled personnel, are not needed. But if they are fired they will provide the core for a political fifth column which could provide a focal point for discontent.

Fifth, by remaining in illegal occupation of Walvis Bay – Namibia's only deep water port – after independence, South Africa would ensure that it has a choke point. Until Namibia creates alternative ports (for example, by reactivating Swakopmund) or gains access to others (via Angola or Zambia), South Africa at Walvis Bay controls its basic access to the outside world and can prevent diversification of trade and transport away from South Africa.[35]

Sixth, similar considerations apply to road and rails transport. Rolling stock is highly mobile and, like many of the lorry fleets, is South African-owned. Major repair facilities are in Upington in South Africa, or Walvis Bay, but not Windhoek. Roads and rail lines without lorries and rolling stock, and without maintenance and repair capacity, do not constitute a transport system.

Seventh, the sea bastion of South Africa's Orange river line at Alexander's Bay is within mortar or launch range of Namibia's premier economic asset – the Oranjemund diamond complex. Furthermore, the 'boundary' of the Walvis Bay 'enclave' is within range of the alternative port at Swakopmund. The implications are only too clear.

This analysis of the infrastructure for destabilization reveals two things. The infrastructure is alarmingly strong and multifaceted but several, perhaps all, of its elements could be rendered less effective by priority attention to their dismantling or neutralization. The seven elements are as identified above.

First, despite South African claims to the contrary, most of the 'external debt' seems to be held by South African financial institutions, and all is fully guaranteed by their government. Thus, repudiation backed by the International Court of Justice opinion and precedents for ex-colonial debts – plus a firm commitment to honour any debt Namibia incurred – would seem likely to defuse the threat of bankruptcy or of lack of access to normal credit. This is especially so as the 1983 Vienna Convention on 'Succession of States in Respect of State Property, Archives and Debt' would – even were the South African administration lawful – ban imposition of colonial debt on Namibia without the independent government's consent.

Second and third, financial and administrative reform plus training and upgrading Namibians and securing replacement expatriates, are priorities for independent Namibia. To some extent these can be planned and programmed before independence in the knowledge that an orderly, leisurely transition (of the type which characterized most British colonies at independence) is a luxury Namibia is unlikely to enjoy. Similarly, some professionals will stay if assured of terms and conditions of service, and some have had initial discussions with Swapo on such issues.

Fourth, an income policy and an approach to mobilization of professional and skilled Namibians, at the least, not to expect white salaries can be begun even before independence. Frank dialogue on constraints is not hopeless in respect to the middle class fractions with real skills. The politicians, clerks and home guard are not an economic, but a conversion or security, problem; buying them off would be an economically as well as politically bankrupting approach.

Fifth, interim port facilities can be available within months, probably by reactivating Swakopmund via dredging, artificial break-waters, lighters, etc. and by road links to Angola and Zambia created over the same period, if the priority is accepted and planning begun before independence. The diversion of resources would remain a severe cost but less of a danger and constraint than seeking to operate via a South African-held Walvis Bay.

Sixth, similarly, vehicles, rolling stock and maintenance/repair equipment can be in place in a limited period of time – if needs are identified early and priority given to ordering.

Finally, action on the economic front cannot prevent cross-border raids; that is primarily a diplomatic and security issue. However, the careful choice of partners (for example, a continuing De Beers presence at Oranjemund, North European technical partnership at Rossing, a Dutch or Nordic interim port management at Swakopmund) would raise the costs to South Africa of random sabotage attacks.

Thus, although South Africa has a potentially paralysing economic destabilization apparatus already in place, there are a number of obvious measures that can be implemented to reduce its potential to do harm. It is also clear that the planning for this defensive action must begin sooner rather than later.

Resolution 435 is not a perfect solution to the problem of South Africa's illegal occupation of Namibia. From the outset SWAPO has taken the view that, should the proposals being presented offer the opportunity for a settlement which would broadly reflect what the vast majority of Namibians want, SWAPO would co-operate in this, even though the proposals make considerable concessions to Pretoria. SWAPO has been only too aware of the numerous political risks resulting from the concessions made in Pretoria's favour, but has consistently urged early implementation of Resolution 435. SWAPO's flexibility arises from a position of strength reflected in its very evident support among Namibians.

Namibia is not approaching independence in a vacuum. The difference between implementing Resolution 435 in 1978 and at some future date is not simply a matter of a difference in time. Pretoria seeks to make nonsense of the resolution by changing the structures within the country and by setting impossible parameters for its implementation. Without great vigilance on the part of SWAPO and the UN – whose responsibility it would be to ensure fair implementation of Resolution 435 – Pretoria could create a situation where the process would be sabotaged, destroying any possibility of future implementation. They could attempt to wipe out the SWAPO leadership, or create a situation where the government emerging would find it effectively impossible to govern the country. Basically Pretoria is busy laying the groundwork for a massive destabilization of Namibia if, at some point, it is forced to bow to the pressure to implement Resolution 435. The only circumstances under which Pretoria might willingly agree to such implementation would be those in which it perceives the opportunity of making gains for itself: by using the process to set up a puppet government; by trying to destroy SWAPO; or by so destabilizing Namibia that the government of the newly independent country would be forced to capitulate to Pretoria's demands.

The UN plan makes provision for the South African administration to organize and run the election with the UN taking on a role of 'supervision and control' of the electoral process. Originally, no specific provision was made for the nature of the electoral process. It would therefore have been possible for Pretoria to determine the electoral system and to make it known only at a time of its choice – even after the beginning of implementation. However, this was superceeded by Resolution 539 (1983) which required that Pretoria communicate its choice of an electoral system 'prior to the adoption by the Security Council of an enabling resolution for the implementation of the United Nations Plan'. In November 1985, Pretoria informed the Secretary-General that it had adopted proportional representation but gave no further details.

There are numerous ways in which the South African administration in Namibia may attempt to rig the registration of voters or election itself, and make campaigning difficult for SWAPO. Pretoria may attempt to rush the registration of voters at a time when a considerable number of SWAPO personnel are still out of the country, in the hope of excluding a substantial part of SWAPO's organizational capacity from being engaged in the process and directly excluding those still outside Namibia from the registration of voters. It could produce misleading information in selected areas, disqualify candidates, intimidate the population, stuff ballot boxes prior to the beginning of the election, or insist that illiterate voters are 'assisted' by its own officials. The administration will almost certainly create bureaucratic difficulties for SWAPO in importing the vehicles it has in neighbouring states which are essential for campaigning in Namibia. Likewise it will prevent or greatly delay campaign materials or paper supplies coming in from abroad. Similar barriers were put in the way of ZANU and ZAPU in the Zimbabwe independence elections.

Today there are few people, even in conservative, anti-SWAPO circles internationally who would deny the mass support that SWAPO enjoys in Namibia. Certainly South Africa believes SWAPO does have support – otherwise it would have held less implausible internal elections or agreed to internationally monitored elections long ago. SWAPO has also amassed unparalleled support within the OUA, the Non-Aligned Movement and within the UN itself.

Assuming SWAPO wins two thirds or more of the seats in the constituent assembly, Pretoria may still seek to impose procedures in the constituent assembly making progress difficult. Much would depend on the organizational readiness of SWAPO to cope with these eventualities, the adequate training of SWAPO cadres to provide its own effective monitoring of the election, the integrity and independence of UNTAG and the arrangements made by the UN Security Council in its enabling resolution. For example, if this Security Council action to enforce changes in South Africa's administration of the election requires a positive vote it would be subject to a veto. However this could be avoided by requiring positive approval of the stages in the process. The enabling Security Council resolution required to begin implementation of Resolution 435 should provide for reports to be made to the Security Council on the implementation, for example at the end of the first 12 weeks and again shortly before the election date. The enabling resolution should require that the procedure be temporarily suspended pending acceptance by the Security Council that each stage has been satisfactorily implemented.

The mass resistance so evident within South Africa itself also serves to weaken the capacity of the regime to retain its illegal occupation of Namibia. The regime is forced to commit more and more of its troops and police within South Africa; and its violence and brutality are becoming more evident to the international community as the regime tries to quell that resistance. As a result, South Africa is steadily gaining a reputation among Western business investors as an area of too great a risk for their investments. In addition, these investments have too great a 'hassle factor' (in terms of negative image domestically) to be worthwhile if they are secondary from an overall business point of view. Coupled with an economy in a state of deep structural crisis, South Africa is not able to attract the external financing it needs.

For South Africa, as already outlined, Namibia is a fiscal and military personnel drain. The gross cost of holding down Namibia is already 10 per cent of South Africa's state budget, about half of its annual external borrowing, and over R500 per white South African. That is a heavy cost now and is likely to become more difficult for Pretoria to handle.

Related to this is the narrowly military set of issues. South Africa has over half of its front line infantry tied down in Namibia. Both logistical and military considerations make their speedy redeployment to meet threats to the regime at home virtually impossible. From a military security point of view, a much smaller force on the more easily defensible Orange river line and a substantial home-based tactical force available to meet domestic threats would clearly make more sense. This is increasingly so if the current level of physical resistance to *apartheid* is sustained.

Pretoria's attempt to create a Namibian facade for its military presence there through the establishment of SWATF has run into considerable difficulties. The regime's objective is to establish an army in Namibia, capable of replacing the official South African forces, which can claim to be 'Namibian'. To attain this, the force would have to be largely black, would need to be fairly well trained in order to handle the technical sophistication of South African military equipment and would need to produce a reasonable level of morale. On all three fronts Pretoria has problems.

The declared intention of the Pretoria regime is to conscript all Namibian males between the ages of 16 and 65. The first attempts, which avoid conscription of those in the northern regions of Namibia, judged by Pretoria to be more committed to SWAPO, brought strong opposition from Namibians in the central and southern regions. They objected to being drafted into a military force illegally in occupation of Namibia and set against fellow Namibians. Many potential conscripts chose to leave Namibia and join the People's Liberation Army of Namibia (PLAN). The more recent attempt to conscript Namibians began with a sudden order that all males in the Sector 10 area (Tsumeb, Otavi, Grootfontein) would have to register within two weeks. In spite of assistance offered by companies who forced reluctant workers to register, Pretoria again seems not to have followed through with the process. The underlying problem for Pretoria in conscripting Namibians is the overwhelming support they know SWAPO has throughout the country. They realize that conscription of the indigenous population holds grave risks for the regime of having its forces thoroughly infiltrated by SWAPO sympathisers. Minutes of a South African military intelligence conference held in May 1984 and released to the press in Britain by SWAPO, recognized that 'SWAPO internally is organized on a wide terrain on different levels and possesses the infrastructure to collect information over a wide spectrum.'[36] They fear that valuable information could be leaked to PLAN or that trained military personnel might desert to join PLAN.

In an attempt in part to counter this problem it can be expected that

SWATF will retain a very large South African and mercenary component. This can already be illustrated by the extensive use of a South African mercenary officer corps for forces which are otherwise largely indigenous. The process will also continue as illustrated in the recent transfer of *Koevoet* from the SAP to the 'South West Africa Police', where South African members of *Koevoet* were 'transferred or seconded' to these supposedly Namibian forces.

The South African regime's presentation of a Namibian face to its military occupation is not going to reduce costs to the South African treasury unless, of course, they choose to reduce the size of their military machine, an option which would seriously weaken their current tenuous hold on Namibia. The alternative of retaining the current real levels of military expenditure in a very severe economic climate will become increasingly difficult unless the decline of the South African economy can be reversed.

South Africa's closest allies are finding it harder and harder to defend the regime. This has become particularly apparent in the case of the United States. In spite of vigorous support for Pretoria by the Reagan administration, the latter is now coming under   unprecedented domestic pressure to apply sanctions. The British government, while not under the same degree of domestic pressure, is isolated within the Commonwealth in its refusal to apply sanctions against South Africa, and cannot ignore the very strong opinions in favour of sanctions being expressed by the Non-Aligned Movement and the OAU.

Whatever antics Pretoria may get up to with the intention of avoiding a SWAPO government in Windhoek, the regime will eventually be forced to capitulate and then the Namibian people, under SWAPO's leadership, will achieve the liberation of their country and genuine national independence. South Africa's occupation of Namibia is clearly on dead end roads on the economic, political and military fronts. How fast it can be pushed down the remaining distance – and forced to accept Namibian independence – depends primarily on the Namibian people and their liberation movement, SWAPO, but this can be influenced significantly by both domestic (internal to South Africa) and external pressures on the Pretoria regime.

Similarly, how successful South Africa can be in perpetuating economic dependence relations and in destabilizing a genuinely independent Namibia will depend primarily on alertness, planned vulnerability reduction, and commitment to continued struggle by the people of Namibia and their government. But this can be influenced significantly by the price South Africa has to pay in terms of external national, enterprise and international actions (not just statements) taken in response to aggressive destabilization.

CHAPTER 5

Lesotho, Botswana, Swaziland: Captive States

'In a quiet valley of aloes, wattle and poplar trees below Lesotho's parliament lies a curious little graveyard. It has 27 low headstones with the names of the dead and the blunt epitaph: "Massacred by the SADF, 9/12/82". Six newly turned graves alongside them are unmarked, but when the headstones are erected they will probably carry a similar statement ...

The graveyard is fenced off with barbed wire and separated from Maseru's main cemetary by the Seputana River, a little tributary which runs a few hundred yards into the Caledon River, the border with South Africa. The separation from the main cemetary is deliberate. The dead are all South Africans, members of the African National Congress (ANC). And the plan is that when "liberation" comes to South Africa they will be leaving, making the trip across the Caledon to some final resting place, another of Africa's "heroes acres".

In the meantime the graveyard serves as a reminder of this tiny mountain kingdom's invidious position, caught between the millstones of white South Africa and black nationalism, and of its diplomatic dilemma.

A couple of miles down the road at the Maseru border post a handful of South African police in paramilitary uniforms make minute examination of vehicles and baggage in search of explosives, guns and ANC desperadoes which they know will not be found, but which provide a convenient excuse to reduce a puny neighbour to a state of seige.'[1]

In those four descriptive paragraphs written from Maseru on 14 January 1986, Mike Pitso encapsulated the dilemma facing Lesotho in particular, as well as Botswana and Swaziland (known collectively as BLS or Boleswa) – the captive states of southern Africa.

Lesotho

After the ANC was banned in South Africa in 1960, Lesotho became one of many countries where its members and other South Africans sought refuge and shelter. Twenty years later the South African refugee population in Lesotho had reached 11 500, mostly refugees from the social system of *apartheid* – people who left because of the ban on racially mixed marriages, children escaping from 'Bantu' education, students looking for university places – and 100 new arrivals were registering each month at the Interior Ministry.

Then, in the early hours of 9 December 1982, the haven for refugees turned into a charnel-house. South African Defence Force (SADF) commandos, supported by helicopters and armoured trucks, sped through border posts on the outskirts of Maseru and shot up several residences, slaughtering 42 people, including Lesotho nationals, some of them women and children. A government minister said it was a 'traumatic' experience that 'destabilized us psychologically'.[2] The dead included 30 South African refugees; and 27 of them now occupy those marked graves on the banks of the Seputana river.

The other six graves, as yet unmarked, are those of refugees who died in another attack on Maseru on 19 December 1985. They were killed while attending a Christmas party.[3]

Of the three captive states, Lesotho is the most vulnerable. It is a tiny, impoverished nation of 1.5 million people, completely surrounded by South Africa and almost entirely dependent upon the capriciousness of its hostile neighbour. Only 13 per cent of the country's 30 355 square kilometres is suitable for cultivation. Its economy is essentially a remittance and subsistence on

About 150 000 of its people – more than half of the adult population – work on mines, farms and industries across the border, and most rural households rely on income from the remittances of these migrant workers. The money they remit accounts for over half of Lesotho's gross national product. All of Lesotho's imports and exports pass through the republic; shops and businesses are branches of the South African system and so is the railway; 95 per cent of the tourists, as well as most investment and all electricity, come from South Africa. Lesotho is dependent upon South Africa for 97 per cent of its imports and on the Southern African Customs Union (SACU) for nearly 70 per cent of government revenue. As much as half of Lesotho's national budget is subsidized by foreign aid.[4]

Since the mid-nineteenth century when Boer commandos from the farming communities of the neighbouring Orange Free State began raiding them, the people of Lesotho have lived under the threat of siege. Twelve days after the murder of the six refugees, South Africa imposed yet another economic blockade. Queues of vehicles built up at border posts while South African customs officials laboriously searched every item, deliberately causing lengthy delays. At one crossing point, a truck driver was forced to open all 1 050 cases of cooking oil sent from the United States as food aid. The truck was held up for 24 hours as the officials refused to let other people in the queue help the driver to unload the cooking oil or put it back on his truck. In Maseru and elsewhere, shops were soon emptied of food-stuffs, and the fuel stocks dwindled to one or two days' supply. On 20 January, the government led by Chief Leabua Jonathan fell in the first military *coup d'état* in southern Africa.

It is still too early to say to what degree the South African government was actually involved in the *coup d'état*, but it certainly created the conditions through its economic blockade. By playing upon Lesotho's geographic and economic vulnerability, South Africa created pressure that inflamed internal contradictions and led directly to the downfall of Jonathan, once Pretoria's favoured candidate. To understand the *coup d'état* and the destabilization of Lesotho, it is necessary to put into perspective the country's historical evolution and the contradictory forces arising from this history which gave the South Africans the opportunity to intervene.

Throughout the colonial period, Pretoria sought to incorporate BLS into South Africa. In the mid-1960s, when it became clear that Britain as the colonial authority would not allow this, Pretoria designed new strategies. The most obvious one was intervention in the political system to create a political climate favourable to South Africa. In Lesotho, the dominant political party was the Basutoland Congress Party (BCP), formed in 1952 by Basotho activists in the ANC of South Africa. Although radical and pan-Africanist, the BCP was predominantly a party of the emerging black middle class – the intellectuals, traders and senior civil servants. Both London and Pretoria imagined they saw 'red' in its ranks.

It was in these circumstances that Pretoria, acting through the agencies of the local Catholic church, provided the financial and organizational support to found a new party of the right. The Basotho

National Party (BNP) was formed in 1959, explicitly as a counter to the BCP, with a 'moderate' political platform to which the British government could bequeath power on its departure.[5]

Another important party in this period was the Marema Tlou Freedom Party (MFP), a breakaway from the BCP. The MFP became a royalist party favouring an executive monarchy, and it is people who have been associated with this party who occupy many important positions in the new government today.

Although banned since 1970, the influence of the Communist Party of Lesotho (CPL) is acknowledged within the left of the BCP as well as in the BNP. Yet another smaller party was Charles Mofeli's United Democratic Party (UDP), also a splinter from the BCP, and staunchly pro-Pretoria, particularly after Mofeli was fired from Jonathan's cabinet.

Hefty financial support from Pretoria enabled the BNP to win 42 per cent of the votes in first general election in 1965, and a razor–thin majority of 31 out of 60 seats, thus enabling Jonathan to form the first post-independence government. He became the first black leader of an independent country to visit South Africa.

The point about the BNP, at least the BNP of 1966–1970, is that it was a party of the minor chieftaincy and the conservative Catholic intelligentsia. This period saw the domination of South African, mainly commercial, capital in the mainstream of the Lesotho economy, extending its tentacles through the newly formed National Development Corporation. The trading outlets were farmed out to the Portuguese and Indian merchant class of South African extraction. Labour exported to the South African mines expanded in this period to an average figure of 250 000 migrant workers a year. To circumvent the emerging BCP intellectuals in the civil service, the senior positions were packed with South African bureaucrats. So in the first five years of independence, Lesotho very much resembled a 'bantustan'.

This staunchly pro-Pretoria policy, and the fact that there was nothing to show for five years of close collaboration with *apartheid*, eroded the BNP's electoral base. The outcome of the 1970 election was a foregone conclusion although, surprisingly, the BNP managed to retain 23 seats. The BCP won a clear majority with 36 seats, but Jonathan refused to relinquish power. He annulled the election, suspended the constitution and declared a state of emergency. This was the beginning of a political crisis that was to span the next 15 years.

Between 1970 and 1973, Jonathan ruled through a personal dictatorship without any semblance of democratic process. Then, under pressure from international donors, he reintroduced the parliamentary process in 1973, through the Interim National Assembly consisting predominantly of his party and of nominated opposition personalities. The formation of the Interim Assembly caused a political crisis for the opposition, splitting the BCP down the middle. The deputy leader, Gerald Ramoreboli, led a faction into the assembly, while the leader, Ntsu Mokhehle, and the secretary-general, the late Koenyama Chakela, fled the country after an abortive BCP uprising in 1974.

Even as the opposition was being scattered into exile, a shift in Lesotho's relationship with South Africa was beginning to take shape. The first signs of this appeared as early as 1973 when Jonathan told the newly constituted assembly that 'Lesotho would not cease to give moral support and any other possible support to our fellow men in the liberation movement who are still struggling to free themselves from the yoke of colonialism and racial oppression'.[6] In the same speech, he attacked Western countries for continuing to sell arms to South Africa. The BNP's change of stance has been a subject of debate ever since.[7]

The pro-Pretoria policy and the violence which accompanied Jonathan's paramilitary *coup d'état* in 1970 had isolated the BNP and made it very unpopular. By 1973, the government was ruling from a very narrow political base. In order to broaden that base it was necessary to undermine the political influence of the opposition BCP, and Jonathan set out to do this by appearing to distance himself and his party from Pretoria. The BNP also needed to shed its collaborationist tag in order to gain admission to African diplomatic circles and to establish proper credentials within the Organization of African Unity (OAU).

In addition, new class forces emerging within the BNP began to question the economic rationale of collaborating with *apartheid*, saying it was 'too expensive politically and yet unrewarding economically'. Pretoria had shown that it was content to retain Lesotho as a market outlet but was not willing to consider serious investment. After the Transkei border crisis in 1976, when the Federal Republic of Germany (FRG) raised its development aid to

R4.6 million, Britain to R11 million, and the European Economic Community (EEC) earmarked R22 million to assist Lesotho to reduce dependence on South Africa, the new policy came to be widely accepted within the BNP ruling circles.

If party stalwarts needed any further convincing, it came from the changing balance in the subcontinent following the collapse of the Portuguese empire and the liberation of Mozambique and Angola. This convinced the inner circle of the BNP ruling class that the future in southern Africa did not lie with Pretoria.

As the rewards of the disengagement process began to percolate in, Lesotho's pronouncements against Pretoria became more bold and assertive. One week after the Soweto uprising in 1976, the Lesotho government issued a strongly worded statement condemning *apartheid*. Later in the same year, Lesotho refused to recognize the 'independence' of the Transkei bantustan and when Pretoria exerted pressure to this end Lesotho took its case to the United Nations (UN), thus internationalizing the issue, much to the embarrassment of Pretoria.

Another source of conflict with Pretoria was the development of relations with Mozambique. Jonathan visited Maputo in 1978 and annoyed the South Africans by posing for a photograph with President Machel giving the clenched fist salute. Pretoria was further annoyed by the introduction of a twice weekly direct air service between Maputo and Maseru. In the following months, Jonathan improved his relations with the ANC at both government and party level. His government then declared its intention to adhere to the UN protocol of accepting and protecting refugees from South Africa. By the end of 1978, Pretoria was fed up with these antics and decided that Jonathan must be 'persuaded' back into the fold.

The exiled leaders of the BCP had succeeded in launching a diplomatic onslaught that isolated the Jonathan regime, but by 1976 the frustrations of exile politics had begun to set in and the once powerful opposition party was heading toward its final destruction through collaboration with Pretoria. According to the late secretary-general, Chakela, his split with Mokhehle in 1976 was the final rupture of a struggle which had gone on for nearly two years within the BCP. This struggle centred on two main issues: Mokhehle's involvement with South Africa's state security through its then boss, General Hendrick van den Bergh, and the involvement of some BCP members in support of anti-government factions in the Angolan civil war.[8]

Chakela and his following refused to collaborate. He returned to Lesotho in 1980 under the Amnesty Act and, until he was assassinated in July 1982 within metres of the South African border, he led the progressive faction of the BCP.

The Mokhehle faction, on the other hand, formed the basis upon which Pretoria established the Lesotho Liberation Army (LLA). There is no evidence that the South Africans intended to replace Jonathan with Mokhehle by this means, but rather to shake him back into the fold. The first LLA attacks occurred in early May 1979 in Maseru. The targets were the central post office and two high-tension electricity pylons, as well as the headquarters of the electricity corporation. These were followed by a spate of bombings in the northern part of the country, damaging bridges and isolated telephone and electricity poles. A representative of Mokhehle's faction of the BCP, through the South African news media, claimed responsibility for the LLA, which he described as the military wing of the party whose aim it was to topple Jonathan's government. Thereafter, the LLA expanded its operations to include assassinations and attacks on police and paramilitary posts. The South African press launched a parallel onslaught of disinformation.

Although the initial attacks were not too serious, the South African strategy of 'persuading' Jonathan seemed to work and, in August 1980, he agreed to meet P.W. Botha at the Peka bridge. Although the results of this meeting were not made public, there was a thaw in hostilities and the activities of the LLA came to a temporary halt.[9]

At the beginning of 1981, the LLA attacks resumed on a broader scale and intensity. This came in the wake of increasing internal and external pressure against the Pretoria regime, particularly the more spectacular acts of sabotage by ANC guerrillas. Ruling circles in Pretoria popularized the theory of the presence of ANC 'military bases' inside Lesotho, largely to find justification for military intervention, as it did with other neighbouring countries. The resumption of attacks on Lesotho also coincided with the inauguration of a new US president, Ronald Reagan, and with the build-up and subsequent South African occupation of southern Angola. There were sporadic attacks on the residences of ANC refugees at various places in Lesotho, and the house of the ANC representative in Maseru was attacked on at least three occasions before the invasion of December 1982.

The UDP leader, Mofeli, a close confidante of Pretoria, was at the forefront of verbal attacks against the ANC. The Mofeli stance was soon appropriated by a right-wing student's group at the university and an Evangelical church newspaper. The strategy appeared to be to cause a rift within the BNP, while at the same time isolating the ANC, so that the extreme right within the ruling party would force a showdown and demand the expulsion of the ANC. But this misfired with the assassination of a cabinet minister and senior party man, Jobo Rampeta; the attempted assassination of Peete Peete, then heir apparent to Chief Jonathan; and finally the assassination of Chakela, which aroused strong anti-South African sentiment within the country. These events forced the party to close ranks around Jonathan, who then began to mobilize international opinion against South Africa and to seek support from socialist countries. The resolve to resist *apartheid* and to oppose interference in the sovereignty of Lesotho hardened after the December 1982 raid on Maseru.

Internationally, the raid exposed South Africa's regional policy of aggression. For the BCP/LLA, it marked the beginning of the final demise. For Jonathan and the centre left of the party, it heralded the final rupture with Pretoria. Thereafter, the Chief established diplomatic relations with the Soviet Union, China and North Korea; he fired his pro-Pretoria foreign minister, C.D. Molapo, and expelled diplomats representing Taiwan and South Korea, declaring he did not want 'small boys' in his capital.

Pretoria, also, seemed to reach a final decision at this stage: that Jonathan had to go. But it took another four years to dislodge him from power.

The post-Maseru-raid period can be justifiably defined as one of 'undeclared war' against Lesotho. Pretoria's intensified destabilization of the kingdom had two main objectives: to pressure the Lesotho government into signing a non-aggression pact; and to overthrow Jonathan and replace him with either a more malleable politician from his own party or a candidate of the opposition alliance which Pretoria was busily assembling.

The pressure exerted on Lesotho, as on other countries in the region, was both economic and military. Initially, South Africa withheld millions of rands in revenue due from SACU, as well as helicopter spare parts, to encourage Lesotho to re-negotiate the customs union to include the 'homelands' of Transkei and Bophu-tatswana. That would have amounted to recognition of their South African-bestowed 'independence', and Jonathan's government refused. Lesotho was also invited to join a regional development bank with the 'homelands' in the hope that recognition by one independent African country would lead to recognition by others. Again Lesotho refused.

Early in 1983, the Maseru abattoir and the city's water storage were bombed. This was followed closely by a helicopter attack on the town's oil depots. The government alleged that the attack on the oil depots was carried out with SADF support, and independent investigations confirmed these allegations. It was the first provable case of direct attack by South African military personnel on an economic target in Lesotho.

Shortly after this came the car bomb explosion in Pretoria which killed several members of the South African military and was claimed by the ANC. Pretoria's response was to impose strict checks on all traffic between Maseru and the republic, which, in reality, amounted to the imposition of sanctions. The embargo was lifted briefly after meetings at ministerial level. But major incursions by South African surrogates soon followed, designed to stretch Lesotho's tiny paramilitary force.

The new wave of LLA activity included the destruction of a military barracks and a plot to assassinate the prime minister with a car bomb. Pretoria accused Lesotho of turning a blind eye to ANC activities and imposed border restrictions, demanding the expulsion of 3 000 South Africans. At about this time, Pretoria's assembly of an alliance opposed to the BNP came to fruition with the creation of the Basotho Democratic Alliance, led by the former foreign minister, C.D. Molapo.

Jonathan was walking a political tightrope and the onslaught finally forced him to concede on 'matters of mutual interest'. It was widely believed that he had entered into some 'understanding' with South Africa, but the nature of this remained a matter of speculation. The result, however, was the so-called 'voluntary deportation' in which about 60 South African refugees were evicted from the country. Pretoria then eased the blockade.

After signing the Nkomati Accord with Mozambique in March 1984, Pretoria again stepped up the pressure on Lesotho. But this period witnessed only sporadic and isolated LLA activities. The LLA had by then split into three different groups and was, for all practical purposes, a spent force. Any armed incursion mounted against Lesotho at this stage would have forced Pretoria to use its own military or an assortment of mercenaries. So, predictably, in 1984, the South African government relied almost exclusively upon economic pressures.

They went all out in this period to force Jonathan to sign an Nkomati-type pact, resuming border restrictions on Lesotho nationals and threatening to repatriate migrant workers in the mining industry. In addition, Pretoria 'withdrew' in this period from the Highlands Water Scheme, under which impoverished Lesotho would sell its only natural resource to its thirsty neighbour. The pact Pretoria wanted Lesotho to sign was called a 'security agreement' rather than a 'non-aggression pact', and reportedly required Lesotho to notify South Africa of every refugee entering its territory and to provide for deportation or repatriation if Pretoria insisted.[10]

Jonathan's government resisted pressure to sign a pact, however, and in July accused South Africa of imposing sanctions by withholding a shipment of light arms from Britain. Jonathan subsequently claimed that the South African government offered him a million rand. At the end of August, P.W. Botha again threatened to cancel the Highlands Water Project, saying that Lesotho was unwilling to meet Pretoria's security needs.[11] However, discussions resumed in October on the 2 000-million-rand project to provide drought-afflicted South Africa with a vital new source of water by the mid-1990s. On 1 October, Lesotho's information minister, Desmond Sixishe, announced that the ANC had agreed to 'withdraw', and two days later the delayed shipment of weapons left Durban.

The pressure, however, continued to mount and, a year later, Lesotho was under seige. South African commandos attacked Maseru in December 1985, killing nine people of whom six were South Africans; and the republic reimposed border restrictions that amounted to a full-scale blockade. A delegation from the 1 500-man Lesotho paramilitary force visited Pretoria; so did five opposition politicians. On 20 January 1986, the paramilitary staged a *coup d'état*, in the name of their commander, Major-General Justin Lekhanya, but pledging loyalty to King Moshoeshoe II, who became the executive head of state, governing on the advice of the military council and the council of ministers.

The *coup d'état* in Lesotho resulted from the cumulative effects of destabilization which exposed fractures within the BNP. These divisions centred around two forces: the generation of technocrats who had entered government in the early 1970s and used the state to accumulate property; and the younger generation of ministers who were still relatively 'empty-handed'. The older technocrats were represented by Evaristus Sekhonyana, removed by Jonathan as foreign minister in 1984, and later minister of finance in the post-*coup* government. The younger generation came to be represented by Vincent Makhele, foreign minister in the government which was overthrown.

The power struggle that emerged in 1985 was primarily directed at the control of state power in the post-Jonathan era. Fought against the backdrop of destabilization on the one hand, and the less reactionary foreign policy that had been championed in recent years, the battle for accumulation was recast in ideological terms between the 'left' and the 'right'. The Makhele faction, the 'left', consolidated its position by taking a strong anti-*apartheid* stance, no doubt favourable at this point to Jonathan. The Sekhonyana faction tended to favour some form of pact with Pretoria.

The main instruments of the battle seemed to be control of the party, particularly the youth league, and proximity to the prime minister. When Sekhonyana was removed from the foreign ministry in 1984, the 'left' had won the first battle. But the second round, which was to prove fatal for the whole party, was yet to come.

The general election set for September 1985 was of great importance to the BNP, and to Chief Jonathan in particular, for a number of reasons. First, it was necessary for him to establish legitimacy both at home and abroad. Secondly, he wished to use the election as a referendum to confirm confidence in his policy toward Pretoria. And finally, he hoped the outcome would give him a chance to select a successor and retire, a desire he had expressed on a number of occasions over the previous five years. The warring factions of the BNP viewed the elections in the same light, particularly with respect to the question of succession.

By 1985, it was widely believed that Sekhonyana, although isolated within the cabinet, retained the following of the party rank and file. Thus the only way for his opponents to dislodge him was through the ruthless and violent tactics applied by the youth league during the campaign. Another important factor is that the BNP 'left' were personalities without a sizeable political base and were therefore vulnerable to a charismatic candidate from another party. This explains their unwillingness to give the opposition the opportunity to participate in the elections. However, with the exception of the CPL and the newly formed United Fatherland Front, the opposition parties had no political base either. In the circumstances, it was considered politically astute for the BNP to defeat them in an open election and discredit them once and for all. This was not the calculation of the BNP 'left' who considered themselves within a whisker of power. The non-election that returned the BNP unopposed (after other parties refused to participate) was the final straw.

The country emerged from the election exercise divided, and the BNP even more divided. The Makhele 'victory', mirrored in the new cabinet, was for all practical purposes hollow. From the election in September until the fall of the government in January 1986, the party could not hold itself together.

In the final analysis, it was South Africa, playing upon Lesotho's internal contradictions, particularly those between the paramilitary force and the youth wing, which finally ousted Jonathan's government. Even then, in many ways, the *coup d'état* was very much a family affair. Nominally, executive power passed from Jonathan to his uncle, King Moshoeshoe II (who had gone into exile in 1970 and returned the same year after pledging to remain politically passive – a promise he kept until 1986). The officers who seized power were nominally led by the head of the paramilitary force, General Lekhanya, who on hearing the announcement of the take-over on the radio is said to have telephoned the prime minister and claimed he knew nothing about it.[12] The real power on the council appeared to rest with two brothers, both Lieutenant-Colonels called Letsie. They retain the name of their forebear, Letsie, the eldest son of Moshoeshoe I, the great Basotho king of the nineteenth century (1786–1870), whose diplomatic skill kept his kingdom intact, eventually under British protection. Moshoeshoe I tried to ensure future unity by betrothing the daughter of his first son, Letsie, to the son of his second son, Molapo. But in the polilitcs of present day Lesotho, it would appear that the sons of Lestie have taken over from the sons of Molapo.

It is probably still to early to guage the meaning of the changes in terms of Lesotho's policies. The internal policy is unlikely to change. Nor, given the historic animosity of the citizens of Lesotho towards the

Boers, do the incumbents have much room for manoeuvre if they are to retain a popular base. Early South African pressure on the new regime to hand over leading ANC figures was resisted and they were flown further north into exile in Zambia. A member of the military council who toured the Frontline states soon after the *coup d'état* told African leaders that Lesotho remains committed to SADCC and opposed to *apartheid.* But he said that, first and foremost, the new government must consider economic and geographical realities. The implication was that while Lesotho would continue to admit refugees from South Africa they would be removed rapidly northward, that official ANC presence would be curtailed, and the decibel level of opposition to *apartheid* muted.

Botswana

Gaborone, the capital of Botswana, has the charm of a large, rather sleepy, village. Its central feature is a colourful broad shopping mall. There politicians, civil servants and cattle owners rub shoulders free from the racial tension and segregation less then 10 kilometres away across the border in South Africa.

The tranquillity was rudely shattered in the early hours of 14 June 1985, when residents were awakened by bursts of automatic rifle fire, mortars and grenades. Gaborone had become the latest victim of the South African government's strategy of armed attacks on neighbouring capitals.

The raid lasted 45 minutes. Ten houses and an office block in different parts of the city were destroyed. South African soldiers stormed the houses, spraying bullets as they went, and residents who came to their doors were gunned down. Polaroid pictures were taken of the dead. In all, 12 people died.

Later that day, in Pretoria, the head of the SADF, General Constand Viljoen, claimed the targets were certain 'key' activists of the 'control centre of the Transvaal sabotage organization of the ANC'. Every effort had been made, he said 'to get at the enemy, and not at the Botswana police or members of the public or innocent members of the terrorists' families'.[13]

But a very different picture emerged as the identities of the victims became known. The people caught asleep in their beds were all civilians – a six-year-old boy from Lesotho, his uncle, a recently arrived computer programmer from Somalia, a young government social

worker, her husband and a friend visiting from South Africa, a pacifist
university student, two teachers, a typist and a domestic worker. Four
of the 12 may have had connections with the ANC but none were likely
candidates for guerrilla training. By no stretch of the imagination
could they be construed as 'key' ANC activists.[14]

The true motives for the attack seemed to be to try to silence a vocal
community of South African exiles as well as frightening and alienat-
ing the Botswana community from the exile community, exerting
pressure on the government to expel South African exiles, and
generally boosting morale in South Africa by dramatizing the attack as
a 'successful' offensive against 'terrorists'. Botswana would continue
to receive refugees under the Geneva convention, a senior official said:
'There are conditions which the [refugees] observe and may not be
expelled from a country without any evidence that they have con-
travened such conditions ... The only way we could stop receiving
refugees is if they do not come.'

The attack on Gaborone was highly embarassing to the Reagan
administration, coming as it did only three weeks after the foiled
Cabinda raid in Angola in which a South African officer was captured
and confessed that the mission had been to destroy American-owned
oil installations. The US ambassador in Pretoria, Herman Nickel, was
recalled 'to review the situation'. Nickel observed that the raid made
'it virtually impossible for President Reagan not to sign' the divestment bill then before congress. The State Department called in the
South African ambassador-designate, warning him 'If you [South
Africans] want to bring down the wrath of God on your head, I couldn't
think of a better way of doing it'.[15] The British Foreign Office
described the attack as 'indefensible'.

Until that day, Botswana had been left in relative peace by the
South Africans. There had been a number of car bombings and other
explosions, killing several ANC members. But, for nearly 20 years, the
Botswana government had been able to maintain a 'dignified pattern
of independence' and a 'good working relationship with South
Africa'.[16]

Botswana gained its independence from Britain on 30 September
1966, having been a British 'protectorate' since 1884. From the
following year until independence, the 600 372 square kilometres of
sparsely populated and largely arid territory was known as Bechuana-

land. The first prime minister of independent Botswana was Sir
Seretse Khama, chief of the Bamangwato tribe. Under pressure from
South Africa, the British colonial administration had exiled him for
marrying a white woman. But he returned in 1962, entering the
Legislative Council as head of the Bechuanaland Democratic Party
(BDP) which worked for a multi-party, democratic, non-racial state
and won an overwhelming majority in the pre-independence elections.
He was later knighted by the British queen.

Despite his conservative traditionalist background, Khama was to
play a significant role in southern African politics over the next 14
years before his death in 1980. He was part of the Frontline states
grouping, which also included the leaders of Angola, Mozambique,
Tanzania and Zambia, and which played a prominent role in the
Zimbabwean liberation struggle. As leader of one of the Frontline
states, Khama stood in the forefront of opposition to *apartheid*. While
his role was more muted than that of some of his colleagues – and his
country's economic and geographic position more difficult – there was
no doubting the principles he stood for.

He was one of the leading advocates of the Southern African
Development Coordination Conference (SADCC), and his country
hosts the SADCC secretariat. On 3 July 1979, at a Frontline states
meeting in the northern Tanzanian town of Arusha, called to discuss
plans for establishing SADCC, he made his position very clear.
Political freedom had been won, he said, but economic liberation
remained to be achieved. He called for the development of the
subcontinent as an integrated region 'rather than a cluster of
impoverished little chauvinistic entities', adding that there was a need
to improve regional transport facilities so the African nations could
'lessen their dependence upon the racist and white minority regime of
South Africa. This economic dependence has in many ways made our
political independence somewhat meaningless.'[17]

Nine months later, on 1 April 1980, he chaired the summit meeting
in the Zambian capital, Lusaka, that launched SADCC, and he
sounded an ominous warning. 'The struggle for economic liberation
will be as bitterly contested as has been the struggle for political
liberation,' he said. But he emphasized that SADCC, while seeking to
lessen its dependence on South Africa for trade and transport, was not
seeking outright confrontation. 'It is not our objective to plot against
anybody or any country but, on the contrary, to lay the foundation for
the development of a new economic order in southern Africa and forge

a united community.'[18] As stated elsewhere, Pretoria had no intention of allowing that dependence to be reduced and it thus embarked on a programme of economic and military destabilization.

Traditionally, the people of Botswana have held their wealth in cattle and at independence the pastoral sector was the only significant foreign exchange earner. While the cattle industry still generates 10 per cent of the country's export earnings, it is now in third place behind diamonds and copper-nickel matte.

Fifteen years ago, Botswana was one of the poorest countries in sub-Saharan Africa. Today, largely because of diamonds, it is one of the five richest, with foreign exchange reserves equalling more than a year's government spending. Since diamond deposits were found in Orapa in 1967, Botswana has become one of the world's three largest diamond producers – with South Africa and the Soviet Union – and over 70 per cent of its export earnings come from diamond sales. This has generated an annual economic growth rate of over 11 per cent for the past five years. In 1985, Botswana had its first trade surplus with exports of US$ 684.9 million and imports of US$576.8 million.[19] If the Trans-Kalahari railway to Windhoek could be constructed it would provide Botswana with the economic incentive to exploit its large coal reserves; but this is unlikely until Namibia is independent.

While Botswana has achieved rapid economic growth, it still has a host of economic problems including, as Khama realized, its dependence on South Africa. Another key problem is that, due to a colonial legacy lacking in adequate planning for future development, priority must be given to the expensive task of creating an infrastructure, to providing education and rural training, and to expansion of productive employment. Third, the droughts in the early 1980s ravaged the country, reducing the national cattle herd by 20 per cent and diverting state funds from development to relief projects. Water shortages and unreliable rainfall continue to cause serious difficulties, with small harvests necessitating large imports of food.[20]

South Africa likes to give the impression that the withholding of food is a weapon which can be used against its neighbours, that 'more and more black states will depend to some extent on this country for basic foods' and that 'full grain silos will mean that we can talk and negotiate from a position of strength'.[21] First of all, South Africa is responsible for the critical shortage of food in some neighbouring countries, such as Mozambique and Angola, where its surrogates have been sabotaging transportation routes, damaging rural infrastructure, and destroying crops and food relief supplies. Secondly, South Africa's own weakness on this issue was exposed during the same period of drought, when it was forced to import supplies of the staple food, maizemeal, from one of its independent, black neighbours, Zimbabwe.

Botswana's economic turnabout has been based in large part upon the development of its mineral wealth by the state in conjuction with, largely, South African capital. Anglo American, a South African transnational, and the American Amax Corporation have a controlling interest in the copper-nickel mine at Selebi-Pikwe. De Beers have joined the government in the development of the diamond fields at Orapa, Letlhakane and Jwaneng, and De Beers' Central Selling Organization markets Botswana's diamonds abroad. This leaves Botswana's vital foreign-exchange-earning sector highly dependent upon forces outside the government's control.

Botswana is also heavily dependent upon South African transport, and industrial and processing sectors, with upwards of 80 per cent of its imports passing through or originating in South Africa. Twenty per cent of its electricity comes from the republic, and all of its oil. Unable to absorb its own growing labour force and school leavers, over 25 000 nationals of Botswana work in South Africa. Only four times that many are in formal wage employment at home. The Botswana government receives almost 40 per cent of its revenue from the joint customs union, which has in fact arrested industrial development in Botswana. In a less precarious position than Lesotho, Botswana is still dependent upon the good will of South Africa and its corporations to keep its cars and lorries running, its lamps lit, its shelves stocked and its people employed.

Physically, Botswana is a country of great contrast. To the west, the sweeping sands of the Kalahari desert spill over into Namibia. To the north, close to the border with Angola, there is the stark beauty of the Okavango Swamps teeming with wildlife. To the east, the arable lands and ranches with their long-horned cattle adjoin Zimbabwe and South Africa. The reality of the geographical location of land-locked Botswana is that it has been surrounded by war for most of the past 20 years. Consequently, it became a refuge for people fleeing from Namibia, Rhodesia and South Africa.

By the end of the Rhodesian war, there were about 20 000 Zimbabwean refugees in Botswana and, on at least 100 occasions, Rhodesian troops violated the border. Today, there are about 5 000 Zimbabwean refugees in Botswana, some as a result of the conflict in Matabeleland, others economic refugees fleeing the drought that ravaged that area. Relations between Botswana and Zimbabwe have improved markedly in the past two years after some tension and today Botswana extradites people known to be using Botswana as a rear base for operations against the Mugabe government.

Tension increased along Botswana's northern border in early 1982, when there were a number of overflights by South African aircraft near Namibia's Caprivi Strip. At about this time there were also a number of attacks on South African exiles in Gaborone, including the kidnapping of one young man who was taken back to South Africa. A disinformation campaign in the South African press claimed there was a build-up of Soviet personnel in Botswana. The president, Dr Quett Masire, said this disinformation was used to provide Pretoria with a pretext to 'eliminate enemies' in Botswana. 'I think they're trying to make a Lebanon of us,' he observed.[22]

Since that time there has been considerable pressure on President Masire, as there was on Chief Jonathan in Lesotho, to come to some agreement with Pretoria which would ensure that the ANC did not use Botswana as a 'launching pad' for operations in South Africa. This pressure has taken at least three forms – diplomatic, economic and military.

Early each year since 1983, a list of 'ANC terrorists' has been given to the Botswana government by Pretoria, who urged them to 'take appropriate action'. In each case, the Botswana government has asked for evidence to support the allegations. After signing the Nkomati Accord with Mozambique in March 1984, the South Africans increased pressure on Botswana to sign a similar pact and, at a SACU commission meeting the same month, they produced 'the full draft of a non-aggression treaty – all ready for signing'. A number of points were discussed, including South Africa's demand for the right of 'hot pursuit', the proposal for the 'homelands' to join the customs union, and bilateral economic matters. Botswana officials were 'appalled' and refused to sign.[23]

The Botswana government later assured South Africa that 'subversive elements' would not be allowed to use its territory but maintained its refusal to sign a formal security pact, giving as an example the MNR's continued infiltration of Mozambique despite the Nkomati Accord and saying it would be 'difficult to have confidence in what it [South Africa] says it will do'. When President Masire met President Reagan at the White House in early 1984, he asked for Washington's support to prevent South Africa from forcing him to sign an agreement.

But Pretoria needed evidence of support in the region, and it is therefore not surprising that, on the eve of P.W. Botha's trip to Europe in June 1984, his officials boasted that Masire was ready to 'design measures to prevent the planning and execution of acts of violence, sabotage and terrorism'. 'Pik' Botha told parliament that he was negotiating with neighbouring countries in search of agreements that each other's territories would not be used as 'springboards for subversion'. He said an agreement in principle had been reached with Botswana to allow each country's security forces to enter the other country in 'hot pursuit of terrorists', and that Pretoria was waiting to hear from Gaborone on how the accord would be implemented.[24] But this was merely a propaganda exercise for European, American and South African audiences. Masire's office said he had 'no knowledge of the negotiations, let alone the agreement in principle'.

British and American pressure 'behind-the-scenes' was credited with relieving South African insistence on a signed agreement. Instead there was an agreed public statement 'in which the foreign minister of South Africa said his government no longer required Botswana to sign an agreement because it accepted assurances that it does not allow use of its territory as a launching pad against South Africa. He said that South Africa also undertook not to allow its territory as a launching pad against Botswana.'[25]

As opposition to *apartheid* boiled over in the urban townships toward the end of 1984, Pretoria, wishing to carry on the charade that their enemy was external but no longer having Mozambique to blame, claimed Botswana had become the 'channel for sabotage and refuge for saboteurs'.[26] Botswana, they argued, was incapable of controlling activities of the ANC, or preventing widespread crossings after the blocking of the Mozambique infiltration routes. Early in the New Year, with Pretoria threatening 'hot pursuit', the Botswana foreign minister, Dr Gaositwe Chiepe, met 'Pik' Botha to get some 'practical arrangements' underway. But Botswana maintained its refusal to sign any kind of pact with Pretoria.

The most public example of the use of economic leverage on Botswana was South Africa's vacillation in supporting the US$ 300 million Sua Pan soda ash project. At Makgadigadi, 150 kilometres north of Francistown, there is a massive dry salt lake containing enough salt, soda ash and potash to supply the subcontinent for the next century. But, to make the exploitation of the deposits economic, the South African market is needed. A clause in the SACU agreement guaranteeing Botswana exclusive marketing rights in territories belonging to the customs union, means that South Africa should stop its importation of soda ash from the United States and cancel its own proposed soda ash project. But Botswana has not been able to get a firm South African commitment to the project and 'Pik' Botha has made it clear why: Botswana will not get co-operation 'on certain economic projects' without first coming to an 'acceptable understanding' regarding security.[27]

Other economic pressure included a threatened re-negotiation of the terms of the customs union. The South African finance minister ordered an investigation into all aspects of the SACU agreement, saying it 'does not meet the needs of the eighties'. P.W. Botha said in a public speech: 'We see the customs union not in isolation as a revenue-sharing arrangement, but as part of a *comprehensive regional development strategy*'.[28]

As with the other countries on the frontline, diplomatic and economic pressure from Pretoria is accompanied by sabotage, disinformation and military force. Without a surrogate force to do its dirty work, the South African military has had to use its own commandos and undercover agents to destroy and kill in Botswana. A spate of bombings took place in the months prior to the massive June 1985 raid on Gaborone. Two South African refugees living in Gaborone were hurt in February when a bomb exploded at the home of one of them, and they left Botswana soon after. A few weeks later, a car bomb killed a South African refugee working for a Western aid organization in Botswana. Marius Schoon, a longtime anti-*apartheid* activist and ANC member who spent 12 years in prison for his views, was forced to leave Botswana when the British organization for which he worked cancelled the post in the wake of threats against his life. He and his family moved to Angola, followed by a parcel bomb which killed his wife and six-year-old daughter.

Botswana has maintained throughout that while it finds *apartheid* abhorrent and it will continue receiving refugees from South Africa, it has not given ANC activists sanctuary or permitted the country to be used as an infiltration route. 'There is no allegation of bad faith by South Africa against Botswana,' Major Craig Williamson, of the South African security police, stated in June 1985. 'We believe Botswana is doing everything it can. But we are dealing with a sophisticated terrorist organization ... [which] is not, perhaps, in the experience of a small Third World country's intelligence organization and police force.'[29]

In the first days of 1986, South Africa threatened Botswana again after several land-mine explosions near their common border which killed nine people. A number of South Africans living in Botswana were arrested and the Botswana Defence Force (BDF) was put on full alert. Masire, while continuing to resist a security agreement with Pretoria, noted that if a blockade similar to the one imposed on Lesotho were to be applied to Botswana, the economy 'would be terribly crippled ... and our lives would be turned into misery' [30]

The BDF was created in 1977 to try to combat Rhodesian incursions and today it numbers only 3 500 men. It was powerless to prevent the June 1985 raid on Gaborone. However, its defence capabilities are being improved and – in what appeared to be a clear signal to Pretoria to refrain from attacking Botswana – it was announced in February 1986 that a British Special Air Service (SAS) team had arrived to assist in training the BDF.[31] The presence of a British military training mission in Botswana, as in Zimbabwe, should make Pretoria think twice about open incursions.

Swaziland

On 31 March 1984, while Botswana and Lesotho continued to resist signing formal security pacts with South Africa, the pressure on them to do so took a new turn. Two weeks earlier the governments of Mozambique and South Africa had signed the Nkomati Accord, and now 'Pik' Botha and his counterpart from Swaziland, Richard Dlamini, met in Pretoria and announced the existence of a two-year-old hitherto secret security agreement. It had been 'decided to make public,' their statement said, 'the existence and contents of an Agreement relating to Security Matters'.

In the agreement the two governments agreed to 'combat terrorism, insurgency and subversion individually and collectively as well as their right to call upon each other for such assistance and steps as may be deemed necessary or expedient to eliminate this evil'. They undertook to respect each other's independence, sovereignty and territorial integrity, to refrain from the threat of use of force against each other and not to allow foreign military bases or units in their countries except in self-defence, and then 'only after due notification to the other'.[32]

Unlike the Nkomati agreement, which the Mozambique government insisted must be a public document, the agreement between Swaziland and South Africa has never been made public, despite the joint statement revealing its existence. The agreement in fact comprises a series of three letters which are published here for the first time as Appendix 4.

The first letter is dated 12 February 1982 and was written by P.W. Botha to Swaziland's monarch, King Sobhuza II. Botha begins the letter by referring to various discussions and correspondence between the foreign ministers of the two countries which resulted in agreement 'that international terrorism, in all its manifestations, poses a real threat to international peace and security and that our respective Governments should take steps to protect our respective states and nationals against this threat.'

To this end, Botha proposed an agreement containing four articles, the essence of which, with one omission, was contained in the statement issued by 'Pik' Botha and Dlamini two years later. The exception is the reference to the UN Charter giving nations the right to call for foreign military assistance in the event of their being attacked.

The Swaziland prime minister, Mabandla Fred Dlamini, quoted P.W. Botha's letter verbatim and then signed it, saying that the exchange of letters would constitute an agreement between the two governments. His reply was dated 17 February 1982, the same date which appears on a short note on headed paper over the signature of Sobhuza II, Ingwenyama, King of Swaziland, addressed to 'My Dear Prime Minister', authorizing him to sign the 'Letter of Understanding on Security Matters' between the Kingdom of Swaziland and the Republic of South Africa.[33]

Inevitably, comparisons have been made between the agreements with South Africa signed by Mozambique and by Swaziland. But, in a number of important respects, there is little similarity. In the first place, although a captive state, Swaziland was not confronted with the massive onslaught that the South African authorities were orchestrating against Mozambique, directly or through surrogates. Thus, there is no similarity between the plight of the two states at the time they signed the agreements. In February 1982, Swaziland, had there not been an ulterior motive, could have resisted an agreement as Botswana and Lesotho continued to do, but by March 1984 Mozambique almost certainly could not. Further, Mozambique insisted on conducting its negotiations with public knowledge and signing an agreement that was open to scrutiny. Swaziland chose to do so in secrecy and only agreed to it being made public – without publication of the full document – once its actions would be overshadowed by the attendant post-Nkomati publicity.

There are also fundamental differences in the actual agreements. The agreement with Swaziland is virtually a police agreement giving the South Africans the right to operate in Swaziland. The Nkomati Accord does not. In fact, as revealed in the earlier chapter on Mozambique, the SADF had specified that they would not operate in Mozambique against their surrogates, the MNR. In addition, the Swaziland agreement clearly places the ANC in the category of 'international terrorism'. In contrast, the Mozambique documents contains a clear condemnation of the *apartheid* system when it refers in the preamble to 'the principle of equal rights of all peoples'.

The intricacies of Swaziland's arrangement with South Africa may never be widely known, but there would seem to have been something in it for everyone, all of course advantageous to the South African government. Within four months of the security agreement being signed, South Africa announced its intention to formally cede to Swaziland two border regions which King Sobhuza had historically laid claim to – wishing to bring 'all his children together' into a Greater Swaziland.[34] By late 1981, the *quid pro quo* was obvious: a crackdown on ANC activities in Swaziland in exchange for the land.

Although ethnically related to the Swazis, Kangwane on the northern border of Swaziland, and Ingwavuma to the south-east, are designated 'homelands' in South Africa (the latter is part of Kwazulu). The 'chief minister' of Kangwane, Enos Mabuza, one of the more forward-looking of the 'homeland' leaders, was offered a post as deputy prime minister of Swaziland, or ambassador to South Africa, in return.for his support of the annexation, but the incentive failed to move him.[35] He and other 'homeland' leaders initiated a political and legal battle to prevent the transfer, keeping the issue in the courts until long after Sobhuza's death in 1982.

Their argument rested on *apartheid* legislation, which dictates that before any measure affecting them is implemented, they must be consulted. Since they had not been consulted, the court upheld their case. Pretoria responded by establishing a commision of enquiry, the Rumpff Commission, which reported that the free will of the people of the two areas could not be accurately determined and that the leaders of Swaziland and of the 'homelands' ought to deliberate the matter themselves. South African authorities publicly abandoned the plan in June 1984, three months after signing Nkomati and making public the security pact with Swaziland.

The land deal would have given Swaziland an outlet to the sea at Khosi Bay, and would have greatly increased the size of the tiny kingdom. But it would have favoured South Africa's ethnic 'homeland' policy, enabling it to dispose of almost one million citizens with one stroke of a pen. The annexation also would have provided a 'buffer zone' for South Africa along the southern border of Mozambique. In addition, the cost of administering the territories would have been transferred to Swaziland, outweighing any economic benefit, perhaps one reason why the then prime minister, Prince Mabandla, opposed the deal.

Swaziland was already beset by economic problems which have grown steadily worse, through 1984/5:falling export earnings(especially for sugar, its main commodity export), increased costs for imports (especially oil), the resulting high rate of inflation, rising unemployment and so on. After the death of King Sobhuza, Swaziland moved even more firmly into the South African economic orbit and in late 1984, nine months after revealing the existence of their security pact, the governments of South Africa and Swaziland signed an agreement facilitating the exchange of trade representatives with full diplomatic status.

Swaziland's relations with the Boers (the Dutch settlers of the southern tip of Africa) have always been different to those of Botswana and Lesotho. While the latter two countries fought Boer expansionism in the nineteenth century, the Swazis gave them land in the north and west of their country in exchange for cattle.

In the 1860s, Swazi leaders helped the Boers to put down a rebellion of their black subjects, and, in the next decade, the Boers intervened to ensure the succession of a claimant to the Swazi throne. Until the 1880s, the Swazis and the Boers (or Afrikaners, literally, speakers of Afrikaans) treated each other as equals. Since that time, though, with the political subjugation of the African kingdoms in the region by the British and with the development of an industrial economy centred on the gold-mines, South Africa has dominated the 17 363 square-kilometre kingdom.

On 6 September 1968, Swaziland ceased to be a British colony and became an independent state, with King Sobhuza II, who had been monarch since 1899, at its head, and with a political system based on the British model. Five years later, in April 1973, Sobhuza abolished the parliamentary system in a royal *coup d'état*. He banned all political parties, introduced a state of emergency, announced the formation of a national army and vested all state power in himself. In 1979, the king created a new state structure in which power remained with him while the Liqoqo, or inner council, had an advisory role. A cabinet of government ministers was created, including a prime minister, but decision-making rested firmly with King Sobhuza until his death in August 1982.

The power of the royal family rests upon its traditional role and upon the wealth it controls through the Tibiyo TakaNgwane Fund, created before independence to act as a depository of mining royalties. The money has been used to buy land – much of which is under sugar for export – and to establish joint ventures with transnational corporations, many of them South African. The fund is exempt from taxes, is not accountable to parliament, and revenue accrues to the royal family, not to the nation as a whole.

The population of Swaziland numbers less than one million, the vast majority of them peasant farmers living at a subsistence level. Not surprisingly, South Africa dominates the economy, buying 20 per cent of the exports and providing 90 per cent of imports. About 60 per cent of government revenue derives from the joint customs union. South Africa also provides employment and, because only 30 per cent of school leavers are able to find employment in the local wage economy, the South African job option is vital. About 17 000 Swaziland nationals work in South Africa, sending home about R11 million each year (US$ 4.5 million). More than a third of Swaziland's electricity comes from South Africa and all of its fuel.

Swaziland is land-locked and therefore reliant on its neighbours for port facilities. Until 1985, about one third of its trade went through South Africa, and the remainder through Mozambique. However, a new rail link which opened in February 1986 will tie Swaziland even more firmly into the South African transport system – instead of moving away from it as SADCC colleagues would prefer. Its construction raises questions about Swaziland's – and South Africa's – future plans for utilizing the port of Maputo. The cross-country railway is plugged into South African railways at both ends, carrying traffic from the mining, industrial and agricultural areas of the eastern Transvaal to the port of Richards Bay in Natal. While revenue from the railway is expected to boost the Swaziland treasury, it will have the parallel affect – like Lesotho's water project – of assisting the local economy while making it more dependent on South Africa.[36]

As in the case of Lesotho, political and financial relations with Pretoria have caused deep divisions within the government of Swaziland, although they have taken a different form. Divisions over the security agreement, the resultant actions against the ANC, the land deal and other economic considerations have developed into a struggle for supremacy in the post-Sobhuza era. In 1982, a strong, conservative economic lobby emerged which hoped to use the death of the king to clamp down on ANC activities in Swaziland and revitalize relations with South Africa to great economic advantage; and no doubt South Africa saw fit to encourage those whom it counted among its allies.

The struggle for power amongst the financial and political elite in Swaziland was over the direction of the state, in terms of socio-economic and political philosophy as well as personalities. This power struggle can be identified in three broad phases. The first phase deals with the subordination of the prime minister to the Liqoqo, which was accomplished in early 1983 when Prince Mabandla fled with his family to Bophutatswana. His successor, Prince Bhekimpi Dhlamini, an ardent supporter of the land deal, was put into office by two powerful members of the Liqoqo, Dr George Msibi and Prince Mfanasibili.

The second phase saw the subordination of the queen regent to the Liqoqo. This was orchestrated in 1983 when the existing regent, the 'old she elephant' Dzeliwe, was removed and Princess Ntombi La Thawala was ensconced. The new queen regent signed an agreement limiting her powers, an agreement the previous regent had refused to sign. By the end of 1983, power lay with a small clique within the Liqoqo, a group that was supportive of closer ties with South Africa. Richard Dlamini, another leading proponent of the land deal, was appointed minister of foreign affairs. But it was not long before there was a falling out among the power brokers.

A multi-million-rand customs fraud involving the SACU caused considerable political, as well as financial, damage when it came to light in mid-1984. The finance minister of Swaziland, Dr Sishaye Nxumalo, revealed in June that the customs union had been defrauded of about R13 million (US$ 5 million), depriving the member countries – Botswana, Lesotho, Swaziland and South Africa – of that revenue.

The fraud, involving South African businessmen, consisted of the importation of almost 270 container-loads of textiles, electronic equipment and other goods worth about R50 million (US$ 20 million). The goods were dutiable and were released by customs at the South African port of Durban only because they were consigned to a bonded SACU warehouse in Swaziland, where duties would be paid when the goods were released. However, papers had been falsified, the bonded warehouse did not exist, and the goods remained in South Africa where they were sold without duty being paid.

Dr Nxumalo announced that a thorough investigation would take place which he expected would unmask people in 'high places' in Swaziland. Within days he was arrested and charged with treason. Several of his associates were also detained, or removed from office, including the minister of foreign affairs, Dlamini.

P.W. Botha, then on his European tour, was informed of these actions by letter and, within days of his return, sent the South African foreign minister, 'Pik' Botha to Mbabane. He was assured that the changes in government did not reflect a shift in Swaziland's policy of prohibiting its territory from being used by the ANC.[37]

In early 1985 a number of other officials were forced into 'compulsory retirement' while others were arrested and charged with sedition. Among the latter were the commissioner of police and his white deputy, both of whom were regarded locally as 'straight' highly professional policemen. They had antagonized Mfanasibili when they were involved in Mabandla's attempt to detain him, and were supposedly instrumental in helping Mabandla escape to South Africa. Shortly after their arrest, the Liqoqo leadership claimed that there were plans for a *coup d'état* led by relatives of the men in detention, but none materialized.

A commission of enquiry was set up to investigate the customs fraud, headed by the ombudsman, Robert Mabila, who was also secretary to the Liqoqo. His report concluded that 17 South African companies were among the 21 involved, and that 'the architects of the customs union fraud are largely, if not entirely, South Africans'. The remaining four companies were registered in Swaziland. The ombudsman's report also recommended legal action against the companies and personalities implicated in the customs fraud.[38]

During the second half of 1985, the power struggle reached its third phase when the queen regent moved to reassert her authority and that of the monarchy, and ordered the arrest of some of those who had put her in power. A group of disgruntled members of the royal family led a march on parliament in August, demonstrating their opposition to the excessive powers of the Liqoqo which they said had been 'highjacked' by Msibi and Mfanasibili. The two were removed from the Liqoqo in October and their hand-picked police commissioner was dismissed.

Within a few weeks, the former finance minister and other political detainees were released, and so were senior police officers arrested earlier for treason. In early 1986, it was announced that Mfanasibili would be taken to court for 'subverting justice' by contributing to false statements which led to the arrest of his opponents. This activity was basically an attempt to reassert royal authority and to counteract measures taken since Sobhuza's death to subordinate the monarchy to the power of the Liqoqo. The early installation of the new king, 18-year-old Prince Makhosetive, in 1986, is seen as an attempt to consolidate that power. But there is no reason to believe that the new king will initiate any major changes in the economic or political structures of Swaziland, nor is he likely to change Swaziland's policies toward Pretoria.

The growth and activities of the ANC provide some understanding of the development of relations between South Africa and Swaziland. Since the early 1980s, *Umkhonto we Sizwe*, the military wing of the ANC, has stepped up its actions against *apartheid*. According to South African government figures, the number of incidents rose from four in 1976 to 12 in 1979, then increased significantly to 60 in 1981. The number decreased in 1982 to 39, but the following year it rose again to 56. For some months after the signing at Nkomati, the incidents of ANC armed attacks decreased but, by the end of 1984, the ANC had made up for the lost time and they have been escalating their struggle ever since.

South African military forces, which invaded Angola in 1975, began violating the sovereignty of other neighbours in the early 1980s, on the pretence that the threat was external – despite the evidence of increasing and sustained internal resistance to *apartheid*. Hence, the ANC offices in Swaziland, as elsewhere in the region, were a target. The harassment of ANC members in Swaziland culminated in late 1981 in a series of raids on their residences, the detention of the ANC representative in Swaziland, and a shoot-out near the Mozambique border. In October 1981, the South African defence minister, General Malan, threatened to open a 'second front', and, privately, South African authorities warned Swaziland that it would be turned into an 'operational area' if it did not take action against the ANC.[39]

There were some arrests and harassment of ANC members whom the Swazi authorities claimed were 'violating the terms of their exile'. Tough, new legislation was introduced, to restrict opponents of the government as much as to restrain members of the ANC, but relations in the country, long a safe way-station for refugees from South Africa, remained 'politely tolerant' until about the time the security agreement with Pretoria was made public at the end of March 1984.

In early April, a bomb exploded in Durban, killing three people. The bombing, and the influx of ANC members from Mozambique, led to strong South African pressure on Swaziland to fulfill its commitment under the agreement. The government of Swaziland responded by ordering police to round up and jail ANC members who crossed the border. A few weeks later, the police claimed that several ANC members had stormed a police station, releasing four of their colleagues. The ANC denied this and insisted that the guerrillas had been handed over to the South African police. Within weeks, more than 100 ANC members had been flown out to a safer haven further north.

ANC members interviewed later said four of their number had been turned over to the South Africans and another six were unaccounted for. 'Whites in camouflage uniforms were seen at all the big raids,' they said. 'It seems clear that most of the whites were South Africans and that they actually directed an assault on a house in Manzini which led to a seven-hour gun battle, and killed at least two men.'[40]

The situation continued to deteriorate and, late in 1984, students demonstrated at the university campus against the deportation of a

student leader to South Africa. Then the deputy chief of the
Swaziland security police, Chief Shibi, was murdered and the government alleged that the killer was Solly Ngcobo, whom they described as
an 'ANC hit man', a claim the ANC denied. But Shibi's murder was
used to justify another crackdown on the ANC, resulting in several
arrests, as well as a deportation order for the ANC representative.
More than 300 ANC members were deported from Swaziland in 1984,
and 23 others were threatened with deportation if they did not
surrender to police.

Early in the new year, Solly Ngcobo was shot and killed by police.
Seven other ANC members 'vanished' from the Mbabane police
station following threats made by one officer that ANC guerrillas
would be handed over to the South Africans. The Swaziland police
claimed there had been another ANC break-in to free the missing men,
a claim the ANC again denied. The ANC blamed South African
agents, calling the whole affair a Pretoria-inspired provocation aimed
at sabotaging ANC talks with Swaziland. Relations deteriorated
further in 1985 with the expulsion from Swaziland of students and
academics belonging to the ANC.[41] Several ANC guerrillas and at least
two Swazi policemen have been killed, and South African forces often
cross the border in 'hot pursuit', raiding villages and threatening
villagers to report any ANC presence.[42]

Another 38 ANC members were deported in January 1986.[43] By
continuing to deport ANC personal, Swaziland will hope to ensure
that Mbabane is not invaded as Gaborone and Maseru have been and
that the new king receives support from Pretoria.

South Africa's relations with Lesotho, Botswana, and Swaziland have
been based primarily upon their geographical proximity and almost
total economic dependence, and dominated by South Africa's overwhelming military might and its willingness to use it against its
weakest neighbours. Each of the three states also has a different
relationship with Pretoria, depending on its varying political structures and composition of government.

Certainly Jonathan's refusal to allow opposition participation in the
1985 elections, in the face of the growing strength of his opposition,
gave Pretoria the chance to meddle in Lesotho's affairs. In Swaziland,
the financial alliance between the local elite and South African capital
has moulded political relations between those two states. While there

is antagonism based on national interests – for example, Swaziland businessmen protest that South Africa's bantustans offer economic incentives that take opportunities away from them – the alliance is secure enough for Swaziland to have stated publicly its opposition to international sanctions against the *apartheid* regime on the grounds that these would threaten Swaziland's interest as well.[44] In Botswana, there is a democratic and open political system which leaves the Pretoria regime less opportunity to foster surrogate dissident groups or opposition political parties, although in the last election one opposition party campaigned vocally in favour of a formal security pact with South Africa and there were strong suggestions that South African money was involved in the campaign.

The escalating spiral of violence within South Africa will inevitably mean more and more citizens seeking refuge in Botswana, Lesotho and Swaziland. The majority of them, as in the case of the majority who remain within the republic, support the ANC which, confronted with the obduracy of *apartheid*, has no alternative but to continue its struggle. For as long as there is *apartheid* there will be destabilization, not just for the BLS countries but for all of the independent black-ruled states of southern Africa. They are caught in *apartheid*'s crossfire and, until the shooting stops in the republic, they are victims of the whims and excesses of the last bastion of white supremacy.

Perhaps the best summation of what the future holds in store for the three captive states of Boleswa was given by Botswana's foreign minister, Dr Chiepe, who said the 'sole source of tension is apartheid policy ... Until apartheid is dismantled lock, stock and barrel, the confusion which this vile system generates inside South Africa will continue to spill over across the borders and threaten the peace and stability of the region.'[45]

END OF PART ONE

The cover photo of the train approaching a broken track is from the Namibe Railway in Angola. The picture typifies South African sabotage actions throughout the region, using military tactics to achieve economic and political goals, keeping its neighbours dependent upon trade routes through South Africa by destroying their transport infrastructure. One example of South Africa's economic sanctions against the region. Photo: Department of Information, MPLA-PT

top Tunnel on the Namibe Railway where 15 metres of track were destroyed and another 20 metres mined by South African troops transported by helicopter. Photo: DIP, MPLA-PT

and The gutted shell of a train sabotaged in Mozambique's Sofala Province. The focus of Pretoria's sabotage activity in the region is the transport and communications network, particularly the railways in Mozambique and Angola, thus ensuring the dependence of all neighbouring countries on routes through South Africa.

Photo: Carlos Cardoso, AIM

top A burnt out truck in Manica province of Mozambique. Many thousands of people died of hunger in Mozambique in 1983–84 because food relief transported by truck and train was destroyed with South African weapons. Photo: Paul Fouvet, AIM

and One of the blocks of flats in a Maputo residential area damaged when a powerful car bomb exploded near the centre of the city on 21 April 1986. Photo: Alfredo Mueche, AIM

top left Clinic destroyed by South African troops in Cahama in Angola's Cunene province. Photo: Marga Holness
and A bridge on the Serra da Loba Highway in Huila province of Angola sabotaged by South African troops landed by helicopter. SADF Special Forces units often attribute their acts of sabotage to Unita. Photo: MPLA-PT
above The town of Ngiva, capital of Cunene province, burns after a South African bombing raid. Photo: MPLA-PT

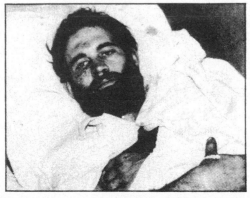

Captain Wynand du Toit, commander of a SADF Special Forces unit caught in the far north of Angola while attempting to sabotage an oil installation belonging to Cabinda Gulf, partly owned by the US transnational, Gulf Oil. Du Toit admitted that the action was to be claimed by Unita. Photo: COSAWR

Defeated South African troops
retreating from Angola in March
1976 after the unsuccessful
invasion to try to prevent the MPLA
from coming to power. Photo: IDAF

S.A. WEERMAGSIDENTIFIKASIE
KAART
S.A. DEFENCE FORCE IDENTITY
CARD
77295103BG
No.
Rang SKTR
Rank
Van
Surname SMIT
Voornaam MARTHINUS
Christian names HERMANUS
Geboortedatum
Date of Birth 61/05/22
Uitgereik
Issued 79/08/09
Saam
H. Adm
Hoof van Staf Personeel,
Chief of Staff Personnel,
57766

insert Identity card of Rifleman
Smit, a South African who was
killed in Angola. Photo: DIP, MPLA-PT

Mass grave of Namibian refugees
murdered by the South African
army at Kassinga in Angola on
4 May 1978. Photo: MPLA-PT

The tactics of South African proxy forces in each country are similar and include murder, maiming and rape as well as destruction of economic infrastructure. These photographs show two of the many victims of MNR mutilations in rural Mozambique. This woman had her ear cut off in Manica province in 1985.

This man, Joaquim Mapinda, a teacher in Sofala province, had his ear and his nose cut off. His nose has since been rebuilt by surgery.

Photos: Anders Nilsson, AIM

When the MNR main base at Casa Banana, in central Mozambique,
was overrun in August 1985, many rural people being held by the
MNR were freed. The only material they had in which to clothe
themselves was from the parachutes the South Africans had used to
drop armaments. Photo: Tommy Sithole, The Herald

A view of the Casa Banana airfield from inside a helicopter after the
storming of the MNR headquarters. This landing strip was built by
the South Africans for ferrying supplies to their surrogates in central
Mozambique. Photo: Tommy Sithole, The Herald.

Armoured vehicles and anti-aircraft guns parachuted in to the MNR by South Africa and captured at the main Gorongosa base, Casa Banana. Photo: Tommy Sithole, The Herald

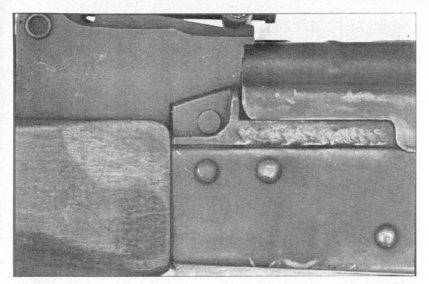

top An AK 47 rifle supplied by South Africa and captured from bandits operating in Zimbabwe's Matabeleland province. The number is obliterated in an attempt to make it difficult to trace the weapon to South Africa.

and An AK 47 round stamped '22-80' captured in a contact with bandits in Matabeleland. South African-supplied ammunition of this type was used in the murder of Rhodesian Front senator, Paul Savage, and other white farmers in Matabeleland.

TO THE PEOPLE OF ZIMBABWE

SOUTH AFRICAN TROOPS HAVE CARRIED OUT AN ATTACK AGAINST
OFFICES AND HOUSES USED BY ANC GANGSTERS IN YOUR COUNTRY

THESE GANGSTERS INFILTRATE INTO OUR COUNTRY TO MURDER
INNOCENT WOMEN AND CHILDREN OF ALL RACES.

WE REGARD THE PEOPLE OF ZIMBABWE AS OUR FRIENDS AND
NEIGHBOURS. WE HAVE NO FIGHT WITH YOU, AND WE WISH TO
LIVE IN PEACE WITH OUR NEIGHBOURS.

UNFORTUNATELY, YOUR GOVERMENT ALLOWS THESE ANC GANGSTERS
TO TERRORISE INNOCENT PEOPLE IN OUR COUNTRY. FOR YOUR
OWN SAFETY YOU SHOULD NOT ALLOW ANC GANGSTERS TO OC-
CUPY HOUSES AND OFFICES IN YOUR COUNTRY, FROM WHERE
THEY CAN PLAN THESE VICIOUS, COWARDLY ACTS AGAINST IN-
NOCENT PEOPLE IN OUR COUNTRY.

IF THIS HAPPENS IT IS OUR RIGHT TO SEEK OUT AND DESTROY
THESE ANC GANGSTERS WHEREVER THEY MAY BE. SELF DEFENCE
IS NOT ONLY OUR RIGHT, IT IS OUR DUTY.

top left The house in a Harare surburb where the ANC representative, Joe Gqabi, was assassinated in 1981. The house itself was destroyed in a South African attack in the early hours of 19 May 1986.
Photo: The Herald

and Prime Minister Mugabe outside the ANC offices in central Harare which were destroyed by South African saboteurs who hired cars from a local touring company for their early morning attack. They escaped by helicopter from a rendezvous point outside the city.
Photo: Alexander Joe

above One of the leaflets scattered in Harare by South African soldiers. The simultaneous raids on three Commonwealth capitals – Gaborone, Harare and Lusaka – were condemned worldwide as an act of 'international terrorism'.

Police and troops of the occupying South African forces break up a SWAPO rally in Windhoek. The South Africans are creating their own military and economic infrastructure in Namibia in preparation for future destabilization. Photo: IDAF

ANC President Oliver Tambo pays his respects at the coffins of some of the 42 people massacred by the South African army in Maseru, Lesotho, on 9 December 1982.

'In a quiet valley of aloes, wattle and poplar trees below Lesotho's parliament lies a curious little graveyard. It has 27 low headstones with the names of the dead and the blunt epitaph: "Massacred by the SADF, 9/12/82". Six newly turned graves alongside them are unmarked....' The dead are victims of two South African attacks on the capital, Maseru, and their graves serve as a reminder of Lesotho's vulnerability, completely surrounded by South African territory and totally dependent upon it.

CHAPTER 6

South Africa's Military Build-up: The Region at War

In the ornate assembly halls of the United Nations in New York, the Security Council continues to debate whether South Africa constitutes a 'threat to international peace and security'. In southern Africa, there is no doubt. Every day people are dying – or being maimed, injured or displaced – through South African military actions. The *apartheid* regime is at war with its neighbours, as well as with its own population.

Despite a UN arms embargo, the regime has built up an arsenal of sophisticated weaponry that includes nuclear armaments. The defence budget has doubled over the past five years. And the decision-making process is dominated by the military since the accession to power of the former minister of defence in what is often described as a 'constitutional *coup d'état*'. The South African authorities now use military force to counter resistance to *apartheid* within the country, and have systematically extended its use far across international boundaries. As we have seen earlier, the targets are not primarily guerrillas of the African National Congress (ANC) or even South African refugees but include transportation routes and other economic installations as well as citizens of neighbouring countries, both black and white, and other foreign nationals.

The white-power system in South Africa has survived through the use of repressive laws and brutal violence against the majority of the population. The long history of more than 300 years of colonial domination has recorded many brave challenges which were put down by the use of overwhelming force, in a pattern similar to other colonial situations. But the crude methods of the colonial era were not suitable for a rapidly developing economy in the post-War years; and thus more elaborate

and comprehensive techniques of repression were deployed especially after the accession to power of the National Party in 1948. Race
rule and white domination were imposed more systematically to cover
every aspect of human behaviour so as to ensure the long-term
'survival of the white man'. A series of draconian laws and other
measures began to be introduced during the 1950s in order to create
the new *apartheid* society.

This was also the decade of mass mobilization and extra-parliamen-
tary opposition led by the ANC and its allies. The regime took
extensive powers to cope with the new upsurge of resistance and
did not hesitate to use the new laws. The 1952 'Defiance of Unjust
Laws Campaign' resulted in stronger penalties being enacted for any
future campaigns of passive resistance. In 1956, a year after the
adoption of the Freedom Charter[2] at the historic Congress of the People,
156 national leaders were arrested for high treason. After four years all
of the accused were discharged by the courts.

By this time a major confrontation had already developed between
the mass of the population and the regime. The repressive organs of
the state, including the police force, had been expanded to deal with
the growing nation-wide resistance. It became clear that the regime
was determined to answer all protest with the full might of the state
security apparatus. It is in this context that Chief Luthuli, president-
general of the ANC, appealed to the outside world in 1959 to boycott
South Africa and isolate the *apartheid* regime. Luthuli's appeal was
directed mainly at South Africa's major trading partners; if they were
to implement a programme of economic and other sanctions against
Pretoria it could help to prevent a major violent confrontation in
southern Africa.

But Britain and the other major Western powers had no intention of
interfering in the so-called 'internal affairs' of South Africa, let alone
adopting specific measures to help to end the system of white
domination. However, the crisis that was building up could not be
ignored altogether and the British prime minister, Harold Macmillan,
warned the all-white parliament in Cape Town early in 1960 to
recognize the 'wind of change' which was blowing throughout Africa.
Within weeks the world was shocked by news of the Sharpeville
massacre.

In March 1960 a crowd of peaceful demonstrators gathered at
Sharpeville and Langa to protest against the pass laws. The police
fired, killing 72 people and wounding 186, most of them shot in the

back as they were running away. There followed an upsurge of anger throughout the country and thousands of Africans burned their passes. The regime responded by suspending the pass laws, declaring a State of Emergency and detaining over 20 000 opponents.

The ANC and the newly formed Pan-Africanist Congress (PAC) were declared illegal organizations and driven underground. All effective methods of non-violent protest were outlawed and it became clear that the abhorrent system of *apartheid* would have to be removed through armed resistance.

The regime which had itself created this situation then set about utilizing the crisis to deliberately inculcate a 'war psychosis' in the entire white community and to place it on a virtual war footing. White South Africa was to be trained for war against its own black population: housewives were organized into shooting clubs and even school children were given target practice.

'In the same way as the world powers are continually preparing for war, South Africa intends to be ready for internal trouble,' the defence minister explained in 1961. A wide variety of military equipment, including armoured vehicles, tanks, aircraft, naval vessels and large quantities of ammunition, was acquired from abroad. At the same time the regime set about developing a substantial internal armaments and ammunition industry in order to reduce its vulnerability to international boycotts.[2]

The initial expansion of the military forces was intended mainly to suppress internal resistance and to intimidate those who might decide to embark upon guerrilla warfare. It is one of the few situations in the world where a regime was preparing for armed resistance well in advance of such a development taking place.

A second factor which led to acceleration of the military build-up was the process of rapid African decolonization. The newly independent African states felt deeply about the need to eradicate the *apartheid* system and spoke openly about it at the UN and other international forums. Thus, South Africa also developed a second objective: to intimidate the new African states by expanding and displaying its own military might.

A third purpose was to utilize its formal military strength to defy the UN over the occupation of the trust territory of Namibia. Indeed, in later years, those who argued for sanctions to be enforced with a naval blockade in order to remove the South Africans from Namibia were countered by Western claims that such action would be impossible in the light of South Africa's substantial naval and military power.

The fourth reason was that a militarily strong South Africa could also be an attractive ally of the West, not only in the subcontinent but in the Southern Hemisphere as well.

It was for all these reasons, with the central purpose being to maintain the *apartheid* system internally, that the regime embarked on a massive military build-up during the 1960s. This process has continued unabated ever since so that today, with its acknowledged nuclear weapon capability, the Pretoria regime presents a grave threat to international peace and security.

During the post-Sharpeville period the regime relied heavily on its police force to take on the major responsibility for maintaining internal control. Wide powers were given to a reorganized para-military police force which was integrated with the military at various operational levels. At the same time the role of the security police was expanded. Thus a fully-fledged police state came into being to cope with the resistance of the 1960s by means of bannings and banishments, detentions without trial and solitary confinement, well-developed and widely used techniques of physical and mental torture and deaths in detention. The outside world became aware of the nature and type of control exercised by the regime over more than 80 per cent of the population. But the police could not be expected to fully suppress the growing spiral of internal resistance, so the regime, at the same time, began to systematically and deliberately expand the overall capacity of its military forces.

It is by examining the ever-increasing levels of military expenditure that one obtains a clear idea of the true extent of militarization that has taken place since 1960. The figures in Table D, showing military budget estimates since 1960, are based on calculations published by the International Institute for Strategic Studies in London. They are in general underestimates and do not cover expenditure by all government departments. Nevertheless, they give a relatively accurate indication of the rate and scale of military expansion since 1960.

Immediately after Sharpeville the annual defence budget of R44 million in 1960 shot up to R129 million in two years and reached R255 million by 1966/67. In less than 10 years this figure almost doubled again to R500 million by 1974/75, reflecting the growth of armed struggle in the neighbouring Portuguese colonies as well as Rhodesia. There-after, with Angola and Mozambique independent, and following South Africa's invasion of Angola in 1975 with US support, the budget estimate two years later amounted to a staggering R1 300 million.

Table D
South Africa's military budget estimates 1960 to 1986

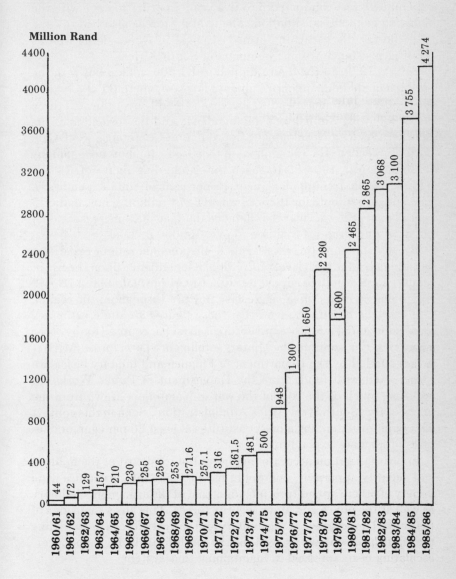

Over the next two years it increased even more sharply by an average
of about R500 million per year to reach the record figure of
R2 280 million by 1978/79. This was because 10 years' defence
expenditure was contracted into five years in order to cope with the
changing geopolitical situation. The military forces also had to cope
with the rapidly escalating armed struggle in Rhodesia as well as
growing resistance within Namibia and South Africa.

During 1979/80 the figure dipped to R1 800 million but with the
creation of an independent Zimbabwe it rose again to R2 465 million
for 1980/81. Defence spending increased steadily over the next three
years, following Zimbabwe's independence and the formation of the
Southern African Development Coordination Conference (SADCC),
until it reached R3 100 million in 1983/84. It shot up again by
R655 million in 1984/85 to reach the astounding figure of R3 755
million, which accounts for about 15 per cent of state expenditure.
The budget estimate for 1985/86 was R4 274 million. Thus, in the 25
years since Sharpeville the defence budget has increased one-
hundred-fold from R44 million to over R4 000 million.

By any standard this represents a phenomenal rate of expansion
and indicates the high level of Pretoria's dependence upon the *use* of
military force – both to impose its authority within Namibia and South
Africa and to maintain an aggressive posture throughout the region.

It must be noted, however, that these figures are underestimates
since substantial military expenditure is in fact accounted for by other
ministries. For example, the Military Intelligence Directorate (MID) is
in fact funded by the Department of Finance and military bases are
constructed with funds from the Department of Public Works. In
addition, much of the cost of the war in Namibia is drawn from the
funds of the 'South West Africa Administration'. Seen in this context
direct military spending alone constitutes at least 20 per cent, or one-
fifth, of all state expenditure.

In order to get an accurate picture of the total cost of the military
and security apparatus, one would have to take into account a wide
variety of other expenditure, including that of the armaments industry
as well as the police and other security forces. This gives some idea of
the central importance of the military and security forces in upholding
the *apartheid* system as well as the prohibitively high and ever-
escalating costs involved in maintaining that system.

The enormous increase in defence expenditure has been accompanied by a substantial expansion of human resources. Most of the military personnel are drawn from the ruling white population and removing them from productive employment adds a further heavy burden to the *apartheid* economy.

In 1965, according to official figures, the military forces numbered 26 500 (army 19 000; navy 3 500; air force 4 000). By 1985 the total number of regular forces numbered 106 400 (army 76 400; navy 9 000; air force 13 000; medical corps 8 000), with another 317 000 reserves and a further 21 000 listed for the South West Africa Territory Force (SWATF). By conservative estimates, Pretoria is able to mobilize a force of well over half a million – mainly white – personnel for military duties. There is a very high cost to be borne for this level of mobilization which is still lower than what the regime would like to have available at its command.

The economy is generally short of skilled white labour and for the military to drain it further produces widespread protest from the business community as well as from those who are enlisted. In addition, active service increasingly involves a risk of death or permanent injury. This and other factors, including conscientious objection, have resulted in hundreds of young white recruits defaulting on the national service and call-up duties, with many deserting the country.

All eligible, young, white males are initially conscripted for a two-year period of national service and thereafter perform regular tours of active duty. Their commitment ends, at the earliest, at the age of 55.

A detailed official explanation about the shortage of human resources was contained in the 1982 Defence White Paper, which said: 'It is in the national interest that the White male should no longer be utilized as the only manpower source. Therefore the SA Defence Forces will be more and more dependent on other sources of manpower, such as White females and members of other population groups, [and]...their utilization is already being based on programmed manpower development plans which extend to 1990.'

The White Paper disclosed the following composition of the full-time force:

Permanent Force	28%
National Servicemen	46%
Voluntary Service Members	3%
Civilians (including black workers)	21%
Auxiliary Service	2%

It went on to state that 'by 1987 the Full-time Force will have expanded by approximately 17%....As regards White females, efforts in the short term will be directed mainly at expanding the Permanent Force' and as far as coloured and Asian males are concerned 'an increase in their numbers is also envisaged'.

With regard to Africans the White Paper specified three categories, 'namely Permanent Force Members, members of Auxiliary Service and civilians'. The permanent force members where trained with those from the 'bantustans' at 21 Battalion at Lenz near Johannesburg.

The White Paper also revealed that, with the exception of a 'multi-national' African unit still to be established, 'Black members who belong to the combat elements of the Auxiliary Service are divided into regional units. These regional units will serve as the nucleus of the independent defence forces of the states concerned.' These defence forces will 'be able to contribute to the protection of their own territories'. It went on to add that the 'expansion of Black regional units in SWA [South West Africa] has been given priority' over those in South Africa and that as for the large number of African civilians serving in the defence force 'the possibility of placing as many of these persons as possible in uniform is being investigated at present'.

Another Defence White Paper in 1984 disclosed that some of the targets mentioned two years earlier could not be met and stated that 'the Permanent Force presently constitutes a smaller percentage of the Full-time Force than two years ago.' The permanent force had been reduced to 25.52 per cent from 28 per cent and the main reason given for this was 'the lack of accommodation for other population groups as well as for White women in certain centres'.

The real reason is undoubtedly the difficulty of recruiting people who do not wish to serve in the armed forces. Another problem is white South Africa's traditional uncertainty about training Africans for warfare when they can so easily utilize those skills to fight the *apartheid* system itself. Thus, the regime is faced with a situation where it needs to recruit more Africans, whose lives it believes are more expendable than those of whites, and at the same time having to balance that with the major security risk involved. How far can it rely upon the victims of the *apartheid* system to protect it, particularly in times of great internal crisis? Understandably, there are powerful forces within the regime who are deeply opposed to any substantial reliance by the military forces on non-white personnel.

The 1984 White Paper stated that while the intake of coloured men had increased by 22 per cent there was no 'growth with regard to Asian men' and 'in the case of Black men there has been an increase of 13 per cent'. According to the 1985–86 *Military Balance*, out of the total

'Regulars' in the Army of 18 400, some 12 000 are white, 5 400 are black and coloured, and 1 000 are women.

From the early 1970s the regime has given serious attention to recruiting women for the military forces. Special study teams were sent abroad and considerable attention was paid to the Israeli system. However, all these efforts have not led to any major intake of white women and since they began to be enlisted on a voluntary basis there have not been many offering themselves for service. Those serving at present are estimated to number about 3 500 and most are members of the permanent force, deployed essentially in non-combat roles. A further 500 white women serve through the small, voluntary, national service scheme.

The failure in enlisting an adequate number of white women for the military forces, with the resultant shortage in total white personnel and the inevitable increase in the intake of African, coloured and Asian personnel, has caused serious misgivings within the ruling National Party. For example, its Cape Congress in September 1983 had before it a resolution calling for compulsory national service for women. This was turned down by Prime Minister P.W. Botha on the grounds that training facilities for the 24 000 eligible white women who turned 17 each year would cost between R600 million and R700 million to establish and 'the country could not afford such expenditure'.[3]

With the establishment of special armies for the 'bantustans' the regime hopes, according to the 1982 White Paper, 'that such defence forces will be able to contribute to the protection of their own territories'. This forms part of the overall strategy to develop a system of 'regional' defence as opposed to 'border' defence only, mainly as a result of the growing success of underground resistance by the ANC.

Since the early 1960s the South African Police (SAP) force has operated in support of the military, and its paramilitary role on 'border duties' in northern Namibia and Rhodesia during the latter half of the decade is well known. This paramilitary role has expanded with the growth of internal resistance and today is equipped with a wide range of weapons which are primarily designed for military purposes.

The 1983 official yearbook on South Africa says 'The SAP is a national force and is the first line of defence in the event of internal unrest.' The nation-wide resistance during 1985 exposed the weakness of this first line of defence and thousands of troops were deployed in the African townships. Even then it became virtually impossible to maintain control and in July 1985 the authorities declared a State of Emergency which gave wide powers to the police.

According to a leading South African lawyer, Sydney Kentridge, under the emergency regulations a policeman 'may do whatever he pleases to maintain what he considers to be law and order... He may shoot, or whip, or tear-gas. However unnecessary or extreme his action, he knows that he is safe as long as he acted in good faith. And he is told anything he does will be presumed to be in good faith.'⁴ The minister responsible for the police, Louis Le Grange, introduced a bill in Parliament in April 1984 whereby acts or offences committed outside South Africa by members of the SAP shall be deemed to have been committed inside the country.⁵

Like the military, the police force is acutely short of personnel, and in October 1985 the regime announced that it would expand the 45 000 police force (of whom about half are white) by 11 000 men, or 25 per cent, during the next 17 months. As the police force has expanded over the years there has been a steady reduction in the proportion of white recruits. The police have their own Maleoskop Counter-Insurgency Training Centre near Groblersdal which by 1983 could handle 5 000 trainees a year in 'all aspects of counter-insurgency, combating of urban terrorism and riot control measures'.

Soon after the Sharpeville massacre, a reserve police force was established, consisting of recruits who perform part-time duties in their spare time. Within this force there are special units, such as a diving unit and a radio reserve consisting of radio amateurs.

The military and police forces are integrated in their operational and command structures and when the first line of defence – the police – cannot cope with internal unrest, the military is called in to assist. On the other hand, specially trained members of the paramilitary police force are deployed in operations beyond South Africa's borders, on sabotage missions and for certain 'border duties'. Both forces are short of personnel and the police have a much larger proportion of black personnel than the military.

In addition to regular police and military units, there are several special forces (such as the *Koevoet* in Namibia). For these and other units the regime has recruited several thousand mercenaries from abroad, with the largest intake coming from Rhodesia on the eve of Zimbabwe's independence. At that time they also recruited a large number of black 'auxiliary' forces from Rhodesia and more than 5 000 were kept in camps in the northern Transvaal.[6]

The mercenaries are not restricted to these special units and also serve in the standard arms of the South African Defence Force (SADF). Some 'special operations', such as the attempted *coup d'état* against the government of President Albert René in the Seychelles in November 1981, include both mercenaries and members of the SADF. That force was led by Colonel 'Mad Mike' Hoare, a well-known mercenary commander, but included a senior officer of the SADF, which had also provided the weapons for the group.[7]

South African legislation requires foreign nationals resident in that country to serve in the armed forces. Legislation enacted in April 1984 meant that immigrants with permanent residence permits automatically became South African citizens by naturalization, so those aged between 15 and 25 were liable for two years' full-time national service plus 12 years on the active reserve.[8] These provisions are not only encouraging a larger group of young white men to resist recruitment but also contribute to the substantial outflow of recent white immigrants as well as deterring others from going to settle in South Africa.

It is quite clear that, despite the various measures taken since 1960, the regime is facing a serious crisis of manpower. Moreover, the crisis during 1985 revealed the extent to which the military and police forces are stretched, with the regime unable to assert its authority in many areas.

P.W. Botha's accession to prime minister in September 1978, after serving as defence minister for 12 years, heralded the growing ascendency of the military in the white political process in which decision-making and planning came to be dominated by security considerations. Soon after taking over from John Vorster, Botha reorganized the power structure and created a 'National Security Management System' which transformed the State Security Council (SSC) into the most powerful decision-making body in the country. He trimmed the bureaucracy, applying the management methods of the SADF to government. Military men became his key advisors, and Botha's takeover of the administration was referred to as a 'constitutional *coup d'état*'.

The SSC was streamlined in 1979 from an *ad hoc* body that met irregularly and was subservient to cabinet into a powerful planning body whose fortnightly meetings precede cabinet meetings.

Technically, the SSC is one of four cabinet committees (the others deal with economic, social and constitutional affairs) but, according to a prominent Afrikaner scholar, the minutes of other cabinet committees are attached to minutes of the full cabinet for circulation, while those of the SSC are not. Decisions of the SSC are not automatically circulated or subject to confirmation by the full cabinet.

The secretary to the SSC who presided over the reorganization was Lieutenant-General A.J. van Deventer, a high-ranking military officer and close confidante of P.W. Botha. He was recently replaced by General Pieter van der Westhuizen, former head of military intelligence. The SSC, and its secretary, act as a kind of 'gate-keeper' through which information is circulated and through which all important government business must pass before submission to cabinet. Technically, the cabinet remains a superior body and may return decisions to the SSC but in practice it rarely does so, due to the powerful representation of cabinet ministers and military leaders on the council.

As a result of widespread speculation about the precise role of the SSC, and to play down claims that the military were taking over the running of the country, some details of its membership, which was hitherto secret, were officially disclosed in September 1983. The SSC is chaired by P.W. Botha, now state president, and includes the next

Table E
South Africa's Security Establishment

The National Security Management System

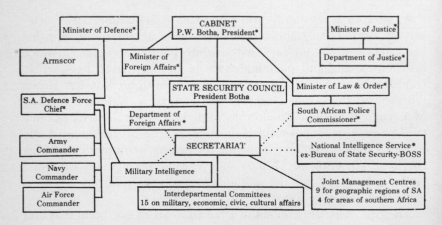

*members of the State Security Council, a statutory body which also includes the senior cabinet minister

senior cabinet minister as well as the ministers of defence, foreign affairs, law and order, and justice. Other members include the head of military intelligence, the chief of the defence force, the commissioner of police, the head of the national intelligence service, and department heads whom the president chooses to co-opt as 'observers', such as the directors of foreign affairs, justice, or information.

The statutory responsibility of the SSC is to advise government on 'national policy and strategy in relation to the security of the Republic' and it concerns itself with a wide range of issues not normally associated with defence and security, including foreign and regional policy, labour, sport, cultural and religious matters, among others.

The secretariat of the SSC consists of four branches: an administrative branch, the strategy branch, a strategic communication branch (responsible for 'advice and co-ordination in the war of words'), and the national intelligence interpretation branch. The latter co-ordinates intelligence provided by the police, the MID, and the National Intelligence Service (NIS, formerly the Bureau of State Security, BOSS). The SSC also has various interdepartmental committees. The 'grassroots' component of the SSC network is the Joint Management Centres which are officially known by their Afrikaans abbreviation, GBS. There are nine GBSs which service the different geographic areas of the country, demarcated according to the nine main areas served by the SADF, while another four cover countries in the region. One study, called 'The Rise of the South African Security Establishment', says the 'most disturbing' result of the shift in power to the security establishment – especially to the defence force – is 'the apparent efforts to destabilize the domestic order of foreign states'.[9]

The pre-eminent role of the SSC in the overall decision-making system means in effect a dominant role for the military and security forces, and diminished responsibility for both the cabinet and white parliament. The establishment of the tri-cameral parliament in an effort to co-opt Indian and coloured people onto the side of the ruling white community thus did not represent any major inroad into the white power structure. The constitutional reform has in fact concentrated substantial dictatorial power in the hands of the president resulting in a major erosion of 'democracy', even for the white electorate.

In the light of these developments it would be true to say that white South Africa's decision-making system has been transformed in order to cope with growing internal resistance. There are very few aspects of civilian life that are not dominated by military and security considerations, and in the process the military has acquired substantial political power. It is therefore true to speak of a 'Botha–Malan' regime since that reflects accurately where effective power lies.

To bring about this transformation, the regime has emphasized during the last decade that the threat to white South Africa is not limited to the border war but represents a 'total onslaught' against the republic which it claims is directed by the Soviet Union. This can only be countered with a 'total strategy' to resist the 'onslaught' at every level. This process has gone through various stages, and in 1982 the chief of the defence force, General Constand Viljoen, announced a new 'area defence system' to meet the growing 'area war' assault by the ANC. He claimed that the ANC was planning an 'area war' of widely spread attacks aimed at creating 'an atmosphere of instability' and at spreading security manpower.[10]

General Viljoen predicted that the military would have the task of holding the ring while the politicians work out a political solution – something that has not happened so far – and he stressed this point again on his retirement in 1985. Inevitably, as the confrontation has grown inside the country, the military has had to take on additional responsibility for the day-to-day physical security of the country and its white population; the loss of political authority and control over the majority African population has had to be overcome by the deployment of massive force throughout the country. Now that the last line of defence, the military forces, are being deployed to maintain civilian order, South Africa has virtually reached its 'security ceiling'.

The ever-increasing annual defence budgets have contributed to the development of a large internal armaments manufacturing industry as part of an overall plan to make South Africa 'self-sufficient' for all its strategic requirements. But even with substantial financial resources at its command the regime has not been able to achieve the intended degree of self-sufficiency in the production of arms and ammunition.

Even before the imposition of an international arms embargo by the UN Security Council in 1963, Western companies had begun to invest heavily in South Africa's new armaments industry. In 1962, Imperial Chemicals Industries (ICI) of Britain joined De Beers in revitalizing the African Explosives and Chemicals Industries Ltd (AECI), and set up three factories to produce tear-gas, ammunition for small arms, and anti-tank and anti-aircraft rockets.

Following the two resolutions adopted by the UN Security Council in 1963 and 1964 to prohibit the supply of arms – as well as technology to produce arms – to South Africa, external collaboration in the development of internal arms production intensified. Items which could not be manufactured in South Africa were delivered openly to the Pretoria regime, as either 'civilian' or 'dual-purpose' products, which were not covered by the way in which certain governments interpreted their obligations under the arms embargo.

In November 1965, Marconi of Britain constructed a modern radar network along South Africa's northern borders and began a 20-year association with the Pretoria regime, regularly updating the radar systems and providing modern equipment for new installations.

South Africa had little difficulty in securing Western co-operation to undermine the international arms embargo, and in 1965 Defence Minister Fouche was able to boast that he had already obtained 120 licences to manufacture weapons locally. South Africa, he said was 'already practically self-sufficient so far as the production of small weapons, ammunition and explosives were concerned'.

Preparations were made in advance to produce military aircraft and by 1967 the Atlas Aircraft Corporation began constructing, under Italian licence, the Aermacchi MB 326 under the name 'Impala'. These aircraft had most of the vital components imported from abroad, including initially the Rolls Royce engines; these were later manufactured in South Africa under licence granted by Piaggio of Italy, which had in turn received the original licence from Rolls Royce in Britain. This was one way to circumvent the partial arms embargo imposed by the British government.

The costly process of developing an internal arms production capability was partially overcome by the massive annual increases in the defence budget. Defence Minister Fouche revealed in 1964 that defence contracts worth R35 million would be placed with South African industries in that year alone. He added, 'The fact that Defence is spending so much is one of the greatest inducements for new industrial development.'[11]

The adoption of the international arms embargo and threats of further boycotts served to accelerate industrial development in certain sectors of the economy and in effect amounted to advance preparations for a siege. At the beginning it was generally considered desirable to promote 'import replacement', but the threat of more effective international measures changed the goal to one of 'self-sufficiency', which was considered vital for national survival. There was, inevitably, substantial state intervention in the economy but, due to the prohibitive costs involved, it was impossible to achieve 'self-sufficiency' even in the arms sector which was considered to be of the greatest strategic significance.

The South African Armaments Corporation (ARMSCOR) was established in 1968 and amalgamated with the government's Armaments Production Board in 1977 to form 'an autonomous government organization'. Armscor has nine main subsidiaries and claims to have more than 1 000 private subcontractors. Annual turn-over in 1984 was stated to be R1 600 million and its assets then amounted to R1 400 million. Armscor's chairman, Commandant Piet Marais, said in an interview published in 1984 that the company itself employed 33 000 people but that a total of about 80 000 people are actually involved in armament production throughout the country.[12] He also disclosed that Armscor had facilities 'to produce the necessary volume of items such as ammunition'. Commandant Marais explained "That was done as a form of insurance which has cost a certain premium, and if we take up some of that capacity for exports it is obviously of tremendous help to us.'[13]

The cost of simply maintaining existing facilities for the production of arms and ammunition is proving to be quite expensive. Since a constantly diminishing proportion of defence expenditure is being allocated to equipment, that raises the costs even further. The assembly and production of new types of equipment is even more expensive, and when taken together with the large sums which need to be paid to smugglers, middle-men and others in order to obtain vital parts and components from abroad, one gets an idea of the prohibitive costs involved.

The Pretoria regime has over the years tried to popularize the myth that it is 'self-sufficient' in arms and ammunition. This is done not only to justify the enormous cost of establishing an internal armaments industry but to discredit the international arms embargo and to give the impression that the SADF is adequately equipped with modern arms. The South African authorities are not alone in perpetuating this impression which is repeated, at times with even greater exaggeration, by various Western defence publications. Thus there exists the widespread belief that South Africa is in fact 'self-sufficient' and meets virtually all of its defence needs from internal production.

The truth is that, despite the development of a substantial domestic weapons production capability, the SADF has been severely hit in certain key sectors, even by the weak and limited international arms embargo.

The South African armed forces acquire military security equipment in a variety of ways. Arms which are 'made' in South Africa are those manufactured under formal licensing and other similar arrangements, or those based on 'borrowed' foreign technology. Those described as 'indigenously developed' items are essentially adaptations of existing overseas products. Most of these involve a large percentage of foreign-made components which are imported either as normal commercial products or smuggled into the country by various devious means.

Secondly, a large quantity of so-called 'dual-purpose' equipment, including sophisticated military radar systems, are acquired on the open market. Where necessary, the overseas government concerned even provides export licences for restricted items on the grounds that these do not amount to a breach of the arms embargo. Export licences are also issued for purchases made directly by the South African military and police forces.

Thirdly, items which cannot be acquired by the above methods are obtained by means of well-established clandestine smuggling operations which somehow are not detected by the respective overseas governments nor by any of their security and intelligence services. The few cases which have been exposed, with some resulting in prosecutions, have been due largely to the vigilance of the anti-*apartheid* organizations and the media, or because of prompt action by customs officials.

Fourthly, some arms and components which are generally prohibited for export to South Africa by the major Western countries are acquired via Israel, Taiwan, Chile or other allies.

Many of the problems faced by the internal armaments industry arise out of the fact that the industrialized sector as a whole is highly dependent on foreign technology and components. A recent Study Group Report issued by the Department of Industries and Commerce confirmed that 'South Africa is largely dependent on imported technology' and went on to state that 'the acquisition of expertise is facilitated by South Africa's close ties with many multi-national enterprises controlled from the developed countries'. The dependence on foreign technology and components becomes a much more serious problem for the internal arms production industry because of the high degree of sophistication involved, together with the relatively low production runs which result in massive overhead costs.

Although there is considerable secrecy surrounding South Africa's overseas arms purchases it is not impossible to make some realistic estimates. According to a finding of the World Campaign against Military and Nuclear Collaboration with South Africa, 'more than half of the total amount spent by ARMSCOR in acquiring military hardware is in fact spent abroad'. Evidence presented to the UN Security Council's Arms Embargo Committee in 1984 stated that 'out of an annual expenditure of R 1.62 billion, over R 900 million is spent overseas and only about R 700 million at home'.[14]

Of course claims of 'self-sufficiency' can be made more easily if one refers to the total payments made by the SADF for its purchases to enterprises based in South Africa *without* taking into account the cost of plant, parts and components acquired by them from abroad. The figures can be further distorted by including items which are made entirely abroad but purchased via either a local subsidiary of a. multinational company or an agent in South Africa. Thus, the degree of 'self-sufficiency' is directly dependent on the way in which the figures are actually calculated.

Moreover, this method of assessing whether all of the needs of the SADF are in fact met by 'internal' purchases does not point to the acute shortages in various critical sectors which are not being met. A close examination of official documents gives some idea of the problem even if, for obvious reasons, they are gross understatements and merely reflect the tip of the iceberg.

For example, paragraph 37 of the 1984 Defence White Paper opens with the following sentence: *'The provision of spares for highly sophisticated equipment in the SA Air Force has been a serious problem.'* The gravity of the situation comes through in a later sentence: 'As regards the provision of spare parts, priorities have been identified in respect of 10 types of aircraft which require specific attention.' When it is realized that the air force has relatively few types of aircraft it becomes clear that virtually the entire air force is affected.

Paragraph 39 opens with another disclosure: 'With the phasing out of the Shackleton maritime aircraft towards the end of 1984 the SA Air Force will have no long-range maritime reconnaissance capability.' The South African authorities have been making strenuous efforts in recent years to acquire new reconnaissance aircraft but have so far failed to obtain any replacements due to the arms embargo. The White Paper describes the situation thus: 'The replacement of the long-range maritime aircraft continues to receive attention.'

The situation in respect of the navy is no better. Although South Africa claims to 'manufacture' a few small, missile strike-crafts, the 1984 White Paper concedes that 'these vessels only meet part of the current and future needs of the SA Navy'. In the next paragraph it is pointed out that the three Daphne submarines 'have already seen thirteen years of service' and that the 'replacement vessel, SAS Tafelberg, has also become obsolescent and is being modernized and modified'. It is expected that this will enable 'the needs of the SA Navy' to be met 'until a new replenishment vessel replaces SAS Tafelberg'. Thus items which would otherwise have to be scrapped are having their service life temporarily extended by costly modifications.

In its conclusion, the 1984 White Paper claims that the success of the SADF during military operations 'can be ascribed to the sound armaments development of the RSA and the manufacturing capability developed over the past decade'. The next sentence explains: 'Achievements in the field of local armaments manufacture include the R4 rifle, the G5 gun, the Ratel infantry combat vehicle, mine-resistant vehicles, missiles and strike craft.' Allowing for the fact that these 'manufactured' items involve a heavy external dependence, that still leaves a large variety of arms and related equipment which has to be acquired directly from abroad – or done without.

Thus the White Paper itself concludes: 'A major problem is that some of the most reliable main armaments are obsolescent.' Earlier, it stated: 'Objectives in respect of preparedness programmes and the manufacture of arms could not be fully achieved owing to a restricted SADF budget during the past five years and also as a result of the economic recession.'

These extracts from just one Defence White Paper point to the serious problems faced by the military forces in terms of simply maintaining the existing level of operational capability in certain crucial sectors, let alone expanding it to meet the growing crisis faced by the regime. It also exposes the grave problems associated with having to keep relying on major items which are in fact 'obsolescent'. Thus it is possible to state conclusively that:

1. Those items which are 'made' in South Africa are highly dependent on external sources of technology, plant, parts and components.

2. Items 'made' in South Africa are not able to meet the overall needs of the SADF and the regime itself admits that 'some of the most reliable main armaments are obsolescent'.

3. Even the limited and weak arms embargo is depriving South Africa of some vital military equipment and forcing it to allocate

massive resources to try to 'manufacture' certain items internally while
acquiring others from abroad through expensive smuggling operations.

4. Despite substantial efforts to recoup some of the costs of
weapons production through exports South Africa has so far failed to
win any important markets and the earnings have not been adequate
to make a significant contribution to the exorbitant costs involved in
internal weapons production.

5. Faced with an acute and growing economic and political crisis,
South Africa is unlikely to be able to proceed with its present weapons
production plans which will have to be seriously curtailed.

6. The SADF will increasingly have to make do with a *smaller*
percentage of its budget available for the purchase of arms and will
consequently have to rely on fewer and more out-dated weapons in
several vital areas, resulting in a serious weakening of its overall
military capability.

The UN Security Council first imposed an arms embargo against South
Africa in August 1963 when it adopted Resolution 181 calling on all
states 'to cease forthwith the sale and shipment of arms, ammunition
of all types and military vehicles to South Africa'. In December 1963,
through Resolution 182, a second decision was taken which also
covered 'equipment and materials for the manufacture or maintenance of arms and ammunition in South Africa'. In 1964 a third
resolution was adopted, reaffirming the earlier decisions and calling
upon all states to implement the embargo.

Britain and the United States applied a limited partial embargo
while France, and later Italy, openly flouted the decisions. The French
newspaper *Le Monde* stated in May 1968 that 'France had become the
principal supplier of arms to South Africa'. By that year South Africa
had become France's third biggest arms customer, after Israel and
Belgium. It is in this period that South Africa ordered from France
modern submarines, radar and missile systems, as well as helicopters
and Mirage fighter planes.

Those early decisions of the Security Council were undermined in
various ways by several Western governments which did not have the
political will to impose a strict arms embargo, with the result that
the South African regime was able to obtain a substantial amount of its
military requirements from abroad. Inevitably, there were repeated
efforts by African and non-aligned states to impose a mandatory arms

embargo but these were all defeated by the joint veto power of Britain, France and the United States.

In October 1977, when yet another triple veto was cast, it produced so much protest that the Western powers felt obliged to submit a much weaker text. This was adopted on 4 November as Resolution 418 (1977).

Despite its weakness, this represented a major success and was the first ever mandatory decision taken by the UN against one of its members. Moreover, the resolution had the potential to make a significant impact since the text of operative paragraphs 2, 3 and 4 is very clear:

2. Decides that all States shall cease forthwith any provision to South Africa of arms and related material of all types, including the sale or transfer of weapons and ammunition, military vehicles and equipment, paramilitary police equipment, and spare parts for the aforementioned, and shall cease as well the provision of all types of equipment and supplies, and grants of licensing arrangements, for the manufacture or maintenance of the aforementioned;

3. Calls on all States to review, having regard to the objectives of this resolution, all existing contractual arrangements with and licences granted to South Africa relating to the manufacture and maintenance of arms, ammunition of all types and military equipment and vehicles, with a view to terminating them;

4. Further decides that all States shall refrain from any co-operation with South Africa in the manufacture and development of nuclear weapons; (for full text see Appendix 5).

In an address to the UN Special Committee against Apartheid in December 1977, a representative of the British Anti-Apartheid Movement stated: 'If the present mandatory decision is applied strictly, then I am convinced that the South African defence forces can be denied any further arms and defence equipment as well as spare parts and components which will make much of their existing weaponry inefficient and non-operational: that is, provided that nobody sabotages the embargo.'[15] However, experience since the adoption of the mandatory resolution is similar to that of the earlier decisions of the Security Council – that the objectives of the embargo are seriously undermined by the way in which it is interpreted and implemented by South Africa's major trading partners and certain other countries.

In order to try to avoid some of the earlier evasions, the Security Council decided to establish a committee to monitor and supervise the mandatory arms embargo. Despite its relatively weak mandate, the committee initially issued some important reports, including one in September 1980 'on ways and means of making the mandatory arms embargo more effective'.[16] After reviewing the various problems encountered in the implementation of the embargo, the committee submitted 16 important proposals to make it more effective.

One of the proposals was that 'the embargo should include imports of arms and related material of all types *from South Africa*'. Acting on this proposal, the Security Council adopted Resolution 558 (1984) which requested member states to 'refrain from importing arms, ammunition of all types and military vehicles produced in South Africa'. (for full text see Appendix 6).

The Security Council has therefore only partially adopted one of the 16 proposals; Resolution 558 (1984) does not cover the importation of military 'related material' and, even more important, it is a non-mandatory decision. The Western countries refused to yield on these two points despite intense efforts by the non-aligned members of the Security Council.

At present, there is no immediate prospect of any further measures being adopted by the Security Council and its 421 Committee has been left with virtually no effective role since 1980, largely due to the blocking role of Britain and the United States.

One of the main deterrents to making the arms embargo more effective is the fact that each UN member state determines how to interpret its own obligations in terms of the mandatory resolution. There is no reference to the Security Council in drawing up the necessary legal measures and no systematic reports are submitted about their actual operation. Thus we have a situation where every country uses different rules to enforce the same embargo; and even the same country has different regulations from time to time, depending on changes in government or in government policy.

The existence of major loopholes in national legislation usually come to light only when specific cases are publicly exposed. Then, in most cases, the government in question explains that the particular transaction is not in breach of the embargo because it is a 'civilian' or 'dual-purpose' item, or that the item is not intended to be used for an essentially military purpose.

Even where there is clear *prima facie* evidence of a breach of national legislation, it still depends on the level of enthusiasm of the authorities in order to ensure that adequate investigations are conducted, the offenders apprehended, and proper criminal proceedings instituted. The general experience of anti-*apartheid* organizations is that most Western governments attach very little importance to enforcing even their limited national embargoes and are reluctant to prosecute alleged offenders.

In the few cases where criminal prosecutions have in fact taken place yet another major weakness in national legislation has been exposed. The penalties provided for offences against the arms embargo are so weak that they do not serve as an effective deterrent. Besides, most offenders calculate from experience that the risk of actually being caught and convicted is so low that they can confidently engage in highly profitable deals on behalf of the South African regime. Even where particular cases are exposed and some lead to prosecutions, the governments concerned do not feel obliged to provide all the available information to the UN.

The World Campaign has repeatedly emphasized the importance of making a comprehensive study of all of the relevant national legislation enacted by individual states with a view to blocking existing loopholes and making the embargo more effective. But the Security Council's 421 Committee has so far not been able to act on this suggestion. As a result, the World Campaign has had to conduct some of its own research about particular aspects of national legislation in order to follow up specific cases. But such information is only of limited value.[17]

In July 1985 the British Anti-Apartheid Movement published the most detailed report so far, *How Britain Arms Apartheid*.[18] This comprehensive study of British policy and legislation provides detailed information about specific breaches and identifies all the existing loopholes and other weaknesses. It also offers concrete proposals for making the mandatory embargo more effective. Similar studies for certain other countries are now being prepared. When these are published they will help to shed light on the gross inadequacy of existing national legislative measures which enable the South African authorities to circumvent and undermine the mandatory arms embargo.

In September 1983, six years after the embargo was imposed, no government had yet informed the Security Council 'about particular licences and patents which may have been revoked or discontinued by companies or other enterprises within its jurisdiction'.[19] The Italian government claimed, in June 1979, that in respect of the licences granted for the Aermacchi MB 326 and the Rolls Royce engines 'the licences were ceded in 1964 *una tantum,* that is, without a provision for their termination. As the supply of technical assistance and spare parts for both the MB 326 and the Rolls Royce Viper engines has been discontinued since 1972, the unilateral withdrawal of the licences at this stage would not affect in the least the production, and in fact would just result in a net benefit for South Africa.'[20]

Thus, it appeared as if the Italian government was claiming that a decision adopted under Chapter VII of the UN Charter to counteract a threat to international peace and security could not be implemented because there was no provision for 'termination' of the respective licences in the original agreement with South Africa. This raises important questions about the binding authority of mandatory decisions adopted by the UN Security Council within the Italian legal system. However, in the above answer, the Italian government appears to be more concerned about the possibility of South Africa continuing to produce the licensed aircraft and engines even if the licences are terminated, claiming that this would 'just result in a net benefit for South Africa'. Presumably their concern was that South Africa would stop payment of fees and royalties to the holders of the licences in Italy.

The arms embargo is extremely weak in the field of licences, patents and other arrangements to provide technology to South Africa for its internal arms production. The situation is made worse by the fact that virtually all of the major Western multinationals have subsidiaries or associate companies in South Africa and are therefore able to pass on technical information easily without any monitoring.

In those areas where it is impossible, or too expensive, to manufacture or assemble particular items within South Africa the embargo is undermined by the way in which 'arms and related material' is defined by individual governments.[21] For example, it was revealed that a British firm, International Computers Ltd (ICL), had supplied computers to the South African authorities for use by the police and for a South African plant involved in weapons manufacture. The British government responded to representations by stating that since the computers themselves did not form part of a weapons system, they were not covered by the embargo.

A second problem related to the fact that although at that time (April 1979) the US administration had announced that it prohibited *all* supplies to the South African military establishment – a policy that was relaxed under the Reagan administration – several other states continued to provide what they considered to be 'non-military' items direct to the South African military.

A third problem related to 'dual-purpose' or 'civilian' items – such as aircraft – which were supplied to various companies or civilian purchasers in South Africa and which later were found to be used by the South African military establishment. A wide variety of aircraft from the United States had been obtained in this way.

There were also difficulties relating to communications and radar equipment. For example, the Advokaat communications system based near Simonstown was described by the South African defence authorities as a joint maritime operations centre from which the operational command of the maritime forces was carried out. However, the Federal Republic of Germany (FRG), from where it was purchased, maintained that the Advokaat was an entirely civilian project and did not have much military significance.

These and other cases show the need for a precise definition of what constitutes 'arms and related material'. It has been suggested that an international check-list of items should be issued in order to avoid difficulties in determining what items are prohibited by the arms embargo. This problem has not been resolved and each country continues to implement its own version of the embargo, enabling the South African military authorities to obtain a substantial quantity of military equipment from abroad.

Some of the major areas in which the embargo needs to be tightened have been described in detail in several expert studies. A comprehensive study about computer exports to South Africa published in 1982 revealed that the policy applied by Washington was not as comprehensive as was generally understood.[22]

In May 1981, a document published in London showed that the Plessey AR-3D radar system supplied under licence by Britain amounted to a breach of the mandatory arms embargo. The foreign secretary, Lord Carrington, stated that 'the equipment is to be used in the South African civil and military air control system' and explained that 'integration of the operation of national air traffic control systems is standard practice in most countries'. Furthermore, when conclusive proof was provided of a South African military officer being trained by Plessey to operate the system, Lord Carrington explained: 'I do not regard the presence of the SADF personnel [in the UK] as having constituted a breach of the government's policy of non-collaboration with the South African government on military matters since they were here as part of a private arrangement directly between the company and their customers.'[23]

A major Marconi contract with South Africa for the supply of a tropospheric long-range communications system came to light in 1975 as a result of the refusal by one of its engineers, Mr Jock Hall, to work on the project. He was suspended, and ultimately left the company, but the system was still exported directly to the South African Defence Department.[24] There was another revelation involving Marconi in 1983, and again it involved radar equipment licensed for export to South Africa. The British government explained to the House of Commons that the licence was granted on the grounds that 'it is for use in air traffic control in South Africa and involves no infringement of the UN arms embargo'. A Marconi spokesman said; 'We are updating the existing S247 surveillance radar system which we installed in the 1960s.' The *Jane's Weapons System Yearbook* describes the S247 as a 'high-power static radar system used for defence purposes'.[25]

A major problem with most of these deals is that Britain and several other Western countries refuse to disclose, even to their own parliaments, details of licences granted for the export to South Africa of listed items. Because of this secrecy, the facts become known only if there is some unexpected disclosure, and so there is no way of knowing how many such deals are negotiated. There is also a wide range of external military and security collaboration with South Africa that is not covered by the existing embargo.[26]

The 1982 Defence White Paper in South Africa stated that due to the over-production of arms in the world, and the difficulty of penetrating 'this highly competitive market', Armscor relied 'mainly on the fact that the products available from the RSA are operationally evaluated and tested and the highest quality standards are maintained throughout'. Its subsequent campaign of advertizing in overseas defence publications was launched under the slogan: 'Born of necessity. Tested under fire'.

In September 1982, Armscor invited foreign news correspondents to a champagne breakfast to announce the launch of the G6 artillery vehicle, with the G5 155mm gun mounted on a mobile six-wheel chassis. Armscor marketing officials claimed it to be a 'world beater' since the self-propelled G6 had speed and mobility not normally associated with heavy artillery, which is usually pulled on trailers or mounted on tanks.[27]

Armscor announced that its arms exports for the previous year amounted to R10 million but that it intended to raise this figure to between R100 million and R150 million per year. A senior official identified the sales target areas as those countries with similar conditions to South Africa in South America, the Middle East, Far East and Africa.[28] Earlier reports that South Africa had made an agreement to supply Morocco with Eland armoured cars were confirmed in the *Military Balance 1981–82,* published by the International Institute for Strategic Studies in London, which stated that delivery for the armoured cars was due in 1980.

Despite all the secrecy surrounding South Africa's arms exports, it is not too difficult to identify some of its major customers. Israel has, over the years, developed a close military relationship with Pretoria; several of its weapons have been sold to South Africa and some have been made there. There are several joint weapons production schemes, and Israel is obviously an important customer as well as a transit point for exports to other countries. Several fellow-pariah nations, including Taiwan, Chile, Paraguay and Argentina, have decorated Armscor officials and South African military officers, and these would seemingly constitute some of its main customers.

During Britain's war over the Falklands there were widespread reports of arms and ammunition from South Africa being airlifted to Argentina. Relying on Armscor sources, one newspaper claimed that the South African frequency-hopping radio devices 'amazed British soldiers who captured them from the Argentines'.[29]

In October 1982, Armscor managed to display some of its products at the Defendory Expo '82 held in Piraeus, Greece. When the Greek government was informed after the second day of the exhibition, the exhibits were removed and the Armscor delegation was expelled from the country. How Armscor managed to gain entry to the exhibition is still not clear. But the chairman, who was also expelled, was reported to be expecting 'good business' despite the premature closing of the exhibit. He added that 'it was especially satisfying that our first international show took place in a NATO [North Atlantic Treaty Organization] country'.[30] Among those items on show were the newly announced frequency-hopping radio devices, the G5 155mm howitzer and the Kukri artillery rocket, as well as videos and slide shows of the G6 and the Valkiri air-to-air missile.[31]

During 1983 and 1984, several Western defence publications carried major feature articles, applauding South African-made military equipment and helping Pretoria to promote its arms exports. They, naturally, also carried expensive Armscor advertisements as part of the overall export drive.[32]

The Samil range of military vehicles and trailers are in fact a mix of several overseas models, owing their origin mainly to the Magirus-Deutz and Unimogs of the FRG. The four-ton Unimog chassis is also the basis for the Valkiri 127mm rocket lauancher.

The Valkiri artillery rocket system, claimed to be indigenously developed, is similar to the Taiwanese Working Bee-6 system. The 'indigenously' developed Skorpioen anti-ship missile was originally the name under which the South African Navy deployed the Israeli Gabriel 11 missiles, which are similar to the Taiwanese Hsiung-Feng naval weapons. The similarities between several weapons system claimed to be 'indigenously' developed by South Africa, Israel and Taiwan indicate the existence of high level co-operation between them on several projects.

The Kukri air-to-air missile which the South African government claims to be 'indigenously' developed is said to have a unique helmet-mounted sight for target designation but is otherwise similar to the Matra Magic missile and uses similar technology. The Kukri is also described as the V3B air-to-air missile.

It is interesting, too, that both South African and Taiwanese missile boats are versions of the Israeli Reshef fast attack craft.

The production of the well-publicized G5 155mm howitzer was first announced by P.W. Botha in April 1979 when he claimed that it was South African-designed and made from local steel with South African know-how. This was considered a 're-markable' achievement for Armscor which had 'taken only 24 months from the design to the production stage'. Subsequently it became known that the gun was in fact acquired from the Vermont-based Space Research Corporation. The elaborate smuggling operations involved South Africa purchasing a share in the company as well as having the system tested in Antigua before arranging for the smuggling of the equipment, as well as thousands of shells, to South Africa. Because of the ease and speed with which much of the equipment was exported via the United States and other intermediaries there were several investigations about possible official complicity in the deal. According to one report issued in Washington by the House of Representatives' Sub-Committee on Africa, there must have been high level involvement in bending the rules on the part of the State Department, the US Army and the CIA to enable South Africa to acquire the system.[33]

In an interview in 1984, the chairman of Armscor, Commandant Piet Marais, disclosed details about the Space Research deal and explained that it arose in the aftermath of the South African invasion of Angola in 1975 when they were 'being outgunned by quite a few Russian weapons'. It is not known how far the G5 has been used in operations by the South African military forces and some experts claim that it is not a system of great value to the SADF. The G6 was only a prototype and estimated to cost over US$ 1.3 million, for the mobile vehicle alone *without* the gun.

The South African Eland armoured vehicles (based on the French Panhard AML 60/90) and the Ratel combat vehicle (similar to the French Berliet VXB-170 but believed to be based on FRG automotive parts) also form part of the export drive.

In March 1984, the South African media reported Armscor's participation in the Fida '84 international military show in Santiago at the invitation of the Chilean Air Force. Following its ejection from the Greek exhibition in 1982 and its failure to participate in any other international exhibitions since then, the Armscor officials were jubilant and said that in 'contrast' with their Greek experience 'our reception has been excellent'.[34] This is not surprising since South African–Chilean relations are at a high military level; the former South African ambassador to Chile, Lieutenant-General J.R. Dutton, was replaced in 1984 with the retired chief of the air force, Lieutenant-General A.M. Muller.

It is important to recognize that with the end of the Rhodesian war South Africa lost its most lucrative arms market. At almost the same time the SADF had to reduce its percentage of arms purchases due to increasing operational costs. Thus, not only were there increasing overhead costs to be met by reduced sales but new plants which needed more funds. For example, in 1982 a R176-million expansion to Pretoria Metal Pressings, one of Armscor's three munitions companies, was completed and these and other capital costs could not possibly be recovered from an expansion of arms exports. The efforts to penetrate the international market since 1982 have not produced any significant results and consequently investment in new production facilities have virtually come to a halt. Short production runs inevitably result in very high costs and when the items produced have in turn to be offered at low prices, in order to compete on the international market, Armscor is forced to bear massive losses.

The South African arms industry is facing an extremely serious crisis and to continue to produce at the existing level, let alone expand any of its facilities, it will have to be allocated an increasing proportion of very scarce resources.

In the confrontation that is building up in the region, the Pretoria regime is becoming very anxious about the improved ability of several neighbouring states to protect themselves militarily. For over two years, senior South African officers have been warning that Angola, Mozambique and other states in the region have improved their defences, and are now equipped with modern MiG jet fighters and early warning radar systems.[35]

Towards the end of 1985 these concerns became so acute that South African defence publications printed lengthy reports on the relative force strengths of neighbouring states and military officers began to give special briefings on the subject. In November 1985, one Western defence publication reported warnings by South African military experts 'that a sophisticated radar network has been installed by the front-line African states capable of monitoring aircraft movements within South Africa'. They were also reported as believing that 'missile fighter aircraft in hostile African states may now outnumber the South African Air Force by as much as two to one'.[36]

The SADF is clearly in some difficulty. While it may be able to inflict considerable damage to the economies of individual African states through destabilization and acts of aggression, it has long borders with these states and cannot possibly entertain any comfort from the prospect of turning them into hostile countries.

According to its own admission, it can no longer count on total air superiority. Shortage of tanks is overcome by concentrating on equipping itself with anti-tank missiles. Lack of new fighter aircraft means that it relies instead on fitting the existing old ones with new types of missiles. Shortage of naval vessels, submarines and helicopters has for years been answered by claims that it is soon going to manufacture them locally.

Meanwhile, there is such a ground swell of nation-wide resistance that the police and military forces are already stretched. To that has to be added the massive military deployment in Namibia involving over 100 000 soldiers. The strains on the SADF, and on the military-industrial complex, taken together with the grave crisis faced by the economy has created a formidable problem for the regime and it is difficult to see where it will move. By its own actions it has removed any room for manoeuvre.

The South African authorities have anticipated the problem of not being able to maintain the white power structure by themselves and have made strenuous efforts to secure formal treaties with the major Western powers so as to guarantee direct external military support at times of crisis. In order to forge a closer alliance with the West, Pretoria has always emphasized the 'strategic' importance of the Cape Sea Route and even offered the use of the Simonstown Naval Base to Nato.

South Africa entered into a formal defence agreement with Britain in 1955 in the form of the Simonstown Naval Agreement, which was based on an exchange of letters between the two countries. Twenty years later, Britain was forced to abrogate it as a result of domestic and international anti-*apartheid* pressure. The agreement has been used not only to facilitate extensive naval co-operation but also to supply a wide range of military equipment to South Africa on the grounds that there was a legal obligation to do so under the Simonstown Agreement. Under this guise, the Heath government even wanted to supply helicopters during the early 1970s and this almost led to the break-up of the Commonwealth at the Singapore summit in 1971.

South Africa wanted something more than the Simonstown Agreement and, during the late 1960s, set about preparing for a hemispheric pact to include not only countries across the South Atlantic but also Australia and New Zealand to cover the Indian Ocean. South African ministers visited various South American countries and developed close military links with Argentina. The South African press began to speculate about the establishment of a South Atlantic Treaty Organization (SATO).[37]

The 1969 Defence White Paper stated that: 'The considerable harbour and repair facilities at Simonstown and elsewhere in our country, as well as the modern communication and control facilities, all provided at great expense, are indispensable to Allied naval forces in the Southern Atlantic and Indian Ocean areas.' It then disclosed that a world-wide communication network was to be constructed to enable South Africa's maritime command to keep in touch with any ship or aircraft operating between Australia and South America. This project together with the new tidal basin and submarine base at Simonstown involved enormous expenditure, all aimed at making South Africa a more attractive ally.

The Advokaat military communications system was inaugurated in March 1973. It was built at a cost of over R15 million by FRG companies with components obtained from a number of Western countries.[38] At that time it was reported that it had substations in Walvis Bay in Namibia and was directly linked by 'permanent channels' with the Royal Navy in Whitehall and the US Navy base at San Juan in Puerto Rico.[39]

The British Anti-Apartheid Movement submitted several documents to the UN Security Council in 1975 which revealed details about the construction of the Advokaat system with the use of official Nato forms. In the face of conclusive evidence that South Africa had been provided with the Nato Codification System for Spares and Equipment it was claimed that this did not amount to military collaboration with the Pretoria regime.

Australia apparently stopped using the Advokaat system by early 1975 and South African press reports complained openly about this. Pretoria thereafter claimed that its system extended only to the Bay of Bengal in the Indian Ocean.

Whenever Nato officials and members have been asked about links with Pretoria the standard answer has always been that South Africa is outside the Nato area and therefore there is no question of military relationship. However, by 1973, Nato had authorized the Supreme Allied Commander Atlantic (SACLANT) to undertake special studies for operations outside the Nato area and especially covering 'the sea lanes for petroleum or other vital supplies'.[40] The British parliament was told in November 1974 that 'Studies have been made, but there is no commitment on the part of NATO members to engage collectively or individually in activities outside the NATO area.'[41]

It is interesting that the Advokaat system, which became operational in 1973, covers the northern point of the South Atlantic where the Nato area ends – the Tropic of Cancer. Because of the extensive operational area of the system, South Africa claims that it acts as the virtual nerve-centre for Western defence in that part of the southern hemisphere.[42]

In November 1975 the chairman of the Nato Military Committee, Admiral Sir Peter Hill-Norton, suggested that three or four Nato members could combine with a group outside the alliance to monitor what was going on in the Indian Ocean and in this way a Nato 'area of interest' could be established, in addition to Europe.[43] One month earlier, in October 1975, the FRG representative on the Nato Military Committee, Lieutenant-General Gunther Rall, was forced to resign by the Bonn Government when the ANC disclosed that he had visited various atomic and military installations in South Africa during 1974, under an assumed name.

One issue on which repeated assurances have been sought from Nato is the question of meetings with South African officials. When its secretary-general refused to give clear assurances the British Anti-

Apartheid Movement took up the matter. As a result, Secretary-General Luns wrote to the Anti-Apartheid Movement on 9 June 1976 and stated: 'There are no contacts between members of the International Staff of the Alliance with the Republic of South Africa'. However, the World Campaign established that Dr Luns himself met secretly with Foreign Minister Botha in Brussels on 14 November 1980. Dr Luns then informed the World Campaign that it did not amount to a breach of his undertaking since it was a private meeting at his own residence.[44] There was increased anxiety about Nato links with South Africa when it became known that this was in fact the third such meeting between Secretary-General Luns and Foreign Minister Botha, all in clear breach of an official written undertaking. The British government explained that the South African foreign minister had met 'Dr Luns, not in his official capacity as Secretary-General of Nato, but as a respected and experienced European Statesman'.[45]

Several press reports in 1983 once again created serious concern about the Nato links with South Africa. The commanding officer of the Simonstown Naval Base, Dieter Gerhard and his wife, Ruth Gerhard, were charged with spying for the Soviet Union. This followed the arrest of Dieter Gerhard by US authorities who handed him over to South Africa. After a secret trial, they were both convicted of high treason in December 1983. Various press reports disclosed that Gerhard had access to highly sensitive Nato information as well as detailed technical knowledge about the Seacat missile system, the Sea Sparrow surface-to-air missile, and the Selenia fire and weapon control system.[46]

On the basis of reports about the Gerhard case as well as other substantial evidence it is difficult to avoid the conclusion that there exists substantial military and security collaboration between South Africa and certain major Nato powers as well as with Nato itself. However, despite these and other links, it has not been possible so far for Pretoria to obtain replacement naval surveillance aircraft for their aging Shackletons. This is due largely to the current strength of international anti-*apartheid* opinion and the vigilance of committed organizations and individuals.

The overall relationship that exists between the major Western powers and *apartheid* South Africa raises an important question as to the nature and degree of future external intervention that can be expected on the side of the Pretoria regime – particularly when the survival of the white power system is seriously threatened. There is no

doubt that in the growing internal confrontation the number of white
casualties will begin to increase and then both Pretoria and its allies
will try to subvert Western public opinion by appealing for support
against 'terrorist violence'. Pretoria will try to mobilize anti-
communist sentiment in other countries by suggesting that any
success for African freedom will represent a serious threat to vital
Western interests. Whether, and how far, this succeeds will depend on
many factors including the way in which the Western media presents
the situation.

For the Pretoria regime it is almost past the point of no return; it
cannot put the clock back. In September 1981, Defence Minister
Malan told the white parlimanet that 'the next five years are of vital
importance in the history of the Republic of South Africa and our
actions in many spheres will be decisive'. He explained that he was
'not speaking only of the sphere of security, but also of the constitutional, diplomatic and economic spheres' and concluded: 'I believe
that time is an extremely important factor, and I also believe that there
is not much time left.'[47]

It is abundantly clear that despite the various measures taken by
the regime since then to consolidate its power through so-called
constitutional reforms, 'Rubicon' promises and other manoeuvres
none of them have succeeded to date. Virtually all such initiatives
have had a boomerang effect and have served instead to mobilize
increased resistance on the part of the majority of the population.
Armed struggle and nation-wide resistance are now permanent
features and these processes cannot be easily reversed.

Western bankers and business people have realized that South
Africa is no longer safe for their loans and investments and, like many
South African white business leaders and others, they are looking to
an   alternative future and seeking meetings with the ANC.

If the economic and political crisis persists, the regime may decide,
instead of making major concessions, to simply put the shutters down
and operate as a garrison state with a siege economy. It may respond to
various critical developments by resorting to massive military retaliation and the fact that it has nuclear weapon capability makes it
extremely dangerous. However, while it is important to correctly
assess its military capability, it is also vital not to exaggerate it.

On the basis of past experience it is possible to say that the ability of
the Pretoria regime to survive for so long is related in part to the
massive political, economic and military support that it has received
from its external allies. The future is also dependent on the nature and
degree of support that it is able to enlist from its major Western allies.

CHAPTER 7

South Africa's Nuclear Capability:
The Apartheid Bomb

There is no longer any doubt about South Africa's nuclear weapon capability. What is not known is the number of devices it has in stock and the precise nature of the weapons.

Most of the 200 aircraft operated by the South African Air Force can easily deliver nuclear weapons. In addition, it has both ground-to-ground and air-to-ground missiles, and there are even reports that it is working on the deployment of cruise missiles. Thus, it has no problem as to the means of delivery.

There is a long history of Western nuclear collaboration with South Africa. Under the 'Atoms for Peace' programme the United States and South Africa signed a 50-year agreement for nuclear co-operation in 1957. In 1961, South Africa purchased the Safari 1 research reactor from the United States and has received extensive assistance in the nuclear field from that country. But Britain, West Germany and France are also heavily involved and there has been more recent collaboration with Israel, which has given a new dimension to the growing international concern and anxiety about South Africa's weapon capability.

In 1976 the then president of the South African Atomic Energy Board, Dr. A.J.A. Roux, said 'We can ascribe our degree of advancement today in large measure to the training and the assistance so willingly provided by the USA during the early years of our nuclear programme, when several of the Western world's nuclear nations co-operated in initiating our scientists and engineers into nuclear science ... even our nuclear philosophy, although unmistakably our own, owes much to the thinking of American nuclear scientists.'

All the available evidence confirms that South Africa's nuclear programme has been initiated, supported and developed to its present level as a direct result of the ready assistance provided by its Western nuclear partners. It is these western nations that bear the full responsibility for the development and manufacture of the *apartheid* bomb.

Although South Africa may by now have several bombs in its cellar, it is still highly dependent on external sources of know-how, plant, technology and finance in order to proceed with its ambitious nuclear plan. Most of this assistance continues to be provided by the major Western powers in various forms. When challenged by anti-*apartheid* protests, each one individually insists that its own collaboration with South Africa is 'exclusively for peaceful purposes' – a claim persistently made for over 25 years.

It is of the greatest importance to ascertain the nature and scale of all external nuclear collaboration. If all of the evidence could be assembled together it would help to throw light on the specific current needs of the *apartheid* regime, indicate more clearly the nature and scale of its nuclear plan, and focus attention upon those companies and countries most directly involved.

However, because of the general secrecy surrounding nuclear relations – and especially those connected with South Africa – it is impossible to establish *all* of the facts. Even a cursory examination of the available information reveals that the Reagan policy of 'constructive engagement' has made a substantial contribution to enhancing South Africa's military and nuclear capability. If this process continues, then, within a few years, the major Western powers will enable Pretoria to emerge as a significant, and highly dangerous, nuclear-weapon power.

South Africa is known to have substantial uranium resources. According to the latest official figures, its known 'reasonably assured resources' amount to over 313 000 tonnes whilst those in occupied Namibia are 135 000 tonnes, making a total of around 450 000 tonnes under its control. This is a conservative figure and other more general estimates are much higher, reaching an amount that is double the above figure for South Africa. These calculations relate to uranium recoverable from existing production centres at costs of less than US$ 130 per kilogram.

In addition, there are substantial quantities of uranium resources which have not been tapped so far. If all the potential uranium-bearing deposits are taken into account, then the estimated *additional* resources amount to a further 1 351 000 tonnes in South Africa, and just under 200 000 in Namibia – all still considered to be recoverable at costs of less than $ 130 per kilogram. Of course, if the calculations are made at higher costs of recovery then that substantially increases the quantity of uranium resources.

South Africa has been producing uranium for over 30 years. Its current level of production is around 6 000 tonnes per year, having almost doubled since 1977 when it produced 3 360 tonnes. Most of its production is for long-term contracts with a small quantity being sold on the spot market, making it less vulnerable to short-term price variations.

South Africa is considered to be the western world's third biggest producer of uranium, after the United States and Canada. However, when one adds Namibia's production of almost 4 000 tonnes to that of South Africa it makes a total of 10 000 tonnes under the control of the Pretoria regime, which is close to the 10 300 tonnes and the 10 500 tonnes produced by the US and Canada respectively.

This reveals the important role conferred upon South Africa, over the years, as a producer of uranium, by the major Western powers.

These figures take on an added significance in the context of the overall Western uranium production capability for 1984, estimated at around 45 000 tonnes. Of the major consumers the US alone accounts for over 12 000 tonnes for its reactor requirements, followed by France (6 700 tonnes), Japan (5 000 tonnes), West Germany (2 800 tonnes), Britain (1 550 tonnes), Canada (1 500 tonnes), and Sweden (1 300 tonnes).

Multinational enterprises based in the US, Canada, Japan, and Western Europe are directly involved in South African and Namibian uranium production and sale. Some of them have a long record of collaboration with the *apartheid* regime, the most notorious being the British-based Rio Tinto Zinc which manages the Rossing mine in Namibia and has South African, British, Canadian, West German and French shareholders. The fact that South Africa's occupation of Namibia has been declared 'illegal' by both the United Nations Security Council and the Hague Court has not deterred foreign interests from exploiting Namibian uranium. Indeed, encouraged by the 'business-as-usual' policy of their own governments towards Namibia, they have effectively become partners with the *apartheid* regime in imposing its illegal rule over the Namibian people.

South Africa's role as a major producer of uranium has not only helped to legitimize its illegal occupation of Namibia but has also provided Pretoria with substantial – and much needed – foreign

exchange earnings. Moreover, taken together with its huge reserves of
uranium, it amounts to a formidable advantage in securing extensive
Western support for its own nuclear programme.

The main governmental research body concerned with nuclear matters is the National Nuclear Research Centre, which is based in
Pelindaba, not far from Pretoria. Its main facility is the US-supplied
Safari 1 research reactor, which began functioning in 1965. Under
the general nuclear co-operation agreement with the United States,
South Africa has received substantial know-how, training and technical assistance since 1957. This included adequate quantities of enriched uranium for operating the Safari 1 reactor until 1975 – when
deliveries were suspended in an effort to get South Africa to sign the
Nuclear Non-Proliferation Treaty (NPT).

Also at Pelindaba is Safari 2, claimed to have been designed and
manufactured by South Africa, which began to function in 1967. Its
enriched uranium and other needs were also provided by the United
States, and the two research reactors enabled South Africa to acquire
vital experience for the subsequent development of its nuclear
programmes.

The Safari 1 reactor, as a result of an agreement between the
United States, South Africa and the International Atomic Energy
Agency (IAEA), was placed under international safeguards in 1967.
The reactor is at present operating on fuel which is manufactured by
South Africa itself.

At Pelindaba, a hot-cell complex is being built in order to carry out
post-irradiation examination of fuel as well as materials irradiated in
the Safari reactor and the two French Koeberg power reactors.

South Africa had been working secretly since 1960 on a uranium
enrichment research programme and in 1970 Premier Vorster disclosed that they had developed their own 'unique' process for enriching
uranium. A year later the Uranium Enrichment Corporation was
established to make South Africa an independent manufacturer of
nuclear fuel.

No one really believed the South African claim of a 'unique' process
and very soon evidence was forthcoming of close nuclear collaboration with enterprises in West Germany. The African National
Congress (ANC) of South Africa published several documents and
concluded that the enrichment plant was developed with the co-
operation of the 'State-owned Society for Nuclear Research, Karls-

ruhe, the State-controlled company STEAG in Essen and with the
agreement and active participation of the Federal Government in
Bonn.'

There were vehement denials from Bonn, and by 1976 there were
reports about STEAG's withdrawal of co-operation with South Africa.
South African officials admit that their enrichment process is related to
the West German 'jet nozzle' method but also point out that it owes
more to the US vortex-tube concept. With such origins it is certainly
not possible to claim that the enrichment process is 'unique' to South
Africa.

A pilot enrichment plant was established at Valindaba, very close to
Pelindaba, and Premier Vorster disclosed its existence in April 1975.
It was also intended to construct a commercial enrichment plant with
possible financial backing from the Shah of Iran in return for supplies
of enriched uranium.

In June 1975, South Africa announced that it had completed a pilot
plant to produce uranium hexaflouride, which is the 'feed material' for
the enrichment plant. Thus, it was now in a position to do the entire
enrichment process itself and the objective was not only to meet South
Africa's own needs but to become a major exporter of enriched
uranium.

However, the cost of a commercial enrichment plant turned out to
be prohibitive and by 1978 the pilot plant had to be expanded into a
'relatively small' production facility. This plant, which is not under
international safeguards, enriches uranium to 45 per cent and
provides fuel for the Safari reactors.

In place of the commercial plant, a 'semi-commercial' enrichment
plant was under construction in 1985 with a planned productive
capacity of about 300 tonnes separative work units per year. This is
intended to provide adequate enriched uranium for the two
Koeberg power reactors, with some left for export. Because of
shortage of funds it is not likely to become operational before 1987
and this means that fuel for Koeberg will have to be obtained from
others sources until then.

It is also important to note that South Africa has shown interest in
the use of lasers for uranium enrichment and that, among others,
Israel is conducting research into this method.

The details about South Africa's uranium enrichment process are
secret and its enrichment plants are not under any bilateral or international safeguards.

South Africa has built a nuclear power plant some 30 kilometres
north of Cape Town at Koeberg. France has supplied the two
pressurized-water reactors, each able to generate 920 megawatts of
electricity. Koeberg 1 was due to become operational at the end of
1982, with Koeberg 2 following a year later.

However, on 18 December 1982, a series of four bomb explosions
caused extensive damage to the R 1.8 billion nuclear power station.
The ANC claimed responsiblity for the blasts, in retaliation for the
South African military attack on Maseru nine days earlier in which 42
people – South African refugees and Lesotho nationals – were killed.

The Koeberg plant suffered substantial damage with the result that
the commissioning of its first reactor was delayed until March 1984. It
became fully operational a few months later.

Earlier there was a serious problem about the supply of fuel for the
Koeberg reactors in view of the suspension of deliveries by the Carter
administration in an attempt to induce South Africa to sign the NPT
and place all its nuclear facilities under international safeguards
operated by the IAEA. South Africa refused to comply with the
requirements stipulated by the US Nuclear Non-Proliferation Act of
1978.

In November 1981, the Pretoria regime announced that it had
obtained the fuel required for the Koeberg plant. It transpired that
deals arranged by South Africa's Electricity Supply Commission
(ESCOM) – via two US-based companies – resulted in enriched fuel
belonging to the Swiss nuclear unit, Kaiseraugst, being delivered to
the French company, Framatome, for fabrication into fuel rods. The
130 tonnes of uranium fuel had originally been enriched for the Swiss
plant at the Tricastin facility in France where it had been stored until it
was delivered to Framatome.

Since Framatome is partly state-owned, the French government
must have known about the deal but refused to do anything to try to
block it. When US legislators raised the possibility of taking action
against companies which undermined its Non-Proliferation Act, the
Reagan administration refused to act, claiming that it had no
jurisdiction over commercial activities which take place outside the
US and in any case did not believe in actions which would 'produce a
deteriorating relationship' with South Africa.

The Koeberg nuclear power plants are the subject of a safeguards
agreement entered into between France, South Africa and the IAEA.
The plutonium produced by these reactors can in theory be secretly
diverted to uninspected facilities for reprocessing so that it can be

used for manufacturing a plutonium bomb. However, most experts point to the enriched uranium route as being the most likely one for the *apartheid* bomb.

South Africa has obtained considerable benefits from its membership of the IAEA, which it joined in June 1957. Much of its nuclear programme, and particularly its exploitation of South African and Namibian uranium resources, has been advanced as a result of the direct and indirect advantages of membership.

As the most advanced member from the African continent, South Africa was accorded an important role within the IAEA and served as a member of the Board of Governors until June 1977. Its growing nuclear weapon capability led to increased pressures from other African and non-aligned members, and, at the IAEA General Conference in New Delhi in 1979, its credentials were rejected.

Representations had been made earlier (by the World Campaign Against Military and Nuclear Collaboration with South Africa) to several member states calling for the exclusion of South Africa from the IAEA in view of the substantial benefits that it obtained from membership. Although South Africa was prevented from participating in the 1979 conference and has not been allowed to attend any of the subsequent annual conferences, it still retains full membership of the IAEA and continues to enjoy all of the benefits that accrue from it.

The UN General Assembly has adopted numerous resolutions calling for an end to all forms of nuclear collaboration with the *apartheid* regime, but until recently these did not result in any special initiatives being taken with the IAEA. However, due to increased anti-*apartheid* pressure and growing concern about South Africa's nuclear weapon capability, some limited measures were taken during the 1980s. The first action by the Board of Governors was taken in September 1981 when it decided to exclude South Africa from participation in the Committee on Assurances of Supply (CAS).

All efforts to exclude South Africa from the IAEA itself have so far not succeeded because of the determined opposition of the Western governments that it remain a full member on the grounds that international bodies should be 'universal' and open to all states. It is also claimed that, by retaining South Africa's membership, the international community is likely to have a restraining effect on the *apartheid* regime, which should also be encouraged to sign the NPT and place its unsafeguarded facilities under international inspection.

In May 1982, the World Campaign ascertained that the Director of the South African Atomic Energy Board was a member of the Nuclear Energy Agency Group on Uranium Exploration Techniques, which was organized jointly by the IAEA and the Organization for Economic Co-operation and Development (OECD). This was in clear breach of UN resolutions calling for an end to all forms of nuclear collaboration with the *apartheid* regime. Despite protests, South Africa was not excluded from any symposium on Uranium Exploration Methods organized by the group in Paris from 1–4 June 1982.

Further investigations by the World Campaign revealed that South Africa's membership of the IAEA was of even greater importance to the *apartheid* regime than was at first expected. The IAEA confirmed that South Africa was a member of several special working groups on uranium. In one category of six groups established jointly by the IAEA and the OECD, South Africa was a member of all six and served as chairman of two. It therefore played a central role within all of these groups and it was remarkable that this was permitted when everyone knew of South Africa's illegal occupation of Namibia and the plunder of its uranium resources. Representations made to the relevant authorities in the OECD produced the response that South Africa became a member of the joint working groups as a result of its membership of the IAEA and that all representations should be addressed to the latter organization.

The World Campaign appealed to the IAEA Board of Governors at its June 1982 meeting to remove South Africa from the joint IAEA/OECD Working Groups on Uranium Resources and Exploitation Techniques but no action was taken by the Board. It was later explained that it needed a decision of the full IAEA General Conference.

On 17 September 1982, a letter was addressed to the General Conference, repeating the request to exclude South Africa from the Working Groups. The UN Special Committee against Apartheid sent a supporting cable to the IAEA and stated that it was 'most concerned that South African regime is enabled through these groups to obtain nuclear technology and maintain close relations with nuclear experts from other countries'. It called for 'immediate action to exclude South Africa from IAEA Working Groups and joint Working Groups in which IAEA participates'.

Despite these representations no action was taken by the IAEA General Conference in September 1982. It became clear that much more needed to be done to get the matter even raised within the organization. The World Campaign thereafter worked in close co-operation with African and non-aligned countries so that by the next General Conference, in 1983, it became impossible to avoid the subject.

Nigeria submitted a resolution on behalf of the Group of 77 States which recalled some of the earlier resolutions of the UN General Assembly, demanded that 'South Africa submits all its nuclear installations and facilities to inspection by the Agency', and called upon states to 'end all nuclear co-operation with the South African regime'. It further requested the Board of Governors and the Director-General to consider implementation of the relevant resolutions of the General Assembly 'in what relates to the Agency and especially the request to the Agency to refrain from extending to South Africa any facilities which may assist it in its nuclear plans and in particular the participation of South Africa in the technical Groups of the Agency'.

The resolution was adopted on 14 October 1983 with 50 in favour, 6 against and 19 abstentions. This created a serious problem for the IAEA and its members since the resolution called for action which would be firmly opposed by South Africa and its close friends. The matter came to be handled in an unusual manner: it was suggested that since most of the working groups were about to complete their task it was not necessary to exclude South Africa from any of them but simply to wait for the groups to stop functioning. The major Western countries claimed that any action to remove South Africa from the groups would be tantamount to restricting its membership rights and privileges, which they would not permit.

A few months after the 1983 General Conference, the South African regime sent a letter to the IAEA, stating that South Africa's nuclear customers 'will have to guarantee that the technology, material and equipment will not be used for nuclear explosives, but only for peaceful purposes'. It also went on to state that South Africa was prepared to 'resume' discussions 'on safeguards in respect of its semi-commercial enrichment plant but not its pilot enrichment plant'. This response, though limited and without much real substance, confirms that the South Africa regime cannot normally be persuaded to comply with international requirements unless some action is taken against it.

The stalemate that had developed regarding the working groups was reflected in the resolution adopted at the 1984 General Conference which repeated some of the earlier points. However, it made the important new call that all states 'stop all purchases of Namibian uranium'. The vote this time was 57 in favour, 10 against and 23 abstentions.

By 1985 South Africa still had not been removed from any of the working groups and, as the IAEA itself explained to its General Conference that year, 'South Africa, as a member of the Agency, has the right under the Statute to participate in activities open to all Member States, including attendance at meetings'.

Meanwhile, as efforts were being made to secure South Africa's exclusion from the various technical and other groups, another development came to light. In the 1982 edition of the Uranium 'Red Book', published by the OECD and prepared by the joint OECD Nuclear Energy Agency and IAEA Working Party on Uranium Resources, there was a special entry for the 'Republic of Bophutha-tswana' with the South African bantustan described as 'a newly independent state in Southern Africa'.

This entry apparently went unnoticed for almost two years until the World Campaign protested to the IAEA about it in October 1983. A request to insert a correction in unsold copies was refused but an assurance was given that the next edition would not contain the 'erroneous' entry.

The next edition, published in December 1983, contained a map of southern Africa which had *three* bantustans listed with Lesotho and Swaziland, and all five described as 'independent states'. Once again the matter appears to have gone unnoticed by anyone within the IAEA or the OECD until it was raised at an IAEA Board meeting by Nigeria on 8 June 1984. An assurance was given that a correction would be made.

It is not too difficult to ascertain how these illegal entries came to be made. The joint Working Party responsible for preparing the 'Red Book' has South Africa as a member represented by Dr P.O. Toens, head of its Atomic Energy Board (later known as the Nuclear Development Corporation of South Africa (Pty) Limited).

Western governments which insist on retaining South Africa as a full member of the IAEA do not appear to notice how the Pretoria regime stretches the 'universality' principle to gain international recognition for its bantustans. Even after this is done there is no public protest, let alone censure, about such a gross abuse of membership – not even after their attention has been drawn to the specific improper entries.

At the 1985 General Conference, the resolution submitted by

Nigeria on behalf of the African Group took matters a few steps further. It repeated some of the earlier demands and made the clauses on Namibian uranium more comprehensive. However, two crucial new clauses were added, requesting the IAEA 'to exclude South African participation from all expert meetings, panels, conferences, seminars, etc. where such participation could assist South Africa to persist with its exploitation of Namibian uranium', and 'to stop publishing the entry provided for Namibia by South Africa in the Red Book' and 'also to ensure that no reports or information relating to Namibian uranium extraction, production and exports are published without the full consultation of the United Nations Council for Namibia'.

This time the resolution was adopted without any votes against, though several Western members abstained. Some of those which had abstained in earlier years now voted in favour but explained that they still had reservations about excluding South Africa from any activities of the IAEA since that would amount to interfering with its membership rights. This shift in voting pattern was due to the fact that it was becoming politically impossible for even the staunchest defenders of South Africa's membership to appear to vote against a resolution dealing with nuclear relations with the Pretoria regime.

With regard to the 'Red Book', it is in future to be prepared not by the Working Party which includes South Africa but instead by the secretariat of the OECD/NEA and the IAEA. Once again, special arrangments are made to end the role of the Working Party and make the two organizations responsible for the publication rather than exclude South Africa.

The way in which the South African question has been dealt with within the IAEA shows the powerful pressures which prevail when it comes to simply excluding South Africa from several uranium working groups and technical conferences, etc. These difficulties persist despite the fact that none of the resolutions, so far, have called for the suspension or exclusion of South Africa from membership of the IAEA. All of the working groups of which South Africa was a member have had their activities terminated rather than excluding South Africa from any of them.

At the time of the controversy, the IAEA maintained that the working groups were in any case coming to the end of their use and that there was therefore no need to exclude South Africa from any of them. However, the OECD Nuclear Energy Agency explained to readers of one of its publication in March 1985: 'At this point in time, the sixth Newsletter "R and D in Uranium Exploration Techniques" should have been issued.' It mentioned that the previous one had appeared in January 1984 and continued: 'However, during the intervening period, developments of a political nature led to the disruption of the NEA/IAEA joint work in the uranium area.'

There is no doubt that membership of the IAEA provides a great benefit for the South African regime and specifically for the development of its nuclear programme. Through membership it is invited to take part in all the technical meetings and other activities organized by the IAEA, and is able to participate in the same way as other member states. Through such links South Africa is able to acquire vital technical and other know-how and to make contacts which are invaluable for its nuclear plans. It is able to recruit experts to South Africa, not only for employment there but also to participate in conferences held in that country. In a very real sense membership of the IAEA enhances South Africa's all-round nuclear capability – including its capacity to develop and manufacture nuclear weapons.

Some argue that by retaining South African membership it is possible to restrain its nuclear ambitions. There is no evidence that membership over all the years has had this effect. Besides, the arrangements made for IAEA inspection of the Koeberg nuclear plants arose out of formal agreements made with France, the supplying country. These arrangments can be retained.

Another related argument is that if South Africa is excluded from the IAEA it will not sign the NPT. Despite strong pressures from some of its closest friends, including the US and Britain, South Africa has persistently refused to accede to the NPT. Repeated calls by the international community, including several resolutions of the IAEA which have demanded that South Africa submit 'all its nuclear installations and facilities to inspection by the Agency' have had no effect.

In any case, there is considerable doubt as to how far South Africa would abide by any international undertaking since it has a unique record of violating most of its international obligations. All moves to try and persuade South Africa to sign the NPT apparently involve continued co-operation with it in the nuclear field. In some cases where such collaboration is increased it is even suggested that it can serve as an inducement for Pretoria to sign the Treaty.

In terms of its obligations to the work of the IAEA it is important to note that South Africa has, since 1979, refused to make any voluntary contributions to the IAEA's Technical Assistance and Co-operation Fund. Even more significant is the fact that by 1984 its outstanding

contributions to the regular budget of the Agency amounted to over
US$ 930 000. It made a payment of about half this sum during 1985,
aware that its default in meeting contributions would result in
increased anti-*apartheid* pressures during the 1985 IAEA General
Conference. Though its default was not raised by any delegate it is an
added reason for suspending or excluding South Africa from membership of the IAEA.

This account of South Africa–IAEA relations gives some indication of the powerful role played by South Africa in the nuclear field,
largely due to its importance as a producer of uranium – and the
controller of Namibian uranium – as well as the general political
attachment of the major Western powers to the Pretoria regime. It
also illustrates the enormous pressures and vested interests that come
into play in favour of South Africa once any anti-*apartheid* initiatives
are taken to reduce or end external nuclear collaboration with the
Pretoria regime.

Although the Carter administration attempted to impose certain
limitations on nuclear deals with the South African regime, the Reagan
administration has reverted to more comprehensive nuclear collaboration with Pretoria.

Early in 1982, the US secretary of commerce, Malcolm Baldridge,
stated that the Administration would permit the export of some
nuclear-related items to South Africa and disclosed that five licences
for specific items had been approved in the past two years. Among
these were: vibration test equipment which can be used to test war-
heads and ballistic re-entry vehicles; the Cyber 170-750 computer
which can be used to model a nuclear explosion; multi-channel
analysers for processing data from cables at a nuclear test site; 95
grams of helium 3 which can be used to manufacture tritium for
thermo-nuclear weapons; and a hydrogen re-combiner for the
Koeberg nuclear power plant.

In addition, the Commerce Department also intended to permit the
sale of a hot isostatic press that can be used for making vital
components for nuclear weapons, but this (together with the helium 3)
has been held up due to congressional pressure.

In September 1983, the US Administration approved a request
from seven companies to provide an estimated $50 million worth of
technical and maintenance services for the Koeberg plant.

In November 1983, reports were published about US attempts to prevent the smuggling of VAX computers from South Africa to the USSR. Certain items were impounded in West Germany and the rest were eventually confiscated in Sweden. This advanced computer system was said to be useful for conducting nuclear weapon tests as well as for tracking cruise missiles. Apparently US agents were able to act in time to prevent the equipment from reaching the Soviet Union but what has not been established is how many such systems have in fact been supplied to South Africa and for what purpose.

The Reagan policy of 'constructive engagement' with *apartheid* has already resulted in substantially increased US nuclear and military collaboration with South Africa. With the support emanating from other Western powers, the Pretoria regime is determined to press ahead with its ambitious nuclear programme.

On 6 August 1977 it was revealed that the Soviet Union and the United States had confirmed, through satellite pictures, that South Africa had made advanced preparations for an underground nuclear test in the Kalahari Desert. President Carter and several West European government leaders appealed to Premier Vorster not to proceed with the detonation. There was no explosion recorded at that time.

However, two years later, on 22 September 1979, the US Vela reconnaissance satellite detected, in the South Atlantic, a double flash of light, resembling the signals from an atmospheric nuclear explosion. This information was kept secret by the United States until the following month when it was revealed by the ABC television network. The State Department then asserted that it had 'no corroborating evidence' to verify the explosion and 'no independent evidence' to link it with South Africa.

Because of considerable domestic and international pressure, the White House appointed a special panel of experts, who, after their first meeting, according to the Washington Post of 1 January 1980, ruled out almost every other explanation for the event except an atomic explosion. Subsequently, the same panel met again and produced several revised findings, eventually deciding that the evidence was 'inconclusive'.

Meanwhile, the media reported that, according to the Central Intelligence Agency (CIA), a force of South African naval ships had been conducting a secret exercise at sea on the night of 22 September 1979, at about the same latitude and longitude as the recorded explosion. In addition, a US radio observatory at Arecibo, Puerto Rico, detected a disturbance in the ionosphere, a ripple coming from the right direction and the right velocity to have been caused by a nuclear explosion.

Moreover, at the Los Alamos Laboratory in New Mexico, scientists were in no doubt that the Vela satellite had accurately recorded a small atomic explosion, about seven kilometres up in the atmosphere in the remote ocean, east of South Africa, on the night of 22 September 1979.

All the available evidence pointed overwhelmingly to the fact that a nuclear explosion had been carried out and most experts allocated the the responsibility to South Africa, with some suggesting that it could have been done with Israeli involvement.

If the United States or any other Western power had placed the blame on South Africa they would have had to cease their nuclear collaboration with Pretoria and would have been under serious domestic and international pressure to take further action against the *apartheid* regime. The consequences for South Africa would have been extremely serious, hence the later 'indeterminate' findings of the White House panel where very convenient for both Washington and Pretoria.

Nevertheless, there is no doubt that the major Western powers. like the rest of the world, in fact believe that South Africa does have nuclear weapons. There is also general consensus about this among international scientists, and some have even suggested that the 22 September explosion could have been a neutron bomb.

There was further anxiety when, in December 1980, a US reconnaissance satellite was reported as having sighted another flash over the South Atlantic, with underwater detectors recording unexplained heat and sound originating from the same point. By February 1981, US intelligence experts once again discounted reports of a possible nuclear explosion and explained that the underwater recordings were probably caused by the descent of a large meteorite.

Even if South Africa has not actually tested any nuclear devices, it is the confirmed judgement of the United States and the other Western powers that Pretoria has nuclear weapon capability. There are thus more than adequate grounds for ceasing all forms of nuclear collaboration with the *apartheid* regime.

Yet the major Western powers persist in their nuclear collaboration and the Reagan administration has increased its support for the South African nuclear programme. Why do they do this when they know of the instability and desperation of the *apartheid* regime?

Is it to enable South Africa to intimidate and blackmail African states in the region to submit to the will of the *apartheid* regime? In the context of overall Western security is it intended that South Africa should provide a nuclear 'umbrella' in the southern hemisphere? Moreover, can the threat of an *apartheid* bomb be used to persuade the world, at a future date, not to impose effective sanctions or support the African liberation struggle, for fear that it may provoke a deadly form of retaliation by an increasingly desperate regime?

It is vital that the world understand and appreciate to what extent the South African bomb is intended to ensure the survival of the *apartheid* system and the grave implications of this for the international community.

CHAPTER 8

Rising Cost of Apartheid:
The Economic Crisis

Contrary to the claims and pretensions of South African business the economy is not and never has been entirely capitalist in nature nor in the manner it mobilizes and deploys the forces of production. True enough there is a market economy in which private property relations predominate. But it is also an economy dominated by wide-ranging institutionalized barriers to the right of the black population to sell their labour freely in the highest market, or to gain access to the world of capital accumulation, or even the right to own land and other property freely. These barriers emerged not by accident nor by the spontaneous evolution of the economy; they are the outcome of a consciously designed socio-economic system. The objective of this system has been, and remains, the production of a unique rate of surplus extraction. Its essential function is to sustain the costly superstructures of white minority privilege, the high rate of return on investments, and the commanding power of capital in the South African economy.[1] It is the cheap labour system which stands at the heart of the *apartheid* economy.

The system itself was substantially the product of British colonial policy in the years before the Act of Union in 1910. All subsequent *apartheid* laws and policies have their roots in this colonial past and it is this fact which continues to give the South African economy its essentially colonialist character. Since 1910, this colonial form has been systemically extended and enforced to the point where today the African worker and the black population are little more than objects of labour – unequal and without rights in their relations with capital, and allowed to earn an income barely sufficient to reproduce their labour and to subsist.

As long as the black population remained subdued or were cowed into accepting their miserable existence, the *apartheid* economy

flourished, at a rate which transformed that economy into the most
advanced on the African continent. It has evolved a substantial
industrial base and capacity, technologically advanced and with a
supporting infrastructure of banking, finance and a service sector.
The country's economic growth has been accompanied by a remarkably high level of capital concentration, with some 10 major corporations today controlling over 75 per cent of the assets traded on the
Johannesburg Stock Exchange. South Africa has been the recipient of
vast inflows of foreign capital, accounting in the post-war years to
about 20 per cent of domestic capital formation, as well as of transfers
of foreign technology and know-how, all on the basis of a rate of return
on capital of around 22 per cent a year. This is *three times the average
rate in the advanced industrial countries.* In South Africa, the state
itself has traditionally played a major role in fashioning the broad
parameters of the country's economic modernization process, with its
parastatal corporations entering into organic relationships with
private domestic and foreign corporations in managing and enhancing
that process.

However, this burgeoning industrial power, and with it the high-
cost privileges of the white minority, have always rested on a narrow
colonial-type economic base: the mineral, mining and agriculture
sectors and those branches of manufacturing and distributive industries which remain heavily dependent upon an unconstrained supply
of cheap black labour. The profitability, and indeed the viability, of
the more advanced modernizing sectors of South Africa's economy
have been critically dependent upon the intensity and scale of the
surplus extraction rate. This in turn depended on the intensity of black
labour exploitation so that – as in the gold-mining industry – the
volume of profits extracted remained about twice the aggregate wage
bill of the mining companies and four times the wage costs of their
black work-force. In agriculture, the systems of bonded labour
relations, hitherto protected by law and now by convention, ensured a
similar high rate of surplus extraction.[2]

This describes the dual nature of the South African economy, in
which an active internal colonialism produces the resources required
for a fast-developing industrial economy. The latter has all the
trappings of a banking, financial and overblown service sector, with
exceptional living standards for the white minority and a degree of
openness which has firmly integrated the economy into the world
capitalist market.

Sustaining this dualism in the past decade or more has not been easy, in the face of rising black political consciousness, opposition and struggle, increasing workers' militancy, the collapse of Portuguese colonialism, the pressures for Namibia's independence and the international movement of boycotts and sanctions. All of these factors put a new, much higher price-tag on the sustaining of the political status quo and the structures of the *apartheid* economy.

The regime and capital generally responded to the emerging difficulties and costs in diverse ways. The state's involvement and intervention in the national economy was sharply accelerated. The instruments of coercion and repression were perfected and considerably enlarged. The bureaucracy required to manage and administer the ever-increasing body of legislative controls and restrictions on the black population was similarly increased. A specific militarist social formation aimed at securing military self-sufficiency and controlling the southern African region was set in train, with the armed forces occupying an increasingly political role in directing the state's policies. In these essentials, the massive growth of the *apartheid* state machine emerged from the difficulties of keeping the economic dual in place.

Those difficulties have now reached the point of crisis – the gravest yet in the history of the state. The 1985 State of Emergency signified that the dual economy was under severe threat. This threat came from three sources. First of all, the transformation of the black population's alienation into open revolt, including labour strikes, cast doubt on the capacity of the regime to govern. Second, there was a ground swell in favour of international sanctions, and the ban on bank loans was beginning to bite. Third, and most damaging, was the fact that the costs of managing the *apartheid* system and sustaining the dual economy were beginning to exceed the surpluses generated by the system. In a word, the *raison d'être* of the *apartheid* economy was now in question.

For capital, both domestic and international, South Africa suddenly became a high-risk and high-cost investment. The profit rate slumped. The inflation rate, at 15–16 per cent, eroded the real value of assets. And the collapse of the currency suggested a breakdown of confidence on a substantial scale with large amounts of capital leaving the country. The refusal of foreign banks to extend credit or grant new loans to South Africa was traumatic; it meant that this source of funding to meet the rising costs of *apartheid* and the wars in southern Africa had been interrupted. With the economy in a deep slump, it became clear that overpowering economic and political forces had combined to produce a comprehensive structural crisis for the *apartheid* economy, generating schisms of varying significance within capital, the regime and some sections of the white population.

Unmistakably, it is the totality of the crisis which now generates within the structures of capital (inside South Africa and among Western corporations) the pressures for what is called 'political reform'. 'Reform' has become the magic word for ending the crisis. By definition, 'reform' consists of an adjustment of the variables within a given institutional structure or simply 'reform' through changes within the system. In the case of South Africa this would amount to no more than rearranging the furniture of *apartheid* and opening certain windows to make the system *appear* more equitable, without altering it in any fundamental way. This, quite clearly, is not what the majority of the people and their liberation movement can or will accept. A prairie fire has been ignited and there now exists in South Africa's body politic more inflammable material than is within the fire-fighting capacity of the Pretoria regime to extinguish. In this sense, there exists no serious long-term hope for the *apartheid* economy.

Resting as it has been on the narrow base of a traditionally high-profit primary goods sector, the South African economy has expanded through a substantial growth in the country's industrial base. Today this accounts for over 32 per cent of the gross domestic product (GDP). Between 1963 and 1981 the manufacturing sector expanded at an average annual rate of around 7 per cent. But the slump in the economy since 1981 has caused a reduction in manufacturing output and thus a sharp increase in unemployment. The primary goods sector – agriculture and mining in the main – has been more or less stable, contributing 20 per cent of the GDP since 1963, growing in terms of output by 2.3 per cent in the period of 1963–72 and by 0.8 per cent between 1973 and 1980. Since then sharp declines have occurred, largely as a result of the drought which caused the 1983 farm output to fall by 20 per cent.

The past three years to 1986 have seen little change in real output in either of these sectors of the economy. But what little growth there has been in the GDP (in real terms) has been due to sharp increases in government spending, associated directly with the rising costs of the Namibian occupation, the armed interventions in southern Africa and the intensified repression within the country. Between 1980 and 1984 state expenditure more than doubled, reaching almost 18 per cent of

The Economic Crisis   225

Table F

South African economy in crisis

	1981	1982	1983	1984	1985*
Value of Gold Exports (US$ billions)	10	8	8.7	8	6.5
GNP (US$ billions)	74	72	72	70	68
Value of the Rand (Annual average, in US cents)	110	90	80	60	51
Inflation Rate (per cent)	15.2	14.8	13.2	15.1	16
Government Deficit (rand billions)	1.9	2.4	4.0	4.3	?
Treasury Bill Rate (per cent)	9.8	15.6	13.4	19.3	23.0
Foreign Currency Holdings (US$ millions)	666	485	823	242	310
US Bank Claims on South Africa (US$ billions)	1.2	2.2	2.8	2.9	?

Source: SA Reserve Bank and International Monentary Fund   * estimated

the nominal GDP. The state budget, incurring deficits rising to R4.3 billion in 1984, has been financed in large part from domestic and foreign borrowings. This deficit is now running at over 4 per cent of the GDP compared to around 2 per cent in 1980. While military expenditure is officially put at R3.7 billion, or 20 per cent of the total state expenditure for the 1984–85 financial year, actual expenditure may be considerably larger since much of military spending is hidden in what is described as 'other current' and capital spendings. Taken with the expenditure on the police force these total about 40 per cent of the state budget, or about R10 billion.

The substantial decline in real private capital investment in the years since 1980 is reflected in the absorption by the state of a growing share of domestic savings – of which a large part is business profits. Gross fixed investment (in real terms) fell in 1982 by 1.1 per cent over the previous year, by a further 8.6 per cent in 1983, and by almost 15 per cent in 1984.

The disequilibrium in the economy was compounded by the

Table G

GDP volume change by sector 1963–1984

	1983	1963–72	1973–80	1980–83	1983–84
	R millions at current prices	per cent change in volume			
Primary Sectors	16 129	2.3	0.8	– 14.5	– 3
Industry	26 012	8.9	5.0	– 0.3	– 2
Service Sectors	39 206	5.6	3.9	6.7	1
GDP at Factor Cost	81 347	5.4	3.6	0.4	– 2

Source: SA Reserve Bank, Quarterly Bulletin.

seemingly confused monetary policy pursued by the authorities. On the one hand the money supply was sharply increased to around 20 per cent a year, which is undoubtedly an easy way to fund the state deficit. On the other hand, money market rates of interest were pushed to unprecedented heights of as much as 25 per cent in a bid to reduce the high rate of inflation and to force public and private corporations to arrange short- and medium-term loans from foreign banks. Within three years such borrowing totalled at least US$ 14 billion. International estimates put the figure even higher. The South African authorities also floated long-term bonds in Europe which have raised an average of R2.9 billion a year since 1977.

South Africa's aggregate debt at the end of 1983 (short-, medium- and long-term) was estimated by the International Monetary Fund (IMF) at $26.8 billion. More recent estimates put this debt at $32 billion, of which about $14 billion is in short-term loans. The ratio of this debt to the GDP is now over 33 per cent and to annual exports 115 per cent.

One key factor which contributed to the growing pressures on the economy, and to prolonging the slump, has been the shift in the wage-profit relationship following the militant upsurge of the black trade union movement and the passage of legislation which, for the first time, permitted black workers to organize legally. The membership of black trade unions has tripled since 1979 to about 700 000. The country's industrial relations system, once employer-dominated and arbitrary, has suddenly become the centre of agitation and militancy, with wage demands increasingly linked to quasi-political demands. The outcome was that while money wage earnings rose by 15–20 per cent a year until 1983, this was immediately offset by consumer price

Table H
Gross fixed investment 1983

	1983	1983	1981–83
	R million at current prices	Per cent of Total	Per cent Change in Volume
by Private			
Enterprises	12 780	54.9	+ 8.3
Public Corporations	4 569	19.6	−23.9
Government	5 926	25.5	+ 2.9
Total	23 275	100	− 1.6

Source: SA Reserve Bank, Quarterly Bulletin.

increases of 15–16 per cent a year. Between 1980 and 1983, unit labour costs (adjusted for productivity gains) rose annually by 18 per cent, while wholesale prices direct from factory rose by 10–12 per cent a year. The impact on the level of profits must have been considerable, especially if account is taken of the fact that throughout the 1970s wholesale price increases in South Africa were always ahead of changes in unit labour costs.

Another key factor which transformed the recession into a structural crisis was the change in the traditional cushion of flexible black wage earnings which had hitherto absorbed the shifts and changes in the terms of trade (the relation between prices paid for imports and prices received for exports). This cushion may no longer exist, in view of the wage pressures coming from the black trade unions. Since 1980 the unit value of South Africa exports (export prices) has fallen by 22 per cent whereas import prices have come down by only 11 per cent. Since 1979, when the price of gold rose to a peak of US$ 840 an ounce, the terms of trade have fallen by over 20 per cent. The outcome has been a persistent decrease in the exchange rate, not only to maintain the volume of exports but to try to increase it. The exchange rate was brought down in the hope of overcoming the damaging impact of the deteriorating terms of trade on the profitability of exports, especially the export of gold and other minerals. At the same time, imports were sharply reduced. In 1983 imports fell by over 11 per cent, in part due to the recession in demand and in part due to the efforts of the authorities at enhancing the level of import subsitution by producing more goods locally. The depreciation of the rand and the temporary imposition of an import surcharge in 1982 (reimposed in

late 1985) on some 60 per cent of imports sharply reduced the demand
for foreign produce. The balance of payments was kept stable but at
heavy cost in terms of domestic inflation (in part the result of the
currency devaluation) and growing international indebtedness.

The stability of the balance of payments has thus been largely
contrived. In 1981 and 1982, the sharp fall in the price of gold and
other mineral prices sent the South Africa current account balance into
sharp deficit. This led to a major borrowing from the IMF amounting to
$1.2 billion, and other borrowings on the international capital market.
However, this did not stop the steady outflow of private capital
because confidence in the South African political situation and in the
value of the rand was already eroding as early as 1982, reaching crisis
proportions in the first half of 1983. At this point, the capital balance
(inflows minus outflows) went into a R1.3 billion deficit. The situation
worsened in 1984. According to IMF statistics, the 'errors and
omissions' item in the capital balance – an estimate of capital flight
out of the country – amounted to $2.09 billion (about R5.5
billion). The flight of capital continued in the first half of 1985; and,
when the international banks became reluctant to either extend new
credits or roll over existing debts, the crisis became more acute. This
caused the collapse of the external value of the rand, the temporary
closure of the foreign exchange and stock markets, and the reimposi-
tion of exchange controls. The two-tier value of the rand was restored
– with one rate for trade/current transactions and the other a
depreciated rate for capital transactions – in an effort to prevent
further outflows of foreign and domestic private capital.

The third factor contributing to the transformation of the recession
into a structural crisis concerns the growing absorption of the
country's resources by the state machinery. These resources had to
come from somewhere, but they could not come from further
exploitation of the black population as that had been pushed to its
limits. Nor could the resources come from some miracle increase in
black labour productivity since such an outcome is dependent upon
the wholesale dismantling of the structures of *apartheid*. Finally,
recent developments suggest that resources available from international borrowing have now dried up and are unlikely to be resumed
for some years to come. Public pressure against bank loans to
apartheid has become a major political force in the United States and
several countries of Western Europe. Hence, the needed resources
can now come only from corporate profits – and from the white
minority through a calculated cutback in their privileged living

standards. (P.W. Botha actually called for cuts in the salaries of white civil servants, but was firmly rebuffed!)

It is in this context that, for the first time, the major multinational corporations are forced into an agonizing reassessment of the value of their interests in South Africa, and into making a choice as to whether they will continue the risk of remaining committed to the *apartheid* system. There are at present about 300 American companies operating in South Africa with an estimated capital stake of $3 billion. In 1985, 18 such companies halted all or part of their South African operations, three times the number a year earlier. It is estimated that American companies now employ about 70 000 black and white South Africans (less than 1 per cent of the labour force), compared to 90 000 four years ago. Several American companies are gradually reducing their South African exposure by selling out to South African corporations. British multinational corporate exposure in South Africa is of course extensive. Of the estimated direct foreign investment, now amounting to about $25 billion, some 60 per cent comes from Britain and other member countries of the European Economic Community (EEC). The latter's trade interests are substantial and their profit income from South African operations has in the past been a major component of their aggregate income. But even here there are indications that a choice of sorts is under way. A number of British companies have liquidated their holdings in South Africa by selling to South African interests; and, of some significance, Barclays and Standard Chartered Banks have reduced shareholding in their South African associated banks. Whereas, in the past two decades, about a third of the growth in the domestic product was attributed to the operations of foreign capital, this has markedly declined in the past three years to around 10–15 per cent.

How choices will ultimately be made now depends upon whether the costs of managing and administering the cheap labour structures of the *apartheid* economy can be contained, and it is here that some serious doubts exist. The mining of gold and other minerals as well as farming, has traditionally provided the riches which sustained not only the 20 per cent rate of return on capital but also the vast state machinery needed to administer the maze of race laws.

Even in good times the system was expensive. The country maintains the expense of 15 different education departments, one for each of the so-called 'homelands' and several others. The administration of the pass laws, which determined where blacks could live, work and travel, cost over US$150 million a year (almost R400 million).[3] The

Table I
The big investors in apartheid

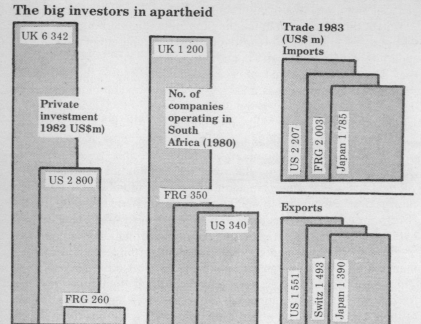

Foreign investment in South Africa in 1982 totalled US$ 20 billion, of which 54 per cent was from Britain and other EEC countries. In the first half of 1983 disinvestment totalled $650 million.

Source: The Guardian, 15 September 1985

budget of the Department of 'Co-operation and Development', in the ministry that controls black affairs, came to $1.15 billion (or almost R3 billion) in 1984. That amounts to 10 per cent of the total state budget. These funds were used largely for the forced removal of thousands of blacks from urban townships to the barren and jobless 'homelands'. The cost of running these 'homelands' was expected to reach $1.1 billion in 1985, nearly 9 per cent of the state budget. Another $500 million will be paid out to industrialists for relocating factories in the 'homelands'. These funds do little more than finance puppet officials and the bureaucracies concerned with controlling the black population. The provision of facilities such as segregated toilets in factories, separate canteens, separate coaches and other segregated railway transport simply adds to the cost. Military costs have been spiralling and have increased by over 800 per cent in the past decade. To this must be added the $1 billion annual military costs of occupying Namibia (although there is some return from mineral exploitation) and waging wars of destabilization against the Frontline states. In addition, vast sums are spent on propaganda to prop up South Africa's increasingly embattled society and win friends abroad.

Into this equation of the rising cost of *apartheid* must be added the increasingly parasitic profile of white employment. Well over 60 per cent of white adults are now directly or indirectly involved in managing the institutions of *apartheid* – in the police and armed forces, in the various departments of state, in executive and managerial positions of the economic infrastructure, and in other forms of non-productive employment. As opposition to the regime mounts, this sector of white employment can only become more extensive and, since the distribution of income heavily favours whites, more expensive. Capital will ultimately have to bear these costs without any certainty of social and political stability or a resumption of high rates of return on investment. However, when an Afrikaner millionaire – such as Anton Rupert, owner of the Rembrandt tobacco empire and much else – declares, as he did following Botha's 'Rubicon' speech, that 'time has run out for South Africa', he is clearly indicating that capital may no longer be willing to meet the costs of the *apartheid* system. This fact and its potential implications give a particularly severe twist to the structural character of *apartheid's* economic crisis.

How far will capital, both domestic and foreign, go towards abandoning the Botha administration? This is certainly the central problem confronting the regime. The regime is aware that its *apartheid* policies have supported the profit rate and provided a system of security for the cheap wage structures which produced the exceptional economic surpluses that made South Africa such a profitable area for international investment and accumulation. Capital is equally aware that keeping the lid on a revolt by the majority of the population through mounting repression and armed violence not only puts in question that security but undermines the capital accumulation process. For domestic business and international corporations, South Africa certainly remains too important a prize to surrender. Unless driven by overwhelming pressures, they will not easily accept as a solution anything approaching a far-reaching redistribution of wealth, income and power – or anything which could have a damaging effect on profitability. Despite all the past rhetoric of business about codes of conduct and the need for advances in the relative position of black workers, they do not countenance any basic change in the relative endowments of wealth and economic power

between black and white or in the political superstructures required to
entrench those endowments. It is here that a difficult but seemingly
necessary set of compromises from capital may be available for barter.
These doubtlessly aim at producing elements of reform of the kind
defined above – rearranging the furniture of *apartheid*, making it
superficially less abhorrent and less inequitable, and creating a small
black middle class which can either control or absorb the tensions
inevitable in an otherwise continuing cheap labour economy. As Harry
Oppenheimer of the Anglo American empire declared in a recent
interview with *Fortune* magazine, if the ANC 'will be willing to think
again about the use of violence and about the *rate of change*' then
clearly a deal in favour of stability becomes possible (emphasis
added).

The pressure in favour of a specific reform process – which, like the
Red Queen in *Alice*, would produce all the signs of movement in an
otherwise unchanging and entrenched situation[4] – is critically dictated
by the requirements of the mining industry in South Africa.

Gold remains of supreme importance to the South African economy. This is the position today as it has been for the past 100 years.
In 1983, the value of mining output amounted to R12.2 billion or 15
per cent of the GDP. Of this mining output, gold production amounted
to 64.5 per cent. The mining industry absorbs some 700 000 workers,
or 14 per cent of total non-agricultural employment. Over 90 per cent
of these workers are black and over 60 per cent are employed on the
Witwatersrand-Orange Free State mining complex. Mineral exports
now contribute over 60 per cent of the total value of exports; and gold
exports alone account for 45 per cent of aggregate exports. Thus, gold
production is, and has been, the principal engine of overall economic
growth and the dominating force in shaping the dual structures of the
apartheid economy, with its unique system of labour mobilization and
control. All industrial growth has depended on the continued viability
of the gold-mining industry, a fact which has led South African
economists to view the economy as taking the shape of an inverted
pyramid, with gold and other mining activity supporting the
expanding industrial sector and the privileges of the white minority.[5]

The domestic and international significance of gold arises from its
very nature – the historic money-commodity which, by virtue of its
scarcity and other properties, instantly commands purchasing power
and has for a long period served as the central medium of international

monetary settlements. The South African goldfields of the Witwatersrand, Evander, West Wits, Klerksdorp and the Orange Free State – extending in a 300-mile arc – represent the largest known concentration of gold reserves in the world. This is today controlled by 38 large mining companies and managed by seven South African mining 'houses'.

With South Africa's gold production running at 650 tons a year in recent years, comprising about 51 per cent of world output, the mining industry is very large by any standard. The seven interlocking mining (and finance) houses control 100 per cent of the gold output, as well as the output of uranium and several other important minerals. They manage assets of over R40 billion and employ in gold-mining alone some 400 000 workers. Few industries in the world can boast of such overwhelming power – in the national economy, in the degree of capital concentration, in the command of labour and in fashioning the institutions of the political, economic and social order. In this fundamental sense, all South African politics since 1886 have been dominated by gold and by the requirements of the gold-mining industry. The wider question of black labour mobilization is directly associated with this, and so are the economic and political superstructures which it necessitates. The central theme of South Africa's recent history has been the interaction between the gold producers, the flow of capital investments from abroad, and the regime and infrastructure required to mobilize black labour. This is as much true today as it has been over the past 100 years.

A major problem for South Africa and its mining industry is that the price of gold is largely determined by the outside world. The relationship between domestic costs of production and the externally determined price governs the viability of the industry – and hence the inflow of foreign exchange and foreign capital – and the overall stability of the economy. As long as production costs are constantly minimized in relation to the fixed gold price, the inverted pyramid and the economic base stay in place. Since 1886 this cost-minimizing exercise has led to the mine owners acquiring the right to control the recruitment of labour and to fix the wage rate in a manner which prevented any competition in the market for black labour in general. In time this was institutionalized, with a supporting structure of race laws, in a system of contract labour. The system involved formal controls over the freedom of movement of black workers, concentrating surplus labour in the 'reserves' or 'homelands', and imposing on the economy a wage-setting mechanism which deliberately seeks to

Table J

Sources of labour on gold mines, 1911–1982

Year	South Africans	Foreign Migrants						Grand Total	% For. Migr.
		Les.	Bots.	Swaz.	Moz.	Others*	Total Foreign Migrants		
1951	113,092	31,448	12,246	6,322	91,978	31,602	173,596	286,688	61
1961	146,605	49,050	20,216	6,784	100,678	65,012	241,740	388,345	62
1971	86,868	64,056	20,498	5,640	95,430	98,055	283,679	370,547	77
1973	81,375	76,403	20,352	4,826	83,390	112,480	297,451	378,826	79
1975	101,553	75,397	17,440	7,356	91,369	28,731	220,293	321,846	69
1978	204,318	91,278	17,647	8,269	35,234	32,048	184,476	388,794	48
1982	257,954	99,034	18,148	9,422	47,150	16,262	190,016	448,170	42

Source: M. Lipton, Capitalism and Apartheid, 1985.   * Mainly Malawians.

minimize mining costs and maximize the surplus generated from gold production.

This system now faces serious difficulties. A sharp downturn in the gold price since 1979 has forced the South African authorities to pay the mining companies for gold produced in a depreciating rand currency. This gives the mines sufficient income but leaves the state to face the problem of declining foreign exchange revenue from sales of gold abroad. A second factor has been the growing wage demands by black mine-workers. In 1982, the Chamber of Mines, the mining industry's wage setting and labour-recruiting cartel, finally extended recognition to the black unions. In 1984, the Chamber was confronted with its first legal strike by black miners (the last strike, an illegal one, took place in 1946 and was violently suppressed with the support of the armed forces). The 1984 strike was quickly settled, though not without violence, deaths and police intervention, and a 20 per cent wage increase was won. In 1985 another strike was rapidly halted with threats of mass sackings and lock-outs, though average wage rates were increased by a margin just below that demanded by the black union. These wage increases led to a rise of about 30 per cent in the cost of producing a kilogram of gold between 1983 and mid-1985. In 1983 the average cost was R7 680 per kilogram; in the first half of 1985 it was R10 280. And this despite the increased exploitation of higher grade mining ores.

An important outcome of this pressure on gold-mining profits has been the reduced flow of mining taxation of the state coffers. In 1984 the state received gold-related tax revenue of about R2.2 billion, amounting to 11.7 per cent of total revenue. In 1985 this revenue declined to about R1.8 billion, or 8.4 per cent of total state revenue.

Another factor affecting the mining industry has been the sharp cutback in international investment, as reflected in the steady liquidation of foreign holdings of mining stocks and shares until the recent official clamp-down on such capital flight. This was done through the imposition of the two-tier exchange rate for the rand and the limitation of payment of dividends on shares held abroad. Finally, the growing international ban on the importation of Krugerrand coins is having a serious effect. Until recently, well over a quarter of the country's gold output was converted into coins for sale abroad as part of a $2 million advertizing and sales campaign, crucial for holding up the price of gold in general.

In this situation the mining houses cannot easily consider the ending of the migrant labour system. For them the costs of creating a stabilized labour force, involving the provision of housing and services, would be too onerous to contemplate in the context of the uncertainties mentioned above. The traditional rhetoric about the need for a skilled black labour force rings hollow so long as the companies and the white trade unions maintain a 'colour bar' which provides white workers with an implicit monopoly to occupy all the skilled jobs in the industry.

Table K

Gold/mining – wage costs and working profits 1983

Number of white employees	47 083
Number of black employees	440 678
White salaries and wages (R million)	904.9
Black salaries and wages (R million)	1 514.1
Average annual cost per white worker (R)	19 220
Average annual cost per black worker (R)	3 435
Working profits of gold-mining companies (R million)	4 732
Profit: Black Wage Ratio	3.1

Source: Chamber of Mines, Annual Report 1985.

In the past decade several of the major mining houses have sought to extend their investments abroad in wide-ranging primary and secondary activities. Anglo American has become a major investor in Latin American mines and, through its shareholding in the New York commodity house Philbro, has acquired a small but important stake in Salomon Bros., the powerful New York investment bank. Consolidated Goldfields, through its London arm, has been acquiring shareholdings in mines and other ventures in the United States, Australia and elsewhere. Barlow Rand and Central Mining are similarly expanding abroad. But this expansion has now come up against rising international opposition to business links with South African companies. For example, Salomon Bros., despite its links with Anglo American, has ended its banking and capital-raising connections with South Africa. While these sanctions pressures are still in their infancy, it is clear that the mining companies are now caught in a double squeeze coming from within and from without. This undoubtedly augurs an escalating crisis for the colonialist base of the *apartheid* economy.

Shifts and changes in the level of employment are generally associated with swings in the capitalist business cycle, and with technological and other structural changes arising from increases in capital-labour ratio in the production process. In South Africa this association manifests itself with a vengeance. The black worker bears virtually the entire burden of each cyclical adjustment, and this burden multiplies as capital searches for lower production costs and labour-saving production systems. Thus the crisis since 1981, first cyclical and then structural, has produced a sharp deterioration in the economic and social conditions of the black working population.

South African economists, even of progressive persuasion, have been discussing the process of 'capital restructuring' in the economy following the onset of the recession and the wider crisis of profitability. They see some movement towards both further capital concentration and greater reliance on capital-intensive production processes, and, most remarkably, in the hitherto labour-intensive sectors of white-owned agriculture and mining. These are the sectors which, historically, have been organized along essentially colonialist lines. There is no doubt that there have been some increases in the capital-labour ratio in mining and agricultural production; but there must be some doubt as to whether this transformation towards a capital-intensive primary sector has proceeded to the point where the colonialist character of the South African economic base has been drastically eroded. In mining and farming, as in certain areas of manufacturing there has never existed the easy option for capital to engage in a systematic trade-off between black labour inputs and increasing capital investments. Rather, the dependence on cheap black labour has remained crucial since without such a dependence the surpluses required to support the high-cost industrialization process, the privileged standard of living of the white population and much else would be virtually impossible to generate.

It may well be that capital is in a dilemma. Any move towards higher capital investment is an act of confidence – that markets will expand and that profits sizeable enough to repay the capital within a reasonable time-scale can be generated. That confidence has been put into serious doubt since the onset of the recession and may indeed have collapsed. By contrast, all labour-intensive processes are by nature flexible. Shifts in market demand can be easily absorbed by hiring or firing elements of the labour force. In the latter case, the costs to capital of changes in confidence or of market demand are minimal.

This seems a necessary context for defining what happened to the South African labour market in the period since 1980. The liberalization of trade union regulations in 1979 opened a new period of adjustment in the wage-profit relationship. This was followed by severe recession and a structural crisis (whose causes were of course wider than this factor alone). Hence the crisis may be seen as functional in nature in the critical sense that it was needed in order to produce the counteracting tendencies of high inflation and a sharp increase in black unemployment – that is, counteracting tendencies for reasserting the cheap wage structure of the *apartheid* economy. However, where the capital restructuring argument has validity is in the fact that the recession and the crisis have led to a quantum leap in capital concentration and centralization. Huge conglomerates of capital now dominate all key sectors of the economy, with balancing interests and stakes in both the colonialist and the modernizing sectors. This reinforces the traditional 'inverted pyramid' structure of the economy – with giant monopolies now decisively managing the economic dual. Their power has risen sharply and without their support the Botha regime cannot survive.

The regime does not collate statistics on black unemployment nor of unemployment in the unskilled sectors of the economy. Unemployment among the white working population has remained insignificant at no more than two per cent despite falling output and declining

markets. On the other hand, unemployment among the black population has risen to unprecedented heights. Out of a total black
population of 27 million, some 9.5 million are what is described as
'economically active'. According to an IMF report in 1984, 'unofficial
but highly regarded estimates put the number of black unemployed at
between 2½ and 3 million'. The *Rand Daily Mail* of 29 October 1984
also used the figure of 3 million. This amounts to an unemployment
rate of 30 per cent. The South African Research Service (SARS) has
estimated that unemployment in the bantustans – in particular the
Ciskei, Bophuthatswana, KwaZulu and Gazankulu – has climbed to
more than 50 per cent.[6]

When confronted with these facts the regime, and business people
generally, argue that the trend is for black wage earnings to rise,
suggesting something in the nature of a catching-up process. Between
1976 and 1983 monthly earnings in the mining industry rose by 350
per cent to an average level of R304 a month; in manufacturing the
monthly earnings rose by as much again to R385 a month. The gap has
been narrowing between black and white wage earnings although
white earnings are still four times higher on average. In the past eight
years the cost of living has tripled, however, leaving real wage incomes
only marginally higher.

Wage rates may continue to go up as they have since the legalization
of black trade unions in 1979, but the rising unemployment also
suggests an absolute decline in *per capita* incomes for the black
population and hence in substantial increases in poverty and
inequality. According to a paper presented to the Carnegie enquiry,
93 per cent of poverty manifests itself in the bantustans and among
African families working on white-owned farms. In the Transkei – the
most developed of the bantustans – some 60 per cent of families live
below subsistence level.[7] A total of 1 430 000 people in the bantustans
have no income and nearly nine million people (or one-third of the
black population) live below the poverty line. The conditions of life in
the urban townships are only marginally better. In Soweto, with a
population of well over one million, between 20 and 40 per cent live
below the poverty datum line.

Despite the notional improvements in black wage rates, the
pressures on living standards take diverse and insidious, though
seldom acknowledged, forms. For example, in the bantustans,
thousands of African farmers have been systematically dispossessed
of their land, with the best land being taken over by state and private
businesses for commercial agriculture. Significant segments of the

population have been – and are being – converted into landless peasants with little or no prospect of employment. Compensation is rarely given for the loss of these lands, and where given is often pocketed by chiefs who work closely with the regime. Next, wages for black workers are negotiated on the basis of changes in the cost of living index. The index is an inflation measure and has little to do with social needs or the burdens placed on the employed by increasing unemployment within families and communities – the 'dependency ratio' – or from the loss of subsistence earnings resulting from the forced removals programme. In these terms it has been estimated that employed workers require annual wage increases of 34–40 per cent annually just to maintain existing living standards.

There is no doubt that today the bantustans are key instruments in the hands of the regime and of capital for enforcing the relative poverty of the black population. The concessions made to the urban working class tend to be immediately counter-balanced by a reduction in social conditions of the people living in bantustans. Indeed, as a recent study establishes, the bantustans are now the 'bulwarks of white domination. ... ironically, the security and longevity of apartheid lies not so much in the South African police but in the black government appointees' in these bantustans. They serve to 'fragment black solidarity' and are 'concentrations of irrepressible black frustrations'.[8]

The black trade union movement has made notable strides since 1979. Today nearly 1.5 million workers of all races, or 15 per cent of the working population, are unionized (compared to 50 per cent in Britain). Despite the fact that there exist on the statute books some 17 laws which can still be used to restrict the freedom of the trade union organizations and harass trade union officials (the most notorious being the Trespass Act), the black unions have become a potent force in securing changes in the wage-profit relationship and in providing a substantial workers' base to the general liberation struggle. In the three years 1982–84 there have been 1 199 strikes and work stoppages. The State of Emergency has been employed to detain a large number of trade union officials and to cripple their trade unions. Lock-outs and mass dismissals of striking workers have become a feature of business policy as became evident in the mineworkers' strike of August 1985.

The further development of the trade union movement remains heavily circumscribed by legal restrictions and contraints on the occupational mobility of workers, the freedom of association and the geographical mobility of workers under the influx regulations and the pass laws. These restrictions have been enjoined by the disparities in education and training, producing virtually insuperable barriers to the movement of black workers into skilled jobs. As Table L shows, there was no dramatic change in the racial and occupational composition of employment between 1970 and 1980. Apart from the legal impediments, there persists a range of informal and social conventions which also entrench the concentration of black labour in the most menial and unskilled of jobs. It has been suggested that with the general elevation of the white worker into the managerial classes and into the burgeoning bureaucracies of the *apartheid* system, the resulting shortage of skilled workers opens new opportunities for black workers to rise up the ladder of skilled jobs. However, what in fact appears to be happening in the manufacturing industry is the continuous de-skilling of the labour process, thus producing built-in barriers to African advancement.

Table L

Composition of the labour force in 1970 and 1980

Per cent in each category

	1970	1980
Skilled Workers		
White	68.3	59.7
Black	21.1	28.5
Administrative and Management		
White	94.1	91.7
Black	1.7	2.9
Semi-skilled		
White	72.9	61.0
Black	15.9	24.2
Unskilled		
White	8.5	10.5
Black	79.7	77.2

Source: SA Central Statistical Services – Bulletin of Statistics.

The structural crisis of the 1980s has spawned considerable debate on whether or not South Africa's *apartheid* laws and structures have now emerged as major constraints on the evolution of a liberal 'capitalism' and on further economic growth. The industrialists and businessmen who met Oliver Tambo, president of the African National Congress (ANC) of South Africa, in Lusaka in September 1985 undoubtedly held to this view. According to press reports at the time, they argued that economic growth and the creation of wealth were now critically necessary for improving the condition of blacks and that this improvement is only possible through the proclaimed 'rationalizing' process of the market economy. They see that process as both a necessary and sufficient condition for making the institutions and structures of *apartheid* increasingly irrelevant. In a word, they said that capitalist industrialization will be a sure factor in dissolving the significance of race in South Africa's economic and political life.

The arguments they used are deceptively simple. Capitalism and free market relations place a premium on economic productivity and the efficient operation of all useable resources. Thus workers are hired solely on the basis of industrial aptitude, management personnel are selected on the basis of managerial efficiency, contracts are awarded to the lowest qualified bidder, industrial opportunities exploited on the basis of entrepreneurial ability, and so on. In this impersonal world, factors such as class origin, family connection, and race become irrelevent. South African economists such as Horowitz, Hutt and O'Dowd hold to this position.[9] It also underlies the current pleading of South African capital to the outside world to avoid imposing sanctions, and to assist instead by providing capital, technology and trade which would allow South Africa to cross over from *aparthied* to non-racist but full-blooded capitalism. Gavin Relly, chairman of the Anglo American Corporation, presented the philosophy this way:

> Which economic system would best create wealth? Which political system would best secure the stability required *inter alia* to encourage investment both local and foreign? The answer of the ANC to these questions (universal suffrage with a measure of nationalisation of the commanding heights of the economy) would have a devastating effect on the country and subcontinent .... Growth will depend on a great number of factors, investment confidence, the availability of capital and the untrammelling of the people to participate fully in a free enterprise society.

M.C.O 'Dowd, also of Anglo American, has argued that capitalism and *apartheid* are incompatible and predicted that by the 1980s economic growth would so erode *apartheid* that a Western-style welfare state would be the inevitable outcome. He wrote this in 1965 and we are in the 1980s already.

Some of these positions were considered in a seminal essay by Herbert Blumer, published in 1965.[11] He examined a number of countries including his own, the United States, and found that the

claim that industrialization dissolves the racial factor was not borne
out by the facts. In the southern United States, in South Africa, and in
many colonial and ex-colonial countries, the prevailing pattern of
racial alignment and its accompanying codes become firmly fastened
to the industrial structure. He concluded that,

> The picture presented by industrialization in racially ordered
> societies is that industrial imperatives accommodate themselves
> to the racial mould and continue to operate effectively within it.
> We must look to outside factors (political struggle and interna-
> tional pressure) rather than to the maturation of these impera-
> tives for an explanation of the disintegration of racial mould.

What Blumer does not discuss are the factors which entrench this
racial mould, namely how race becomes more than a surrogate of class,
given the fact that race is more easily defined and easier to manipulate
through the instruments available for propagating the ruling ideology,
including education and social policy. It is this which gives the racism
of *apartheid* its distinctive character, and this is why South Africa's
industrialization has been built around and within the 'racial mould'.

Despite this definitive analysis, the debate goes on and in fact has
been heightened by the extraordinary nature of the crisis now
engulfing the country. A new book by Merle Lipton takes up the case
of Gavin Relly in what is described as the 'dynamics of South African
capitalism'.[12] This argues that the trend of capitalist opposition to
apartheid is accelerating, that the power of the capitalist class has not
grown in step with their opposition to *apartheid*, that capitalist
dependence on cheap unskilled labour has been declining with the
alleged increasing capital-intensive nature of production, and that
these, with other factors, have led to the surprising situation where
apartheid is sustained not by capital as such, but by politics. This is
the political power of what she calls the 'oligarchy'. In a word, there
exists no simple correlation between economic and political power in
South Africa.

What is absent from this account is clear recognition that a decisive
change has occurred in the relative costs and benefits of *apartheid* for
capital in general, arising not so much from the dynamics of South
African capitalism but from the challenge to the hegemonic mould in
which *apartheid* has been historically structured. This challenge arises
from the transformation of the mood of alienation of the black majority
into one of active revolt and of struggle for liberation, from the
Namibian people's struggle for independence, and from the collapse
of the southern African colonial system. The costs of holding the fort

against these profound changes have become an exceptional burden on capital itself. It is this which explains the desperate efforts by capital to restore stability through 'reforms', and prevent the further economic and political isolation of South Africa.

That there is no hope for the *apartheid* economy is now no longer in question. But its break-up and collapse could well take time and will surely be accompanied by even greater violence and killing. The speeches of P.W. Botha suggest that the capacity of the South African system to undergo fundamental, or even meaningful, changes remains severely limited. Even the exercise of intra-systemic change – rearranging the furniture of *apartheid* – is proving extremely difficult and complex. The influx controls, the pass laws and the group areas regulations are difficult to abandon, as are the separate and unequal education system and the bantustan structures. What remains of 'reform' are a series of cosmetic and irrelevant shifts here and there, such as bringing in a few black faces in the largely advisory 'President's Council' and acknowledging a national citizenship for the urban black population. Gavin Relly speaks vaguely about the need to alleviate deprivation and poverty, but fails to define the structural changes required for this in terms of the distribution of wealth, income and political power for the economic liberation of the black populations.[13]

The people's liberation struggle is sure to escalate. Further, the international pressure for sanctions is certain to be important as an associated force, causing a more acute phase in the crisis of power and the ability of the country's ruling forces to govern. The Western powers have been pushed by public opinion into adopting partial sanctions measures, which by themselves will have only a limited effect. The ending of new commercial bank loans and the inability of South Africa to borrow from the IMF, however, are serious attacks on the country's financial stability, as is the spreading ban on the import of Krugerrands.

In these terms, the liberation struggle within the country has been enjoined by the internationalization of the crisis of the *apartheid* economy, and the West is clearly engaged in a complex and difficult damage-limitation exercise. The scale of their capital's stake in *apartheid* and their trade links are certainly important factors in determining crisis-management policies, and in this respect they are very much on the defensive. If it becomes evident that South Africa is

ungovernable, Western capital will be forced into a policy course
which, as in Zimbabwe and elsewhere, accepts the new reality while
striving to sustain their influence, and strategic and economic interests.
At the same time, Western capital is transfixed by other equally crucial
and wide-ranging strategic calculations. These concern sustaining the
surrogate imperial role of *apartheid* South Africa in the southern
African region, with the aim of transforming the region into an anti-
communist bastion – even at the risk of costly military forays by South
African armed forces into the Frontline states. But here again the
West faces severe problems. Their policy of 'constructive
engagement' with the *apartheid* regime has thoroughly aliena-
ted the black population throughout the region who now view
Western capitalism as their enemy. In this respect, the dilemmas
facing South African capital as a result of the explosive contradictions
within South Africa are compounded by the contradictions and
dilemmas implicit in Western policy. At some moment of time, and
this is not far off, these contradictions will have to be resolved and in a
significantly new way – will the West move towards negotiations with
Oliver Tambo and the ANC in much the same way as Britain was forced
to negotiate with Robert Mugabe and his colleagues for a settlement in
Zimbabwe? This possibility, if not eventuality, is now clearly on the
political agenda for South Africa. And it is certain that this possibility
will concentrate the minds of those inside South Africa who manage
and benefit from the *apartheid* economy.

CHAPTER 9

Political Economies in Conflict:
SADCC, South Africa and Sanctions

The most dramatic forms of conflict in the Republic of South Africa, and between it and the independent states of southern Africa and occupied Namibia, are military. However, the major underlying contradictions in South Africa itself, and between it and the southern African region, are economic. These contradictions are fundamental and (often violently) antagonistic. They arose out of the European conquest of southern Africa; and they centre today on attempts by the South African regime to sustain and expand white economic supremacy at home and in the region, while the independent states of southern Africa, with Namibians and black South Africans, struggle to overcome it.

Clearly not all South African goals or tactics are, at least in any narrow sense, economic. Indeed some have significant economic costs to South Africa. The raid on Gaborone and the political blockade of customs union negotiations would appear to be counter to Pretoria's economic interests. In the same sense, not all military-political tactics are pursued for solely security or power reasons; sabotage, especially in respect of transport, is an integral tool of South Africa's regional economic policy.[1] Nor are all of the tools used to preserve political-economic hegemony necessarily violent. The customs union, export credits, and discount rates on rail traffic are in any normal sense non-violent. But they are all instruments used to maintain an exploitative regional economic supremacy and this by its nature inevitably leads to violence.

The separation of South African political-economic goals, strategies and tactics from those more narrowly related to security and power is, therefore, somewhat artificial, even at an analytical level. As the chapters on each country have demonstrated, South African regional policy is based on a 'total strategy' aimed at what is perceived

by the South African regime as a 'total threat' to its basic interests –
and ultimately to its survival. However, it is useful to look more
specifically at political-economic aims and instruments, both to
understand a central element in the regional struggle and to underline
the fact that the conflict in southern Africa is not merely a tale of
random, episodic violence. The present economic relationship
between South Africa and the independent southern African states is
sustained and sustainable only by the threat and reality of quite overt
economic and military violence. South Africa's economic relations
with its neighbours, so long as it retains the *apartheid* system, cannot
be basically complementary nor mutually beneficial. At best, the
'partnership' South Africa seeks is that which Lord Malvern
described as existing in the Federation of the Rhodesias and
Nyasaland: a white rider on a black horse.

South Africa's basic objectives in the region are economic, political
and security hegemony. The three interlock and are mutually reinforcing, even if they may conflict in any one particular case.

Economic hegemony is important because it pays. South Africa's
economic growth in the 1970s was relatively modest, under four per
cent annually. The most dynamic element was exports to independent
southern African states, which accounted for as much as a quarter of
total growth.[2] Further, the South African economy is constrained by
its domestic market and by foreign exchange. The relatively small
home market is even more constrained for many products than its size
would suggest because of *apartheid*'s impact on black incomes and
therefore, purchasing power. Consequently, export expansion is
critical to sustained growth and profitability, particularly in manufacturing. Furthermore, while South Africa has a relatively internally
integrated economy (remarkably so for a country of its economic size
and level of development), it is crucially dependent on imports of fuel,
certain capital goods and a number of intermediate inputs. The
demand for these imports tends to grow more rapidly than overall
output.[3] Therefore, rapid export growth is necessary to avoid crippling import capacity constraints. Despite its diversified raw
materials and traditional gold export base, South Africa can sustain
the needed rate of export growth only if it can build a dynamic export
sector in manufactured goods. The most logical markets for many
products – due to lack of domestic alternatives as well as physical and

institutional proximity-are in the independent states of southern Africa.

Regional economic predominance is perceived by the current South African regime (as it was by its Afrikaner republic and British colony predecessors) as far too important to leave to market forces, let alone to 'free' market forces. This economic predominance is the result of systematic, selective state and enterprise policies in transport, fiscal matters, enterprise structuring, investment, and provision of personnel and knowledge.[4] Present South African state and enterprise regional policy is in large measure directed toward consolidating, protecting and expanding that pattern of economic predominance and dependence.[5]

Security hegemony interacts with economic. Economic hegemony reinforces South African security because it renders attempts to effective liberation in any sphere difficult. This is especially true in respect to transport, where denial of access to South African routes could at present throttle the economies and state apparatuses of Lesotho, Botswana, Swaziland, Zimbabwe, Malawi and probably, Zambia. However, it is also the case in respect to revenue for customs union members and to import sources and export markets (including that for labour). All of these dependencies could be reduced, but their multiple existence allows South Africa to impose high initial costs in sectors of its choice. It is no accident and no frivolity when Pretoria brandishes the threat of economic sanctions against its neighbours in an attempt to defuse the growing international trend toward sanctions against itself. Those economies would be much weakened by forced, instant disengagement by South Africa.

Equally, however, violence by South African 'security' forces and their proxies is critical to the maintenance of economic hegemony. Dominance in the key transport sector is neither geographically nor economically natural. Ultimately it can be ensured only by action to keep other southern African routes wholly or partially non-functional.[6]

Both the Southern African Development Coordination Conference (SADCC) and South Africa perceive transport as vital. For SADCC countries, transport is the key to liberation; to South Africa, it is a tool for continued domination.[7] South Africa has used sustained violence, as well as direct economic means, to ensure that the transport links to Lobito Bay, Maputo, Beira and Nacala have been intermittently available, limited in capacity, or closed entirely. The war on the Beira–Zimbabwe transport links, for example, is a war about economics as well as politics.

Political dominance is also linked to economic hegemony in a two-way relationship – at least in the sense of ensuring that independent states do not seriously pursue economic liberation, successfully mobilize international pressures on Pretoria, or provide effective external support to the South African liberation struggle.

Since economic disengagement is costly in the short term, it can only be carried out by a government with a clear political programme. It is South Africa's strategy — using whatever means possible from economic incentives through sabotage deterrents – to ensure that such programmes are not pursued on a sustained basis. Thus, influential groups in neighbouring countries must be convinced that disengagement from South Africa is not in their interests so that such programmes will lack a firm national base, and may even cease to be canvassed seriously.

Economic power can also be used as a weapon for influencing other political programmes. Economic pressures, as well as terror raids, can be applied against those who support the South African liberation struggle or mobilize external pressures on South Africa. Lesotho's experience in January 1986 is a case in point. Conversely, acceptance of South African consent, or mild disapproval, as a binding constraint on political programmes would guarantee that these did not threaten South Africa's regional economic interests. The seminal consultancy study in South Africa by Deon Geldenhuys, outlining the uses and tactics of economic destabilization, related primarily to limiting political projects of independent states and not to the defence of economic interests as such.[8]

This relationship between politics and economics presumably underlies South Africa's vehement, and often violent, antipathy to SADCC and passive attitude toward the Preferential Trade Area (PTA).[9] SADCC is overtly political and has an explicit political project of economic disengagement for which it mobilizes external and domestic resources. The PTA is much more technically economic, more market and less state interventionist; perhaps as a result, it is far less oriented to any political project of economic liberation.

South Africa's regional objectives are interlocking; therefore, it needs a strategic approach to achieving them, not an episodic tackling of one case at a time without regard to the broader picture. South Africa has perceived this requirement. Even if the 'total strategy' and 'constellation' formulations include a good deal of rhetorical overkill for domestic purposes (and in their fullest presentations seek the impossible), they do constitute operational stategies which may be, to a substantial degree, attainable.[10] They form a framework for particular actions and for gauging their relative success or failure, their strengths and limitations. This fact can be missed because there are at least five strategic elements, and these are not totally consistent in the abstract: economic incentives, economic threats and penalties, a dual outward-looking approach involving a forward or 'strike kommando' policy coupled with one of 'constellation' or political-economic domination, and an inward-looking *'laager'* approach.

The first strategic element is the provision of economic incentives to co-operation. South Africa, and especially (but not only) its business community, has a preference for this approach when it does not perceive its interests to be under severe and immediate threat. One reason for this preference is that the use of force disrupts exports and related profits, while incentives do not. Another reason is that the use of incentives or 'carrots' – and of 'mutually advantageous' agreements – when successful, gives a degree of consent and stability unlikely to be achieved by either naked economic force or physical violence.

The range of possible incentives is very broad. The Southern African Customs Union (SACU) – whereby railway income, import duty and other related charges are collected jointly and distributed by South Africa to other members (Botswana, Lesotho and Swaziland) – is a major example.[11] So are the various arrangements providing locomotives, wagons (over 3 000 in the case of Zambia and 6 000 in total) and technical assistance to southern African state railways; and preferential rail rates offered to exporters and importers using South African Transport Services (SATS) railways and ports.[12] Export credit is another 'carrot' and one which is increasingly effective in the current foreign exchange crisis in most of southern Africa. Even if prices are marked up 20–30 per cent to cover the credit cost, 18 months to pay is a major incentive to an importer or central bank with almost no foreign exchange to hand and little or no access to normal commercial credit. Specific, and often transitory, incentives are also numerous, such as the South African market quotas given for television sets and fertilizer made in Swaziland (since effectively withdrawn).

It should not be assumed, however, that the incentive element of the overall strategy is benign. In the first place, benefits to one southern African state may be highly damaging to the economic

interests of others – and may increase the difficulty of operating a
regional project of political-economic liberation. The customs union,
for example, protects South African exports to Botswana, Lesotho
and Swaziland from competition from other SADCC states (except for
Zimbabwe and Malawi). South African credit facilities greatly hamper
Zimbabwean exports to Zambia even when they are substantially
lower in cost. The contract rates on external traffic are carefully
tailored to undercut those of the Mozambican rail and port system.[13]

Further, the appearance of generosity is often either totally unreal
or at the least conceals a radically unequal division of gains. Because
SACU payments are effectively made two years in arrears, inflation
and import growth fully cancel out the apparent 41 per cent revenue
bonus. In most years, Botswana, Lesotho and Swaziland would derive
more revenue from an independent tariff and excise system than
they do from SACU.[14] However, the barriers to greater domestic
production, increased regional trade through SADCC or PTA, and
imports from low cost sources outside Africa, are very real. Even in the
short term, these entail higher import bills and transportation costs;
and in the medium and long term, there are significant obstacles to
structural change and development. Provision of rolling stock and
technical assistance to railways also serves South African interests.[15]
It creates an incentive to, and a body of lobbyists for, using South
African routes; and it improves the efficiency of the southern African
railways using SATS – a necessary condition for avoiding
chaos on SATS itself. As SATS has a surplus of obsolete equipment,
the rental fees almost certainly exceed any alternative earnings on the
loaned equipment.

These 'positive' incentives have always been combined with
'negative' aspects, such as penalties and deterrents – the second
strategic element. The threat or reality of withdrawal of the incentives
is in itself a powerful 'stick', as shown when SATS withdrew
locomotives loaned to Zimbabwe in 1980–81. As with incentives,
deterrents are varied. Cutting back on the hiring of migrant labour or
reducing the terms of transfer of earnings are weapons which have
been used against Mozambique and, less systematically, against
Lesotho. Selective interruption of the flow of key goods – especially
petroleum products, fertilizers and grain – to SADCC states
assertedly for 'technical' reasons has in fact been linked to political
and security demands. All of the independent states of southern
Africa, except Angola and Tanzania (which do not import or export via
South Africa), have been beaten with this stick more than once since

the formation of SADCC in 1980.[16] 'Technical problems' in relation to moving exports, such as Zimbabwe steel and Botswana beef, are the complement to similar import delays.[17]

The most dramatic deterrents are specific acts of economic sabotage and the promotion of general insurgency. These have formed the core of the strategy with respect to Angola and have become the dominant element in respect to Mozambique. In Zimbabwe and Lesotho these tactics have been used selectively, and elsewhere in the region they have been used on a more occasional basis. This 'outward-looking strategic orientation' runs parallel to incentives and deterrents, and its most dramatic variant is the forward or 'strike kommando' policy. This is the third strategic element, typified by the raids on Maseru, Maputo and Gaborone at the single strike level and by the repeated invasions of Angola at the level of sustaining advances beyond South Africa's frontiers.

This strategic element makes use of economic sabotage against targets such as bridges, dams, railroads, pipelines, mines and oil installations; and it makes use of general economic destabilization through direct actions by the South African Defence Force (SADF) combined with surrogate activity. Thus the cost of this policy to the target states and their people is very high, in both military and econo mic terms.

The aims of this 'strike kommando' policy are not entirely economic in terms of gains sought by South Africa. Indeed in narrow economic terms it is costly to South Africa; extra military expenditure probably exceeds US$ 2 billion a year; freight costs escalate from non-use of the Maputo port; power shortages result from loss of Cahora Bassa supply, and so on. Only if one supposes that South Africa's aim in Angola is to install a regime which would resume trade and provide a dependable petroleum supply do its forward policy tactics there appear to have specific economic benefits for South Africa. However, the outward-looking strategy is designed to protect the political economy of *apartheid* by keeping opponents far from the frontiers and by reducing to rubble the economies and polities of unfriendly neighbours especially those which contain alternative outlets to the sea and little South African investment. In that sense, it is economic.

The other aspect of the outward-looking approach – the fourth strategic element – is political-economic. This is complete South African regional hegemony, as articulated in P.W. Botha's 1979 Carlton Centre presentation of the 'constellation plan'.[18] This strategy seeks a 'co-prosperity sphere' with common economic policies, co-

ordinated security, and at least tacit acceptance of South African
political leadership in a region stretching from Zaire through
Mozambique and from the Cape to the Ruvuma and Congo rivers. In
less ambitious variants, the political element is reduced to demands
on neighbouring states to prevent mobilization of opposition to
Pretoria, and the security aspect is cut back to refusing bases, or
presence, to South African liberation movements and to external
armed forces. The economic elements – trade, transport, technical
and financial assistance – are then dominant and the number of
regional participants flexible, with Botswana, Lesotho, Swaziland, a
'multi-party' Namibia, Zambia, Mozambique and Zimbabwe as the
core.

This approach is most attractive to the private sector, and from the
point of view of production, export and profit expansion. As already
noted, it is not by any means benign and does not confer equal gains.
By strengthening economic links with South Africa, it in fact increases
the leverage against a political economy of liberation. An example of
this is the 1980–81 threats by Pretoria to end its trade agreement with
Zimbabwe. Further, while primarily based on incentives and benefits,
this approach can and does make use of threats or penalties as a means
of securing specific policy changes by southern African states.

Finally, the fifth strategic element is an inward-looking or 'into
laager' approach. This element seeks to concentrate South African
strength within its borders, behind strong defences and with minimum
dependence on external sources of supply.

South Africa has few critical imports from the region, with the
short-term exception of labour for the gold-mines. The reduction in use of
the port of Maputo, Cahora Bassa power and migrant labour, and the
freezing out of certain Swaziland, Botswana and Zimbabwe goods
could be viewed as inward-looking. On the export side, a comparable
strategy of retargeting away from the region does not appear to exist.
Indeed, the thrust of the South African Foreign Trade Office
(SAFTO) is in quite the opposite direction.[19] However, a strategy
highly inward-looking in respect of security, political stance, and
South African imports could also seek to preserve export markets,
especially those for transport services, as a means of creating
dependency and retaining vital foreign exchange income.

The tactical instruments used to implement South African strategy
are numerous and varied, as the presentation of strategic elements

suggests. Tactics vary in channels of operation and therefore in degree of co-ordination and control. For example, the customs union arrangements are government to government, regularly reviewable and instantly terminable. In contrast, existing South African investment in other African countries is historically determined, not speedily (if at all) removable, and owned by private enterprises whose interests may or may not be consistent with Pretoria's overall strategic concerns. An example of the latter point is Anglo American's stake in Angolan diamond mines which are a target of South African surrogates. However, because the continued operation of many South African investments is critical to the host economies (such as the diamond mines in Botswana), their continued operation could be put at peril by Pretoria. Thus, existing investment is to some extent a lever the South African regime can use.

New investment is an intermediate case. The South African authorities can directly (via pressure on companies) or indirectly (by creating economic chaos in the potential host country) ensure that such investment does not take place. But it has no power to ensure this unless the investor is a South African state corporation. Private firms will not rush in unless they see a realistic prospect of stable profits (including a continuation of the South African economic tactics which led it to favour the investment). Thus, when Pretoria favoured – or appeared to favour – investment in Mozambique after Nkomati, there was a flurry of visits but very little actual investment because the general economic situation was unpromising and because businesses were sceptical of how long the *détente* might last.

South Africa has used several tactics simultaneously or in sequence to achieve its goals in relation to particular countries or sectors, and it has developed multi-purpose tactics suitable for furthering several strategic elements. The first point is well illustrated by the transport sector and the second by Renfreight, the South African clearing and forwarding agency dominant in the region.

As stated earlier, the bottom line in blocking the implementation of SADCC's transport liberation has always been sabotage. The financial and dependence costs of using the SATS system have been perceived to be so high that most states in the region are firmly committed to SADCC routes to the sea and will not divert their traffic unless forced to do so. The exceptions are Lesotho, which has no overland options, and Swaziland, which benefits from South African transit traffic. From the 1975 blockage of the Benguela railway to Lobito Bay, Angola, which has never been effectively reopened, through the current

war by Mozambique and Zimbabwe against South Africa's proxy forces
to keep the Beira route open, much of the South African violence has
centred on transport disruption and blockage.

However, a variety of other tactics have been used, such as the provision
and then withdrawal of railway rolling stock, as already mentioned.
A new development is the use of 'fighting rates', or cut-price contracts,
designed to offset the advantages of the Mozambique rail and port
routes. This is a relatively recent tactic and a potent one, especially in
relation to Zimbabwe.[20] The emergence of 'fighting rates' has been
facilitated by SATS' increasingly commercial orientation and by the
increasing overvaluation of Mozambican meticais and undervaluation
of the rand. In late 1985 and early 1986, as the Mozambique
government moved to offer counter rates, the rand rose from US$0.35
to US$ 0.46, undercutting the SATS campaign.[21]

Trade promotion also reinforces transport dependence, as imports
from South Africa and exports to South Africa must go via SATS
routes. Further, SATS insists on relatively balanced traffic, in its own
commercial interest. This means, for example, that Zambian imports
from or via South Africa lead to effective pressure to balance traffic by
rerouting copper exports away from the Tanzanian port of Dar es
Salaam to South African ports at East London and Grahamstown.

The last major tactic in the transport sector is a less evident one:
clearing and forwarding. South Africa's two major clearing and
forwarding groups, Rennies (a SAF Marine subsidiary, and thus
SATS) and Manica Freight Services (an Anglo American group) have
been merged as Renfreight. The new company is controlled by Old
Mutual (an insurance company), which has acquired SAF Marine,
with a significant minority holding by Anglo and additional cross links
via Barclays National. This company dominates not only South
African clearing and forwarding but also that of the land-locked
SADCC members and of Mozambique. Its links with SAF Marine and
its dominance of shipping agency work mean that it directly and
indirectly dominates the South African Shipping Conferences which
cover Beira and Maputo as well as South African ports.[22]

Renfreight is a multi-purpose instrument. At the simplest level it
earns profits and foreign exchange because clearing and forwarding is
lucrative. It is also in a position to route freight via SATS (with whom
SAF Marine has strong mutual interest links even if now separately
owned) because, in practice, shipping agents have wide latitude in
recommending and choosing routes for their clients. Renfreight has
every reason to use that position since its associates in SATS – Anglo,

SAF Marine, Old Mutual and Barclays National – stand to profit from business routed via South Africa, through rail and port charges, insurance, ancilliary services, related goods purchases, ship cargoes and so on. In gross terms, these gains are larger than the clearing and forwarding fees themselves. Further, Renfreight prefers to take its profits in rand, not in inconvertible regional currencies.[23]

Finally, the internal commercial logic of a regional clearing and forwarding company means that detailed data on cargo by nature, bulk and weight, value, source and route must be on a computer in Johannesburg. Effectively, this means it could be available, through one means or another, to South African authorities for analysis (of sources and prices to counter with trade credits or data to SAFTO, and of stocks and flows of key commodities) and, when desired, as a means for implementing selective delays and/or sabotage.

As the country chapters have shown, South Africa does not act in an identical way against all independent southern African states. Dominant strategic elements and tactics differ markedly, and are used in different combinations.

In the case of Zambia, the dominant strategic element has been the 'co-prosperity sphere' with a systematic campaign since 1965 to build up export trade and transport linkages. This has been notably successful despite Zambia's very real effort to identify alternative sources of imports and to develop intra-SADCC transportation routes.[24] An additional factor is that South Africa has perceived the Zambian president, Kenneth Kaunda, not as sympathetic, but as committed to dialogue. Therefore he is seen as a potentially valuable interlocateur with the leaders of liberation movements and other Frontline States, but also as one who would react very negatively to sustained economic and military aggression.

This is not to overlook a persistent sub-theme of more violent actions, such as the campaigns in south-western Zambia adjacent to Namibia, the training of the Mushala gang, delays in goods deliveries, and the threatening 1985 raid on the Lusaka ANC offices. These appear to have been designed to warn Zambia of the dangers of more active support for liberation movements, of breaking off dialogue or failing to develop economic links.

From a South African perspective, the approach has worked rather well. First, Zambia's severe economic and technical problems –

flowing primarily from the sanctions imposed on Rhodesia and the collapse of the copper market – have made the government unable and unwilling to incur additional costs. Extended trade credit and massive rolling stock loans are critical to Zambia. Second, South Africa has built up a perception of itself as a relatively fair economic dealer and a competent economic partner in the eyes of elements of the Zambian elite and even of the urban labour force.[25] These perceptions have been critical to its trade and transport campaigns.

A somewhat harder line has been taken in respect to Zimbabwe – one constrained by the fact that Zimbabwe is an important export market and investment site. Another constraint is the reality that a prosperous Zimbabwe using Mozambique transport routes and taking SADCC export markets away from South Africa would be a major disaster for both the economic and security aspects of the political economy of *apartheid.* South Africa has apparently had difficulty in identifying ways to reconcile this dilemma. But the strategy seems to be to exacerbate internal conflict in Zimbabwe, to prevent the use of Mozambican transportation routes, and to keep its (much more resilient than Zambia's) economy off balance.

One aspect of South Africa's policy toward both Zambia and Zimbabwe that is physically external to those states is the blocking of intra-SADCC transportation routes. In the case of Zambia, this means primarily the Lobito Bay line; and in the case of Zimbabwe, the Beira and Maputo links. Here, too, Zimbabwe's response has posed a dilemma for Pretoria. The Zimbabwe army not only defends the communication routes to Beira and Tete, but acts with the Mozambican armed forces against South Africa's proxies, the MNR.

South Africa's stance in respect to the three small BLS states also varies. With Botswana, it has been largely 'co-prosperity sphere' use of economic dependence (markets in, investment in and mine workers from Botswana matter to South Africa but also keep Botswana dependent). This has been backed by threats in order to deter government from pursuing any political-economic liberation beyond the verbal level. However, Pretoria has begun to perceive this approach as increasingly unsuccessful. Botswana has rejected advantageous customs union revisions linked to recognizing bantustans, turned down water export deals even when this imperilled other desired investiments, begun to canvas alternative import sourcing and transportation routing. Botswana has been a driving force in the formation and promotion of SADCC, which is headquartered in Gaborone. Each step has been cautious and limited, but the direction is the same and the impact cumulative. The 1985 attack on Gaborone, and the crescendo of threats preceeding and following it, represent a fairly desperate effort to force Botswana to reverse its course. As there is no evidence it has succeeded in that, South Africa is presumably considering what new coercive tactics might be more effective and meanwhile threatening more and bigger raids.

Swaziland perceives itself as so vulnerable to South African sabotage and economic destabilization that the overt strategy has been overwhelmingly one of offering – though often not delivering – incentives. The covert strategy has been that of seeking to manipulate government and business leaders.

In respect to Lesotho, the South African blockade amounted to the imposition of sanctions, and there have been few incentives other than limiting the contraction of market access for Lesotho labour. The bottom line of the proposed water project is that South Africa needs the water. Coercion until 1986 mainly involved raids, both direct and by proxy. These were partly for domestic political reaction, partly through genuine belief in some quarters that ANC military operations were mounted from Maseru, and partly to remind Lesotho of its vulnerability. The blockade, the most serious form of economic destabilization, was used in spite of the fact the economy is almost entirely South African owned and supplied.

The question arises as to whether South Africa's strategy and tactics for regional hegemony form a seamless web of diabolically clever Machiavellian (or Kissingeresque) cunning; a wandering minstrel show lurching from one piece of crisis management to another; or a mass of internal contradictions and insoluble conflicts among South African objectives. The answer is probably none of the above by itself, but some of each combined.

South Africa does have regional interests which have been defined in fairly stable terms for almost 200 years, since the early nineteenth century. Regional strategy since 1970 has been intensely ideological and remarkably consistent in objectives – the preservation of *apartheid* at home and the acquisition of *lebensraum,* especially economic and security, throughout the region. However, the balance among strategic elements and tactics has shifted sharply over time with temporary, selective reversals of course overlying a secular trend toward rising levels of violence. The political economy of regional hegemony has been operated pragmatically, responding to perceptions of attainable targets based on changes in domestic and regional, national and international contexts, and adjusted in light of the results.

While a coherent regional policy has emerged from the consistency of objectives, the interests of white South African individuals, subclasses and institutions are not identical nor are their perceptions of the most effective ways of pursuing them always congruent. Indeed, as the Gorongosa documents demonstrate, there can be quite antagonistic fractions within the same institutions. It is worth reviewing some of the divergences and shifts in balance to gain insight into their underlying causes.

At an individual level, for example, the Gorongosa documents suggest that the hardline militarist advocates of the 'strike kommando' approach viewed some politicians as sharing their perceptions while seeing other politicians and some military leaders as having different and antagonistic perceptions. The debate within the armed forces among advocates of the forward strategy, a mixed approach, or an inward-looking approach has been visible for over five years. While apparently emotionally attracted by a 'strike kommando' forward policy stance, President Botha has a real concern for direct economic interests and a perception that Portugal's overextension on the colonial periphery led to its collapse at the centre. He and his colleagues on the State Security Council (SSC) have developed from their divergent individual opinions a mixed approach, involving the five strategic elements.

Institutions have interests and perceptions which are not necessarily identical to those of the state. SATS, particularly under former General Manager Loubser, is a clear example.[26] SATS' view of 'transport diplomacy' as a hegemonic tool and of itself as a major, quasi-independent actor, has led it to take a fairly consistent 'co-prosperity sphere' approach. Loaning wagons and rolling stock, setting rates and discounts to get business, and strengthening the role of SAF Marine (then a SATS subsidiary) in regional clearing and forwarding have been among its tactics.

SATS needs traffic, especially for its Eastern Cape ports, and has limited chances of finding this domestically.[27] Thus reasonably functional internal rail services in the independent states funnelling into the SATS network provide the necessary volume of operations. However, SATS' perceptions are not based in narrow self interest, nor are they benign. It sees continued regional transport dependence as critical to South Africa's economic and regional dominance and itself as an agent able to work for those ends with independent African states and institutions which could not or would not readily negotiate or work with the South African government.[28]

It also sees provision of rail links and rolling stock in terms of the leverage provided. A decade-long programme of constructing the two link lines which make Swaziland a rail corridor from the Transvaal to the Natal ports increases flexibility for SATS in respect to South Africa's own external trade. It is a means of ending South African dependence on the port of Maputo and increasing SATS' ability to compete against Mozambique's transport system for Zimbabwean cargo.

Sub-class interests also differ. The standard presentation is business versus the military. That is an oversimplification. There are three distinguishable capitalist sub-classes in South Africa, which broadly correlate with the main white political groupings.

The first can be termed 'high capitalism' and encompasses the South African transnational corporations (especially the Anglo American–De Beers and Rembrandt groups), the large domestic corporate groups (Gencor, Old Mutual), some local subsidiaries or affiliates of transnational groups headquartered abroad (Barclays National, Shell, BP) and certain parastatals (notably SATS, Electricity Supply Commission and SAFTO). For this sub-class, the bottom line is the preservation of capitalism in South Africa (with *apartheid* dispensable if necessary for that end) and expansion within the region. Violence and destabilization are perceived as costly and damaging to profitability, though not unacceptable as tactics to attain a 'co-prosperity sphere' or 'constellation' in the region or to avert socialist revolution at home. Economically, this sub-class totally dominates South Africa. Politically – for historic reasons and because its perceived interests are distinctively different from those of most white South Africans – it is surprisingly weak and able to influence state policy only at the margins.[29] It is the colonial capitalist class, primarily English-speaking, 'liberal' and most often aligned to the Progressive Federalist Party (PFP).

'Middle capitalism' comprises a greater number of firms, ranging from moderately larger corporations to efficient family enterprises, and is predominantly Afrikaner in nature and culture. It is less able to perceive its capitalist viability as separable from an *apartheid* state domestically or from South African regional hegemony. Exports are important to many firms in this group (who are SAFTO's main clients) and for some (such as the Kirsch Group which was born in Swaziland) regional links go deeper. While broadly in favour of a 'co-prosperity sphere', this sub-class is less certain of its ability to cope with independent African states or to compete with domestic or other foreign interests in them. Politically, this sub-class in National Party (NP), with all of the contradictions which characterize that party.

What the above interest (high and middle capitalism) have in common is the promotion of export markets to generate profits, with government support for their expansion. Economic destabilization and sabotage designed to force economic policy changes (though not similar measures related to purely political objectives) can be useful in that context. However, this is true only if the pressures are effective, the 'sanctioned' state reverses its policy, the destabilization is wound down and the independent state's economy snaps back. Permanent destabilization directed at creating and perpetuating economic chaos as an end in itself (as in Angola and Mozambique) has little attraction for these profit-centred enterprises.

'Petty capitalism' can be typified by the community commercial establishments and the small capitalist or large-scale peasant white farmer. Its direct interest in regional economic links is low and its perception of any broader class or national interest almost equally so. This is numerically the largest, though economically the weakest, of the capitalist sub-classes, and it does not perceive itself as able to survive in any context except *apartheid*. For these 'petty capitalists', P.W. Botha's domestic 'reforms' are much too radical and far-reaching; and the basic aim of their desired regional policy is to combat the '*swaart gevaar*' (black peril) by force and outside South Africa's borders.

That South African strategy is flawed and its tactics unevenly successful – or on occasion counter-productive – is no reason to write it off as insignificant or easy to overcome. Neither is the fact that domestic resistance and regional animosity cannot be cured by 'co-prosperity spheres' or 'strike kommando' policies, but only through an end to *apartheid*.

South Africa is much more powerful than the independent states of southern Africa, both economically and militarily; it is willing to use that power to inflict damage on its neighbours and to reward acquiescence. Its identification of its own interests may be flawed and its post-1975 (and especially post-1980) strategy largely a series of *ad hoc* responses to unexpected (but not always unpredictable) external events. But its identification of methods of inflicting costs on SADCC (in terms of human suffering as well as $) has been only too accurate. Its ruthlessness in inflicting these costs – especially in respect to transport which both South Africa and SADCC perceive as the backbone of regional political economic hegemony – is apparently virtually unlimited.

SADCC is the symbol and tangible embodiment of the political economy of southern African liberation. It is a political-economic project of the independent states of the region – Angola, Botswana, Lesotho, Malawi, Mozambique, Swaziland, Tanzania, Zambia and Zimbabwe – perceived by *apartheid* South Africa as a dangerous enemy of its regional hegemony. If SADCC is able to carry out its programmes, especially in transport, it represents a potentially mortal threat to South Africa's political-economic predominance in the region. To assess this programme for economic liberation, a more detailed analysis is necessary of SADCC's historical, institutional, and operational issues.

In 1979 there was hope that Zimbabwe would soon be independent under black majority rule. The cost of the war was becoming too high for Rhodesia, and right-wing attempts in both Britain and the United States to recognize the internal 'Zimbabwe-Rhodesia' settlement had been forestalled. But the leaders of the Frontline States (Angola, Botswana, Mozambique, Tanzania, Zambia) knew that Zimbabwe's political independence did not mean economic independence. President Seretse Khama of Botswana, who became the first chairman of SADCC, summarized their assessment that '... economic dependence has in many ways made our political independence somewhat meaningless.' In July 1979, the finance ministers from the Frontline States met in Arusha, in northern Tanzania, to discuss a new type of economic co-operation, which would include independent Zimbabwe, recognizing its geographical and economic centrality in the region.

SADCC was launched in Lusaka on 1 April 1980, a few days before Zimbabwe's independence celebrations. The new group had been expanded in the interim to include Lesotho, Swaziland and Malawi in order to encompass all the independent states in the region. The African leaders were fully aware of the difficulties of the new venture. Their economies had suffered from the crisis of the international economic system. Terms of trade for their major exports, such as copper, cotton and coffee, had deteriorated by 50 per cent in just four years, 1975–1979. Foreign debt had risen to over 30 per cent of export earnings for most.[30] They had no illusions that regional co-ordination could change that global context. Zambia and Mozambique had been victims of economic sabotage as their bridges, rail lines, and irrigation works were bombed by Rhodesia during the Zimbabwe independence talks at Lancaster House; and the Frontline leaders realized that a desperate South Africa would use the same tactic.

It was also clear by 1980 that 'autonomous' national development projects were not working in the Third World, particularly for low income economies. The Frontline economies were fragmented, dependent on primary commodities, and very much tied to their ex-colonial masters. Three (Botswana, Mozambique, Zambia) were dependent on South Africa for regular food supplies, trade and transport. International sanctions against Rhodesia left the Zimbabwe economy more fully integrated into South Africa, for the *apartheid* regime abrogated the sanctions. However, the members brought to SADCC experience of bilateral co-operation among their economies. The most innovative example was the Tanzania-Mozambique Permanent Commission of Co-operation, which directly influenced some SADCC provisions, such as production complementarity and counter-trade, as discussed below.

President Machel of Mozambique summarized the nature of the new regional co-operation when he said, 'we have built an organization from our own realities and experience and not from patterns imported from abroad.'[31] The Southern African Development Co-ordination Conference is a multi-government organization, not a supra-national one set up with a life of its own. Decisions in SADCC are made by consensus. Implementation is decentralized, as each project is the responsibility of one or more states. Projects do not proceed without the state(s) enacting it. Consequently, the central bureaucracy is small (although technical personnel in the sectoral co-ordinating units and associated programme bodies number almost 100).

The choice of this decentralized series of consensual conferences reflects the bitter experiences of Tanzania in the East African Community (EAC), of Zambia and Malawi (before independence) in the Central African Federation (CAF), of centralized rule of 'Portugal in Africa' and of SACU. The EAC became an entity in itself, almost a fourth state in East Africa. The CAF drained revenue from Zambia and Malawi to expand production in Rhodesia. SACU is (and Portugal in Africa was) for the benefit of South Africa (Portugal).

SADCC is explicitly political, not in the sense of any overall domestic ideological congruity – that could be counterproductive even to try – but in declaring that economic links are not made in a vacuum.

Economic conditions and relations in southern Africa had never been left to 'market forces'. In addition to the bias of the economic unions mentioned above, the colonial states intervened regularly to force labour production from Africans and to limit access of their goods to markets. Lucrative subsidies from the colonial governments went to white farmers and mining companies, while Africans were taxed to the point of malnutrition. Examples abound from each state,[32] but a few can serve as reminders. The Kyle Dam was built in Rhodesia to aid the sugar industry. Huletts Corporation (of South Africa) persuaded the government to finance construction of the dam ($4 million), with the corporation contributing only $600 000.[33] Data from independent Zimbabwe shows that white commercial farmers were not particularly 'efficient', with many continuing to farm solely because of the largesse of the state, through price subsidies, extension services, provision of irrigation, and other inputs.[34] As far as their contribution to state revenue, even in 1980 three in four paid no income tax.[35]

SADCC analysts are not fully convinced, therefore, of the conventional wisdom of 'apolitical', expert-controlled, cost-benefit analysis, for it has been high cost and low benefit to Africans for centuries. 'Efficiency' is a contributory factor but not a sufficient condition for economic growth and in any case can be defined only in relation to specified objectives. Diversity in production, sources and markets, and distribution of goods and services are greater priorities of economies trying to emerge from colonial domination. SADCC, therefore, sees the ultimate goal as 'restructuring' the southern African economies. The colonial legacy in infrastructure, production, and distribution is not acceptable, economically or politically. However, equally important, no supra-national organization will impose any changes; restructuring will occur only as much as each government determines. SADCC's more modest role is to create a new regional economic context for national change – with the new infrastructures, agricultural research, shared training facilities, production co-ordination and intra-regional trade expansion. SADCC is equally committed to constructing equitable patterns of regional interaction in order to pursue common interests.

This SADCC analysis clearly complements its first stated goal: to reduce economic dependence on South Africa. It is a practical goal, for even with a free South Africa, the linkages would have to be altered. However, it is also a political expression of repugnance for a regime and an economy which survives solely by repression of the majority at home and of its neighbours regionally. Again, SADCC is not unrealistic about the difficulty of this goal. First, it is to reduce, not eliminate, dependence. Second, SADCC members include Botswana, Lesotho and Swaziland whose economies are captive of South Africa, and Malawi whose government has chosen to build monumental projects with South African capital and technology. The economic ability and political will to reduce dependence varies considerably; yet at the Harare annual conference in January 1986, held just days after the South African blockade provoked a *coup* in Lesotho, the new minister of planning and economic affairs, Michael Sefali, said Lesotho would 'resist any attempts aimed at reducing her to a status of subserviance ... and fully participate in all SADCC programmes.'[36]

The objectives of SADCC to increase economic development through regional co-ordination and to reduce dependence, not only but especially, on *apartheid* South Africa, were not simply left to vague declarations. The steps toward these long term goals have been many, but small; they have been determined, but practical. SADCC now has 398 projects, costing US$ 4.8 billion, of which half are either completed, implemented or actively under negotiation.[37] Transport is considered the first priority – to refurbish old lines, build new ones and improve training and operational co-ordination. Mozambique can serve five of the other states for ports to overseas markets, and the Southern African Transport and Communications Commission (SATCC), co-ordinated by Mozambique, has been praised by the donors. Of 111 projects ($ 2 742 million), 28 are financed, 30 are partly financed and 40 projects are under discussion. Since 1982, 17 projects ($113 million) have been completed, including a microwave link of all the states.[38]

Second on the priority list is promotion of food production to reduce economic vulnerability; only Zimbabwe and Malawi are likely to be food exporters in the near future. Thirty-five agricultural projects have secured funding ($125.9 million) and another 37 are under negotiation.[39] One indication of the type of food projects is the sorghum-millet-groundnut-legume research, all peasant-produced, drought-resistent food crops. The field tests are occurring at multiple points in the nine countries with emphasis on small peasant usability.[40]

The agriculture sector also co-ordinated requests for relief during the drought (1981–84) so that the different countries would not be competing with each other ($23 million was secured and $113 million for rehabilitation is under negotiation).[41] This co-operation continues to be important for drought persisted in 1986 for Botswana and parts of Angola, Lesotho, Mozambique and Zimbabwe. In 1986, the early warning system to detect impending food shortages nationally and for the whole region will be in place; it is the first regional system of its kind. Each member co-ordinates one to three sectors.[42] For example, Botswana is in charge of agricultural research and animal disease control while Lesotho is responsible for soil and water conservation.

The third priority is industry, co-ordinated by Tanzania. The objective is to set up production complementarity, with industry promoted in all the economies, but planned to avoid competition. For example, each state will produce textiles, but textile chemicals will be produced only by Botswana and Tanzania.[43] All but Botswana, Lesotho, and Swaziland produce cement, with SADCC potentially able to export cement. No new plants will be started, and studies will ascertain demand for additional cement products. Movement toward co-ordinated implementation of national fertilizer production plans appears to be progressing. In contrast, plans to co-ordinate tractor production seem to have failed.[44] Licences to transnational corporations have been given for the same product: Leyland has spent 3.6 million kwacha in Zambia to make the same type and range of vehicle as the Mutare plant in Zimbabwe.[45] Production complementarity can be seen as an attempt to preclude Zimbabwe's potential domination as it presently accounts for 37.5 per cent of SADCC industrial output and 54 per cent of SADCC heavy industry.[46]

Mining, directed by Zambia, is a vital sector to many of the economies, but co-ordination began late and has not yet progressed very far. The mining sector is the most fully integrated with South Africa and more particularly with one corporate group. As one SADCC official joked, 'SADCC does not have to worry about regional co-ordination of mining; Anglo American Corporation already does it!'[47] Or as economist Duncan Clarke points out, 'Investment linkages thread a financial and economic pattern of regional interdependence which is deeply rooted' – and which has survived major upheavals in the region.[48] To date, SADCC has not even addressed minerals marketing or mining legislation, but has concentrated on the easier decisions of inventory of mineral resources, small-scale minerals studies, training and identification of diversification, down-stream processing and production.

In a real sense, SADCC will always be on the brink of failure, for its goals are very long term, but its projects and its new 1986–1990 perspective plan look only to the next five years. Development and dependence reduction constitute an ongoing process, and there is no 'final victory'. Partly due to the drought, the international economic crisis, and poor national planning – but also substantially related to South African aggression – seven of the SADCC economies had declines or stagnation in output per capita since 1980; real Gross Domestic Product (GDP) of SADCC as a whole has fallen. Several SADCC members have reduced imports since 1979.[49]

Yet the first years of SADCC also show real successes. SADCC seems to have passed the first test of economic co-ordination in that co-operation, not rivalry, has increased. Member states attend meetings enthusiastically to argue through problems; counterparts in specific ministries know each other personally and learn to resolve differences more easily. This intangible benefit now has some tangible results. The Malawi road spur to the Dar es Salaam road in Tanzania was completed in six months, and a fishery project is assessing possibilities for co-ordinated exploitation of Lake Nyasa/Malawi's marine resources. A few years back, Malawi and Tanzania had very limited relations and argued acrimoniously over their precise boundary.[50] In October 1984, Zimbabwe ameliorated the Malawian fuel crisis (caused by MNR attacks of the rail line) by shipping 3.5 million litres of petrol to Malawi.[51] Capital has entered the region which might not have come otherwise; certainly, aid to Angola and Mozambique has been higher than they would have received bilaterally.[52]

As regioinal co-ordination moves into the second half of its first decade of existence, more difficult questions will arise. The co-ordination of SADCC has not threatened the political *status quo* of any of the states. In fact, the decentralized nature is designed exactly to avoid that issue. However, if the ultimate goal is to 'restructure' economies, elements of the ruling classes and of basic national economic interests will be challenged at some point.

The crisis of the international capitalist system will not go away; since the 1970s the 'upward swings' have been shallow and for short periods. To deal with the crisis situation, SADCC economies will have to make hard choices about production, not simply promote full capacity of existing industries. It may not make sense to rescue parts of the Tanzanian industry or to modernize parts of the antiquated Zimbabwe industry. As SADCC is organized now, those decisions will be made solely at the national level. For the region to ameliorate the vagaries of the international crises, however, such national decisions should more regularly and fully include co-ordinated consideration of the regional context. If not, SADCC will remain quite vulnerable to outside forces.

SADCC also has not established an investment code for the region. Until a uniform code is signed, international capital can play one economy against others; but to sign one code would mean far greater economic congruence than SADCC can envisage today or perhaps ever.

Foreign exchange shortages in all member states except Botswana have deterred trade; SADCC has responded with encouragement of bilateral counter-trade. If Mozambique's trade is in deficit to Tanzania, it is up to Mozambique to find goods to export that Tanzania needs. The deficit is paid by additional trade. SADCC says that the foreign exchange crises will only be resolved by beginning with greater production and then promoting trade to validate that production – the opposite of normal common market theory.

Questions which SADCC has not even addressed also affect its longevity. It has not discussed the wage differential among workers on various projects from different countries. The nature of management is not discussed by Swaziland which co-ordinates manpower training or by SATCC which is busy training its technical unit.[53] It appears that SADCC is accepting, without question, hierarchical management, with the technically skilled in quite superior salary categories and with little worker role in decision making, or at least the member states pursue various formulations and modifications of that model. The preoccupation seems to be to find and train personnel, not to raise questions about social relations of production. This approach avoids controversy in the short term, but may undermine SADCC, as the process of development even at present differs greatly between economies with capitalist production and those which are trying to pursue a transition to socialism.

Dependence on South Africa may be reduced only at the price of greatly increased dependence on Western capital. Until recently, the Soviet Union ignored SADCC, stating that the problems arose from colonialism and preferring bilateral links. However, all the developed socialist countries, except Hungary, attended the 1986 Harare consultative conference and discussions are under way for the Council of Mutual Economic Assistance (CMEA) to relate to SADCC. The People's Republic of China is helping to repair the Tazara railway and a line in Botswana. The vast majority of the funds, however, are coming from Western donors. For example, the sectoral offices, such as SATCC and the food security office in Zimbabwe, have only small

portions of their budgets provided by the members. The Nordic countries
are the primary sourse of SATCC finance, and the US, Australia,
Canada and Federal Republic of Germany (FRG) are supporting the
food security division. SATCC officials admit that there are no short
term plans for full financing by members. One suggested that
technicians could be seconded to SATCC as a contribution, but that
has not yet occurred, even from Zimbabwe which has qualified
personnel who might be spared from national requirements.[54] The
contribution to SATCC by each member was only $6 000 per year in
1984.

In addition, the local currency component of each project remains
modest. For example, in food security, 87.1 per cent of the budget is in
foreign currency; for agricultural research, it is 100 per cent.[55]
In industry, 75.5 per cent of the budget will take foreign exchange to
finance.[56] In several cases, however, domestic inputs and national
contributions have clearly been understated or left out because the
published information was designed to attract the external funds
needed to complement them. Flows of capital to SADCC to implement these projects are a success but only for the short term. Plans
for regional self-financing are necessary to sustain SADCC.

To date, donor interference has been limited, and SADCC has
protested sharply and effectively when it has occurred. The United
States financed the sorghum-millet research project at the regional level,
but put in an exclusionary clause saying that Angola, Mozambique and
Tanzania could not benefit. This precipitated several discussions as
well as condemnation by President Nyerere who singled out the US for
reprimand at the July 1984 Gaborone summit meeting.[57] The US
altered its formulation to one specifying what it would (as opposed to
what it would not) finance, accepted that all findings would be
available to all SADCC members, and financed the regional and six
country components. But it took another year before other donors,
such as Canada, agreed to support the three initially left out.

The Western donors will continue to offer funds to try to insert their
own agendas into SADCC. The United States Agency for International Development (USAID) prides itself in promoting small
farmers, but translates that to mean private farmers who may become
'master farmers'; producer co-operatives are not on the agenda. The
Nordic countries have criticized SADCC members for their agricultural policies, without mentioning the role of international commodity prices in contributing to the African food crisis.[58]

The SADCC leaders are quite aware of outsiders' agendas. The question, which will only be determined by the process, is whether SADCC will reject, modify or accept the 'suggestions'. To date it has acted on its stated view that all suggestions, comments, criticisms and dialogue are welcome but that, because SADCC and its members are responsible to their peoples, decisions must be southern African.

The answer may be different for energy, co-ordinated by Angola, than for forestry, co-ordinated by Malawi. The decentralized nature of SADCC makes funding procedures complex for donors, but on occasion gives them much room for manoeuvre. One critic of SADCC's dependence on Western capital stated that Western strategy is no longer to divide and rule, but to 'regroup and dominate; SADCC is only co-ordination of donors, for donors'.[59] Certainly, in its first six years, SADCC has set its own priorities and has halted the more blatant attemps at interference. Further, its annual conferences are the only regular multilateral consultative group meetings called, organized, documented and run by the recipient side. However, plans for a greater share of national capital in the projects and for national experts as consultants must become serious before it will escape criticisms like the above.

To concentrate solely on overall foreign funding proportions, which SADCC itoolft hao oaid wcrc unsustainably and undesir- ably high (in its 1985 OAU Summit paper), is to miss two critical points. First, they are higher than evisaged in 1979–80 because the external economic position of SADCC's members has been much worse than could reasonably have been foreseen – largely as a result of world recession, drought and South African aggression. To make a rapid start and to sustain concrete action, SADCC had to resort to increased use of external resources. While this does lead to a medium-term problem, any other choice would have led to no significant operational programme.

Second, SADCC's dependence reduction objective is not theoretical and undifferentiated. It is contextual and specific. Dependence on South Africa is the immediate enemy. Substituting dependence on grants and soft loans from a range of donors (to restore and upgrade the five SADCC port corridor transport systems) for dependence on SATS is seen by SADCC as a step forward. In the words of a Confucian saying adopted by Chairman Mao and used in several SADCC addresses and publications, 'Even the longest journey begins with the first step'. SADCC's claim is not that it has arrived but rather that it has taken the first step.

South Africa initially ignored SADCC, apparently in the hope it would fade out, but has since decided that SADCC is an enemy. At Nkomati in March 1984, Prime Minister Botha called it the 'counter-constellation'. In contrast, Pretoria sees the PTA as posing no threat; and it can be easily penetrated by South African transnationals, for they can maintain 49 per cent ownership of their subsidiaries and still benefit from the lower tariffs. The rules of origin code allows major exceptions to local origin content rules for products. This means that Swaziland, for example, could help South African goods enter the PTA via SACU.[60] Finally, the history of preferential trade areas shows that the stronger sectors dominate. What may look like a surge in Zimbabwean trade could well be South African, with Zimbabwean products largely produced by South African subsidiaries in Zimbabwe. Zimbabwean public and private capital might have 51 per cent or more of the shares, but corporations such as Anglo American have no problem controlling production and financial decisions with limited ownership interest if they dominate management and external marketing, and determine access to technology (via licensing and patents).[61] The PTA only requires that a 'majority' of the management be nationals.

The result of years of economic sabotage from South Africa underlines the necessity for SADCC. As the Botswana vice-president, Peter Mmusi stated, 'It has been said that good fences make good neighbours. We know the hard realities of living with bad neighbours – and we will keep our fences in good repair'.[62] Certainly, SADCC needs peace for the new transport links to work and for production to increase. Mozambique has had to 'hug the hated hyena', as ANC leader Oliver Tambo said, and has no peace to show for it. But the 1984 Nkomati Accord did not mean the demise of SADCC. Mozambique wants to return temporarily to the transport, tourism and power trade it had with South Africa in 1980, which South Africa cut off. If substantial new investment comes via subsidiaries in South Africa, then Mozambique will increase its links to *apartheid,* although the likelihood of large enterprise investments seems remote. On the other side, investment will enter on Mozambican terms, which are more stringent than those in Botswana, Swaziland, Malawi, Lesotho or Zambia. SATS and South African users are contributing $15 million to increase the capacity of the Maputo rail and harbour, ironically perhaps, a SADCC priority. One could view this as a SADCC 'sell out' to South Africa, or as necessary South African compensation for the SADCC projects it has destroyed or as a product of internal contradictions in South African strategy and tactics.

The choice by South Africa to bomb SADCC projects shows, in fact, its vulnerability to co-ordinated economic links in the region. As shown earlier, having most regional external trade in goods and services flow through *apartheid* South Africa does not make good economic sense. (The shippers praise the Beira line when it is open; the 1984 Zimbabwe tobacco crop went through Beira quickly, at low cost.) The estimate is that Zambia, Zimbabwe and Botswana could save $100 million per year on transport cost alone, if the Mozambican lines were open and problems arising from current rand and meticais valuation were phased out. With appropriate government policy, growing food is cheaper than importing it from South Africa. SADCC industry found that importing small tools costs 10 times more than if artisans made them.[63] For many imports, South African sources are more expensive, even with tariff preferences, than regional or global sources.

The first comprehensive estimates of the cost to its neighbours of South African aggression were prepared by SADCC for the 1985 OAU summit.[64] These cover the period 1980–84 and total just over $10 billion. For comparison, this exceeds total foreign grant and loan aid to the region, 40 per cent of exports from SADCC countries and 10 per cent of their GDP for the five year period. In fact, the SADCC estimates appear to be low; $12–13 billion is still a conservative figure. By 1985 the annual loss was running at $4 billion a year, about $70 per capita for a group of countries whose average annual output is perhaps $500 per capita. For Mozambique the costs now exceed 50 per cent of GDP, and for non-oil GDP in Angola the share is close to half. The six-year total to 1985 is of the order of $16–17 billion.

The economic costs do not stand alone. As many as 250 000 people have lost their lives as a result of South African aggression. The vast majority died because economic and military aggression has created famine in southern Angola and Mozambique by disrupting agricultural production, preventing famine relief food distribution, and destroying the rural water, health and education networks. About 100 000 refugees have crossed borders, mostly Angolans into Zambia and Mozambicans into Zimbabwe; but this figure is dwarfed by up to five million people displaced from their homes in Angola and Mozambique by the tidal waves of war and famine.

SADCC's estimate of the cost of South African aggression is detailed in Table M, with adjusted figures in brackets. The direct cost of war damage has been calculated from Angolan and Mozambican official data, as have the relief and refugee costs. The extra defence expenditure is estimated by country – but excludes Mozambique, Zambia and Tanzania for which it probably totals at least $250 million – by comparing defence budget levels and increases with probable spending in a more peaceful setting.

Table M
The price of defying Pretoria

Direct war damage	1 610 000 000	
Extra defence expenditure	3 060 000 000	(3 310 000 000)
Higher transport, energy costs	970 000 000	
Smuggling, (looting)	190 000 000	
Refugees	660 000 000	
Lost exports, tourism	230 000 000	(250 000 000)
Boycotts, embargoes	260 000 000	
Loss of existing production	800 000 000	
Lost economic growth	2 000 000 000	(4 000 000 000)
Trading arrangements (plus 'fighting' transport rates, export credits)	340 000 000	(590 000 000)
	10 120 000 000	(12 940 000 000)

Smuggling and looting by South African and proxy forces centres on diamonds, ivory, timber and semi-precious stones from Angola and Mozambique. Lost exports and tourism revenue is calculated on the basis of Mozambican coal and sugar, Angolan non-oil exports, Malawian and Swazi sugar, and Mozambican tourism. This is certainly an underestimate as Zimbabwean steel and agricultural exports have also been affected.

Higher transport and energy costs, and lost revenue from geographically and financially artificial routing via South Africa have been estimated from SATS' revenue on regional transit traffic and higher costs to Malawi on non-SATS routes, such as the road via Zambia and Zimbabwe, air and road/rail via Tanzania. Boycotts and embargo costs, as estimated, are dominated by the loss of Mozambican revenue on South African cargo diverted from Maputo. Other items relate to disruption of trade from the seven southern SADCC countries.

Loss of production is necessarily highly approximate. Partial official data from Angola and Mozambique suggest $650 million for these countries. SADCC estimates for Zimbabwe, Zambia and

Malawi appear low, offsetting any double counting with lost exports or transport revenue.

Trading arrangements costs in the SADCC paper are estimates of the additional annual and arrears payments which would have been made to Botswana, Lesotho and Swaziland under re-negotiated SACU terms had South Africa not blocked implementation. The special impact of 'fighting' transport rates (perhaps covered in the transport cost item) and of export credits to block growth of intra-SADCC trade (not covered in export loss estimate as made by SADCC) probably add another $250 million.

The largest and most speculative item is loss of economic growth. In the absence of the costs outlined above, fixed capital formation would have been much higher as would the provision of productive and basic services. SADCC's estimate of $2 billion over 1980–84 is based on assumed resources freed for investment if extra military expenditure had been unnecessary and war damage had not taken place. Even on that basis, they appear rather low, and adding in the other costs suggests a 1980–84 total of about $4 billion and an annual loss of $2 billion by 1985 for this sector.

SADCC is not a mode of production or a transition to socialism project. There is no consensus among its members for such a project and to promote it would abort its programme of economic liberation, for which consensus does exist. Equally, however, while SADCC operates on the basis of consensus it is not a least common denominator organization. Its ruthless condemnation of South African aggression and destabilization – and its growing involvement in the question of sanctions against South Africa[65] – clearly are less radical than those some of its members take nationally, but also go well beyond the purely national positions of others. These co-ordinated statements and actions do have more impact than a collection of purely national – and disparate – ones. Further, in the process of co-ordination (and, some would say, consciousness-raising), SADCC members now see more clearly the overall nature of South African political economic hegemony, as well as the different national abilities to bear costs and assume risks to overcome that dominance.

Sanctions against South Africa as a means of inducing or coercing changes in its internal system, its occupation of Namibia or – less frequently – its regional aggression have been advocated more or less seriously for over 20 years. Action, however, has been limited and concentrated on military equipment, sport and entertainment, and in certain professional fields. A parallel oil sanctions effort by the Organization of Petroleum Exporting Countries (OPEC), while imposing real costs on South Africa, was systematically evaded and dissolved in the buyer's market of the early 1980s. Only for a brief period at the end of the 1970s did extensive economic sanctions on a global or near global basis appear even remotely likely.[66]

The position changed sharply in 1985, when there were greater and more general demands than ever before for economic sanctions against South Africa. This was due to the increasing use of violence to protect the *apartheid* system at home and the continued duplicity of 'reform' promises, combined with a growing realization by the international community that *apartheid* was inherently evil and not reformable. There was also the failure of attempts to negotiate South Africa out of Namibia and the rising tide of regional aggression, notably the strikes against Gaborone and the Gulf Oil installations in Cabinda.

Actual steps began to be taken on transport, trade, finance, technical co-operation and oil.[67] While not in themselves crippling, these measures did impose costs and create momentum for further pressures. Ironically, the most effective sanctions came from investors and lenders. The rising crisis of *apartheid* at home and the costs of regional aggression have rendered South Africa's economy less dynamic and more constrained by foreign exchange. Increasingly, corporations have seen it as prudent business to phase down or sell all or part of their South African interests,[68] while world currency and financial markets have passed a resounding vote of no confidence with the rand falling 50 per cent against the dollar.

As a result, South Africa has been forced to declare a moratorium on external loan repayments and has negligible prospects of securing net new loan or investment capital from abroad until its domestic situation and international image alter radically.[69] In this period, the foreign exchange earnings from trade and transport with SADCC countries have been crucial to South Africa and the magnitudes now estimated suggest the net earnings are roughly equivalent to amounts needed to pay the interest on outstanding debt.

Economic sanctions against South Africa would impose heavy costs on its neighbours, and would certainly include the tightening of South African retaliatory sanctions in the region as well as intensification of 'strike kommando' strategies. This would cause great difficulty for several SADCC states and would bring some economies to the verge of collapse.[70] However, studies carried out at the end of the 1970s suggested that the costs to the region could be sharply reduced, especially once Zimbabwe attained independence.

South Africa has threatened to ensure that economic sanctions against it will be matched by retaliatory actions against its neighbours – most specifically by expelling hundreds of thousands of migrant and seasonal workers from Lesotho, Mozambique, Botswana, Malawi and Swaziland, and by cutting off flows of petroleum products.[71] What action the regime might actually take is less clear. Petroleum supplies would be halted because they are based on imported crude oil. Exports based on South African inputs might well continue since sanctions evasion requires maximizing, not minimizing, export earnings. Transit traffic restrictions might be selective for the same reason. Even labour import cutbacks would probably be selective; neither the crippling of the gold-mining sector (the one export which is, in practice, sanctions proof), nor the creation of an explosive enclave of desperate people in Lesotho, would seem a rational course of action. Upgrading of 'strike kommando' raids would be likely.

Pretoria's reaction would depend on whether it believed that damage to a particular neighbour would cause them to collaborate in sanctions evasion and/or to press the world community to relax sanctions. Just as South African threats have added to the global chorus of voices saying that sanctions would be bad because they would injure the independent southern African states, so acting on the threats might undermine global support for sanctions once imposed.

SADCC's response to the potential reality of economic sanctions against South Africa has evolved rapidly. At the 1985 Arusha Summit, seven member states, including Lesotho, made clear their support for sanctions.[72] Two remained silent, but did not dissent. Claims that the seven have said otherwise in private are clearly fraudulent. SADCC members have also made clear their belief that the basic cause of violence in the southern African region, as in South Africa itself, is *apartheid* and that South Africa's attempts to sustain *apartheid* are imposing crippling costs on governments and people in the region.[73]

SADCC has commissioned studies and consultations on the impact of sanctions against South Africa, and probable South African response, with a view to identifying concrete measures to speed up the process of reducing economic dependence on South Africa and vulnerability to South African action. SADCC has chosen to view the sanctions question within the parameters of intensified struggle and the opportunity for advancing the political economy of liberation, not capitulation and subordinated co-operation in sanctions-busting.

The costs to the region of economic sanctions against South Africa can
be broken down into six main components: transport and communications, imports, exports (including labour), finance, security
and Lesotho. Lesotho requires attention as a special case because it is
not just land-locked but 'South Africa-locked' and there is a
qualitative difference in possible cost-containing measures.

Any costing at present has to be schematic and tentative for three
reasons. First, detailed information has not been collected and
analysed. Second, the extent and nature of the sanctions will affect
the costs; and, third, so will the nature, extent, timing and effectiveness of southern African responses. The following analysis pre-
supposes that sanctions would cover at least petroleum, military and
technology imports. It also presumes that SADCC states will not serve
as sanctions-busting conduits nor will they sever all economic
links with South Africa, and that South Africa will, for its own reasons,
continue some links. The analysis also takes account of the fact that
South Africa will almost certainly increase 'strike kommando' raids on
key economic targets, especially transport and energy, and continue
high levels of support for proxy forces (UNITA, MNR, LLA, Super-
ZAPU), but will stop short of full-scale invasions except in the case of
Angola.

Transport relates to the six SADCC members crucially dependent
on South African routes. Only Tanzania and Angola would be
unaffected. Of the others, only Mozambique, Swaziland, Zambia, and
perhaps Malawi, could survive economically using presently
functional transport routes which do not transit South Africa. In
respect to petroleum transport, however, only Lesotho could not be
supplied – assuming that both the Beira and Dar es Salaam pipelines
were functional as well as the refineries at Dar es Salaam, Ndola,
Maputo and Luanda. Similarly for air transport and communications,
the SATCC project has already reduced the use of South African
facilities and links to the point that total severence would be
inconvenient rather than crippling.

In respect to imports, South Africa is a major source of several
countries, but in every case alternative sources exist and quite often
at a lower cost. Some examples of regional sources are: Zimbabwe and
Malawi for grain; Zimbabwe and, to a lesser degree, Malawi and
Tanzania for manufactures; Mozambique for coal, cement; Angola for
petroleum, and so on. The problems are twofold. First, no source is

effective unless functioning transport routes exist. Second, in Botswana, Lesotho and Swaziland the pattern of 85 to 95 per cent of imports coming from or via South Africa has meant that there is virtually no commercial capacity to source globally, a gap compounded by South African (Renfreight) dominance of clearing and forwarding.

South Africa is not the primary market for the goods export of any SADCCmember except Lesotho. Most exports to South Africa could be redirected, albeit at a cost. Again the question of transport routes for exports other than to South Africa is crucial. For labour, the situation is different. Lesotho is totally dependent on the earnings from migrant workers in South Africa, and the dependence of Mozambique, Botswana, Swaziland and Malawi is also significant.

Financial flows from South Africa to SADCC states are primarily of two types: via SACU and export credits. SACU flows are critical to Botswana, Lesotho and Swaziland, but the underlying import/ excise revenues themselves depend on there being imports to tax not on their sources or the fiscal structures used. For the heavily indebted countries with limited access to trade credit, a rupture in South African supply could cripple imports.

Lesotho faces very particular problems. All ground transport is via South Africa. Virtually all imports are from or via South Africa. About three-quarters of employment and foreign exchange earnings flow from migrant labour exports to South Africa and SACU payments. Total sanctions against Lesotho by South Africa could, without corrective action, quite literally mean economic strangulation and widespread starvation.[74]

The nature of the costs in effect outlines the countermeasures required. The transport requirement is easy to identify. Except for Lesotho, it consists of reopening, rehabilitating and protecting the Nacala, Beira and Maputo (via Limpopo Valley Line) trade corridors. Rehabilitating and protecting the Luanda trade corridor is highly desirable but not essential. In effect, this would reverse the effects of South Africa's sustained campaign against SADCC transportation routes by implementing the priority project in the SATCC programme on a selective and accelerated basis. The problems beyond that are logistical and manageable. These involve re-routing Botswana traffic, developing onward transit facilities for petroleum products from Mutare and Ndola, co-ordinating traffic flow and route capacity allocations, adding to rolling stock, locomotive and lorry fleets. While SATS would likely recall loaned equipment, presumably its return could be denied or phased to allow arrival of replacement units.

Trade problems, apart from labour, turn on transport and commercial institutions. Alternative sources exist. The basic problem is getting the goods to and from the land-locked states. In the special case of electricity, the basic requirement is three high tension lines: Cahora Bassa to Maputo; Maputo (or the Cahora Bassa-Maputo line) to the Swaziland grid; and connecting the Zimbabwe and Botswana grids with a high capacity link.

To use external trade sources and markets, Botswana, Swaziland and Lesotho each needs an independent import/export house with global information sources and contacts. The practical way of creating them rapidly would be joint ventures of the respective development corporations either with northern trading houses (including major international trade co-ops such as the Scandinavian Wholesale Co-operative Federation) or with existing Zimbabwe external trade houses. Similarly, in respect of clearing and forwarding, joint ventures with non-Renfreight firms with external contacts are needed along the lines of Mozambique's joint venture with Agence Maritime Internationale (AMI of Belgium). These steps are desirable and would pay even in narrow cost terms, sanctions or no sanctions.

Reducing the costs of loss of jobs in South Africa requires forward planning of alternative employment, especially in rural areas. Numerous public works programmes for afforestation, irrigation, anti-erosion, water supply, schools and clinics, roads, local warehouse and community centre projects can be undertaken largely by unskilled and semi-skilled labour. The problems are in identifying programmes and their design, determining the requirements for skilled personnel, tools and materials, then mobilizing these and the finance to procure them.

In respect to finance, the 'loss' of SACU can be fully offset by fairly moderate upgrading of existing national customs and excise services to undertake collection. National import and excise tariffs must also be instituted, if import flows are maintained. Alternative trade finance would need to be mobilized – possibly from non-commercial sources – to substitute for South African.

The transition to new transport and trade patterns would not be instantaneous or problem free. Thus, reserve stocks would be needed for key goods such as fuel, food, fertilizer and tools, inputs into manufacturing, spare parts (especially for the transport sector). These stocks should be built up to 90–120 day levels in the land-locked southern African states. Given the present uncertainties in delivery dates, and South African engineering of shortages to exert pressure, such reserves are desirable whether there are sanctions or not.

Lesotho's survival will require international support including an airlift capable of carrying 150 000 to 500 000 tonnes a year, depending on whether only petroleum products or all imports have to be moved. This could be mounted from Maputo to the new Maseru international airport. There is nothing physically impossible about this; in fact, the Tanzania/Zambia airlift after sanctions were imposed on Rhodesia was technically much more difficult. The problem is one of cost. Similarly, to provide income for 50 000 to 200 000 workers expelled from South Africa and to sustain the foreign exchange for imports (and therefore tax revenue) would require major external financial support.

Security aspects of sanctions relate to the fact that, to survive, SADCC states need operative transport, communication and energy installations. South African strikes against existing, rehabilitated or new facilities in the context of sanctions could be even more devastating than its existing pattern of armed aggression. Security issues extend well beyond the scope of this chapter. However, the recent past makes two points clear. First, sabotage can render many projects key to the political economy of liberation unimplementable or non-operational. Second, national and co-ordinated southern African security operations, such as those undertaken by Mozambique and Zimbabwe, can limit the damage done by South African aggression.

The implications are that without improved security, all cost reduction measures and projects, especially in transport and energy, will be vulnerable to South African military strikes; but broader regional defence co-ordination could substantially reduce the damage of such strikes as well as increasing the costs to South Africa in fuel, personnel and equipment. Further, it is likely that the interposition of multi-national or northern blocking force (Commonwealth or Nordic) with real damage infliction capacity would deter South Africa from carrying out a high-profile strike programme.

It would be dangerously romantic to assume that, even if these steps are taken successfully, sanctions against South Africa would not impose severe costs on Lesotho, Botswana, Zimbabwe, Swaziland and Zambia. But these steps could reduce them to bearable levels. Furthermore, almost all of the sanctions cost-reduction measures are part of the political economy of southern African regional liberation and once completed would provide substantial gains.

Finally, with the present annual cost of South African aggression and economic destabilization already running at $4 billion a year – and rising with no end in sight – it serves no practical purpose to talk of the costs to southern Africa of imposing sanctions on South Africa. The costs of co-existing with *apartheid* are immeasurably higher, and the region is already suffering from selective sanctions imposed by its powerful neighbour. The imposition of comprehensive international sanctions would mark another stage in the struggle for regional economic liberation and, to the extent they succeeded, would further the welfare of the states and peoples in southern Africa.

CHAPTER 10

Destructive Engagement: The United States and South Africa in the Reagan Era

There is enormous wisdom in this land, and one prays it will be granted the necessary time to manifest itself... The machine gun will guarantee reasonable time, I think. When you return to America assure your people that Afrikaners will use their machine guns if forced to do so...[We can] buy time, probably through the remainder of this century. But with every moment gained, more wisdom is gained too. And the day will come when the bright lads from Stellenbosch and Potchefstroom will lead the way in conciliation.

Our Zulu and Xhosa – they're the most patient, wonderful people on this earth. ... I think they can wait, intelligently, till the sick white man sorts things out.

> – Mrs Laura Saltwood, in James Michener, *The Covenant*[1]

Mrs Laura Saltwood, Michener's fictional English South African liberal, is banned in the book by the South African government after a 1979 speech advocating that Africans should learn English, not Afrikaans, so that they can read 'the greatest body of learning and literature in the world'. Saltwood's offence is an improbable one for a banned person. And so are the opinions she expounds to her distant American cousin Philip, the visiting geologist. Her words would fit more appropriately in the mouth of a South Africa Foundation executive, or of Chester Crocker, who, by 1979, was already sketching out policies he would oversee as President Ronald Reagan's assistant secretary of state for African affairs.

Michener's mammoth book, published in 1980, incorporated wholesale the prevailing historical myths characterizing South Africa's racial groups. His saga gives the leading role to the Afrikaners, portrayed as intolerant and racist but far more vivid as individuals than his black characters or even the English. South African history is portrayed as an epic of warring tribes, the problem the prejudice of the more backward Afrikaners. But there is still hope. 'The Afrikaner politicians I've met are at least as prudent as the American politicians I know', concludes Philip Saltwood. 'I'm going to put my faith in them.'[2]

Under President Reagan, the United States did place its faith in South Africa's political leaders, relying both on their guns and their wisdom. Reassuring Pretoria that the two powers shared a common interest in a Soviet/Cuban-free stability in the subcontinent, Washington urged that long-term security also required movement toward power-sharing at home and an international settlement in Namibia. With an activist diplomacy of 'constructive engagement', the United States tried to persuade South Africa and pressure its African opponents into a settlement.

Other Western countries were more sceptical about the possibility of solutions, but they were willing to let Washington take the initiative. No major power took active steps to disengage from Pretoria. By the end of 1984, it was clear that Western policies had again helped to buy time for the South African state. South Africa's neighbours, meanwhile, the victims of intensified attack, had lost time for desperately needed development. Steps toward *détente* on Pretoria's part proved tentative at best. Namibia was no closer to freedom. In South Africa the reform process had produced a new constitution excluding Africans, which the overwhelming majority of blacks saw as entrenching a slightly modernized *apartheid*.

As Reagan's second term began it was increasingly difficult to maintain even the pretence that US engagement was 'constructive'. Sustained rebellion in South Africa's black townships, beginning in early 1984 and continuing through 1985 into 1986, ignited an unprecedented response abroad, not least in the United States. Daily demonstrations by the Free South Africa Movement at the South African embassy in Washington expressed outrage at US complicity as well as South African repression. The drumbeat of publicity sapped the confidence of foreign bankers and businessmen, who feared both continued instability and critics at home. As several Western countries banned new investments in South Africa, even Reagan was forced by members of his own party to accept limited sanctions to head off stronger action by Congress.

As the pressure for sanctions against *apartheid* grew, however, both Congress and the administration acquiesced to a campaign from within their ranks to increase aid to South Africa's Angolan surrogate Unita, thus bolstering Pretoria's regional aggression. This seeming contradiction was in fact deeply rooted in patterns governing US policy long before the advent of Reagan, and reflects the diversity of forces in US society affecting Africa policy.

The Policy Context

The faith which the Reagan administration placed in Pretoria, first of all, was not an original invention. The tendency to analyse policies by contrasting one US administration with another pays insufficient attention to the tendencies, policy lines and coalitions which persist from the term of one president to another. There is a continuity in policy which sets parameters and limits significant new directions. Serious sanctions against South Africa, on the one hand, and open proclamation of support for *apartheid*, on the other, are ruled out of the policy debate in advance. Within any one period, policy is not totally unified — the State Department, the Central Intelligence Agency (CIA), the White House and other executive agencies, Congress, transnational corporations and private pressure groups each have different emphases and separate effects.[3]

The difference lies in the balance of emphasis within each administration. This in turn depends on both its internal political base and on the changing objective reality in southern Africa. Since 1960, the dominant tendency in US policy, under both Democratic and Republican administrations, has been conservative *Realpolitik* or pragmatism, which subordinates most foreign policy issues to preserving US world leadership vis-a-vis the Soviet Union and the more general threat of social revolution. The most common corollary is that the United States should stick with familiar allies, even if they be colonial powers, white settler regimes or right-wing dictatorships. Adjustments to rising nationalism or concern with racism or human rights are, within this perspective, sentimental distractions from the real business of defending US interests.

With respect to southern Africa, the most explicit formulation of this perspective was in the Nixon-Kissinger National Security Study Memorandum of 1969, which postulated that white regimes were destined to stay in power and control the pace of change.[4] In practice, this assumption dominated policy both before and after 1969, until it was rudely challenged by the fall of Portuguese colonialism. Even then, it remained the operating assumption when dealing with South Africa itself.

The dominance of this assumption, in Democratic as well as Republican administrations, is reflected above all in consistent US opposition to substantive sanctions against Pretoria. Even the arms embargoes adopted by Presidents Kennedy in 1963 and Carter in 1977 were primarily symbolic and hedged with qualifications. They also left Pretoria's economic lifeline to the West – and thus the basis of its military power – intact.

What did distinguish Democratic administrations was their relative openness to the variant theme of 'establishment liberalism'. This perspective can be summarized in the theses that adjustment to 'moderate' nationalism is the best bulwark against radicalism and Soviet-bloc expansion, that the United States must be flexible and non-dogmatic in analysing Third World developments, and that there must be some effort to identify with Third World aspirations. Democratic sensitivity to African opinion and greater willingness to take symbolic steps offending Pretoria was heightened by the need to pay attention to black opinion and human rights sentiment at home.

Yet the more liberal variant of Africa policy held only a marginal position within the foreign policy mainstream. It had most influence in the opening years of the Kennedy and Carter administrations, which coincided with the periods of uncertainty following Sharpeville in 1961 and Soweto in 1976. But in each case idealism lost its bloom and reform became less urgent as the white regimes in the early 1960s, and South Africa again after Soweto, re-established 'stability'. The Carter administration did persist with negotiations on Zimbabwe and Namibia, but these rested on the premise of co-operation with South Africa. Reform in South Africa, officials argued, could be encouraged by the progressive involvement of Western capital, under such reformist codes as those for factory workers advocated by the Reverend Leon Sullivan.

For Democrats as well as Republicans, moreover, the common axiom of anti-communism and *de facto* ties with South Africa paved the way for regional intervention which had the effect of buying time for Pretoria. In the 1960s it was the Republican Eisenhower administration that made the strategic decision to eliminate Patrice Lumumba in the Congo (Zaire), for fear that his non-aligned stance might give advantages to the Soviet Union. But Eisenhower's Democratic successors also gave priority to securing a pro-Western Congo over advancing the demise of white minority rule to the south. As an Africa Bureau memo from the Johnson administration put it, 'the need to prevent a major Communist success ranks above almost every other consideration.'[5] The maxim was well-illustrated by US co-operation (albeit embarrassed) with white mercenaries in repressing the 1964 Congo rebellions.

A decade later, Act Two of direct US intervention in the region was played out in Angola, again at the initiative of a Republican administration. Among the factors which led to a different outcome was the greater strength of anti-interventionist and pro-African sentiment in the United States, stemming both from the Vietnam experience and from the growing influence of blacks among Democrats in Congress. But the legislative check to US intervention was an exceptional event. The Cold War mainstream among Democrats as well as Republicans saw Angola primarily as a case of Soviet/Cuban gains against the United States rather than in the context of African liberation and South African invasion.

In the aftermath of Angola and Soweto, anti-*apartheid* sentiment in the United States continued to grow, with solidarity groups supporting Zimbabwe, the divestment movement blossoming in universities, churches and local governments, and the formation of the national black lobby, TransAfrica. In Congress, both the Black Caucus and the House Subcommittee on Africa became more prominent loci of expertise and sympathy with African concerns. But such views had little direct influence on foreign policy. As the Carter administration finished out its term, old Cold War priorities were already snuffing the flickering flames of greater sensitivity to African opinion.

US policy-makers with a more liberal bent could congratulate themselves on the outcome in Zimbabwe. Against strong pressure from the right to endorse the internal settlement of Smith and Muzorewa, a wavering US administration and British realists had listened to African insistence that the guerrilla leadership could not be excluded from power. Pro-African lobby groups and congressional liberals helped prevent the premature lifting of sanctions. In the end, a classic British decolonization scenario had been played out, ending the guerrilla war and the prolonged international legal crisis. With vigorous diplomacy, the West had provided the framework for a settlement, pressuring black guerrilla movements to compromise and reassuring whites·that their essential interests could be preserved. Mugabe's victory smashed the expectation that 'moderate' Africans chosen by whites could win a free election against guerrilla victors, despite South African subsidies and the sympathy of an interim administration. Yet the new government was ready to co-operate with the West.

There was even some indication that leading circles in the United States might apply a liberal reading of the Zimbabwe outcome to South Africa. If violence comparable to that in Rhodesia should engulf the South African heartland, the results would be unpredictable, greater international involvement inescapable. The United States, with its assumed global responsibility and history of racial conflict, was particularly concerned. 'The formulation of new approaches to the problem is urgent,' said an influential US report in early 1981, adding that violence could intensify and spread. 'Time is running out', it warned.[6]

Time Running Out was the most prominent result of liberal Establishment efforts to find an appropriate US response. The Study Commission on US Policy towards Southern Africa, sponsored by the Rockefeller Foundation and chaired by Ford Foundation head, Franklin Thomas, had begun its work in early 1979 with a budget of over $2 million. As the Rhodesian drama moved to its climax, the commissioners undertook an elaborate process of study and consultation on the crisis in South Africa.

In spite of the urgency of its title, the report issued two years later went only marginally beyond the policies of the early Kennedy or early Carter periods. Moreover, it came when Washington opinion was moving in the opposite direction, against expanding symbolic disengagement from white rule. Its conclusions were destined to serve less as a guide to government policy than as a marker of the leftward limits of respectable opinion.

Strikingly, the commissioners made no recommendations on Namibia or on South Africa's role in attacking Angola and backing Unita guerrillas there. Avoiding this controversial topic, they proposed the general regional goal of aiding economic development in black states. On South Africa, the commissioners concluded that white minority rule was doomed and affirmed the need for 'genuine power sharing', preferably achieved with a minimum of violence. Allying the United States with such constructive change could minimize growth of communist influence and the prospect of all-out civil war, they argued.

The commissioners rejected sanctions such as trade embargoes or divestment, while acknowledging that these eventually might be needed. Instead they recommended far more limited actions. The US government should broaden export restrictions on arms and nuclear ties, continue strong public condemnation of *apartheid*, expand contact with blacks and aid for black organizations within South

Africa, and prepare for possible cut-offs of minerals from the area. US firms should refrain voluntarily from new investment and abide by the 'Sullivan principles'.

Even measures such as voluntary restrictions on new investment were seen as daring, in the context of mainstream opinion among US leaders. Public opinion might have been willing to go further, as indicated by opinion polls. But a survey among members of the elite Council on Foreign Relations showed no significant support 'for any action that might bring effective sanctions in any form against South Africa'.[7]

As the commissioners recognized, the military threat facing South Africa was far from that which had defeated Ian Smith. New student demonstrations and strikes in 1980 marked the most intense internal resistance activity since 1977. Guerrillas of the African National Congress (ANC) of South Africa carried out their most dramatic sabotage attack to date, inflicting some $8 million in damage to the SASOL coal-to-oil plant. In Namibia, South Africa had failed to eliminate the guerrilla capacity of the South West Africa People's Organization (SWAPO), in spite of repeated claims to have destroyed their base camps in Angola. But there was no immediate challenge to South African control. Time had not yet run out.

Without the expectation of an imminent collapse of South African authority, the liberal call to adjust to a future of majority rule was easily drowned out by the clarion calls of anti-communism. The caution of the post-Vietnam era had limited staying power in the US political arena; and Africa policy was inevitably affected by the resurgence of Cold War perspectives.

This trend was already well in evidence under the Carter administration, where National Security Advisor Zbigniew Brzezinski rivalled his predecessor Henry Kissinger in his willingness to give priority to superpower rivalry over all other issues. A striking indicator of the rising influence of this perspective in African matters came in May 1978, when Brzezinski hinted that the United States should restore aid to Unita and Carter denounced Cuba as being responsible for the uprising in Zaire's Shaba province. Simultaneously, a South African raid killing hundreds of Namibian refugees at Kassinga went without effective US rebuke. The message was clear : in the US policy context, the Cuban 'threat' to Africa far outweighed the threat from South Africa. US negotiators gained South African agreement to the principle of independence for Namibia, but Washington was unwilling to exert similar pressure to implement the plan.

More generally, events far removed from southern Africa – in the Horn, Afghanistan, Iran and Central America – were all by 1980 pressed into service to portray the need for the United States to stand up against the threat of Soviet-backed world revolution. Reagan's election both reflected and reinforced this trend.

In the Carter administration, the Cold Warriors had to pay some attention to more cautious, even pro-African constituencies in the administration, the Democratic party or among the public. In Reagan's Washington, however, such voices were excluded from internal policy debate. The 'regionalists', the human rights advocates, the moderates advising recognition of the limits of US power, lost the fragile beach-head they had won during the Carter administration. Instead, the right wing contended with an even more conservative right wing for influence in the halls of executive power, while radical, liberal and even centrist forces could only build counterweights and check the tilt from the outside. The Reaganauts were riding a rising wave to the right, their only question how far and how recklessly to ride it.

The Reaganaut Line-up

Most accounts of Reagan-era Africa policy have focused on the ideas of Assistant Secretary of State Crocker. As important and skilled at bureaucratic survival as Crocker has been, this emphasis is misleading. In previous administrations, the Africa Bureau generally held a perspective more accommodating to African interests than other power centres within the government. Although its political spectrum was shifted considerably to the right, the Reagan administration was no exception to this general rule – its ideological center of gravity has been to Crocker's right.

Reagan himself provided the best characterization of his own regime when he joked in mid-1981, 'Sometimes my right hand doesn't know what my far right hand is doing'.[8] The Africa Bureau's *Realpolitik* evolved within the context of more extreme views. The right hand accommodated itself to the far right, seeking to achieve what was realistic of the goals they shared.

The internal balance between right and far right was affected by a variety of factors – the stance taken by different individuals within the administration, the weight of public and congressional pressure to the left or to the right, the objective constraints of events overseas.

Although the media's rough categorization of Reagan's men as 'ideologues' and 'pragmatists' was generally a useful guide, individuals could and did shift their positions. In comparison to Central American policy, where the far-right campaign to overthrow the Nicaraguan government clearly dominated any tendency towards *détente* or negotiation, the Africa Bureau gained greater protection for its professedly conciliatory strategy. Compromise was more possible in the case of Mozambique, for example, than in Angola which was already a potent symbol for the far right.

Even at the height of diplomatic conciliation, in 1983–84, the purportedly 'even-handed' constructive engagement still tilted decisively towards Pretoria. But the shifting pragmatist/ideologue balance did affect the nuances and timing of policy. And the results deviated sufficiently from the ideologues' hopes that they repeatedly attacked the State Department's willingness to 'conciliate communists' in southern Africa.

The heart of the extremist approach was a virtually exclusive emphasis on the need to combat revolution and Soviet expansion, combined with lack of embarrassment at alignment with South Africa. The settlement in Zimbabwe was seen as a victory for 'Marxist terrorists', in spite of Mugabe's post-independence moderation and cool relationship with the Soviet Union. The United States should back efforts to roll back guerrilla victories and install pro-Western governments in Mozambique and especially in Angola, a special target because of Cuban troops there and the memory of US defeat.

President Reagan's instinctive sympathies lay with this globalist ideology he had preached for years. 'All he knows about southern Africa,' one of his own officials privately commented, 'is that he is on the side of the whites'.[9] He might have added, without fear of contradiction, 'and against the Cubans'. The hard-line perspective, benefiting from its correspondence to the president's world view, had significant support within the Republican party. Lobbyists for South Africa, such as Donald de Kieffer and John Sears, were well-connected in the Reagan camp.[10] Senator Jesse Helms was the only most prominent of its advocates among Senate Republicans.

Within the administration, 'neo-conservative' Jeane Kirkpatrick at the US mission to the United Nations (UN) preached opposition to the Soviet Union and Third World revolution as fervently as any pure-bred rightist. In a 1979 *Commentary* article that impressed President Reagan and led to her appointment, she argued that rightist 'authoritarian' regimes, whatever their faults, were natural allies and potentially reformable. Leftist 'totalitarian' regimes and movements, however, were irredeemable.[11]

Another advocate of giving priority to anti-communist causes was William J. Casey, the director of the CIA.[12] Casey, one of the founders of the CIA, had been a tax lawyer, head of Nixon's Securities and Exchange Commission, and a founder of the National Strategy Information Center, a right-wing 'think tank' in New York. Casey took over as Reagan's campaign manager for the last six months preceding the 1980 election, and retained close ties to the president. In his confirmation testimony he spoke of the necessity of 'unleashing the ability of the organization to initiate and carry out its objectives', and during his tenure the pace of covert operations quickened, despite the caution of some experienced CIA professionals. According to Leslie Gelb, writing in the *New York Times* on 11 June 1984, covert operations had increased fivefold since 1980, to an ongoing total of 50. About half were in Central America, 'with a large percentage in Africa as well'. Casey repeatedly argued for increasing support to Unita in Angola.

At the State Department, the abrasive and forceful Alexander Haig initially filled the top post.[13] The general, with a résumé including deputy to Kissinger, White House chief of staff during Nixon's final days, and North Atlantic Treaty Organization (NATO) supreme commander, was well-positioned in his views between right and far right. Several of his appointments, including Crocker, disappointed right-wing ideologues.

In many respects, however, Haig faithfully hewed the extremist line, earning the praise of neo-conservative pundit Norman Podhoretz. He spoke of 'going to the source' in Cuba to stop revolutionary ferment in Central America. In 1979, while serving as president of United Technologies Corporation, he had testified to the House Subcommittee on Mining, echoing a favourite South African theme. The enormous mineral wealth of southern Africa, he said, was threatened by a 'resource war' fostered by 'Soviet proxy activity in the Third World'.[14] The 'loss' of southern Africa 'could bring the severest consequences to the economic and security framework of the Third World'. His racist insensitivity was well-illustrated by his habit, in Nixon's National Security Council (NSC) staff meetings, of playfully beating the table like jungle drums whenever African topics were discussed.

Starting out at the NSC was Reagan campaign advisor Richard Allen, considered an asset by the far right. One of the founders of the

conservative Georgetown Center for Strategic and International
Studies in Washington DC, Allen had served a short stint in the Nixon
White House, where Kissinger reportedly regarded him as a member
of the 'sandbox right'. From 1972 to 1974 Allen acted as a foreign
agent for the Overseas Companies of Portugal, trying to improve the
image of Portuguese colonialism in Washington.[15] He resigned from
the NSC under a cloud of suspicion over financial dealings in January
1982, becoming a Distinguished Fellow at the far-right Heritage
Foundation in Washington. But he was present for the crucial first
year, which set the tone of US hostility towards black Africa. Allen's
Africa aide, Fred Wettering, who had served as CIA station chief in
Mozambique from 1975 to 1977 and was a leading advocate of a
hostile US approach to Marxist regimes, continued to hold the NSC
Africa post until late 1984.

Allen was replaced at the NSC by William P. Clark, a Reagan crony
from California who admitted he had no knowledge of foreign policy
before he was appointed as under secretary of state in 1981.[16] Clark
shared the president's hard-line instincts. Since he was a forceful
advocate of increased military intervention in Central America and of
a posture of increased 'strength' towards the Soviet Union, Clark's
high position was a reassurance for ideologues who feared the
influence of 'moderates' on the White House staff.

. The arrival of George Shultz as secretary of state in mid-1982, and
Clark's replacement by Robert McFarlane at the NSC the following
year established a somewhat more favourable climate for more
pragmatic right-wing views, already established in the State
Department's Africa Bureau.[17] Sharing the objectives of global
counter-revolution, these practioners of *Realpolitik* argued that a
successful US policy had to take account of limits posed by real
conditions in southern Africa, using the 'carrot' as well as the 'stick'
with left-wing regimes. Keeping an anxious watch over their right
shoulders, the Africa Bureau pragmatists managed to win
administration tolerance, if not always enthusiastic backing, for
negotiations.

Crocker, the strategy's chief spokesman, had directed African
Studies at Georgetown University's Center for Strategic and
International Studies from 1976 to 1981. He had written prolifically
about US foreign policy in Africa, offering what he billed as a
hard-headed alternative to the 'romantic illusion' of Carter
'regionalist' policies.[18] US policy, he argued, should take account of

both the Soviet threat and local realities, and 'raise the price of Soviet involvement in both regional and global terms'.

Although he had supported Smith's internal settlement and criticized the liberal realists who had persisted with negotiations, Crocker was willing to see hope in Zimbabwe. Not only were the victors committed to 'moderation', but the dominant Zimbabwe African National Union (ZANU) had no debts to the Soviet Union which had backed the rival Zimbabwe African People's Union (ZAPU). Perhaps the West could take advantage of the new situation.

The British success, moreover, might provide a model for Namibia. Britain had taken a dominant role as mediator, using its acknowledged bias against the guerrillas as leverage on both sides.[19] The British pressured the Patriotic Front by threatening to accept a settlement excluding them, and encouraged South Africa and Rhodesian whites to make concessions by supporting them on particular issues. A conservative US administration with a sufficiently active diplomacy might play a similar role in defusing the festering war on the Namibia/Angola front. The United States could deliver an independent Namibia to Africa, while reassuring South Africa that it could retain its regional influence. As a special bonus for both South Africa and the United States, Angola could be induced to send the Cubans home. Southern Africa could again become a 'Soviet-free' zone.

The focus on getting the Cubans out of Angola is in part explained by Crocker's need to appease the ideological Cold Warriors. After all, Senator Jesse Helms held up Crocker's appointment until August 1981, bombarding him with questions testing his willingness to sell out the anti-communist cause. Protecting himself against Helms and keeping the support of the president required repeated reaffirmations of anti-communist shibboleths.

But the tilt to South Africa in the Crocker strategy was not merely an internal Washington ploy. It also expressed the instinctive sympathies and underlying strategic assumptions of the so-called 'moderates' themselves. Although Crocker was touted as an Africanist scholar, one can search his writings in vain for either sympathy or detailed knowledge of any part of the continent save white South Africa.

Crocker shares the view – common to right and far right – that the Cubans and the Soviets are the 'destabilizing' factors in the subcontinent. The instability following the Portuguese *coup d'état* in 1974 had led to increased non-African involvement, he commented in a 1979 article, simultaneously noting 'a broad decline in European willingness to support African stability'.[20] Western European involvement, including Portuguese colonialism, apparently did not count as 'outside' involvement. Africans might see gains in the end of colonialism. Crocker, in contrast, revealingly remarked in November 1982 that the major purpose of 'constructive engagement' was 'to reverse the decline in security and stability of southern Africa which has been under way now since the early and mid-1970s'.[21]

The slogan 'constructive engagement' had already entered the South African debate in reference to the role of foreign investment. Merle Lipton, of Britain's Chatham House, had argued in 1976 that industrialization was improving the situation of South African blacks, and that specific reforms by foreign companies could accelerate the process. Crocker's version put the emphasis on political action, explicitly putting his faith in the *verligte* (enlightened) politicians. US political scientist Samuel Huntington, infamous for his diagnosis of an 'excess of democracy' in Western societies, put the thesis to the South African Political Science Association in 1981, citing South Africa's need for skillful and authoritarian leadership to implement reform and avoid revolution. Effective repression, he noted, might contribute to the 'relatively happy outcome' of a 'quadri-racial polity' in which each ethnic group had a share of power, without the drastic consequences of a non-racial franchise.[22]

On South Africa, Crocker argued, the United States should encourage 'white-led change'. The South African government, controlled by Afrikaner reformers, deserved encouragement and reassurance. it needed protection from the threat of violence and Soviet intervention, so it could make changes without fear of losing control. If the United States made it clear it shared those goals, Crocker argued repeatedly, then South Africa's rulers could be persuaded to make concessions that would enhance their own long-term stability and win greater international acceptability. The militarily inferior Africans would just have to wait, be ready to make concessions when necessary, and recognize that the US diplomatic initiative was 'the only game in town'.

Crocker took the diplomatic task seriously, aided after April 1982 by Frank Wisner as his deputy who, unlike Crocker, won respect from African diplomats for his low-key professional stance.[23] But not even the most persistent diplomacy could counter the flawed assumption that stability could come from tilting to Pretoria. South Africa's position was fundamentally different from that of white Rhodesia.

The settlement in Zimbabwe, the advocates of 'constructive engagement' seemed to forget, came only after the Smith regime was decisively weakened by international sanctions and guerrilla war. Sanctions imposed to date on South Africa were far weaker than those inconsistently enforced against Rhodesia. And while guerrilla war was persistent in Namibia and beginning in South Africa, it was not yet a serious drain on South African resources. Without changes in these basic factors, no new 'settlements' were on the horizon.

The advocates of 'constructive engagement' might urge moderation on South Africa's rulers. But their own strategic decision in favour of closer ties, together with the administration's overall stance further to the right, sent a clear signal that there would be no penalty for intransigence. Washington bolstered Pretoria's capacity to delay at home and intervene abroad, emboldening the hawks and postponing the day of reckoning.

Tilting to Pretoria

Only days after Reagan's inauguration, the South African regime launched its largest raid to date on Mozambique, killing 12 people in the capital city. The raid, following a speech by Secretary of State Haig condemning 'rampant international terrorism', was justified as an attack on 'terrorist bases' of the banned ANC. Throughout Africa the action was seen as a dramatic symbol of the new Washington team's support for the *apartheid* regime, an impression that was to be repeatedly confirmed.

'Let this be the new beginning of mutual trust and confidence between the United States and South Africa, old friends, like Minister Botha, who are getting together again.' The specific reference, from Under Secretary of State Clark's toast to Foreign Minister Roelof 'Pik' Botha in May 1981, was to Botha's experience as ambassador to Washington from 1975 to 1977. But the theme of mutual confidence pointed to the future. South Africa's leaders, Crocker had written in a 'Scope Paper' for the May meetings in Washington, 'are deeply suspicious of us, of our will, from the 1975–76 experience and the Carter period'.[24]

In Crocker's view, the first step was to convince South Africa that the United States shared the same regional objectives. The 'top US priority', Crocker told the South Africans in April in Pretoria, 'is to stop Soviet encroachment in Africa'. According to the May 'Scope Paper', the new relationship with South Africa 'should be based upon our shared hopes for the future prosperity, security and stability of southern Africa, constructive internal change within South Africa and our shared perception of the role of the Soviet Union and its surrogates in thwarting those goals'.

Crocker advised the secretary of state to tell the South Africans, 'We cannot afford to give you a blank check [cheque] regionally.' Perhaps the cheque was not entirely blank. But Pretoria could count on both Washington's explicit desire to re-establish 'confidence' and on the unspoken awareness that beyond Crocker, who was still not confirmed in office, were forces even more sympathetic to South Africa. This left room for quite a substantial overdraft. Small print reminders that it would be nice to reach a settlement in Namibia could be postponed for later payment.

Pretoria's 'total strategy' had, by early 1981, suffered setbacks at the regional level. The key to the strategy in 1978 and 1979 had been building a 'constellation of states' under South African leadership, making it possible to rely primarily on economic and political influence rather than direct military power. But this depended on a favourable political outcome in Zimbabwe, an expectation punctured by Mugabe's landslide election victory announced on 4 March 1980. The official launching one month later, on 1 April, of the Southern African Development Coordination Conference (SADCC), a grouping of independent African states in the region, put finis to the idea of a formal Pretoria-centred constellation.

As the Botha regime intensified military intervention against its neighbours, the signals from Washington burned bright green. The attack on Mozambique in January did not elicit a rebuke from Washington. Instead Pretoria could watch as US–Mozambican relations deteriorated. In March the Mozambique government expelled several US diplomats, charging they had been part of a CIA intelligence network that had targeted the government as well as South African exiles. Washington retaliated by cutting off food assistance.

Mozambique's action came only a day after President Reagan had strongly endorsed friendship with South Africa on nation-wide television. In response to a question from broadcaster Walter Cronkite, the president rhetorically declaimed, 'Can we abandon a country that has stood by us in every war we've ever fought, a country that is strategically essential to the free world?' Praising the remark, the South African Broadcasting Corporation (SABC) noted that the US president had 'disposed of the ambiguity and the veiled hostility which in recent years have characterized Washington's approach to this country'.[25]

Two weeks later, five high-ranking South African military officers visited the US at the invitation of a private far-right organization, the American Security Council, meeting with NSC and Defense Department officials as well as with UN ambassador, Kirkpatrick. The State Department was reportedly 'taken by surprise'.

Such incidents in early 1981 might be interpreted simply as evidence of incoherence. Crocker was still unconfirmed, a policy review on southern Africa was begun but not completed, and the stance towards Angola was being contested from all sides. But South African actions soon provided a litmus test for the new administration.

In 1981, the pace of military action in the 'operational zone' of southern Angola intensified, culminating in mid-August in the largest penetration of Angolan territory since 1976. 'Operation Protea', with a force of 11 000 men, went beyond the periodic raids of previous years to occupy much of Cunene province.

Official US reaction, billed as 'even-handed', echoed South Africa's justifications for its action. Deploring 'escalation of violence in southern Africa regardless of its source', Secretary of State Haig reminded a press conference of the threat of Cuban forces, Soviet advisers and Soviet arms. These arms, he added, 'have been used to refurbish Swapo elements that move back and forth freely across the frontier and inflict bloodshed and terrorism upon the innocent non-combatant inhabitants of Namibia'.[26]

The following week the United States, breaking with its European allies, vetoed a UN Security Council resolution condemning the South African invasion, opposing even the verbal condemnation approved on a similar occasion in 1980. Crocker, in a major policy speech two days before the UN veto, said the United States 'should sustain those who resist the siren call of violence and the blandishments of Moscow and its clients'.[27]

Implying that the South African action should be seen as defensive, he blamed the Warsaw Pact for supporting guerrillas in Namibia and South Africa and noted that South Africa 'has clearly signalled its determination to resist guerrilla encroachments and strike at countries giving sanctuary'. Pretoria could clearly read the implied licence in the parallels to US rhetoric on Central America.

Crocker regarded limited South African concessions as a rational strategy to insure greater stability. So advising Pretoria, US policy-makers also sought to decrease the cost of making concessions by promising concomitant gains: closer US ties and ouster of 'Soviet surrogates'. The catch was that the closer ties were proffered in advance. And the prospect that the Soviet–Cuban presence in Angola could be removed by Washington's negotiating strategy was remote. Therefore the cost for South Africa of not making concessions and of escalating its military response was reduced. US pressure for 'internal reform' receded into near invisibility. On the Namibian question, which dominated the diplomatic picture, the United States could not deliver a Cuban withdrawal and a Swapo sufficiently weakened to cajole Pretoria into a settlement.

Most importantly, raising the costs for South African intransigence, by using pressures to make the continued stalemate or escalation less attractive, was ruled out in advance. This option was excluded not only by the premise that South Africa as the dominant regional power must be placated but also because it might conflict with the priority goal of attacking the Cuban presence. Even if the State Department were willing to compromise, Reagan's ideological supporters would certainly object. Whatever South Africa's leaders did, they could be confident that Washington would not impose penalties.

Crocker might have thought he could sell Luanda the idea of linking Cuban troop withdrawal and Namibian independence, holding out the 'carrots' of peace and of improved economic ties, while finding a wording the Angolans could accept. At a simple empirical level, 'linkage' was obvious and accepted by all parties. Angola and Cuba had long taken the position that the troops would leave once the threat from South Africa was removed.

But the meaning of 'linkage' depended entirely on context and timing. To accept a formal linkage between the two issues was to put Namibian independence – a cause with virtually universal international and legal legitimacy – on the same level with Angola's sovereign decisions on self-defence against South Africa. For African and most international opinion, the Cuban presence as defence against South Africa was at least as legitimate as that of US troops in Western Europe. The 'sphere of influence' concepts of Washington or Pretoria, a 'Monroe doctrine' for southern Africa, could not be conceded legitimacy.

Such issues might be finessed by diplomatic wording. But the United States repeatedly reinforced Angolan doubts on the central issue of security. If, in fact, Cuban troops were to be withdrawn while South Africa still occupied Namibia and maintained its support for Unita guerrilla actions, what assurance could Luanda have that its enemies would not try to move in for the kill? This question would remain even if direct South African attacks on Angola were suspended. Angolan acceptance, therefore, depended on building confidence that South Africa was ready to accept an independent Namibia not under its military influence or that the United States would compel South Africa to accept such an arrangement.

In June 1981, Under Secretary of State Clark pledged to the South Africans that the United States would ensure that Cuban troops left Angola, so that South Africa might feel secure enough to accept a Namibian settlement. Instead of pressuring South Africa to leave Namibia so the Cubans could leave Angola, the United States stressed the reverse sequence, giving South Africa a ready-made excuse for delay.

The United States also disqualified itself as a credible mediator by favouring Unita. Although this fell short of the full-scale support the far right demanded, it sufficed to raise suspicions in Luanda that Washington, as well as Pretoria, sought the downfall of the Angolan government.

Candidate Reagan had said he would provide Unita with weapons, 'to free themselves from the rule of an outside power, which is the Cubans and East Germans'.[28] But in 1981, the administration failed to repeal the Clark Amendment, in spite of a 66 to 29 repeal vote in the Senate. The measure was blocked by strong opposition within the Democratic-controlled House Foreign Affairs Committee, and lobbying by US companies as well as Africa-related groups in Washington.

One major caution was the fact that US companies, including the giant Gulf Oil Corporation, had substantial investments in Angola. These companies regarded the Angolan government as a trustworthy 'business-like' partner, and were sceptical about efforts at destabilization. With good working relationships in Angola, they could hardly be expected to sacrifice their profits to satisfy right-wing ideologues in the White House or Senate.

Even some voices close to the South African security establishment warned against going too far in Angola. Mike Hough, director of the Institute of Strategic Studies in Pretoria, noted that aid to Unita would increase Soviet and Cuban involvement. Support 'massive' enough to bring Savimbi to power, he added, would mean the United States would 'have to prop him up as they did the government in South Vietnam'.[29]

Crocker's diplomatic strategy also imposed some caution. If US intervention grew too blatant it could further antagonize African countries and upset European allies with investments in Angola. The Soviet Union might well match the new aid. And if Luanda felt Washington would stop short of nothing but its overthrow, negotiations would be beside the point. Still Crocker endorsed political support for Unita, and tried to use the threat of escalation to pressure Luanda.

Savimbi arrived in Washington for a visit in December 1981. The same month Crocker met the Angolan foreign minister, Paulo Jorge, in Paris, lecturing him on the need to bring Savimbi into government and dismissing Angolan concerns about defence against South Africa.[30] Suspicions repeatedly surfaced that the United States was violating the spirit if not the letter of the Clark Amendment, through CIA encouragement of Unita backers such as Israel, Morocco, Saudi Arabia and Zaire. In January 1982 Savimbi told journalists in Morocco, 'A great country like the US has other channels... The Clark Amendment means nothing.'[31]

The Washington tilt to Pretoria was not only visible on the Namibia/Angola front. Observers noted resumption of previous staffing levels for military attachés, attendance by two South African military officers at a US Coast Guard air and sea rescue mission, and visas issued for October visits for two South African Police (SAP) generals. These measures, commented a State Department official in November 1981, were altering the 'intangible atmosphere' of bilateral relations with South Africa. The critics were wrong in seeing such moves as 'tangible carrots', he added.[32]

More substantial 'carrots' were on the way, however. First the tap was opened wider for strategic exports allowing small exceptions to flow through such as airport security equipment. Revised export regulations in 1982 lifted the ban on sale of non-military items to the South African military and police. Licences were issued for export of two powerful computers to the government's Council for Scientific and Industrial Research.

So loose were the controls that they were, ironically, used as cover for diversion of equipment to the Soviet Union. Two shipments of components for Digital Vax 11/782 system were intercepted by US customs officials in Sweden and the Federal Republic of Germany (FRG) in November 1983. Routinely approved for export to South Africa, the computer became a 'serious security concern' when discovered *en route* to the Soviet Union.[33]

In general, security-related trade with South Africa increased

significantly. Trade in computers, for example, was running at more
than twice the $78 million annual average of the three years after the
Carter administration imposed its 1977 controls. Commerce Department licence approvals for security-related exports totalled $547 mil-
lion in 1981, almost as much as the $577 million for the three previous
years combined. In 1982, with all but the most sensitive items
excluded from licensing requirements, approvals under licence
amounted to $585 million. Sales under separate munitions list regula-
tions rose sharply.[34] Restrictions on nuclear-related exports were also
loosened, despite a continuing dispute over Pretoria's failure to agree
to the Non-Proliferation Treaty.

Equally welcome in Pretoria were US efforts to assuage South
Africa's growing economic woes. Gold fell from an average of some
$613 per ounce in 1980 to $460 per ounce in 1981 and $350 per ounce
in mid-1982. The balance of payments on current account dipped
to a R4 billion deficit in 1981, forcing an accelerated turn to
international capital markets. By mid-1982 financial analysts were
speculating that Pretoria would again turn to special International
Monetary Fund (IMF) credits. In November the IMF approved a
$1.1 billion credit facility. The Congressional Black Caucus had
appealed to the Reagan administration to vote against the loan. But
the United States enthusiastically endorsed the South African
application, deciding the issue with the US 20 per cent share of the
vote. The allocation was comparable to the increase in South Africa's
military expenditures from 1980 to 1982.[35]

The IMF loan was accompanied by a sharp rise in US bank lending.
In the 18 months from January 1981 through June 1982, US bank
loans outstanding to South Africa increased by some 246 per cent.
The total reached $3.7 billion in 1982, $4.6 billion in 1983. Over the
period, US direct investment declined slightly, from $2.6 billion to
$2.3 billion, reflecting the generally difficult circumstances of the
South African economy.[36] The inflow of loan capital, however, was a
sign that South Africa could count on its Western economic backers in
time of need.

Thus, midway through Reagan's first term, the primary effect of
'constructive engagement' had been to encourage South Africa in its
more aggressive regional policy. By 1983, however, it became harder
to postpone the counting of costs. In Pretoria's national security
establishment some argued that it would be better to accept
objectives more limited than the overthrow or constant destabiliza-

tion of hostile regimes, to explore a *modus vivendi* that might cut war costs and win international credit for moderation.

In Washington there was increasing criticism of 'constructive engagement' from Congress and elsewhere. Even among the policy's supporters there was a recognition that the tilt might have gone too far, undercutting the spirit of compromise it was supposed to foster. Not least important, Western European governments were increasingly concerned at the damage done to their interests by the escalating warfare. The United States might be conceded the diplomatic initiative, but Europe had even more at stake in the region than Washington – not only in South Africa but also in the countries that were its targets.

The Halting Détente Track
In 1981 the tilt towards South Africa quickly became the dominant feature of Reagan administration policy. In the supposedly 'even-handed' approach, the 'other hand' stretched out to Pretoria's opponents was, at best, hesitant. There was little effort at a serious dialogue with Angola or Mozambique, and a virtual boycott of contacts with the ANC and Swapo.

Washington initially tried to woo the newly independent Zimbabwe, approving Carter plans for boosting bilateral aid. But parlaying the Harare connection into an asset for Washington's regional strategy proved elusive. Regardless of its tensions with the Soviet Union, Harare would not be recruited to a crusade against Cuban troops in Angola or other efforts to 'reassure Pretoria'. Meanwhile, South African attacks on Mozambique directly imperilled Zimbabwe. South Africa supplied arms to exploit discontent among ex-guerrillas of Joshua Nkomo's Zapu in Matabeleland, and delayed rail shipments to Harare. Such actions fell short of those against Angola, Mozambique or even Lesotho, but the threat of escalation was unmistakable. US development aid was hardly adequate compensation for an overall US policy which encouraged South African aggression.

Gradually, however, regional negotiations gained momentum. In 1982 and 1983 the balance in Washington shifted towards compromise. Professional diplomat Wisner joined the Crocker team in April 1982. Shultz took over from Haig as secretary of state in June. And National Security Advisor Clark, Reagan's far-right watch-dog, was replaced by his 'realist' deputy, McFarlane, in October 1983.

Outside the administration, anti-*apartheid* groups and Africa
sympathizers in the House of Representatives mounted a steady
challenge to Reagan's South Africa tilt. The November 1982 election
brought a larger Democratic majority and a more critical mood to the
House of Representatives. Hearings exposed the loosening of export
controls and questioned US complicity in South African
destabilization. The divestment movement continued a steady
advance over the 1982–1984 period. With states and cities such as
Michigan and Boston joining the drive, public funds being withdrawn
from companies involved in South Africa approached the $1 billion
mark.[37]

The 1982 IMF loan to South Africa led to an extended legislative
battle over US contributions to the Fund's capital. A compromise
resolution, passed in November 1983, mandated that the United
States 'actively oppose any facility involving use of Fund credit by any
country which practices apartheid'. In the same session, amendments
to the Export Administration Act imposing penalties on South Africa
first passed the House of Representatives. The measure had little
chance of gaining Senate approval, but would be contended throughout 1984.

Pretoria, gauging reaction in the United States, increasingly had to
weigh the prospects that Congress and the public might take action on
their own. The administration remained apparently impermeable to
criticism from the centre and left, but its flexibility in granting new
'carrots' was hampered by the prospect of congressional reaction.

Another influence that Washington could not entirely ignore was
the stance of its Western partners. Even with Margaret Thatcher's
Conservative administration in London or the Helmut Kohl coalition
that took over in Bonn in late 1982, Reagan's officials found little
sympathy for hard-line opposition to the Angolan and Mozambican
governments. None of the other members of the contact group on
Namibia – Britain, Canada, France and the FRG – supported the
Pretoria/Washington 'linkage' concept. The European Economic
Community and the Commonwealth secretariat, as well as the Nordic
countries, actively backed SADCC; they could see that their aid
projects and economic opportunities were directly threatened by
South Africa's destabilization campaign.

France, after the election of President Mitterrand in May 1981, was
most outspoken in disagreeing with Washington on southern African
policy. Paris broke with Washington to vote for a September 1981

Security Council resolution demanding withdrawal of South African troops from Angola, and hosted Angolan President José Eduardo dos Santos later that year. An economic co-operation agreement was signed with Mozambique in December 1981. Two years later France officially withdrew from the contact group on Namibia.

Bonn, too, with its special interest in Namibia, encouraged contacts between Swapo and the German community there, and urged Washington to be more forthcoming in negotiations with Angola and with Swapo. Britain, for its part, had especially great economic stakes and other interests in Zimbabwe. British troops had stayed on as advisors and trainers with the post-independence Zimbabwe army. And yet Zimbabwe, as the land-locked hub of SADDC's plans for improved regional transportation, was vitally endangered by South Africa's campaign against Mozambique. The oil pipeline from Beira and rail connections to both Beira and Maputo were repeated targets. London was in no danger of being converted to sanctions against South Africa, which might endanger the enormous British business interests there. But the unrestrained ventures of Pretoria's hawks were also bad for business.

In June 1983, Under Secretary of State Lawrence Eagleburger restated the themes of 'constructive engagement' in a major speech. Some observers attached great importance to the stronger language he used to condemn *apartheid*, and to his avoidance of words such as 'pro-Soviet' and 'linkage'.[38] It was certainly not a red stop light for Pretoria, but the subtle shift indicated a yellow 'caution' light.

By the time of Eagleburger's speech, moreover, Pretoria as well as Washington was having to address some hard questions about the results of the destabilization policy. The far right in both capitals might want to pursue the maximum objectives of 'rollback' or permanent destabilization of neighbouring states, but there were also those who had to add up the price tag.

In 1982 there was no sign of restraint. A new attack on Angola came in June just as US roving ambassador Vernon Walters was in Luanda reassuring the Angolans that there would be no escalation. In December the South African Defence Force (SADF) launched an attack on Maseru, Lesotho, killing 42 people. Simultaneously, commandos targetted the oil depot in Beira, Mozambique, which stores supplies vital to Zimbabwe. In 1983 the military pressure mounted, with a steady escalation of supplies to the Mozambique National Resistance (MNR) and continued occupation of southern Angola.

In August 1982 Mozambique's government put the country on a

war footing and launched a diplomatic offensive to mobilize Western
pressure on South Africa. Maputo aimed at convincing key leaders in
the West that Mozambique was not, and indeed never had been, a
Soviet satellite, and that the blame for escalating conflict in the region,
endangering Western investments as well as prospects for development, lay with South Africa.

Crocker had long argued that the United States and South Africa
could live with the Front for the Liberation of Mozambique (Frelimo),
given the independent role the Maputo leadership had played in the
Zimbabwe settlement and the low-key character of the Soviet military
presence. US diplomacy only began to reflect this view, however, after
a meeting between Secretary of State Shultz and Mozambican
Foreign Minister Joaquim Chissano in October 1982. A State Department statement in January 1983 acknowledging South African
sponsorship of anti-government bandits in Mozambique was another
signal taken seriously in Maputo, leading to further talks between the
two countries.

Mozambique also sought to influence Washington and Pretoria by
appealing to Western Europe. On a European tour in October 1983
President Samora Machel won a sympathetic hearing from Thatcher
and Mitterrand, as well as officials in Lisbon. South African Foreign
Minister 'Pik' Botha, visiting European capitals in the wake of the
Machel trip, was told repeatedly that South African attacks were
damaging Western interests in the area.

This added to the questioning among South Africa's leaders. They
clearly had the military capacity to create ever increasing chaos and
destruction – but at what cost, and to what end?

The advocates of a 'total strategy' had to consider, first of all, South
Africa's increasing economic weakness. In the second half of 1982 the
gold price recovered, rising from a low of $300 per ounce briefly to top
$500 per ounce in January 1983. Still, the real gross domestic product
(GDP) fell one per cent in 1982. Then the gold price began another
steep dive, plunging almost to $400 by the end of February, and below
the $400 mark by the end of the year. Real GDP declined three per
cent in 1983. Other economic indicators showed similarly disturbing
trends. The rand exchange rate against the dollar, which had hit $1.35
in mid-1980, was down to $0.85 by mid-1982. A brief recovery was
then followed by a steady decline in 1983 and 1984, to under $0.60 by
mid-1984. With the added problems of drought, rising interest rates
and inflation, South Africa faced its most serious economic crisis in 50
years.

Consequently the costs of war loomed larger. On the western front, in Namibia and Angola, military and other subsidies cost more than $1 billion a year. Still, the prospect of overthrowing the Luanda government was blocked. The Angolan army was reinforced in 1983 with new Soviet aid and strengthened by internal reorganization. The costs to Pretoria in December 1983 of its latest Angolan invasion were unexpectedly high, in men and material, as the Angolans effectively used new defence equipment including helicopter gunships. The Soviet Union delivered an unprecedented direct and explicit warning to Pretoria that it would assist in countering any new South African escalation.

In the east, the cost was less direct expenditure than lost economic opportunities. Boycotting Maputo port bludgeoned the Mozambican government, but it also made transportation more expensive for South African businessmen in the northern Transvaal. Chaos and bankruptcy in Mozambique removed a potential market. Sabotaged power lines meant South Africa had to do without electricity from Cahora Bassa in Mozambique.

Since 1982 Frelimo had improved its military capacity by reorganizing in smaller guerrilla-style units. But Pretoria was able to continue its escalation by increasing infiltration and supplies to their surrogates, the MNR. A liability for the South Africans was the MNR's character as a mercenary organization. It might cause chaos and even sap confidence in the Mozambican government, but it had no political programme or credible leadership. Its most vocal representatives abroad were Portuguese citizens. In military terms, it could perhaps be installed in power. But then South Africa would have to provide support, and the military odds would change dramatically as South Africa's clients lost the advantage of the offensive.

By mid-1983 a balance-sheet for the hard-line military option showed a mixed picture. The toll of destruction was enormous, particularly in southern Angola and in Mozambique. Drought added to the devastation in Mozambique, while the continuing MNR campaign targetted and largely crippled relief efforts. Both Angola and Mozambique had been forced virtually to suspend development plans while struggling for survival. Confidence in a socialist future, and even in the capacity of the governments to provide basic security and subsistence, was ebbing.

But without the ability to install its clients in power, Pretoria's success in curbing Swapo or the ANC was problematic. Swapo camps in Angola were raided, but its low-level guerrilla warfare in Namibia seemed unimpaired. Politically, the movement continued to erode South Africa's efforts to build an 'internal' political alternative in Windhoek. Pretoria might buy time to boost its protégés, but time could not substitute for political credibility. As for the ANC, its sabotage attacks were gaining visibility and expanding its support among blacks. The widespread geographic dispersion of targets – from the Koeberg nuclear plant in Cape Town to air force head- quarters in Pretoria – implicity refuted the image of cross-border raids. Some guerrilla cadres were captured inside South Africa, others killed in attacks on Maputo and Maseru. But these dramatic incidents not only failed to stem ANC sabotage; they also helped to build the guerrillas' prestige among black South Africans. Most whites might be persuaded by the external threat hypothesis, but that propaganda backfired among blacks. Even some prominent white government supporters began to say that someday it would be necessary to talk to the ANC.

It was this context, more than US initiatives as such, that led to limited successes for US regional diplomacy. Taking advantage of the desire for respite from war in Luanda and Maputo, and of Pretoria's apparent willingness to limit its objectives, US diplomats helped to facilitate negotiations, taking the lead on the Angolan front and responding to the Mozambican initiative on the other side of the continent. To translate the appearance of *détente* into real restraints on Pretoria, however, would require penalties for South African violations. And that was still excluded from Washington's options. Washington as well as Pretoria would accept thankfully the restric- tions placed on Swapo or the ANC, but neither would genuinely accept a bar to further counter-revolutionary intervention in Angola and Mozambique.

The first sign of limited *détente* came in February 1984, with a US- brokered agreement for South African troop withdrawal and restric- tions on Swapo guerrillas in southern Angola. In March, Mozam- bique and South Africa signed the Nkomati Accord, which bound the two states to forbid any violent acts against each other from their territories. Although Maputo pledged its continued 'moral, political and diplomatic' support for the ANC, South African officials and the majority of international observers characterized the agreement as a sign of a new Pax Pretoriana. But the term was misleading, not only because it exaggerated the imminence of peace, but also because it ignored the concessions South Africa would have been making if it had implemented the security treaty and also lifted its economic sanctions against Mozambique.

Given the military and economic odds they faced, even before the escalation of 1981–1983, the Mozambican leadership saw the Nkomati Accord as a victory. In spite of overwhelming material predominance, Pretoria had failed to install a political alternative. Neither South Africa nor the United States had been able to impose a break in Mozambique's ties with the Soviet Union. Maputo would continue moral and diplomatic support for the ANC. Granted, limits would be imposed on ANC use of Mozambican territory to support guerrilla operations in South Africa. But, reasoned Frelimo, that would be a relatively minor tactical retreat for the ANC, with its strong base of support inside South Africa. Moreover, it would be reaffirming the long-held Mozambican position that it was simply not possible for adjacent states to offer the same kind of rear-base support to the ANC that the Mozambican and Zimbabwean movements had enjoyed.[39]

Mozambique, in implementing the treaty, restricted the ANC to a small diplomatic office in Maputo; several hundred ANC members left the country. But probably more significant for Pretoria was the widespread perception of the pact as a victory for South Africa. Most of the Frontline states, as well as the ANC, shared this view that Mozambique had conceded the most; Maputo found it hard to bridge the gap of understanding. This perception was more significant for Pretoria than the additional transit difficulties caused for guerrillas of the ANC. For Prime Minister P.W. Botha, Nkomati bought diplomatic credit and the award of a European trip. South Africa basked in its image as a peacemaker, while the Reagan administration cited the new trend as a victory for their policy of 'constructive engagement'.

The gain was short-lived, however. The focus shifted to the rising internal revolt in South Africa, impossible to blame on guerrilla infiltration. And it quickly became clear that the MNR was still receiving external support, and that material assistance was coming through South Africa. The security situation improved in some areas of Mozambique, enabling new relief supplies to reach the drought- and war-battered countryside. But in other areas of the country – including Maputo province directly adjoining South Africa – MNR attacks on civilians escalated.

Documents captured by Zimbabwean and Mozambican troops when they took the MNR central base at Gorongosa in August 1985 showed that South African military intelligence officers had actively violated the Nkomati Accord by continuing arms supplies, with the approval of their superiors. The evidence revealed disagreements among South Africa's leaders on implementing the agreement. But it was clear that the advocates of diplomacy were either unwilling or unable to stop the parallel military track targetting Maputo.

Machel visited Washington in September 1985, carrying the proof of Pretoria's duplicity. The visit won Reagan's reaffirmation of *détente*, against far-right critics who called for support of the MNR as anti-communist freedom fighters. But the United States, it seemed, was unwilling to mobilize more coercive pressures on South Africa to respect the treaty.

Across the continent, the bloom of *détente* was even more faded. South Africa had taken more than a year for the troop withdrawal scheduled for March 1984. Moves toward explicit US support to Unita had heartened the hawks in Pretoria and derailed talks with Luanda. Pretoria had released Swapo founder Toivo ja Toivo, but was not ready to end the well-practised dance of delay over Namibia. Since Washington itself was reluctant to compromise on its anti-Cuban and pro-Unita stand, South Africa could hardly expect condemnation for its failure to make similar concessions.

By 1985, accordingly, the regional situation had reached a new stalemate. *Détente* had halted far short of independence for Namibia. There had been a retreat from the high point of South African aggression, but that change was only in small part due to Washington's diplomacy. Moreover, it was a precarious and limited accomplishment. Inside South Africa, an unprecedented escalation of internal strife was making a mockery of the claim that 'constructive engagement' was promoting reform. The temporary setback to guerrilla action imposed by slower infiltration through Mozambique proved secondary to the fact that the primary base of opposition to the South African regime lay within the country. Popular resistance, multifaceted and persistent, non-violent and violent, aroused an extraordinary response from sympathizers overseas. It also showed signs of shaking the confidence of Western business and political leaders in the *apartheid* regime.

Which Side Are You On?
In November 1984, Randall Robinson of TransAfrica, Dr. Mary Berry of the US Civil Rights Commission and DC congressional

representative Walter Fauntroy 'sat in' at the South African Embassy in Washington. Their arrest marked the beginning of daily demonstrations at the embassy by the Free South Africa Movement. The symbolic action, with arrests day after day for an entire year, sparked and sustained an upsurge of anti-*apartheid* demonstrations in dozens of cities and universities around the country. The black-led demonstrations symbolized the commitment of US black leadership to have a role in US policy towards South Africa. And the racial and political diversity of the demonstrators symbolized a broad-based rejection of racial division and injustice, a call to the US public to reaffirm opposition to racial oppression whether at home or abroad. The 'constructive engagement' policy of the recently re-elected Reagan administration was pilloried as an unholy alliance with racism.

The popular anti-*apartheid* movement in the United States in 1985 was stimulated by resistance in South Africa, conveyed to the world by unprecedented media attention. It also built on years of anti-*apartheid* work around the country, and was triggered by the blatant Reagan tilt toward the South African regime. It became a force that neither US business nor congress nor even the Reagan administration could ignore. But its very strength held weaknesses as well.

Many of the anti-*apartheid* supporters in Congress were inclined to limit their backing to the most symbolic and least substantive sanctions against South Africa. Moreover, neither the media nor the demonstrations adequately portrayed the links between Pretoria's internal repression and its regional aggression. South Africa incurred little additional penalty for escalation of attacks against its neighbours. Mainstream commentators and politicians joined the far right in portraying the Angolan conflict as only peripherally connected to South Africa if at all. With that connection obscured, policy-makers considering Angola were far more inclined to follow well-worn anti-communist impulses than to make the connection to the novel and perhaps fleeting anti-*apartheid* clamour.

To understand US policy on southern Africa in Reagan's second term, one must pay attention to the unprecented growth of anti-*apartheid* pressure, to the still well-entrenched opposition to substantive sanctions against Pretoria, and to the continued ability of right-wing forces to exploit anti-communist sentiment in favour of a regional tilt to Pretoria.

The advance of anti-*apartheid* forces overseas stemmed both from the failure of 'reform' in South Africa and the steady growth of the South African liberation forces. Unlike the decade after Sharpeville, when repression had imposed a discouraging break in the momentum of liberation, resistance in the post-Soweto decade was too strong and multifaceted to repress successfully.

By 1981, Prime Minister P.W. Botha's reform agenda was taking shape in new legislation, with such steps as legalizing black union membership, and grants of 99-year leases on some homes in black townships. The *verkrampte* (far-right) wing of the ruling National Party in South Africa conjured up visions of a slippery slide from piecemeal reform to black domination. After P.W. Botha expelled the *verkramptes* in early 1982, under strong pressure from businessmen, he presented constitutional proposals billed as the first step towards power-sharing. The changes, however, were seen by blacks less as concessions than as part of a strategy to entrench their subordination.

The rising black trade union movement, for example, made use of the leeway provided by the new labour legislation. But it was also facing harassment leading it to identify the 'state' as a central obstacle to real progress. Purported reform of the pass laws, which lessened restrictions for Africans with urban residence rights, were even more fatally flawed. Pass-law arrests doubled between 1981 and 1983, and fines were raised for employers hiring illegal workers. But the culminating insult to rising African aspirations was the new constitution, approved by white voters in a November 1983 referendum. It provided for three separate parliamentary chambers, for whites, coloureds and Indians, with a white majority and a white veto on matters of 'common interest', as well as a new executive presidency with increased powers. Most significantly, the arrangements excluded any national role for Africans.

The United Democratic Front (UDF), a broad coalition of hundreds of groups of all races, came together in 1983 to oppose the new constitution. The new body campaigned for a boycott of the Indian and coloured elections and for a non-racial vision of the future South Africa. Black consciousness groups and trade unions, while not all willing to join the new coalition, were equally vehement in rejecting the government's plans.

Detaining many UDF leaders just before the vote, Pretoria claimed a mandate for the new system despite a turnout of less than 5 per cent. On 14 September, P.W. Botha was sworn in as the new state president, with Pretoria's Angolan protégé Jonas Savimbi the most prominent African politician in attendance.

As Botha took office, police were battling protesters in black townships, opening a new round of conflict that would rage unabated throughout the next year and into 1986. The rapid growth of the UDF was an indicator of an even broader proliferation of organizations embodying black confidence and militance. The growth of the black and non-racial trade unions established a potentially critical base of political as well as economic influence. The ANC gained increased legitimacy, and demonstrators chanted calls for the exiled leaders to bring them arms. The ANC, for its part, told its followers that the guerrilla cadres and arms infiltrated at high price into the country could only do part of the job. The people themselves, the 1985 New Year's message from the ANC stressed, would have to 'make South African ungovernable'.

Over the next year, before Pretoria banned television cameras from the townships, the pictures of police and soldiers shooting African youths left a powerful impression throughout the world. Funerals attended by tens of thousands served as new occasions for confrontation with authority when police tried to disperse mourners. A mid-1985 state of emergency over much of the country, thousands of detentions, the removal by arrest or sometimes death of a whole stratum of black leadership – all failed to restore order.

The world's view of events was also affected by the powerful media presence of government critics. The UDF's Allan Boesak, who also served as head of the World Alliance of Reformed Churches, eloquently addressed overseas audiences in tones reminiscent of the US civil rights leader, Martin Luther King, Jr. Winnie Mandela, wife of imprisoned ANC leader Nelson Mandela, openly defied her banning order, commanding international attention from press and politicians. Recently unbanned Beyers Naudé, head of the South African Council of Churches (SACC), spoke with dignity and urgency of his white compatriots' failure to understand the depth of the crisis, gaining credibility from his own elite Afrikaner background. Naudé's predecessor, Bishop Desmond Tutu, was awarded the Nobel Peace Prize in October 1984, using the platform it won him to call incessantly for outside pressure to end *apartheid.*

The Free South Africa Movement demonstrations in the United States captured the attention of the media and the public, accelerating both the nationwide divestment movement and the congressional move to legislate sanctions. If the surge of public pressure emerged suddenly, however, it was not without deeper roots, particularly in the burgeoning divestment movement. For over 15 years, sometimes more actively and sometimes less but never stopping altogether, a network of church people, students and other activists had demanded that US companies get out of South Africa. In the 1970s, after the Soweto upheaval, the movement focused on university campuses, where students called for university funds to be removed from companies with South African subsidiaries or loans. The companies responded by arguing that they could stay in South Africa to promote reforms, adopting equal employment codes of conduct such as the 'Sullivan principles'.

As the years passed, the excuse wore thin, while the divestment movement simultaneously broadened its appeal. From 1980 through 1983, states as diverse as Nebraska, Michigan, Maryland, Massachusetts and Connecticut passed divestment legislation. The city of Philadelphia pension fund sold off $90 million in stocks in 1981, and during 1982 cities and states withdrew more than $300 million from companies with South African ties. The Washington DC city council approved a divestment bill in 1983. In August 1984 New York City voted to divest pension funds from companies with South African subsidiaries, potentially affecting some $600 million in assets. Boston enacted a similar measure the same month.

Early in 1985 New York City passed an additional measure forbidding city deposits in banks that loan to the South African government. One of the nation's largest banks, Citibank, immediately announced it would phase out such loans. 'We were talking big bucks here, and money speaks,' remarked the city's assistant controller. Pittsburgh and New York City acted later in the year to restrict purchases from companies involved in South Africa, and divestment action was under consideration in more than half the US states. In March the American Chamber of Commerce in South Africa, still fighting the demand for withdrawal, warned the South African government that failure to eliminate *apartheid* could produce disastrous economic results.

By the end of 1985, divestment actions by US state and local governments had mandated almost $4.5 billion to be withdrawn from companies involved in South Africa, including some $2.6 billion with the concurrence of the Democratic-controlled legislature and Republican governor of New Jersey. A wave of student demonstrations leading to hundreds of arrests increased the pressure on universities. Columbia University finally yielded to student demands late in the year, and almost 30 universities opted for divestment during the year. Free South Africa Movement demonstrators around the United States targetted the sale of Krugerrands, substantially cutting into sales and forcing numerous dealers to stop importing the South African gold coin.[40]

The most substantive escalation in economic pressure came in August 1985 when major international banks, led by Chase Manhattan and other US banks, refused to roll over short-term loans to the private sector in South Africa representing almost two-thirds of South Africa's foreign debt over $20 billion. As the exchange rate of the rand dropped precipitously, Pretoria declared a moratorium on debt repayment into 1986. Bankers denied that political considerations had caused the move, but it came shortly after a speech by P.W. Botha failing to satisfy demands for change, and political reform dominated the agenda as Swiss banker Fritz Leutwiler attempted to negotiate a settlement. The panic had started with banks in New York, where the City Council had already prohibited city dealings with banks making loans to the South African government. And there was no doubt that fear of new domestic repercussions was a factor in the bankers' minds.

The price of gold levelled out a little over $300 per ounce by the end of 1984, but the general economic crisis was reflected in the continued low exchange rate for the rand, which even dipped below $0.40 after the state of emergency was declared. South African economists argued that the economy had a solid base for recovery, but more and more renewed confidence was seen to depend on political reform as well.

Actions from Western governments, more openly political and less easily reversed than those by private bankers, were hotly contested. Scandinavian countries were seriously considering embargoes on all economic ties with South Africa. After the Botha government imposed a state of emergency in July 1985, France recalled its ambassador, announced a ban on new investment in South Africa and introduced a UN Security Council resolution calling for similar voluntary action by other countries. The resolution passed 13 to 0, with Britain and the United States abstaining. The member nations of the European Economic Community, in spite of reluctance from Bonn and London, agreed in September to maintain bans on oil and arms exports, and to withdraw their military attachés from Pretoria.

When Commonwealth leaders met in October, Britain was again the principal obstacle to action, as African states and India argued for comprehensive and mandatory sanctions. A compromise agreement finally included a ban on Krugerrand imports and an end to government loans or financing of trade missions to South Africa. The leaders of the 49-member group threatened stronger action if South Africa had not begun to dismantle *apartheid* within six months.

In the United States, the sustained controversy echoed in the halls of Congress as well as on the streets. In 1984 sanctions measures including a ban on new investment in South Africa had been attached to the Export Administration Act, and passed the House. Leaders of the effort, including Representative William Gray of the Black Caucus, were infuriated when the House failed to stand up to administration and Senate pressure to gut the bill, which died as a result. During the primary election campaign the Reverend Jesse Jackson made southern Africa a prominent issue.

In 1985, congressional sanctions backers launched a major new effort. A bill introduced by Representative Dellums of California mandated comprehensive sanctions. Congressmen Gray and Wolpe introduced the Anti-Apartheid Act of 1985, sponsored in the Senate by Senator Edward Kennedy and others. The draft bill barred new US investment in South Africa, loans and computer sales to the South African government, and the import of Krugerrands. The two provisions – the Krugerrand and the new investment bans – were subject to waiver with approval of both the president and Congress, if South Africa made specific steps towards ending *apartheid* and granting independence to Namibia.

In June the bill won overwhelming approval in the House of Representatives, with one-third of the Republicans joining Democrats in the 295 to 127 vote. After compromising with the Republican-controlled Senate to defer the ban on new investment for possible action a year later, the House passed a revised version by 380 to 48. In September, in a final concession to head off Senate approval and a predicted congressional override of his veto, the president issued an executive order with his version of the compromise measures.[41]

The Reagan team that responded to the new situation in 1985 still contained the same personnel in the essential State Department posts. At the UN the vocal Kirkpatrick had been replaced by the more discreet Vernon Walters, who was however said to share a similar hard-line perspective. The most notable addition to the White House was Director of Communications Patrick Buchanan, a fanatic ideologue who opposed criticism of South Africa and deplored lack of enthusiasm for the anti-communist crusade. In the debate over sanctions in September, McFarlane reportedly prevailed over Buchanan's non-compromise position. In December, largely because of conflicts with White House chief of staff Donald Regan, McFarlane resigned.

Reagan's shift to sanctions, however limited, was a dramatic measure of the impact of public anti-*apartheid* sentiment. As a signal to Pretoria, however, it was decidedly ambiguous. The conceded ban on Krugerrands and new loans to the government acknowledged a situation which had largely been achieved by protesters already. Restrictions on computer and nuclear-related exports provided the possibility, if tightly enforced, for rescinding most of the exceptions opened up during Reagan's first term. But the executive order, subject to discretionary reversal by the president, omitted the threat of future sanctions in the case of South African intransigence.

Even the strongest version of the Anti-Apartheid Act fell far short of comprehensive measures actually intended to weaken the *apartheid* state. They were understood by their sponsors as a first step, a signal that could have an impact only if seen as a portent of stronger actions to come. The president's action instead indicated that Pretoria could regard these measures as the maximum to expect. In November, the message was reinforced when the United States and Britain vetoed mandatory UN sanctions against South Africa on the Namibian question. The package of 'mandatory selective sanctions', on which France abstained and all other Council members voted in favour, included an oil embargo, a ban on new investment and other trade restrictions.

The escalation of the South African crisis and of the international anti-*apartheid* movement had produced dramatic shifts in the Western debate. For the first time 'sanctions' were a serious issue in the political mainstream. The actions of the banks had shown that South Africa was indeed vulnerable to Western economic pressure. But the taboo against comprehensive sanctions was still powerful in Washington, as in Bonn and London. Two late 1985 articles in the prestigious journals *Foreign Affairs* and *Foreign Policy* proclaimed the failure of 'constructive engagement', but still went through elaborate intellectual gymnastics to avoid even considering sanctions as an alternative.[42]

US establishment opinion on South Africa, in fact, seemed closely to parallel that of the business community in South Africa itself. In 1985, as in 1960 and 1976, business criticism of *apartheid* rigidity was heightened. Arguably the dissent was far more serious this time, as more and more business leaders concluded that only substantive black political participation could halt the descent into chaos and create the possibility for South African capitalism to outlive the structures of white racial dominance. But even while preparing for this contingency, they were fearful of the radical potential of a non-racial society. As a means of pressure they rejected not only the ANC's recourse to arms against the *apartheid* state, but also the demand for sanctions. In the end it seemed they still counted on a miraculous advent of wisdom in Pretoria, and some compromise solution by which they could have their cake and eat it too.

The dominant view among both business and government in the West reflected this South African business perspective. As it became more and more difficult to argue that reform actually was happening, increasing weight was given to the claim that sanctions should be rejected because they would harm blacks in South Africa and in the neighbouring states. The credibility of the plea suffered somewhat since one of its most vehement advocates was the South African government itself, but it was bolstered by citing South African homeland leaders such as Chief Gatsha Buthelezi, by polls showing black worker reluctance to lose jobs with foreign companies, and by noting the close economic links that South Africa's neighbours still maintained with Pretoria.

On the other hand the consensus of credible black leadership in favour of sanctions became clearer and clearer. Defying possible legal penalties, leaders such as Bishop Tutu and Dr Boesak pleaded with the international community to take economic action. Not only the UDF but also the SACC and the newly formed Council of South African Trade Unions (COSATU) called openly for economic sanctions. The Frontline states, meeting in Mozambique in September 1985, reiterated their long-standing position that the inability of economically weak neighbours to punish Pretoria should not be used as an excuse by Western countries. Citing over $10 billion in damages from South African aggression in the past five years, they echoed South African blacks in noting that the suffering caused by *apartheid* was an even heavier burden than the effects of sanctions would be. And, whether reflecting shifts in opinion or methodological differences with earlier polls, researchers reported overwhelming support among South African blacks for economic pressures to end *apartheid*.[43]

Reagan's Washington, in contrast, still found itself in the position of the apocryphal English-speaking South African businessman who, it was said, talked Progressive, voted for the 'moderate' segregation of the United Party – and, concealing the thought perhaps even from

himself, thanked God for the National Party. The continuing sympathy
for Pretoria appeared most clearly in the case of regional policy.

Reviving the Cold War

Encouraging signals to counter the chorus of condemnation for
Pretoria came, ironically, from the US congress as well as the Reagan
administration. Even as the Anti-Apartheid Act was making its
tortuous and ultimately inconclusive way through the legislative
process, sentiment was rising for the support of South African military
operations in Angola. Aided in large part by ignorance of the regional
context, but even more by a deliberate propaganda campaign to
change the terms of debate, the far right launched an all-out crusade
for support of anti-communist 'freedom fighters' in Angola and
Mozambique.

The crusade gained little momentum in the case of Mozambique,
although restrictions were placed on aid to Machel's government.
Unlike Angola, Mozambique had neither the legacy of direct US
intervention nor the conspicuous presence of Cuban troops. And
Mozambique's diplomatic offensive had convinced key US policy-
makers that the South African-backed MNR was no credible
alternative. When President Machel visited Washington in
September 1985, far-right ideologues denounced Reagan for meeting
with a 'Marxist dictator', but legislation introduced to aid the MNR
failed to win White House support.

On Angola, the far right found more backing for their effort to
present the conflict as a Cold War battle unrelated to South Africa.
Even in May, when South African commandoes were surprised in the
act of sabotaging oil storage tanks at Gulf Oil installations in Cabinda,
carrying Unita leaflets claiming credit for the attack, neither the South
African connection or Unita's willingness to endanger US lives and
property aroused outrage in Washington. A few days later President
Reagan sent a message of support to a Unita-hosted international
gathering of anti-communist 'contras', organized by New York
Republican millionaire Lewis Lehrman.

Even more helpful for the hawks in Pretoria's State Security
Council (SSC), because less predictable, were subsequent events in
Congress. The Angolan attack played little role in the debate on
apartheid, and in June the Senate voted to repeal the Clark
Amendment, which had banned US intervention in Angola. The margin
was 63 to 34, with 17 Democrats joining the Republican majority.

Both the president and the Senate were signalling support for South Africa's surrogate in Angola instead of moving towards stronger condemnation of South African regional aggression. The day after the Senate action, in a parallel tilt, the House caved in to Reagan's campaign for support to the 'contra' insurgency in Nicaragua. In July the House also repealed the Clark Amendment by a vote of 236 to 185, on the same day the Senate passed its weaker version of the Anti-Apartheid Act.

The simultaneous actions could only confirm African impressions that US southern Africa policy, even when not consistently indifferent or hostile to African liberation, remained hopelessly confused. In Pretoria it made sense to conclude that when push came to shove, the old Cold War verities would take priority over new anti-*apartheid* rhetoric.[44]

In the last half of 1985, in addition to imposing an internal state of emergency, Pretoria again stepped up its attacks on neighbouring countries. SADF chief, Constand Viljoen, justifying a raid on Botswana only days after the Senate repealed the Clark Amendment, said the action was necessary to counter terrorist actions by the banned ANC. Moreover, he added, the possibility of an international outcry had been 'very carefully debated and thought out'.

The US government responded by withdrawing Ambassador Herman Nickel from Pretoria for consultations, a significant diplomatic move. But there was no sign that the Reagan administration would concede 'punitive sanctions' for South African aggression. In three separate votes in late June, the UN Security Council condemned the Cabinda and Botswana attacks and denounced unilateral South African installation of an interim government in Namibia. But Western pressure ensured that no new UN sanctions were adopted.

After Reagan's action in September had checked the drive for congressional sanctions, at least until the spring 1986 session, the interventionist forces gained strength both in Washington and Pretoria. After the South African authorities banned television coverage of black protests in November, the country's internal strife receded somewhat from overseas headlines; while, in Washington, the political momentum built for direct US support, military or 'humanitarian', for Unita.

Congressional sceptics pointed out the profitable US economic ties with oil-producing Angola, and warned against the dangers of being more closely identified with South Africa. The State Department's

Africa Bureau cautioned against going too far and totally upsetting the prospect for continued negotiations. But nominal anti-*apartheid* sentiment was, for many American policy-makers, still consistent with a regional alliance with Pretoria against an imagined 'communist onslaught'. The $600 000 Unita public relations campaign culminated in Savimbi's high-powered lobbying trip in January 1986, and in a decision by the White House to supply at least $15 million in covert aid. Congressional proposals to grant openly far larger sums were held in abeyance, amidst scepticism from Democrats in the House and Senate intelligence committees. But the opposition was too little and too late, and crippled by the prevalent tendency to isolate the Angolan and South African issues.

In Pretoria the connection was obvious, however. Continued internal unrest would provoke escalated criticism, even from Reagan administration officials and congressional Republicans. But regional aggression was unlikely to lose points in Washington, and might even win favour, especially if Angola was the target. South African troops had secured Unita's headquarters against an Angolan government offensive in September. And far from provoking additional sanctions pressure, the South Africans subsequently won an open, albeit still officially 'covert' alliance with Washington on that front.

In late 1985, a number of signs indicated that Pretoria had again decided to escalate its regional aggression. A December midnight raid on Maseru was followed by the economic blockade that brought down the Lesotho government. The MNR was clearly being re-equipped to launch new assaults. Threats against Botswana, Zimbabwe and Mozambique became more ominous. And the prospect that the United States would threaten South Africa with reprisals to protect any southern African state seemed remote.

Prospects

The future course of US policy will depend in large part on the balance of forces in the conflicts in southern Africa itself, and detailed projections are probably of limited value. In mid-1984, for example, few would have ventured to predict the upsurge of the anti-*apartheid* forces which so dominated the scene in 1985. Yet there are several general conclusions which can be drawn, assuming the continued escalation of conflict both inside South Africa and in the region:

● The grass-roots divestment movement and the campaign for congressional sanctions will continue. Proposals for somewhat stronger measures than those already imposed will gain approval at least in the Democratic-controlled House. The Reagan adminis- tration, despite the occasional Africa Bureau hints that such pressures might be useful leverage on Pretoria, will continue to resist such action every step of the way. In attempting to counter the sanctions push, the administration will heighten its public criticism of Pretoria, and step up assistance to selected reformist projects in South Africa.

● Barring a major new escalation in South Africa, however, congressional 'moderates' will join the administration in resisting comprehensive legislative sanctions or even such limited moves as unconditional bars on new investment or computer exports. Only the imminent threat of the Pretoria regime's collapse is likely to upset the well-entrenched taboo against comprehensive sanctions.

● If Unita/South African military collaboration becomes visible and dramatic to US public opinion, anti-interventionist forces in Congress may have some chance of restraining new US aid to Unita. Otherwise the many Democratic and few Republican waverers on the issue will remain indecisive. The State Department might delay or limit expansion of the aid, while trying to nurse along renewed negotiations. But the programme under way will acquire a life of its own, a continuing subsidy to Pretoria.

● South Africa's leaders may decide to step up or momentarily to abate their campaign against their neighbours, based on their perceptions of their own regional interests, and the changing emphases within the State Security Council. If the trend should shift again in the direction of *détente,* US diplomats would again be ready to encourage it. But as long as Washington excludes the option of punishing Pretoria's regional offences, as well as its internal policies, by sanctions that bite, the effect of US policy will be at best marginal and at worst an additional stimulus to conflict.

● Substantive sanctions, if they were adopted by Washington or by the international community in concert, would be unlikely totally to deter South African attacks on its neighbours in the short term. Nor would Pretoria's regime likely soon concede the demands for dismantling its own basis of internal control.

Such measures could, however, make a difference in limiting the destruction in the short run by deterring the most adventurous moves. And most importantly they would accelerate the day when the balance of forces shifts decisively towards the total abolition of *apartheid,* a day which cannot come until its defenders have been far more decisively weakened.

Abbreviations

ANC	African National Congress of South Africa
ARMSCOR	Armaments Corporation (South Africa)
BCP	Basutoland Congress Party
BDF	Botswana Defence Force
BDP	Bechuanaland Democratic Party (Botswana)
BLS	Botswana, Lesotho, Swaziland
BNP	Basutoland National Party
BOLESWA	Botswana, Lesotho, Swaziland
BOSS	Bureau of State Security (South Africa)
CAF	Central African Federation
CAZ	Conservative Alliance of Zimbabwe
CIA	Central Intelligence Agency (United States)
CIO	Central Intelligence Organization (Rhodesia)
CONSAS	Constellation of Southern African States
COREMO	Mozambique Revolutionary Council
COSATU	Council of South African Trade Unions
CPL	Communist Party of Lesotho
DGS	General Security Directorate (Portugal)
DTA	Democratic Turnhalle Alliance (Namibia)
EEC	European Economic Community
ESCOM	Electricity Supply Commission (South Africa)
FAPLA	People's Armed Forces for the Liberation of Angola
FLEC	Front for the Liberation of the Cabinda Enclave (Angola)
FNLA	National Front for the Liberation of Angola
FPLM	Mozambique People's Liberation Forces
FRELIMO	Mozambique Liberation Front
FRG	Federal Republic of Germany
FUMO	Mozambique United Front
GDP	Gross Domestic Product
GDR	Democratic Republic of Germany
GNP	Gross National Product
GRAE	Government of the Angolan Republic in Exile
IAEA	International Atomic Energy Agency
IMF	International Monetary Fund
JMC	Joint Monitoring Commission (Angola/South Africa)
JSC	Joint Security Commission (Mozambique/South Africa)
LESOMA	League of Socialists of Malawi
LLA	Lesotho Liberation Army
MFA	Movement of the Armed Forces (Portugal)
MFP	Marema Tlou Freedom Party (Lesotho)
MID	Military Intelligence Directorate (Rhodesia, South Africa)
MNR	Mozambique National Resistance
MPC	Multi-Party Conference (Namibia)
MPLA	People's Movement for the Liberation of Angola

NATO	North Atlantic Treaty Organization
NIS	National Intelligence Service (South Africa)
NPT	Non-Proliferation Treaty
NSC	National Security Council (United States)
OAU	Organization of African Unity
OECD	Organization for Economic Co-operation and Development
OPEC	Organization of Petroleum Exporting Countries
PAC	Pan-Africanist Congress
PF	Patriotic Front
PF-ZAPU	Patriotic Front-Zimbabwe African People's Union
PIDE	International Police for the Defence of the State (Portugal)
PTA	Preferential Trade Area
RENAMO	Mozambique National Resistance
RF	Rhodesian Front
SABC	South African Broadcasting Corporation
SACC	South African Council of Churches
SACU	Southern African Customs Union
SADCC	Southern African Development Coordination Conference
SADF	South African Defence Force
SAFTO	South African Foreign Trade Office
SAP	South African Police
SATCC	Southern African Transport and Communications Commission
SATS	South African Transport Services
SAS	Special Air Service
SB	Special Branch
SSC	State Security Council (South Africa)
SWANU	South West African National Union (Namibia)
SWAPO	South West Africa People's Organization (Namibia)
SWATF	South West Africa Territory Force
UANC	United African National Council (Zimbabwe)
UDENAMO	Mozambique National Democratic Union
UDF	United Democratic Front (South Africa)
UDP	United Democratic Party (Lesotho)
UN	United Nations
UNITA	National Union for the Total Independence of Angola
UNTAG	United Nations Transitional Assistance Group (Namibia)
US	United States
USSR	Union of Soviet Socialist Republics
ZANLA	Zimbabwe African National Liberation Army
ZANU	Zimbabwe African National Union
ZANU-PF	Zimbabwe African National Union – Patriotic Front
ZAPU	Zimbabwe African People's Union
ZBC	Zimbabwe Broadcasting Corporation
ZRP	Zimbabwe Republic Police
ZPRA	Zimbabwe People's Revolutionary Army
ZNA	Zimbabwe National Army

Appendix 1

Agreement on non-aggression and good neighbourliness between the Government of the People's Republic of Mozambique and the Government of the Republic of South Africa.

The Government of the People's Republic of Mozambique and the Government of the Republic of South Africa, hereinafter referred to as the High Contracting Parties:

RECOGNISING the principles of strict respect for sovereignty and territorial integrity, sovereign equality, political independence and the inviolability of the borders of all states;

REAFFIRMING the principle of non-interference in the internal affairs of other states;

CONSIDERING the internationally recognised principle of the right of peoples to self-determination and independence and the principle of equal rights of all peoples;

CONSIDERING the obligation of all states to refrain, in their international relations, from the threat or use of force against the territorial integrity or political independence of any state;

CONSIDERING the obligation of states to settle conflicts by peaceful means, and thus safeguard international peace and security and justice;

RECOGNISING the responsibility of states not to allow their territory to be used for acts of war, aggression or violence against other states;

CONSCIOUS of the need to promote relations of good neighbourliness based on the principles of equality of rights and mutual advantage;

CONVINCED that relations of good neighbourliness between the High Contracting Parties will contribute to peace, security, stability and progress in Southern Africa, the Continent and the World;

Have solemnly agreed to the following:

ARTICLE ONE

The High Contracting Parties undertake to respect each other's sovereignty and independence and, in fulfilment of this fundamental obligation, to refrain from interfering in the internal affairs of the other.

ARTICLE TWO

1) The High Contracting Parties shall resolve differences and disputes that may arise between them and that may or are likely to endanger mutual peace and security or peace and security in the region, by means of negotiation, enquiry, mediation, conciliation, arbitration or other peaceful means, and undertake not to resort, individually or collectively, to the threat or use of force against each other's sovereignty, territorial integrity or political independence.

2) For the purposes of this article, the use of force shall include *inter alia* –

a) attacks by land, air or sea forces;

b) sabotage;

c) unwarranted concentration of such forces at or near the international boundaries of the High Contracting Parties;

d) violation of the international land, air or sea boundaries of either of the High Contracting Parties.

3) The High Contracting Parties shall not in any way assist the armed forces of any state or group of states deployed against the territorial sovereignty or political independence of the other.

ARTICLE THREE

1) The High Contracting Parties shall not allow their respective territories, territorial waters or air space to be used as a base, thoroughfare, or in any other way by another state, government, foreign military forces, organisations or individuals which plan or prepare to commit acts of violence, terrorism or aggression against the territorial integrity or political independence of the other or may threaten the security of its inhabitants.

2) The High Contracting Parties, in order to prevent or eliminate the acts or the preparation of acts mentioned in paragraph (1) of this article, undertake in particular to –

a) forbid and prevent in their respective territories the organisation of irregular forces or armed bands, including mercenaries, whose objective is to carry out the acts contemplated in paragraph (1) of this article;

b) eliminate from their respective territories bases, training centres, places of shelter, accommodation and transit for elements who intend to carry out acts contemplated in paragraph (1) of this article;

c) eliminate from their respective territories centres or depots containing armaments of whatever nature, destined to be used by the elements contemplated in paragraph (1) of this article;

d) eliminate from their respective territories command posts or other places for the command, direction and co-ordination of the elements contemplated in paragraph (1) of this article;

e) eliminate from their respective territories communication and telecommunication facilities between the command and the elements contemplated in paragraph (1) of this article;

f) eliminate and prohibit the installation in their respective territories of radio broadcasting stations, including unofficial or clandestine broadcasts, for the elements that carry out the acts contemplated in paragraph (1) of this article;

g) exercise strict control, in their respective territories, over elements which intend to carry out or plan the acts contemplated in paragraph (1) of this article;

h) prevent the transit of elements who intend to plan to commit the acts contemplated in paragraph (1) of this article, from a place in the territory of either to a place in the territory of the other or to a place in the territory of any third state which has a common boundary with the High Contracting Party against which such elements intend or plan to commit the said acts;

i) take appropriate steps in their respective territories to prevent the recruitment of elements of whatever nationality for the purpose of carrying out the acts contemplated in paragraph (1) of this article;

j) prevent the elements contemplated in paragraph (1) of this article from carrying out from their respective territories by any means acts of abduction or other acts, aimed at taking citizens of any nationality hostage in the territory of the other High Contracting Party; and

k) prohibit the provision on their respective territories of any logistic facilities for carrying out the acts contemplated in paragraph (1) of this article.

3) The High Contracting Parties will not use the territory of third states to carry out or support the acts contemplated in paragraphs (1) and (2) of this article.

ARTICLE FOUR

The High Contracting Parties shall take steps, individually and collectively, to ensure that the international boundary between their respective territories is effectively patrolled and that the border posts are efficiently administered to prevent illegal crossings from the territory of a High Contracting Party to the territory of the other, and in particular, by elements contemplated in Article Three of this Agreement.

ARTICLE FIVE

The High Contracting Parties shall prohibit within their territory acts of propaganda that incite a war of aggression against the other High Contracting Party and shall also prohibit acts of propaganda aimed at inciting acts of terrorism and civil war in the territory of the other High Contracting Party.

ARTICLE SIX

The High Contracting Parties declare that there is no conflict between their commitments in treaties and international obligations and the commitment undertaken in this Agreement.

ARTICLE SEVEN

The High Contracting Parties are committed to interpreting this Agreement in good faith and will maintain periodic contact to ensure the effective application of what has been agreed.

ARTICLE EIGHT

Nothing in this Agreement shall be construed as detracting from the High Contracting Parties' right to self-defence in the event of armed attacks, as provided for in the Charter of the United Nations.

ARTICLE NINE

1) Each of the High Contracting Parties shall appoint high-ranking representatives to serve on a Joint Security Commission with the aim of supervising and monitoring the application of this Agreement.
2) The Commission shall determine its own working procedure.
3) The Commission shall meet on a regular basis and may be specially convened whenever circumstances so require.
4) The Commission shall–
   a) Consider all allegations of infringements of the provisions of this Agreement;
   b) advise the High Contracting Parties of its conclusions; and
   c) make recommendations to the High Contracting Parties concerning measures for the effective application of this Agreement and the settlement of disputes over infringements or alleged infringements.
5) The High Contracting Parties shall determine the mandate of their respective representatives in order to enable interim measures to be taken in cases of duly recognised emergency.
6) The High Contracting Parties shall make available all the facilities

necessary for the effective functioning of the Commission and will
jointly consider its conclusions and recommendations.

ARTICLE TEN

This Agreement will also be known as "The Accord of Nkomati".

ARTICLE ELEVEN

1) This agreement shall enter into force on the date of the signature thereof.
2) Any amendment to this Agreement agreed to by the High Contracting
Parties shall be affected by the Exchange of Notes between them.

IN WITNESS WHEREOF, the signatories, in the name of their respective
governments, have signed and sealed this Agreement, in quadruplicate in the
Portuguese and English languages, both texts being equally authentic.

THUS DONE AND SIGNED AT the common border on the banks of the
Nkomati River, on this the sixteenth day of March 1984.

SAMORA MOISÉS MACHEL
MARSHAL OF THE REPUBLIC
PRESIDENT OF THE PEOPLE'S
REPUBLIC OF MOZAMBIQUE
PRESIDENT OF THE COUNCIL OF MINISTERS
FOR THE GOVERNMENT OF THE
PEOPLE'S REPUBLIC OF
MOZAMBIQUE

PIETER WILLEM BOTHA
PRIME MINISTER OF THE
REPUBLIC OF SOUTH AFRICA
FOR THE GOVERNMENT OF THE
REPUBLIC OF SOUTH AFRICA

Appendix 2

MESSAGE FROM THE ANGOLAN HEAD OF STATE TO THE UNITED NATIONS SECRETARY-GENERAL ON THE PROBLEMS OF SOUTHERN AFRICA

Handed to United Nations Secretary-General Javier Perez de Cuellar in New York on Tuesday 20 November 1984 by Elisio de Figueiredo, Ambassador of the People's Republic of Angola to the United Nations

His Excellency Dr Javier Pérez de Cuellar, Secretary-General of the United Nations Organisation, New York

Mr Secretary-General:

I have the honour to address myself to Your Excellency to inform you of the steps taken by the Government of the People's Republic of Angola with the essential objective of guaranteeing the independence of Namibia, through the full implementation of United Nations Security Council resolution 435/78, achieving the withdrawal of South African forces from the south of Angola, securing international guarantees for Angola's security, independence and territorial integrity, and contributing to the establishment of lasting peace in Southern Africa.

As I stated publicly on 26 August 1983, on the occasion of your memorable visit to Luanda, the People's Republic of Angola has always shown its willingness to co-operate in the search for an adequate solution to the Namibian problem, thereby taking the first important step towards the establishment of the just and lasting peace we want for our peoples and the international community.

While ratifying the determination of the people and Government of Angola to continue to fight against the racist invaders, I reiterated our willingness to continue diplomatic action to seek a just solution, and I reaffirmed the following positions of our Party and Government:

1. The immediate and unconditional withdrawal of the South African forces occupying part of our territory;
2. The immediate implementation of Security Council resolution 435/78 leading to the true independence of Namibia;
3. The cessation of South African aggression against Angola;
4. The cessation of all logistical support for the Unita puppet bands.

On the basis of these positions, some of which had already been stated in the statement of the Foreign Ministers of the People's Republic of Angola and the Republic of Cuba of 4 February 1982, and are also contained in the joint statement of 19 March 1984 of both governments, we have held both direct and indirect talks with representatives of the governments of the United States and South Africa, with a view to achieving the above objectives.

These principled positions put forward by Angola are a categorical rejection of so-called 'linkage' - rejected by almost every government in the world and by world opinion - which seeks to make the implementation of resolution 435/78 contingent on the prior or parallel withdrawal of the Cuban military contingent legally present in the People's Republic of Angola at the request of its Government and in accordance with Article 51 of the United Nations Charter.

On the contrary, the implementation of resolution 435/78 and with it the independence of Namibia, is a fundamental factor which, together with the cessation of direct or indirect aggression and threats against Angola and help from abroad for the counter-revolutionary bands, will make it possible within an adequate period to ensure our security and the subsequent progressive withdrawal of Cuban internationalist troops from Angola, as stated very precisely in the above mentioned joint statements of Cuba and Angola of February 1982 and March 1984.

In the course of our talks with representatives of the United States held in Luanda on 6 and 7 September, we presented them with a platform for negotiations to be conveyed to the Government of South Africa, containing five points.

I here transcribe the full text of the said platform presented by the People's Republic of Angola:

1. The completion of the process of withdrawal of South African forces from the territory of the People's Republic of Angola and control by FAPLA of Angola's state borders.
2. A solemn statement by the Republic of South Africa in which it pledges to honour and to contribute to the implementation of United Nations resolution 435/78 on Namibian independence.
3. A ceasefire agreement between the Republic of South Africa and SWAPO.
4. A statement by the Government of the People's Republic of Angola reiterating its decision, in agreement with the Government of Cuba, to proceed with the start of the withdrawal of the Cuban internationalist contingent, only when the implementation of resolution 435/78 is under way.
5. The signing, within the parameters of the UN Security Council, which would act as guarantor, of an international agreement between the governments of the People's Republic of Angola, the Republic of South Africa, the Republic of Cuba and a representative of SWAPO, in which would be defined the respective undertakings for achieving Namibia's independence, and the guarantees for the security and territorial integrity of the People's Republic of Angola and lasting peace in South-West Africa.

This agreement would consider:

1. United Nations troops having been established in Namibia, together with the UN authorities, within the prescribed period, the Republic of South Africa would completely withdraw its armed forces from Namibia, withdrawing first the air force and the units on the border with Angola, which would come under the immediate responsibility of the United Nations troops.
2. As soon as the air force had completely withdrawn from the territory of Namibia and there remained of the South African troops only one thousand five hundred infantrymen, Angola and Cuba would proceed with the withdrawal of five thousand Cuban internationalists from the troops grouped in the south, as a gesture of good will.
3. The Cuban troops would not carry out any kind of deployment of military units or any type of manoeuvre south of the 16th Parallel.
4. With regard to the remaining numbers of Cuban troops grouped in the south, they would be withdrawn to Cuba over a maximum period of three years.
5. If any act of aggression or threat of imminent aggression against Angola by South Africa were noted, the entire agreement would be suspended or annulled.
6. The Republic of South Africa would undertake from the very start to cease all support of the Unita bands, and the United Nations authorities would have to verify the dismantling of the Unita bases on Namibian territory.
7. The withdrawal of Cuban troops stationed in Cabinda Province and other regions in the north of the People's Republic of Angola, including the country's capital, would be programmed in accordance with a timetable to be established for this purpose by the People's Republic of Angola and Cuba.

As Your Excellency can confirm, the platform directly states the problems that must be resolved to secure the implementation of resolution 435/78 and, therefore, the independence of Namibia, as well as other steps to guarantee the disengagement of South African forces from our territory and the establishment of lasting peace in the region, which would create the requisite conditions to proceed with the disengagement of Cuban internationalist troops from southern Angola; all this, of course, within the framework of an international agreement subscribed to by all the parties concerned and guaranteed by the Security Council.

Subsequently, and as proof of the seriousness with which Angola is carrying out the negotiations, on 9 October this year we presented a text which complemented the platform and rigorously expressed our precise proposals with regard to the Cuban military personnel.

The full text of the document is as follows:

The People's Republic of Angola and the Republic of Cuba, in exercising their sovereign rights, and within the framework of Article 51 of the United Nations Charter, agree to proceed in the following manner in respect of the internationalist contingent of Cuban

troops, so long as the points formulated in the platform of the **People's** Republic of
Angola for an international agreement on independence, security and peace in South
West Africa (Angola and Namibia) are accepted, carried out and respected

First, on the grouping of Cuban troops in the south of Angola (ATS):

1. Within 24 months of the entry of the UN troops contingent for the implementation
    of Security Council resolution 435/78, the 15,000 men of the present line defending
    the south of Angola – Namibe-Lubango-Matala-Jamba-Menongue – will be
    withdrawn in the following manner:

    - after the 16th week, within a four-month period, 5,000 men.

    - between the 12th and 16th month, another 5,000 men.

    - between the 20th and 24th month, a further 5,000 men.

    During this period, the Cuban troops would at no time cross the 16th Parallel, which
    is 160km from the Namibian border and 1,360km from the Orange River.

2. The remaining troops of the ATS, comprising approximately 5,000 men, deployed
    behind the said line, would be withdrawn between the 32nd and 36th month.

    During that third year, these troops would at no time cross the 13th Parallel, which is,
    more than 500km from the land border with Namibia and 1,700km from the Orange River.
    That is, as from the 24th month, no ATS unit would cross the 13th Parallel.

    Thus, approximately 20,000 men of the total number of Cuban troops in Angola would
    withdraw in 36 months.

Second, on the remaining Cuban troops in Angola:

1. The remaining Cuban troops which have nothing to do with the defence of the south
    of the country, and no relationship to Namibia or South Africa, as pointed out in
    point 5-VII of the platform, would be withdrawn from Angola in accordance with an
    independent timetable to be agreed upon by the People's Republic of Angola and
    Cuba when the time comes.

    These remaining troops would also at no time cross the 13th Parallel.

    Angola and Cuba shall establish the dates indicated as the maximum limits for the
    ATS to stay in Angola, reserving the right to cut short those periods if security and
    territorial integrity so permit. In the same spirit, both governments, exercising their
    prerogatives of sovereignty, shall determine the moment and the appropriate
    timescale for the withdrawal of the remaining forces, once Angola's integrity and
    security are fully guaranteed.

2. Part of those troops are in Cabinda, which is 1,350km from the river border (the Cunene
    River) with Namibia and separated from the rest of the territory of the People's Republic
    of Angola by a strip of Zairean territory and by the Zaire River.
    Cabinda is 2,550km from the Orange River.

    Another part of this force would be in Luanda and the surrounding area (Bengo and
    Kwanza Norte). Luanda is Cabinda's rear, in view of the fact that it is only here that
    there can be the air and naval forces capable of going to the help of Cabinda in the
    event of aggression, as well as the ground forces which would be transported by air
    and ship.

    Luanda is 945km from the river border (Cunene River) with Namibia and 2,145km from
    the Orange River.

    Other units could be stationed in northern and eastern provinces and in strategic points
    north of the 13th Parallel which ensure communications and supplies to those provinces.

3. That is, the remaining forces would be very far from the southern border, and their
    mission, together with FAPLA, is to defend the territorial integrity of the People's
    Republic of Angola against aggression from the north and north-east, and more
    especially against Cabinda, as has already happened.

4. The People's Republic of Angola does not have the organised manpower resources
    with the required educational level, or the available material and financial resources
    to wage a war against the Unita bands and other puppet organisations, and
    simultaneously to replace the Cuban troops and armaments at strategic points in the
    south, centre and north of the country. Angola has to give priority to fighting the
    bandits who, supported trained and equipped from abroad, have caused and are
    continuing to cause the country substantial human and economic losses.

At the same time, and if agreement is reached in the present negotiations, in only 36 months it will have to replace the strength in men and equipment of the grouping of Cuban troops in the south and assume responsibility for the installations and positions occupied by them.

For this reason, it is only after such replacement has been carried out and peace and internal order has been guaranteed, that Angola itself will be able to take on the tasks which, for the country's security and integrity, are performed by the remaining Cuban military personnel.

This will require time, substantial resources and a tremendous effort in the training of skilled and technical personnel. To demand more of our young State, after five centuries of colonialism, fourteen years of struggle for independence and almost ten years of fighting against foreign aggression and subversion organised from abroad, would reflect a lack of realism and a lack of consideration for our people.

Angola has given proof of its good will and seriousness in seeking peace.

Angola cannot make concessions which would be suicidal to its national integrity and its political and social progress, forgetting the sacrifices made by tens of thousands of its finest sons and daughters.

Angola, Mr Secretary-General, has given proof of its willingness and seriousness in seeking peace, but it cannot accept an arrangement which does not take into account the criteria outlined here or which does not fully respond in a satisfactory way to all the issues related to the rapid independence of Namibia, the disengagement of South African troops from our territory and the cessation of all external help for the Unita puppet bands.

In other words, and reaffirming what is stated at the end of the complementary text, it is not possible either to demand or to expect of Angola concessions which would be suicidal to its national integrity and the development of its political and social process, and would mean forgetting the sacrifices made by tens of thousands of its finest sons and daughters.

Mr Secretary-General, conscious of the fundamental role played by the United Nations in respect of the independence of Namibia and the implementation of resolution 435/78, we consider it indispensable not only that Your Excellency should be fully informed of how the negotiations are going, but also that, at an opportune moment in the not too distant future, that your representative should take part in them, so that you may also make your valuable and necessary contribution to our efforts.

Finally, I should like to say to you, Mr Secretary-General, that Angola has carried out these negotiations in close co-ordination with Cuba and has its full support. At the same time, the leadership of SWAPO has also been informed about the evolution of the negotiations.

I should like to request of Your Excellency that this letter be circulated as an official document of the General Assembly and the Security Council.

Please accept, Mr Secretary-General, the assurances of my highest consideration.

JOSE EDUARDO DOS SANTOS
President of the People's Republic of Angola

**Issued by Information Department of the Central Committee of
the MPLA-Workers' Party, Luanda, People's Republic of Angola.**

The Times (United Kingdom) 24th November, 1984

Appendix 3

Resolution 435 (1978)
Adopted by the Security Council at its 2087th meeting
on 29 September 1978

The Security Council,

Recalling its resolutions 385 (1976) and 431 (1978), and 432 (1978),

Having considered the report submitted by the Secretary-General pursuant to paragraph 2 of resolution in the Security Council on 29 September 1978 (S/12869),

Taking note of the relevant communications from the Government of South Africa addressed to the Secretary-General,

Taking note also of the letter dated 8 September 1978 from the President of the South West Africa People's Organization (SWAPO) addressed to the Secretary General (S/12841),

Reaffirming the legal responsibility of the United Nations over Namibia,

1. *Approves* the report of the Secretary-General (S/12827) for the implementation of the proposal for a settlement of the Namibian situation (S/12636) and his explanatory statement (S/12869);

2. *Reiterates* that its objective is the withdrawal of South Africa's illegal administration of Namibia and the transfer of power to the people of Namibia with the assistance of the United Nations in accordance with resolution 385 (1976);

3. *Decides* to establish under its authority a United Nations Transition Assistance report of the Secretary-General for a period of up to 12 months in order to assist his Special Representative to carry out the mandate conferred upon him by paragraph 1 of Security Council resolution 431 (1978), namely, to ensure the early independence of Namibia through free and fair elections under the supervision and control of the United Nations;

4. *Welcomes* SWAPO's preparedness to co-operate in the implementation of the Secretary-General's report, including its expressed readiness to sign and observe the cease-fire provisions as manifested in the letter from the President of SWAPO dated 8 September 1978 (S/12841);

5. *Calls* on South Africa forthwith to co-operate with the Secretary-General in the implementation of this resolution;

6. *Declares* that all unilateral measures taken by the illegal administration in Namibia in relation to the electroal process, including unilateral registration of voters, or transfer of power, in contravetion of Security Council resolutions 285 (1976), 431 (1978) and this resultion are null and void;

7. *Requests* the Secretary-General to report to the Security Council no later than 23 October 1978 on the implementation of this resolution.

Appendix 4

Repubilek van Suid-Afrika · Republic of South Africa

Kantoor van die Eerste Minister
Prime Minister's Office

Privaatsak X83
Private Bag

Pretoria

0001

12 February 1982

His Majesty
King Sobhuza II of Swaziland
Mbabane
SWAZILAND

Your Majesty

I have the honour to refer to various discussions and
correspondence between the Foreign Ministers of the
Kingdom of Swaziland and the Republic of South Africa
which resulted in mutual agreement between our respective
Governments to the effect that both Governments are aware
of the fact that international terrorism, in all its
manifestations, poses a real threat to international
peace and security and that our respective Governments
should take steps to protect our respective states and
nationals against this threat.

Therefore, I now have the honour to inform you that the
Government of the Republic of South Africa proposes the
following Agreement between our respective Governments:

ARTICLE 1

The Contracting Parties undertake to combat
terrorism, insurgency and subversion individually

and collectively and shall call upon each other
wherever possible for such assistance and steps
as may be deemed necessary or expedient to
eliminate this evil.

ARTICLE 2

In the conduct of their mutual relations the
Contracting Parties shall furthermore respect
each other's independence, sovereignty and
territorial integrity and shall refrain from
the unlawful threat or use of force and from
any other act which is inconsistent with the
purposes and principles of good neighbourliness.

ARTICLE 3

The Contracting Parties shall live in peace and
further develop and maintain friendly relations
with each other and shall therefore not allow
any activities within their respective territories
directed towards the commission of any act which
involves a threat or use of force against each
other's territorial integrity.

ARTICLE 4

The Contracting Parties shall not allow within
their respective territories the installation
or maintenance of foreign military bases or the
presence of foreign military units except in
accordance with their right of self-defence in
the event of armed attacks as provided for in
the Charter of the United Nations and only after
due notification to the other.

Should the Government of the Kingdom of Swaziland agree
with the abovementioned provisions, this letter and
your affirmative reply thereto shall constitute an
Agreement between our two Governments.

Please accept, Your Majesty, the renewed assurance
of my highest consideration.

P.W. BOTHA

PRIME MINISTER OF THE REPUBLIC OF SOUTH AFRICA

KINGDOM OF SWAZILAND

Esigodlweni.
P.O. Kwaluseni

17th February, 1982

My Dear Prime Minister,

    You are hereby authorise to sign on behalf of
Swaziland the Letter of Understanding on Security Matters
between the Kingdom of Swaziland and the Republic of
South Africa in reply to the letter dated 12th February, 1982
from the Prime Minister of the Republic of South Africa.

SOBHUZA II

INGWENYAMA, KING OF SWAZILAND

LEGRAMS: PRIME
EPHONE: 2251/2

GOVERNMENT HOUSE,
P.O. BOX 395,
MBABANE,
SWAZILAND.

17th February, 1982

Honourable Prime Minister

I have the honour to refer to your letter of 12 February
1982 which reads as follows:

> "I have the honour to refer to various
> discussions and correspondence between the Foreign
> Ministers of the Kingdom of Swaziland and the
> Republic of South Africa which resulted in mutual
> agreement between our respective Governments to
> the effect that both Governments are aware of
> the fact that international terrorism, in all
> its manifestations, poses a real threat to
> international peace and security and that our
> respective Governments should take steps to protect
> our respective states and nationals against this
> threat.
>
> Therefore, I now have the honour to inform you
> that the Government of the Republic of South Africa
> proposes the following Agreement between our respective
> Governments:

ARTICLE 1

The contracting Parties undertake to combat
terrorism, insurgency and subversion individually
and collectively and shall call upon each other
wherever possible for such assistance and steps
as may be deemed necessary or expedient to eliminate
this evil.

ARTICLE 2

In the conduct of their mutual relations the
Contracting Parties shall furthermore respect
each other's independence, sovereignty and territorial
integrity and shall refrain from the unlawful
threat or use of force and from any other act
which is inconsistent with the purposes and
principles of good neighbourliness.

ARTICLE 3

The Contracting Parties shall live in peace and
further develop and maintain friendly relations
with each other and shall therefore not allow
any activities within their respective territories
directed towards the commission of any act which
involves a threat or use of force against each
other's territorial integrity.

ARTICLE 4

The Contracting Parties shall not allow within
their respective territories the installation
or maintenance of foreign military bases or the
presence of foreign military units except in
accordance with their right of self-defence in
the event of armed attacks as provided for in
the

        Charter of the United Nations and only after due
        notification to the other.

Should the Government of the Kingdom of Swaziland
agree with the abovementioned provisions, this letter
and your affirmative reply thereto shall constitute an
Agreement between our two Governments.

Please accept, Your Majesty, the renewed assurance of
my highest consideration."

Duly authorised by His Majesty King Sobhuza II, I have the
honour to inform you, Mr Prime Minister, that the
Government of the Kingdom of Swaziland agree to the
abovementioned provisions and regard your letter and this
reply as constituting an agreement between our two
Governments.

Please accept, Mr Prime Minister, the assurance of my
highest consideration.

MABANDLA FRED DLAMINI
PRIME MINISTER OF THE KINGDOM OF SWAZILAND

THE HONOURABLE P.W. BOTHA
PRIME MINISTER OF THE REPUBLIC OF SOTH AFRICA
CAPE TOWN

EMBARGOED AND TO BE CHECKED AGAINST DELIVERY

AGREEMENT BETWEEN THE GOVERNMENT OF THE REPUBLIC
OF SOUTH AFRICA AND THE GOVERNMENT OF THE
KINGDOM OF SWAZILAND RELATING TO SECURITY MATTERS

JOINT STATEMENT BY THE HONOURABLE R F BOTHA, MINISTER
OF FOREIGN AFFAIRS OF THE REPUBLIC OF SOUTH AFRICA,
AND THE HONOURABLE R V DLAMINI, MINISTER OF FOREIGN
AFFAIRS OF THE KINGDOM OF SWAZILAND: 31 MARCH 1984

During discussions between the Honourable R F Botha,
Minister of Foreign Affairs of the Republic of South
Africa, and the Honourable R V Dlamini, Minister of Foreign
Affairs of the Kingdom of Swaziland, in Pretoria today, it
was decided to make public, on behalf of their respective
Governments, the existence and contents of an Agreement
relating to Security Matters.

After having been granted full powers by the South African
State President in Council and His Majesty the late King
Sobhuza II of Swaziland, respectively, the Honourable P W
Botha, Prime Minister of the Republic of South Africa, and

the Honourable M F Dlamini, former Prime Minister of the
Kingdom of Swaziland, concluded the Agreement, which came
into force on 17 February 1982, on behalf of the two
Governments.

The introductory paragraph of the Agreement expresses the
awareness of the two States that international terrorism,
in all its manifestations, poses a real threat to
international peace and security as well as their agreement
that they should take steps to protect their respective
States and nationals against this threat. The Agreement
accordingly records the undertaking of the Parties to
combat terrorism, insurgency and subversion individually
and collectively as well as their right to call upon each
other for such assistance and steps as may be deemed
necessary or expedient to eliminate this evil.

The Parties are required to respect each other's
independence, sovereignty and territorial integrity in the
conduct of their mutual relations and to refrain from the
threat or use of force as well as any other act which would
be inconsistent with the purposes and principles of good
neighbourliness.

In order to facilitate the maintenance and development of
peace and friendly relations between the two States, they
are required not to allow any activities within their
respective territories which are directed towards the
commission of any act which involves a threat or use of
force against each other's territorial integrity.

The Parties are also required not to allow the installation
or maintenance of foreign military bases or the presence of
foreign military units within their respective territories
except in accordance with their right of self-defence in
the event of armed attacks and only after due notification
to the other.

PRETORIA
31 MARCH 1984

Appendix 5

Resolution 418 (1977)
of 4 November 1977

The Security Council,

Recalling its resolution 392 (1976) of 19 June 1976, strongly condemning the South African Government for its resort to massive violence against and killings of the African people, including schoolchildren and students and others opposing racial discrimination, and calling upon that Government urgently to end violence against the African people and to take steps to eliminate *apartheid* and racial discrimination,

Recognizing that the military build-up by South Africa and its persistent acts of aggression against the neighbouring States seriously disturb the security of those states,

Further recognizing that the existing arms embargo must be strengthened and universally applied, without any reservations or qualifications whatsoever, in order to prevent a further aggravation of the grave situation in South Africa,

Taking note of the Lagos Declaration for Action against *Apartheid,*

Gravely concerned that South Africa is at the threshold of producing nuclear weapons,

Condemning the South African Government for its acts of repression, its defiant continuance of the system of *apartheid* and its attacks against neighbouring independent States

Considering that the policies and acts of the South African Government are fraught with danger to international peace and security,

Recalling its resolution 181 (1963) of 7 August 1963 and other resolutions concerning a voluntary arms embargo against South Africa,

Convinced that a mandatory arms embargo needs to be universary applied against South Africa in the first instance,

Acting therefore under Chapter VII of the Charter of the United Nations,

1. *Determines,* having regard to the policies and acts of the South African Government, that the acquisition by South Africa of arms and related materiél constitutes a threat to the maintenance of international peace and security;

2. *Decides* that all States shall cease forthwith any provision to South Africa of arms and related materiél of all types, including the sale or transfer of weapons and ammunition, military vehicles and equipment, paramilitary police equipment, and spare parts for the aforementioned, and shall cease as well the provision of all types of equipment and supplies and grants of licencing arrangements for the manufacture and development of nuclear weapons;

3. *Calls upon* all States to review, having regard to the objectives of the present resolution, all existing contractual arrangements with and licences granted to South Africa relating to the manufacture and maintenance of arms, ammunition of all types and military equipment and vehicles, with a view to terminating them.

4. *Further decides* that all States shall refrain from any co-operation with South Africa in the manufacture and development of nuclear weapons;

5. *Calls upon* all States, including States non-members of the United Nations, to act strictly in accordance with the provisions of the present resolution;

6. *Requests* the Secretary-General to report to the Security Council on the progress of the implementation of the present resolution, the first to be submitted not later than 1 May 1978;

7.*Decides* to keep this item on the agenda for further action, as appropriate in the light of developments.

Adopted unanimously at the 2046th meeting.

Appendix 6

RESOLUTION 558 (1984)
Adopted by the Security Council at its 2564th meeting on 13 December 1984

The Security Council,

Recalling its resolution 418 (1977) of 4 November 1977, in which it decided upon a mandatory arms embargo against South Africa,

Recalling its resolution 421 (1977) of 9 December 1977, by which it entrusted a Committee consisting of all its members with the task of, among other things, studying ways and means by which the mandatory arms embargo could be made more effective against South Africa and to make recommendations to the Council,

Taking note of the Committee's report to the Security Council contained in document S/14179 of 19 September 1980,

Recognizing that South Africa's intensified efforts to build up its capacity to manufacture armaments undermines the effectiveness of the mandatory arms embargo against South Africa,

Considering that no State should contribute to South Africa's arms production capability by purchasing arms manufactured in South Africa,

1. *Reaffirms* its resolution 418 (1977) and stresses the continuing need for the strict application of all its provisions;

2. *Requests* all States to refrain from importing arms, ammunition of all types and military vehicles produced in South Africa;

3. *Requests* all States, including States non-members of the United Nations to act strictly in accordance with the provisions of the present resolution;

4. *Requests* the Secretary-General to report to the Security Council Committee established by resolution 421 (1977) concerning the question of South Africa on the progress of the implementation of the present resolution before 31 December 1985.

Notes
CHAPTER 1

1.The photograph was taken by Eduardo Gageiro and appeared in No. 1896 *O Seculo Ilustrado*.

2. This account was given to authors during an interview with Flower. From his personal archives he also supplied a copy of the photograph with the new caption written on it by his deputy, Ken Leaver. Over a three-year period from 14 November 1982 we interviewed Flower on a number of occasions. Some of these were lengthy interviews. Others were brief to check or clarify detail. All of them were conducted in Harare. It is not necessary to all of them by date and throughout the notes or text we simply refer to Flower.

3. Flower, op. cit. Caetano was offended by Flower's suggestion that the Portuguese forces could not contain Frelimo. Although it had been agreed that details of the meeting would be kept secret, Caetano told his commander in Mozambique, General Kaulza da Arriaga, 'that I [Flower] had had the affrontery to suggest they were making a balls up of it'. Flower's second visit to Lisbon preceeded an official visit by Smith. By now Frelimo were threatening Rhodesia's trade link to the sea through Beira. Again Caetano was offended. On 15 November, apparently responding to a British Broadcasting Corporation (BBC) story filed from Salisbury, he said in a radio broadcast: 'Some of our neighbours with less experience do not conceal their fears and [thus] play the game of the enemy. They have been told more than once there is no reason for their great apprehension.'

4. For a fuller account of events leading to this attack see *The Struggle for Zimbabwe: the Chimurenga War*, by David Martin and Phyllis Johnson, published by Faber and Faber, London (hard cover) and Zimbabwe Publishing House, Harare (paperback), 1981.

5. Ibid., p 17.

6. Interview with a CIO officer who asked not to be identified. We interviewed him and another CIO officer in Harare on 25 November 1982, on 8 February 1984 and again on 18 February 1985. At the time of the first two interviews both men were still serving officers in the CIO. It may seem odd to the reader who is unaware of post-independence Zimbabwean realities that people such as these who had served the rebel Rhodesian regime would wish to – and be allowed to – continue working in Zimbabwe's main intelligence organization. In part this arose from constraints imposed upon the Mugabe government by the Lancaster House agreement giving certain protections to Rhodesian civil servants. But, more importantly, it arose from Mugabe's policy of reconciliation and the need to retain professional skills while Zimbabweans were receiving specialist training. Flower, for example, was retained as director-general of the CIO until late 1982 when he retired on health grounds. Thereafter he continued to be used as an occasional consultant and his place was taken by his deputy, Derrick Robinson, until he also retired.

7.In the book *Selous Scouts, Top Secret War* (Galago, South Africa, 1982), the unit's former commander, Lieutenant-Colonel Ron Reid Daly, claims the Cardoso group came under his command. CIO officers insist this is not true. They say the Cardoso group went operational with the RLI to be tested; and the RLI commander, Lieutenant-Colonel Dave Parker, gave them a 'good report' but wrote of difficulties of trying to integrate 'Porks, coloureds and Afs' into his all white unit.

8. Unnamed CIO officers, op. cit.

9. Ibid.

10. The attack cost Mozambique US$ 2 million. Da Silva was sentenced to death by a Revolutionary Military Tribunal established by law only two days before his execution. He was one of a group of 10, the first people to be executed since Mozambique independence. They were found guilty of high treason, sabotage, terrorism and serving as mercenaries for the Rhodesians. Radio Mozambique reported on 31 March 1979 that da Silva had been wounded and captured during an attack on a re-education centre. He was Mozambican-born but with Portuguese nationality and his execution under a retroactive law led to a Portuguese diplomatic protest.

The final irony was that the Mozambique government had to call in South African fire-fighters to extinguish the blaze at the Beira oil refinery. A simultaneous joint Rhodesian/South African attempt to blow up the Maputo refinery failed, Flower says, because dinghies taking the sabotage unit ashore were swamped in rough seas and the mission had to be aborted.

11. In a speech in 1980 Machel referred to people who had subverted soldiers of the national army, the Mozambique People's Liberation Forces (FPLM). 'These were the people who received Frelimo here in Beira. They offered cars and houses, they organized parties and they organized women for the Frelimo commanders.'

The term 're-education centre' may have a sinister ring. But the Portuguese 'centro de reeducação' could equally well be translated as 'reform centre' or 'retraining centre', which do not carry the same 'brainwashing' connotation.

12. The Mozambique government refuses to use the names MNR or Renamo (the latter adopted by the press in 1983), describing them instead as '*bandidos armados*' which, in English, means armed bandits. It is a phrase widely accepted, even by Western ambassadors in Maputo. The British ambassador, John Stewart, interviewed in January 1984 on the external service of Radio Mozambique just before relinquishing his post, said he fully agreed that the MNR were no more than 'armed bandits'. His successor, Eric Vines, in the Queen's birthday party speech on 18 June 1985, said 'Britain and Mozambique would go together in search of peace, dialogue, observance of the law, defeat of the armed bandits and the future prosperity of Mozambique.' Another senior Western ambassador in Maputo described them as 'a disparate group of gun-slingers, thugs, white Portuguese opportunists and other assorted anti-Frelimo types who lack any vision or programme for the future.'

Frelimo's insistence on the phrase 'armed bandits', and the acceptance of this phrase by Western ambassadors, is explained by the way in which the Rhodesian CIO created the MNR, the massive atrocities they have been responsible for, their total lack of any alternative programme and their failure to develop any credible leadership. Matsangaiza, and his successor, Afonso Dhlakama, had both been convicted of criminal offences and sent for re-education. So had almost all of the other people used by the CIO to start the MNR. And the principal targets chosen by the CIO were re-education centres, to gain more 'recruits'. The first attack Matsangaiza led was on his former re-education centre at Sacuze.

The scale of atrocities the MNR have committed is massive and well-documented. Their terrorization of the population has included acts such as cutting off ears, noses or lips and hacking people to death with pickaxes.

13. Over a period of three years we interviewed, on a number of occasions, four of the seven CIO officers involved in the creation and operations of the MNR in its Rhodesian period. Flower has spoken on the record about the CIO role in creating the MNR and has now written his own biography (yet to be published) which includes details of this period. We undertook not to identify the other three. One, whom we refer to by his actual role as paymaster-administrator, is now retired near Harare after continuing to serve in the CIO for some three years after independence. He, and the other two, agreed to be interviewed only after receiving a waiver of the Official Secrets Act. The second, referred to by his role as senior instructor, commands an elite unit in the Zimbabwe National Army (ZNA). The third remains in the CIO. The other two instructors at the Odzi MNR base, Des Robertson and the medic, John Riddick, have left Zimbabwe and taken civilian jobs in South Africa. Of those directly involved, May was the only one of the CIO/MNR team to 'defect' to the South Africans after Zimbabwe's independence. According to Flower there was a 'gentlemen's agreement' in the CIO that none of his officers would be recruited by the South Africans without his knowledge. May broke the agreement, taking a number of files with him to Pretoria. He is reputed to have become a brigadier in the Military Intelligence Directorate (MID) before moving to Britain in late 1984. There he became 'editor' of *Chief Executive* magazine owned by the Dutch shipping magnate, Johan Deuss, who is heavily involved in supplying Middle East oil to South Africa in breach of Arab sanctions.

14. Former CIO officers, op. cit.

15. Authors' interviews with Fernandes in Lisbon, April and June 1984.

16. We interviewed Arouca in Lisbon in April and June 1984. He spoke bitterly against the MNR and particularly against Cristina and Fernandes whom he said had blocked his attempts to obtain a rear base in Rhodesia for Fumo. When Bishop Abel Muzorewa was prime minister of Zimbabawe-Rhodesia, Arouca visited him during the Lancaster House talks in London in 1979 to try to elicit support. But Zanu's election victory in 1980 ended any

hope this plan may have had. Arouca said he went to South Africa to seek support in 1981, after Zimbabwe independence. Again Cristina thwarted him. Later that year, 'after talks with South Africa and after realizing South Africa was not interested in an independent Mozambique but only in putting pressure on Mozambique,' Arouca announced his resignation from Fumo and his withdrawal from politics on the grounds of 'ill health'.

17. Frelimo statement, Dar es Salaam, 25 August 1964. Further details were supplied during an interview in Maputo in December 1985 by Joaquim Chissano, Mozambique's minister of foreign affairs, who for many years during the liberation struggle was Frelimo's head of security. Milas is believed to have gone to Egypt and then Sudan after fleeing Dar es Salaam. The authors picked up his trail again in Ethiopia early in 1974 where he had been news editor of Radio Voice of the Gospel in Addis Ababa for some years. We next traced him to Nairobi where he was at first involved in the Kenya Planned Parenthood Association and he later worked for the UN agency, Habitat. Fernandes said in 1984 that Milas was still in Nairobi and the deputy representative for Africa of the MNR.

18. The only serious attempt to try to explain *Africa Livre* and its background, that we are aware of, was written by Joseph Hanlon for *Africa Confidential* on 28 June 1982. Hanlon traces its origins back to a split in Frelimo in 1965 when a group which later called itself the Mozambique Revolutionary Council (COREMO) broke away. The Coremo vice-president was Amos Sumane, a former member of Frelimo's central committee. In 1967 he headed another breakaway group called the African National Union of Rombezia. This group wanted an independent state in northern Mozambique from the Ruvuma river bordering Tanzania to the Zambezi. The movement is believed to have been created by the Pide and Jardim to establish a buffer zone and thus prevent Frelimo from moving south. Jardim saw the future of Rombezia as part of a 'greater Malawi'.

Little was heard of the movement until after Mozambique's independence when it began mounting attacks on the Milange district adjoining Malawi from bases in that country. In late 1980 the main Rombezia base was captured by the FPLM and in June 1982 it was announced that Sumane had also been captured. Some captured leaders were executed but there has never been an announcement about Sumane's fate. President Kamuzu Banda of Malawi is said to have made an agreement with President Machel in 1981 to stop supporting the Rombezia movement. It appears probable that after the capture of Sumane, and the execution or imprisonment of other top leaders, control of the movement in Malawi passed to South Africa.

19. See Paul Fauvet, 'Roots of Counter-Revolution: The Mozambique National Resistance', *Review of African Political Econony*, Number 29, 1984. In Mozambique the station became known as Radio *Quizumba*, meaning Radio Hyena. In many African languages the hyena is a symbol of evil or treachery.

20. In another of the ironical twists in the MNR story the senior instructor, having set up Gorongosa base in 1978, commanded a ZNA unit which did the reconnaissance and participated in the assault to retake it on 28 August 1985. He briefed Mozambique commanders on the history of the MNR at nearby Chimoio, and when Machel visited a few days later he presented the officer with a Swiss-army penknife with a Frelimo crest on it.

21. The MNR were also widely known as the 'André movement' and the members as Matsangas or Machangas. Frelimo did not know at the time that they had killed him and only learned this later from an MNR captive. There were many who refused to believe that he was dead and during our research we were told several times that he had been evacuated to Rhodesia after being wounded. Another, more bizarre, story was that his body had been embalmed by Frelimo and was in Maputo.

22. Garagua documents.

23. The MNR alleged Cristina had been killed by Frelimo 'agents'. But, in the middle of an MNR training base in South Africa, this seemed highly implausible. A much more probable explanation was that he was a victim of the leadership power struggle and internal feuding which had been a characteristic of the MNR since Dhlakama's take over.

Following Cristina's death, two brothers, Adriano and Boaventura Bomba, both prominent in the MNR leadership, disappeared. Adriano, then a lieutenant in the Mozambican air force, had defected to South Africa in a Mig fighter on 8 July 1981. After a period as a translator for the SADF (this included Russian as he had trained in the Soviet Union) he returned to the limelight as head of the MNR information department and youth wing. His brother was MNR national political commissar. On 18 March 1985, two years after Cristina's murder, João Santa Rita, a former Mozambican journalist who like Bomba, had defected, provided the first detailed report of Cristina's death in *The Star*, Johannesburg. Santa Rita, quoting MNR sources, said both Bombas had been killed.

'Boaventura accused Cristina, who was a white man, of being totally under South African control,' wrote Santa Rita. 'The row reached such a level that the MNR president, Mr Afonso Dhlakama, wanted Boaventura to be executed for treason. Ironically, Cristina convinced Dhlakama that the row wasn't all that serious and Boaventura was spared.' A few weeks later Cristina was killed. According to Santa Rita, Cristina was killed by a four-man group headed by John Macacola, who was arrested near the scene with a 9 millimetre Parabellum pistol, and he said Boaventura had been behind the killing. Boaventura was arrested on 19 April and thereafter 'disappeared'. Adriano was killed at the MNR main base at Gorongosa.

24. These details were supplied by a senior Mozambican official interviewed by the authors.

25. There is a belief that South Africa was involved in the MNR from the outset in 1976. On the basis of lengthy and detailed interviews with the CIO

personnel involved, we do not accept this. Flower is insistent that Vorster rejected his approaches for support and that support was only forthcoming when P.W. Botha took over in late 1978. This assertion appears to be borne out by the statements of CIO instructors at Odzi that no South Africans or South African supplies appeared there until 1979.

26. Flower, op. cit.

27. Ibid.

28. Details of these two phases of the transfer were given in interviews with the CIO paymaster/administrator.

29. Interview with senior instructor, Harare, 16 January 1986.

30. Economic report by the Mozambique National Planning Commission, Maputo, January 1984.

31. Statistical Information 1975–1984 produced by the National Statistical Directorate of the National Planning Commission, Maputo.

32. National Railways of Zimbabwe. By early 1986 this trade was reduce to less than 10 per cent.

33. Captain Eastwood's report, a copy of which he gave to the authors, is a most intriguing document which requires some historical explanation against the background of its timing. At independence, Zimbabwe inherited the Rhodesian army Military Intelligence Directorate (MID) and it is no exaggeration to say that the sympathies of many of its personnel lay more with the South Africans than with Mugabe's government. Zanla had its own security department but while their training was being upgraded those members of the old MID who chose to stay remained in place. Eastwood was one of them. He had moved from South Africa in the late 1970s to join the Rhodesian forces. His June 1981 report, which white colleagues referred to as 'The Bible', was prepared for a briefing for Mugabe on the MNR and the situation in Mozambique. Reading it again in early 1986 we are left with the distinct impression that it was intended to scare the new Zimbabwean government. If this is correct then Eastwood's statistics for the MNR at that time may be too high. The report warned Mugabe against committing troops to Mozambique: 'Should Zimbabwean troops become actively involved in the war in Mozambique it is axiomatic that each of the aforesaid links (to Beira and Maputo) will be forfeited as a reprisal.' Later in the report, Eastwood said, 'The strategic dangers of such involvement on our part have been pointed out on a number of occasions. Worse-case analysis means we will lose both links to the coast. Under such circumstances Zimbabwe may as well apply for Homeland status.'

34. The documents were found in a pit latrine where they were thrown by the hastily departing MNR. When Mozambique made known the contents South Africa dismissed them as forgeries. But other evidence that has come to light since that time, including documents captured at Gorongosa in August 1985, shows they were genuine.

35. Ibid.

36. A report on this meeting was subsequently obtained by the Zimbabwean authorities from villagers crossing from Mozambique.
37. The ZNA commitment was initially limited to the western end of these routes near to the Zimbabwe border. But as the need grew to free members of the FPLM from static guard duties for operations against the MNR the ZNA presence also grew. By 1985 the ZNA contingent guarding these communications routes had increased to 2 000 men operating from the Zimbabwe border to Beira.
38. *The Herald,* Harare, 24 June 1982.
39. Mozambique News Agency, *Agência de Informação de Moçambique (AIM),* feature 'The SADCC summit in Maputo' by Paul Fauvet, July 1983.
40. *The Observer,* London, 20 February 1983.
41. Author interview with one of the managers of the state farm in Mozambique in December 1985. Frelimo officials told us of the abundance of evidence to prove the Malawi/MNR connection, including highly compromising documentation found at Gorongosa. American and British officials are equally open about this connection. Late in 1985 the British government made formal representations to the Malawi government asking it to terminate all support for the MNR.

On 25 November 1984 a report appeared in the *Sunday Tribune* in South Africa saying that the MNR were receiving arms from Oman and Saudi Arabia via Somalia and the Comoro Islands. The report, written by Hennie Serfontein, stressed South Africa was not involved. A week later, on 2 December, a similar story appeared in *The Observer* in London, written by Godwin Matatu. He said he had flown to the Comoros two weeks earlier and had been expelled after 48 hours while trying to make contact with Colonel Bob Denard, a French mercenary who was responsible for the last *coup d'état* on the island. At first sight the story appeared credible. Mozambique has a Muslim population of over 3 500 000 with strong historical ties to the Comoros and Oman. In addition, it was known that the MNR were trying to obtain support from conservative Arab nations and had even put out a rumour (which was untrue) that Machel had entered a mosque wearing his boots. The government of the Comoros insisted the story that they were a conduit for arms to the MNR was untrue and in December 1985 Mozambique officials, while not entirely ruling out the story, said they had not been able to obtain any evidence to support the claim. Arab diplomats insisted the stories were South African disinformation deliberately planted to shift attention from Pretoria's violations of Nkomati, and some Frelimo officials agreed this might be true. A report by Glen Frankel which appeared in the *Washington Post* on 23 January 1985 can be interpreted as lending support to the disinformation theory. Frankel wrote, 'Meanwhile, official South African sources have been leaking to journalists and Mozambican officials information implicating individuals in other nations, including Portugal, which is

Mozambique's former colonial ruler, Oman, Saudi Arabia and the Comoros, in arms shipments to the resistance movement.'

Machel also did not appear to believe that these were the principal sources of supply to the MNR. In a speech in December 1984 he had said, 'South Africa is still the key to the problem. '

42. In May 1984, following Nkomati, the Mozambique News Agency, *AIM*, made public a dossier entitled 'Documentation about the Accord of Nkomati'. The first item was 'The Nkomati Agreement: An historical perspective'. This contains details of the points Crocker made during his visit. Although this was a historical landmark in the process leading to Nkomati the visit went badly with the abrasive Crocker clashing with Chissano. Thereafter, Crocker's deputy, Frank Wisner, an able career diplomat, handled contacts with Mozambique.

43. Address to National Conference of Editorial Writers, San Francisco, 23 June 1983.

44. *AIM*, 'Documentation about the Accord of Nkomati', op.cit.

45. A detailed account of the negotiating process at Mbabane, Maputo and Cape Town was given to one of the authors during a series of briefings in Maputo in December 1985 by government officials.

46. During the meeting Machel told of the atrocities being committed by the MNR who were maiming, mutilating and raping civilians. 'Are these soldiers?' he demanded of Malan. The South African General, outranked by Machel who is a Marshall, snapped to attention and replied 'No Sir'.

47. Statement issued by the ANC Information Department, Lusaka, 16 March 1984.

48. Briefing in December 1985.

49. Matchet's Diary, *West Africa,* London, 2 April 1984.

50. Ministry of Ports, Railways and Shipping as quoted in the Economic Report by the Mozambique National Planning Commission, Maputo, January 1984.

51. Economic Report, op. cit.

52. Ibid.

53. Ministry of Education statistics supplied to author in Maputo in December 1985.

54. Ministry of Internal Trade statistics supplied to author in Maputo in December 1985. Other statistics in this section were supplied by the relevant ministries.

55. Economic Report, op. cit.

56. Details of post-Nkomati meetings and negotiations were given in a series of briefings in Maputo in December 1985 by government officials.

57. During his annual briefing in Cape Town to foreign correspondents, as reported by Associated Press on 21 March 1985, 'Pik' Botha said: 'Elements from abroad contacted [Fernandes] in Pretoria and apparently suggested to him that he ask for an adjournment of the meeting. Ever since then, we've

had increasing difficulties.' He said he knew the source of the foreign pressure but would not name him. 'We came close to an agreement on a document that would have established a date for a cease-fire and a rough framework on what we would do after the cease-fire. Now we have reached a low point, not in contacts, but in ideas on how to proceed.' The MNR had hardened their stance and he had refused to put their latest demands to Machel. 'I know in advance that he [Machel] would not even read halfway before he threw it away.'

Although Botha did not publicly name the caller, Mota Pinto has been named in press reports by Mozambican journalists who accompanied their delegation and by others who were present when Fernandes concluded the call. As far as the authors are aware, Pinto has not denied these reports. However, since the original reports appeared, two other suggestions have been made as to whom the call really emanated from. One is that it was from Manuel Bulhosa, a rich businessman whose interests in Mozambique had been nationalized and who was Fernandes's employer. The other is that it was a fake call from the MID who opposed the Nkomati Accord and were intent upon blocking a cease-fire. In the light of subsequent evidence, particularly that contained in the Gorongosa documents, this last explanation has a ring of truth.

58. Bulhosa had denied to the Mozambique government that he was supporting the MNR. In 1983 he visited Maputo but Machel refused to meet him. Proof of his links to the MNR subsequently emerged in captured documents when the MNR base at Gorongosa was overrun in August 1985. In a message dated 12 January 1985, van Niekerk informed Dhlakama that Bulhosa was in Pretoria and wanted to meet the MNR leader at Gorongosa.

59. Details of the agreement between Machel, Mugabe and Nyerere are from briefings by officials of the three governments. By the end of 1985 both Machel and Mugabe had spoken publicly about the Zimbabwean commitment.

60. *The Gorongosa Documents,* published in two volumes by the Mozambique Ministry of Information.

61. From 1981 to March 1986 at least 34 foreign-contracted workers, known in Mozambique as *co-operantes*, were murdered, 66 kidnapped and five wounded by the MNR. They included nationals of Brazil, Britain, Bulgaria, China, France, German Democratic Republic (GDR), Ireland, Italy, Portugal, Romania, the Soviet Union, Sri Lanka and Sweden. At least 12 priests and nuns were among those murdered and kidnapped. As a result of the South African-directed offensive against foreign aid workers, most were withdrawn from the countryside bringing development projects to a standstill.

62. There has been some confusion as to whether Viljoen described 'Pik' Botha as a 'traitor' or 'treacherous'. This arises from a mistranslation of the documents. The entry in the diary for 12 September 1984 uses the word 'traicoeiro'. The correct translation is 'treacherous'.

63. *Africa Research Bulletin (ARB),* Vol. 22, No. 9, 15 October 1985.

64. Ibid.

65. *Financial Mail*, Johannesburg, 4 October 1985.

66. Briefing by Mozambique government officials, Maputo, December 1985.

67. On 18 August 1982, Ruth First, a well-known white South African opponent of *apartheid*, was killed in a letter bomb explosion in Maputo. At the time First was the deputy director of the Centre for African Studies at Maputo's Eduardo Mondlane University. The bomb which killed her also injured the centre's director, Professor Aquino de Braganca.

A distinguished author and academic, First was a leading anti-*apartheid* activist who had been one of the earliest detainees under South Africa's security laws. In 1956 she had been arrested and charged with high treason, a charge which was dropped two years later. She was later restricted to the Johannesburg area under the Suppression of Communism Act and the two magazines she edited were banned. In 1963 she was detained and from her experience in solitary confinement wrote the book, *117 Days*. Her later works include the acclaimed, *The Barrel of a Gun*, an examination of *apartheid*

The Mozambicans concluded that the most probable assassin was South Africa.

68. The Gorongosa base was retaken by the MNR in February 1986. Reports at the time said the FPLM garrison had not been resupplied for three weeks, and recapture of the base led to a disinformation campaign which claimed that the ZNA were withdrawing from their combat role in Mozambique. However, the Gorongosa base was taken back from the MNR on 12 April, in a mainly ZNA operation.

69. In June 1985, Mugabe advised Machel that he should not negotiate with the MNR; and he illustrated his point with a story about an Arab and his camel in the desert, where it gets very cold at night. The Arab was warm in his tent, but the camel was outside in the cold. The camel asked if he could just put his head in the tent, and the Arab agreed. Then the camel moved in one leg, and then another, until gradually all of his body was in the tent, forcing the Arab out into the cold.

The story graphically illustrated the hazards involved, and Mugabe later repeated it in the Zimbabwe parliament.

CHAPTER 2

1. The names the various parties used in the 1980 elections are confusing. In the April 1979 'internal settlement' election, in which Mugabe's and Nkomo's parties did not participate, Reverend Ndabaningi Sithole had registered and used the name Zanu despite having been deposed as its leader four years earlier. This forced Mugabe's party to run under the name Zanu (PF) in 1980. Nkomo had hoped that his and Mugabe's parties would run under the name Patriotic Front. But this would not have resolved who would be the

leader and Mugabe's party chose to run on its own. In the event, Zanu (PF) took 63 per cent of the votes cast, Nkomo's Patriotic Front 24 per cent and the UANC only eight per cent. In the 'internal settlement' election 10 months earlier the Rhodesians had claimed that the Bishop's UANC had taken 67 per cent of votes cast.

2. *The Real Information Scandal*, by Eschel Rhoodie, published by Orbis SA (Pty) Ltd., 1983. The author was secretary for information of the South African government and was one of the casualties of the information scandal which also brought down the then prime minister, John Vorster. According to Rhoodie, one of South Africa's many secret projects was code-named 'Operation Chicken'. This involved funding some Zimbabwean nationalist leaders and Rhoodie specifically mentions Muzorewa, Sithole and James Chikerema as beneficiaries of South African largesse. Approximately US$ 1 million were committed to the 1979 Muzorewa campaign, and, in 1980, some 400 vehicles costing about US$ 2.5 million. Muzorewa's three seats, a popular joke at the time went, had cost Pretoria US$ 750 000 each.

3. *Free and Fair? The 1979 Rhodesian election*. Report by observers on behalf of the British Parliamentary Human Rights Group.

4. For the background to Sithole's removal see *The Struggle for Zimbabwe: the Chimurenga War* by David Martin and Phyllis Johnson, Faber and Faber, London (hardcover), and Zimbabwe Publishing House, Harare (paperback), 1981.

5. Mugabe displayed considerable statesmanship in trying to retain the confidence of all groups. In addition to Nkomo he brought three other members of Zapu into the government. He also appointed David Smith, who had been deputy prime minister in the RF government, as minister of finance, and the head of the white Commercial Farmers Union (CFU),Dennis Norman, as minister of agriculture. However, he rejected a suggestion by Machel that he include Ian Smith! But, more remarkably, after 30 000 people had died in the liberation war, he retained the services of the Rhodesian army commander, Lieutenant-General Peter Walls, an avowed anti-Marxist. Walls resigned a few months later when Mugabe refused to promote him to full General. He left for South Africa after disclosing that he had asked the British prime minister, Margaret Thatcher, to annul the election results when he learned that Zanu (PF) had won.

6. Rhoodie, op. cit.

7. In early 1986 a senior CIO officer told the authors that the number of ANC infiltrated with ZPRA in 1980 was about 200.

8. Ministry of Information, Harare, 4 March 1980.

9. *Africa Research Bulletin (ARB)*, Vol. 17, No. 6, p 5702, 1–30 June 1980.

10. *ARB*, Vol. 17, No. 7, p 5735, 1–31 July 1980.

11. From information obtained the Zimbabwean authorities are certain that the killer squad were former Rhodesian soldiers who had gone south in 1980 and joined the South African Defence Force (SADF). At a press conference in

Stockholm on 25 September 1981 (*The Herald*, Harare, 26 September 1981) Mugabe said the assassination had been carried out by former Selous Scouts.
12. Zimbabwe *Hansard*, House of Assembly, Vol. 6, No. 28, Ministerial Statement, CIO officers, 10 February 1983.
13. *The Herald*, Harare, 13 September 1981, reporting the minister of state (security) in the prime minister's office, Emmerson Munangagwa. He said the blasts were recorded by seismographic stations as far away as Malawi where they registered between 1.8 and 2.7 on the Richter Scale.
14. Gericke was originally arrested on suspicion of spying for South Africa. It was during questioning that police began to focus on his possible role in the Inkomo sabotage.
15. Varkevisser's role in Gericke's escape continues to raise question marks. He was accompanied to the Central Police Station in Harare by another man who has never been identified. It is thought that Varkevisser's role in the 'hot extraction' may have been 'involuntary'. According to former colleagues, his wife, Marisa, and two children aged nine and five, along with some of his property, had been 'removed' from his home prior to his role in Gericke's escape. His colleagues believe they may have been taken hostage to ensure his co-operation and that the unidentified third man went with him to the police station to ensure that he did what he had been told. One point which may lend credence to this interpretation is that, whereas others involved in operations for South Africa in Zimbabwe were given jobs in the SADF, MID and so on, Varkevisser was not. When last heard of he was a salesman in Cape Town.
16. The extent of the damage at Thornhill has been widely misreported. A SADCC document, 'Estimates of the Cost of South African Destabilization', to the Organization of African Unity (OAU) summit in 1985 said that 13 planes had been destroyed. This is incorrect. In all, 10 planes were damaged, five of which were write-offs. According to Zimbabwe Air Force documents five Hunters were damaged. Three were totally destroyed and the other two repaired in Zimbabwe. Four Hawk fighters which had just arrived from Britain were damaged. One was a write-off, two were repaired in Britain and one locally. In addition a Cessna 337 was completely destroyed.
17. *The Times*, London, 28 August 1982.
18. On 27 April 1980 there were 5 267 guerrillas at Assembly Point Papa. The contents of the seven truck-loads the government found included 15 BIO recoilless rifles, 27 82mm mortars, 34 ZGU–1, five 12.7 anti-aircraft guns, six SAM–7 missiles, 14 assorted missiles ranging from rifle grenades to 122mm rockets, seven 57mm field guns, 13 GRAD–P 122mm rockets, one 60mm mortar and two 75mm recoilless rifles. The discovery of the cache, the authorities presumed, prevented more armaments being brought in on that route.
19. The Zimbabwean government obtained copies of the railways manifests showing the arms that had been unloaded at Dett. In that period, the instruction to unload would have had to come from a white officer in charge.

20. Senior members of Zapu subsequently conducted an internal enquiry into the property purchases to ascertain where the money had come from and who had authorized the expenditures. This report has not been made public. But a document in the authors' possession lists 52 properties purchased by Nkomo in his individual capacity, by Patriotic Front (Zapu) as a party and by Patriotic Front-owned companies. This shows Nkomo as director of Walmer Ranching Company, owner of Walmer Farm (5 139 hectares) and Makwe Farm (2 570 hectares). The Patriotic Front as a party is shown as owning 20 properties. These include 10 farms, two butcheries, two hotels, a manufacturing company, a building, a haulage firm, a garage, a supermarket and a store. The other properties were owned through Zapu companies such as NITRAM, of which Nkomo was a director. Many of these companies were seized by government after the discovery of the arms caches on some of them.

21. *ARB*, Vol. 19, No. 2, p 6362, 1–28 February 1982.

22. Nkomo and Zapu's central committee denied any knowledge of the arms caches. Allegations that the caching was part of a plot was 'a straightforward lie', Nkomo said. Referring to the farms and business purchased by Nkomo and Zapu, Mugabe said 'We have now established that these were not genuine enterprises but places to hide weapons to start another war at an appropriate time.' Eleven of the companies were seized as 'unlawful organizations' and even the Western press, which had become quite hostile towards Zanu, found it hard to believe that there was not a sinister motive behind the caches.

23. Zimbabwe Republic Police (ZRP) records.

24. Dube and Nzima were brought before Harare Magistrates' Court on 4 January 1983. The prosecutor said they would be charged with murder and attempted murder. On 10 August 1983 they were found guilty in the High Court of murder and sentenced to death. Both men denied the charges, claiming they had been abducted and forced to accompany the dissidents. The judge, Mr Justice Waddington, dismissed their claim as 'inherently improbable' and ruled that their original statements to the police were made freely and voluntarily and were admissable as evidence. Appeals against sentence and conviction were dismissed by the Supreme Court on 4 April 1984. Thereafter the two men appealed for clemency. The appeal was rejected and they were executed in Harare on 7 April 1986.

25. ZRP records, details of which were supplied to the South Africans as part of Zimbabwe's case proving Pretoria's involvement in resupplying bandits.

26. Ibid.

27. Dube's statement presented during his trial in the High Court in Harare in August 1983.

28. Ncube's statement to ZRP.

29. Ndhlovu's statement to ZRP.

30. *The Herald*, Harare, 4 February 1984.

31. Briefing to authors by Zimbabwe government officials, Harare, January 1986.

32. ZRP records.

33. From transcripts of Radio Truth broadcasts.

34. Zimbabwe government estimate.

35. *Rhodesia: South Africa's Sixth Province*, by John Sprack, International Defence and Aid Fund, 1974.

36. 'The Impact of War' by Anthony Wilkinson, *Journal of Commonwealth and Comparative Politics*, 1980.

37. 'Zimbabwe's Manufactured Exports and the Ending of the Trade Agreement with South Africa', by Roger Riddell, Confederation of Zimbabwe Industries mimeo, December 1981.

38. *New York Times*, 19 April 1981.

39. *New York Times*, 1 February 1981.

40. This occurred immediately prior to the resumption of pumping. The cost of repairs was US$ 11 million.

CHAPTER 3

1. John Marcum, in *The Angolan Revolution*, Vol. 1 (The MIT Press, Cambridge, Mass.) p 34, provides a full list of those tried. Apart from four officials of the Union of the Peoples of Northern Angola (UPNA , former name of UPA/FNLA) who were tried *in absentia*, it is overwhelmingly a list of well-known MPLA members, many of whom spent years in prison.

2. The author, closely associated with the MPLA since the mid-1960s and working as President Neto's information secretary after independence, bases herself on the testimony of many of those former prisoners.

3. *The Observer*, London, 7 May 1961.

4. This period is well-documented by Robert Davezies, a French priest, in his book *Les Angolais* (Les Editions de Minuit, Paris, 1965) pp 23–30. He describes the links between the capital and the villages, the people who went back and forth, and the leaflets brought from Luanda to the countryside. Ciel, a young man then in a rural area, is quoted: 'The people were fed up. They wanted to rise up... and they wanted to know how to do it.' After the 4 February events in Luanda, he said, armed settlers arrived in jeeps 'to tell the people not to do what the others had done in Luanda', because if they did 'they would finish them all off'. The local population, Ciel said, got wind of a secret settler plan to massacre them on 20 March. The people rose up on 15 March, with whatever crude weapons and implements they could muster, pre-empting the massacre by five days. The commander who mobilized his group, Ciel said, had taken part in the 4 February events in Luanda.

5. Davezies, op. cit., p 35.

6. Davezies, op.cit., p 189, questioned Holden Roberto about this massacre and was told: 'Unfortunately, there were a number of infiltrations. I admit that we killed them. They were marching in a war zone. They should have asked us

for passes. It is a general rule allowing for no exceptions.' Asked if they would have been granted passes had they asked for them, Roberto replies: 'No, no, it's not possible! Without a previous agreement on strategy, nothing like that is possible.'

7. Basil Davidson, *In the Eye of the Storm* (Longman, London, 1972) pp 211–212, quotes UPA chief-of-staff Marcos Kassanga, speaking at a press conference in Kinshasa on 3 March 1962: 'Some days after the beginning of the Angolan people's revolution against Portuguese domination and slave exploitation, it was turned into a carnage fomented by the leadership of that party whose chief is Holden Roberto.... In all its aspects the armed struggle unleashed in the north of Angola is a real fratricidal struggle. A figure approaching 8 000 Angolans were savagely massacred by tribalist UPA elements....This inhuman massacre effected by Angolans against Angolans is born of blind tribalism which presents itself in four aspects: religious, linguistic, ethnic and ideological.... [Among those killed] we must distinguish the case of Commander Tomás Ferreira and his squad of 21 men sent into the interior by the MPLA.... [They were] captured by UPA militants and barbarously hanged. Now there is the sad death of Commander Baptista, Chief of Military Operations in the interior of Angola, a member of the UPA general staff. His death by treachery was motivated by his disagreement with the extermination of Angolans by Angolans, by his not speaking Kikongo, by his not being a native of São Salvador, and by his not being a protestant.'

Interviewed by Davezies, op. cit., p 212, a former chief-of-staff of the FNLA who went over to the MPLA, José Kalundongo, said that there were never more than 3 000 men trained at the FNLA's Kinkuzu camp in Zaire and that they remained there for months, because Roberto 'wanted them at the base at the disposal of photographers, mainly Americans'. Referring to the fact that training was given by Americans, he went on to say: 'Anyway, one wonders why Mr Holden Roberto, after having refused Algerian volunteers, accepted the services of the American officer Bernard Meinherz', a Vietnam veteran engaged to direct the FNLA's military wing.

8. Citing 'four official sources', *The New Times* of 25 September 1975 said that the CIA started to send arms and funds to Roberto in 1962. In an article printed in the *Congressional Record* of 16 December 1975, a former White House aide was cited as saying that during Lyndon Johnson's administration Washington's policy was 'to play both ends against the middle', adding that the CIA 'had the habit of picking out single individuals and making them our guys'. Quoted in Ernest Harsch and Tony Thomas, *Angola, the hidden history of Washington's war* (Pathfinder Press Inc., New York, 1976) p 21.

9. Marcelo Caetano, *Depoimento* (Distribuidora Record, Rio de Janeiro, São Paulo, 1975) pp 180–181.

10. An *assimilado* from Bié province, Savimbi was in Lausanne, Switzerland, in 1962, the year after the start of the armed struggle, studying political

science after dropping out of medical school in Portugal. He joined the MPLA; but later, at a conference at Makerere University in Uganda, he met Tom Mboya, the Kenyan politician known for his strong American ties, who is said to have prevailed upon him to leave the MPLA for the FNLA. A subsequent visit by a US State Department official bearing a cheque-book appears to have convinced him to take that course. A similar offer made at the time to an MPLA official now working with the Angolan government was refused.

Savimbi soon became 'foreign minister' in GRAE, whose overseas mentors doubtless hoped that this would bestow a national image on the FNLA, then headed by elements associated with the royal family of the old Kongo Kingdom. However, in July 1964, at the All-African Meeting of Heads of State in Cairo, Savimbi resigned from the FNLA in characteristically flamboyant style, publicly accusing Roberto of tribalism and of having been a 'United States creation' since 1961. He denounced the US advisers working with the FNLA and the army's lack of activity. The way was open to him to rejoin the MPLA. He travelled to Brazzaville, where he met Agostinho Neto and other leaders, and he stated that his condition for rejoining was to be made vice-president with responsibility for foreign affairs. The answer to this arrogant demand was simply that no appointments could be made without democratic collective decisions. Savimbi did not wait. He returned to Europe and nothing more was heard of him for the next two years, apart from the fleeting creation in Switzerland of something called Amangola, 'Manifesto of the Friends of Angola'.

11. On 5 May 1972, for example, the Tanzanian newspaper *The Standard* announced that Unita had donated 2 000 kilograms of maize, the surplus of its co-operative farms, to Zambia to help that country overcome shortages aggravated by the Portuguese blockade of Zambian goods in the port of Beira. On 12 May, under the headline 'Maize gift "a joke" ', *The Standard* published the MPLA spokesman's refutation. Referring to Unita's 'imaginary people's co-operatives', the spokesman said: 'If they had surplus maize to give away, why not give it to the people of Angola, some of whom are starving in the liberated areas because of Portuguese bombing and destruction of their crops with herbicides?'

12. Interviewed by Phyllis Johnson and David Martin in Lisbon in April 1984.

13. *The Times,* London, 23 August 1982.

14. J. Sotto-Maior, *A história de uma traição* (Edições Alvorada, Luanda, 1985) pp 15–30. This recent book quotes extensively from the documents related to Savimbi's collaboration with the Portuguese military and contains photocopies of many of them.

15. Ibid., pp 31–33. Sotto-Maior quotes a letter published in the Portuguese weekly *Expresso* from a former soldier in the colonial army in Angola: 'In early 1969, I cannot remember the precise date at the moment, I was a member of a military force which passed through Gago Coutinho, headquarters of the battalion, in transit. We received orders to proceed in vehicles to a place

between Gago Coutinho and Cangumbe....We stopped about twenty or thirty kilometres away and mounted security in the area. MPLA operations were becoming increasingly intensive and effective in the east. Two coloured people, I think, went off into the bush. They came back accompanied by local people in a visible state of deprivation and by a number of young guerrillas, ragged and armed, and I even remember one of them was quite debonair. It was a Unita detachment which had long had relations with the PIDE [Portuguese security police] in Gago Coutinho and had given itself up in order to fight the MPLA which, as I said, was already showing itself to be the best organised force throughout the east.... They got into our vehicles and we arrived at Gago Coutinho at night. We were met by a major in charge of operations in the zone, the local head of the PIDE, Martins, and an African aged about 40, bearded, wearing glasses and with a gold chain on his chest, who I learned was negotiating this strange collaboration on the Unita side. It was he who received his colleagues, put them in a semi-circle and made them sing what I learned to be the Unita anthem. We were then ordered to withdraw.'

Commenting on the letter, the Portuguese newspaper *Expresso* said that from many similar eyewitness accounts and documents in their possession, it appeared that the then PIDE director in Angola, Aníbal de São José Lopes, had contacts with Savimbi since before 1969, although it was not known if they had ever met.

16. Statement issued by MPLA in Lusaka on 25 March 1970.

17. An MPLA statement issued in October 1973, announcing the thwarting of the Chipenda plot, went on to say: 'Hand in glove with world reaction, the colonialists were preparing for the final attack. Their aim was the physical elimination of the most illustrious leaders of the genuine liberation movements in the Portuguese colonies. To this end they formed alliances with reactionary forces within the respective liberation movements, in the MPLA's case using the mindlessness of a former leader who, through personal ambition, became a turncoat, giving a Judas kiss while betraying his comrades. Playing the enemy's game of divide and rule, he used tribalism, seeking to drag some members of his tribe along with him in his inordinate ambition. But the colonialists and traitors failed. They had overlooked the fact that the new generation had been moulded by the valiant MPLA and that the youth know what they want and why they are fighting.'

18. Frelimo, the Mozambican liberation movement, also suffered the effects of agents infiltrated into it. But it was fortunate in that the Tanzanian authorities took action against these agents. This was true in the case of Lazaro Nkavandame, who tried to split Frelimo along tribal lines, and of Frelimo vice-president, Uria Simango, who tried to oust the other leaders after the assassination of President Mondlane and who was deported from Tanzania.

19. The South African magazine *To The Point*, 1 June 1974. On a visit to Mozambique soon after the *coup d'état*, Costa Gomes said on several occasions that he was sure the people of the 'overseas territories' would chose

between the 'extremes' of the status quo and independence.

20 *Notícias,* Luanda, 22 June 1974.

21. Communiqué issued in Lisbon on 8 August 1974.

22. The proclamation stated: 'At this time when the people are called upon to assume their historic responsibilities in an independent Angola, concealed interests are busying themselves, seeking to distort the meaning of what you have been fighting for for thirteen years.' It called upon the people and the guerrillas to carry on the struggle 'for a democratic, popular and progressive regime, for one indivisible nation, for territorial integrity and for independent and sovereign participation in the free concert of nations'.

23. Another secessionist scheme was denounced at a press conference in Luanda by Lúcio Lara on 5 December. He said that an individual had presented himself to the MPLA asking to do propaganda work in the Lunda region in north-east Angola. On closer examination, it had been found that he was born in Zaire, had held responsible posts in the Zairean political party, the Popular Movement of the Revolution (MPR), and that, in addition to Zairean citizenship and MPR membership cards, he had an MPLA/Chipenda card. This person, described by Lúcio Lara as a 'good family man' with three wives and a great number of children, also had on him a plan for the establishment of something called the 'State of Moxico', to include Lunda, Moxico and Kuando Kubango, Angola's eastern provinces.

24. *The Times*, London, 7 January 1976. 'Sources in Washington now say that the CIA first decided that steps must be taken to help the anti-communists among the Angolan nationalists in January 1975. The 40 Committee, which supervises the CIA, then approved sending $300 000 to the FNLA.'

25. *The Guardian,* London, 30 May 1974.

26. This was reported to the US secretary of state, Dr Henry Kissinger, by his consul-general in Luanda, Tom Killoran, after a meeting with Neto. Killoran, who opposed US involvement in Angola, was removed from his post by Kissinger and refused promotion thus destroying his diplomatic career.

27. John Stockwell, *In Search of Enemies* (W.W. Norton & Co. Inc., New York, 1978) pp 86–87, 161–162. (Also published by Andre Deutsch Ltd., London, 1978.) Stockwell resigned from the CIA in 1976.

28. *The Argus,* Cape Town, 25 August 1984.

29. Stockwell, op. cit., p 187. 'To the CIA, the South Africans were the ideal solution for central Angola.... Especially in the field, CIA officers liked the South Africans, who tended to be bluff, aggressive men without guile.... Quietly South African planes and trucks turned up throughout Angola with just the gasoline or ammunition needed for an impending operation. On October 20, after a flurry of cables between headquarters and Kinshasa, two South African C-130 airplanes, similar to those used by the Israelis in their raid on Entebbe, feathered into Ndjili Airport [Kinshasa] at night to meet a CIA C-141 flight and whisk its load of arms down to Silva Porto [Kuito]. CIA officers and BOSS representatives met the planes at Ndjili and jointly supervised the transloading. At the same time, St Martin requested and received

headquarters permission to meet BOSS representatives on a regular basis in Kinshasa. Other CIA officers clamoured for permission to visit South African bases in South-West Africa. On two occasions the BOSS director visited Washington and held secret meetings with Jim Potts. On another, he met with the CIA station chief in Paris. The COS, Pretoria, was ordered to brief BOSS about IAFEATURE [code-name for the CIA's Angola operation], and nearly all CIA intelligence reports on the subject were relayed to Pretoria so his briefings would be accurate and up to date.'

30. Interview with John Vorster published in *Newsweek*, May 1976: *Q:* Would it be accurate to say that the US solicited South Africa's help to turn the tide against the Russians and Cubans in Angola last fall? *A.* I do not want to comment on that. The US government can speak for itself. I am sure you will appreciate that I cannot violate the confidentiality of government-to-government communications. But if you are making the statement, I won't call you a liar. *Q.* Would it also be accurate to say you received a green light from Kissinger for a military operation in Angola? *A.* If you say that of your own accord, I will not call you a liar.'

The Washington Post of 24 December 1975 wrote: 'The United States, in its anti-Communist idiocy, seems hellbent on making another of the colossal blunders that brought us Vietnam. The reference, obviously, is to Angola... Incidentally, the United States might have a larger reservoir of Angolan goodwill to draw upon if we had given some small measure of support to the Angolans in their struggle to overthrow the Portuguese colonizers. Instead, we chose to maintain our alliance with Portugal. And now the Portuguese are gone, we are throwing in with the South Africans.'

31. Stockwell, op. cit., p 164.

32. *Granma Weekly Review*, Havana, 14 February 1982, 'The Angola campaign'. This is a very detailed Cuban military history of the events of 1975–76.

33. Ibid.

34. Ibid. Also the Joint Angolan-Cuban Statement of 4 February 1982, which said: 'With a view to achieving its plans to liquidate the Angolan revolutionary movement, on 14 October 1975 the Government of the United States of America sent the South African army against Angola, taking advantage of the fact of the racist South Africans' illegal occupation of Namibia, which still persists to this day. In less than 20 days South African troops advanced more than 700km inside Angolan territory. Meanwhile, from the north, foreign regular and mercenary forces were moving threateningly close to the capital. *It was at that moment that President Agostinho Neto requested Cuban military cooperation.*' (My italics)

The author, in Angola at the time, was told at the highest level of the importance of staving off the invading armies until independence on 11 November, before which date the Cuban combat troop contingents could not arrive in the country.

35. Stockwell, op. cit., 67–68.

36. Daily Telegraph, London, February 1976. 'More than £10m, mainly from the American CIA, is to be spent on the employment of British mercenaries in Angola.'

37. *Jornal de Angola,* Luanda, 14 January 1976.

38. Stockwell, op. cit., pp 234–235.

39. Angolan Government's *White Paper on Acts of Aggression by the Racist South African Regime against the People's Republic of Angola, 1975–1982,* p 12. 'The damage caused to the People's Republic of Angola by the big South African invasion of 1975–76 amounted to an extremely high sum, representing a heavy burden for a young country freed from colonialism which was starting on a new life of independence. In a report submitted to the United Nations at the time, this damage was estimated to be US\$ 6.7 billion.'

40. Stockwell, op. cit., p 204.

41. *Diário de Luanda,* Luanda, 5 January 1976.

42. Stockwell, op. cit., p 204–205.

43. Stockwell, op. cit., p 193.

44. Joint Angolan-Cuban Statement of 4 February 1982. 'The Governments of Angola and Cuba, merely one month after the expulsion of the racist South African troops, on 22 April 1976, agreed on a programme for the progressive reduction of those forces. In less than a year, the Cuban military contingent was reduced by more than one-third, a process which was halted because of fresh external threats to Angola.... In mid-1979, the Governments of Angola and Cuba again agreed to start to carry out another programme for the gradual reduction of Cuban forces. Almost immediately afterwards, in September that year, the South Africans carried out repeated large-scale acts of aggression against Cunene and Huila provinces.'

45. Angolan government's *White Paper,* pp 16–17.

46. Ibid., pp 24–25.

47. *International Herald Tribune,* New York and Paris, 14 February 1981.

48. Interview in *Wall Street Journal,* New York, 6 May 1980.

49. *Sunday Telegraph,* London, 29 March 1981.

50. *The Observer,* London, 17 May 1981, under headline 'Texas guns were for Angola rebels'.

51. From *US State Department documents on Southern Africa leaked to American Press, May–June 1981,* a booklet of photocopies published by the Swapo Western Europe Office.

52. The US biweekly *Africa News* of 10 March 1986 quotes Dr Steve Weissman, staff director of the House Foreign Affairs sub-committee on Africa: 'I think it is unlikely the South Africans will agree to a timetable for Cuban withdrawal that Angola can accept. They want the Cubans there so (South Africa) can be seen to be working alongside the US against the Soviets.'

53. Registered South African military operations against Angola up to August were 1 617 reconnaissance flights, 100 bombing raids, 50 strafing incidents, 26 ground reconnaissance operations, 67 troop build-ups, four paratroop

landings, 34 ground attacks, seven shelling operations and nine mine-laying and other operations.

54. The partial sabotage of the oil refinery cost US\$ 12 550 000 to repair and a further US\$ 24 million in oil not exported between December 1981 and January 1982, when the refinery was again fully operational.

55. When Savimbi visited the United States in January 1986, a Madison Avenue publicity firm was hired at a cost of \$600 000 to project him to an American audience and tell him how to dress.

56. The *Windhoek Observer,* 20 November 1982: 'Dr Jonas Savimbi, the Unita leader, who had become a God-like legendary figure in the eyes of the white South Africans, but who lives at the mercy of South Africa's armed forces, having a very comfortable bungalow complex virtually on the border, from where he can direct his vast business operations with certain South African interests and involving Angolan teak, ivory and other valuables.'

57. Human losses as a result of South African aggression in 1981 were assessed as 206 soldiers killed, 389 soldiers wounded and 1 086 missing, 158 civilians killed and 265 wounded, and 160 000 homeless people, inhabitants of Cunene province who fled north to seek refuge from the bombing, fighting and occupation and were taken care of by the Angolan authorities.

58. In the Central Highland town of Huambo, in March 1983, the author had the occasion to speak to a prisoner, a former Unita political commissar named Teodoro Silva Gideão who spoke of a Unita congress held in the border area in July 1982. Some members, he said, had been expelled at the congress. It was said they wanted to organize a *coup d'état* against Savimbi because they were fed up with fighting a war they could not win. Among those expelled, he said, were Jorge Sangumba and Samuel Chiwale.

59. *Africa News* (USA), 3 December 1984. 'Escalating tensions within the anti-government Unita movement erupted into open fighting earlier this year, with the Ovimbundu [Umbundu] leadership of the rebel group openly executing its opponents. In interviews with recent deserters from Unita in Lubango and in the central city of Huambo, *Africa News* has learned that the South African-backed dissident group, while certainly not on the verge of collapse, is experiencing serious internal difficulties.... In an attempt to capitalize on these problems, the Angolan government has given a great deal of publicity to recent defections by Unita members and has widely publicized its long-standing amnesty for Unita soldiers and civilians who voluntarily turn themselves in. The biggest defection occurred in early November when 46 soldiers and 285 civilians who had been living with the rebel movement for over seven years surrendered to authorities in the southern province of Cunene.... (A farmer), who is of Kwanyama ancestry, charged that Unita members from Angola's largest ethnic group, the Ovimbundu, had been systematically isolating and killing members of other ethnic groups, such as the Kwanyama, the Gangela and the Chokwe.'

60. *Daily Telegraph,* 28 December 1983, 'S. Africa may have to quit Angola': 'South African forces faced the prospect last night of being forced to make a

strategic withdrawal from southern Angola. They have encountered stiff opposition from Angolan and Cuban units.... [There were no Cuban units in the area.] General Constand Viljoen, chief of the SADF, returned to Pretoria on Monday night after spending four days in the operational area with his troops and personally taking over command of a deteriorating situation....General Viljoen said Swapo was...ducking under the protection of Angolan government Fapla and Cuban forces when faced by the South Africans.'
61. *Financial Mail,* Johannesburg, 13 January 1984.
62. *Sunday Times*, Johannesburg, 25 November 1984. 'Pretoria is reportedly furious with a decision by Angolan President dos Santos to send a memorandum to the UN Secretary-General, Dr Pérez de Cuéllar, setting out Luanda's position on the thorny issue of Cuban withdrawal....The leaks contradict the solemn assurances given by all the parties to the Cape Verdean talks that the negotiations would be conducted with maximum secrecy.'
63. *Sunday Express,* Johannesburg, 25 November 1984.
64. *The Observer,* London, 11 November 1984.
65. *The Washington Post,* Washington DC, 9 February 1986, in article headlined 'The selling of Jonas Savimbi: public relations firm paved guerrilla's way'.
66. *The Financial Mail,* Johannesburg, 18 October 1985.
67. Ibid., commenting as follows: 'SA denied having sent troops to help Unita, but intelligence sources allege that the anti-Swapo drive was merely a smoke-screen for the troops sent to Mavinga. These sources also confirm MPLA al-legations that the mechanised Fapla columns advancing on Mavinga were attacked by SAAF bombers, and that SA's 32 Battalion (Buffalo) fought with Unita till the end.'
68. *Sunday Times,* Johannesburg, 22 September 1985. 'Calling for help from the United States, he said the alleged Soviet involvement in the fighting introduced a new element to the civil war.'
69. *The Times,* London, 24 September 1985, carried the headline 'Pretoria seeks US help to rescue Unita from defeat in Angola', and on 28 September the *Daily Telegraph* wrote: 'An urgent diplomatic effort is being made by South Africa to win American help for Dr Jonas Savimbi's pro-western Unita movement in Angola now under pressure from a major offensive by Marxist government forces.'
70. *The Star,* Johannesburg, 29 September 1985.
71. Stockwell, op. cit., p 193.

CHAPTER 4

1. Festus Thomas was interviewed in Windhoek by a number of journalists, including the editors of this book who met him at the Swapo office on 26 June

1978. His story appeared in many publications around the world and, probably because of the corroborating evidence from doctors, nurses and lawyers, was not denied by the South Africans.

2. *Torture – a cancer in our society*, compiled and published by H. Hunke and J. Ellis, P.O. Box 41, Windhoek, Namibia. Both Hunke and Ellis were later expelled from Namibia by the South African authorities. See also D. Soggot, *Namibia: The Violent Heritage*, Rex Collings. London, 1986.

3. *A Dwelling Place of Our Own*, Randolph Vigne, International Defence and Aid Fund (IDAF), London, 1973.

4. Ibid.

5. *The South West Africa/Namibia Dispute*, J. Dugard, ICJ Report.

6. UN General Assembly Resolution 2145 (1966).

7. *Namibia; The Struggle for Liberation*, A.T. Moleah, Disa Press, Wilmington, Delaware.

8. Ibid.

9. *The South West Africa/Namibia Dispute,* op. cit.

10. *Namibia; The Struggle for Liberation*, op. cit.

11. Letter dated 6 September 1978 from 'Pik' Botha to Dr Kurt Waldheim, then UN secretary-general. S/12836.

12. This announcement was made by South Africa's prime minister, John Vorster, who announced his own resignation in the same speech.

13. Walter Cronkite's interview with President Reagan, CBS News, 3 March 1981.

14. US State Department documents on southern Africa leaked to the American press in May 1981 and reproduced by the Swapo office in London.

15. Ibid.

16. Ibid. Memo to Chester Crocker from Paul Hare, 13 May 1981.

17. *New York Times,* various dates in June 1981. US State Department and South African officials have both since confirmed that 'linkage' was an American invention.

18. UN Security Council Resolution 539 (1983).

19. Pretoria continues to claim that Swanu is part of the MPC. However, as reported in the *Rand Daily Mail* on 3 September 1985, the old Swanu leadership were ousted that month and replaced by a new leadership. The new leaders promptly withdrew Swanu from the MPC. Moses Katjiuongua, one of the ousted leaders, continued to lead a delegation to the MPC which he claimed was Swanu. Probably 90 per cent of Swanu now regard themselves as allied to Swapo and opposed to the MPC.

20. *Windhoek Advertiser,* January 1984.

21. Ibid.

22. Details of the meetings in this phase involving Kaunda were given to the editors in a briefing by senior Swapo officials who participated.

23. 'Destabilization and Dialogue: South Africa's Emergence as a Regional Superpower' by John de St. Jorre, *CSIS Africa Notes,* No. 26, 17 April 1984.

24. South African Défence Force (SADF) journal, *Paratus,* January 1979, and *Focus,* No.3, March 1976.

25. Apart from formal control, the officer commanding SWATF, and other senior ranks, are simply transferred between SWATF and the SADF. For further details see *Apartheid's Army in Namibia,* IDAF, 1982.

26. For this section see COSAWR, 'The South African military occupation of Namibia', articles reproduced from *Register* between September 1983 and March 1984. (Paper 11, International Conference on Namibia, 10 -13 September 1984, London.)

27. For further details about Namibia's political economy see *Namibia: Toward National Reconstruction and Development,* Hutchinson, London, 1985; the chapters on Namibia in *African Contemporary Record (ACR).* Africana, New York/London, 1983–84 and 1984–85; *South West Africa, Statistical and Economic Review,* 1983 and 1984; and *Namibia: The Last Colony,* R.H. Green, K. Kiljunen and M.L. Kiljunen, Longman, London, 1981.

28. *Agriculture: Transforming a Wasted Land,* R. Moorsom, Catholic Institute for International Relations (CIIR), London, 1982.

29. *ACR,* 1983–84 and 1984–85, op. cit.

30. This position could be altered if the Kudu gas field off the southern Namibia coast is proven to be large and exploitable.

31. *Namibia: Toward National Reconstruction and Development,* op. cit.

32. See *ACR* 1983–84, op. cit, and *Political Economy and Structural Change: The Case of Namibia,* C. Allison and R.H. Green, Institute of Development Studies (IDS), Sussex, discussion paper, 1985/86.

33. *ACR* 1983–84, op. cit, and 1985–86.

34. See *ACR* 1983-84, op.cit, and 'Namibia 1985: A New Start? Challenge of a Namibian Nationhood Strategy', W. Thomas, 3 June 1985, speech ms. This is a continuation of his attack on South Africa's fiscal policy as irresponsible and on South Africa's claim of inherent Namibian bankruptcy as equally so. These attacks are notable in that they come from the most able economic analyst promoting a 'neo-colonial' or 'moderate' political economic transition.

35. *Namibia: Toward National Reconstruction and Development,* op. cit. and *Walvis Bay: Namibia's Port,* R. Moorsom, IDAF, London, 1984.

36. Denis Herbstein, 'Secret Pretoria fear for Namibia troops', *The Observer,* London, 9 September 1984.

CHAPTER 5

1. *The Guardian,* London, 15 January 1986.

2. The then minister of information and broadcasting, Desmond Sixishe, quoted in the *Eastern Province Herald,* 28 December 1983.

3. South Africa denies responsibility for this raid, but their denial is so inherently improbable that few people give any credence to Pretoria's claim.

4. *Financial Mail (FM)*, Johannesburg, 3 January 1986, as well as various other economic references including the *Africa Economic Digest (AED)*, London and the *Africa Research Bulletin (ARB)*, Exeter.

5. Khakhetla's *Lesotho 1970* has documented these developments.

6. See *Assembly Debates*, National Assembly, Maseru, 30 April 1973.

7. See Hirchman, D., 'Changes in Lesotho Policy Towards South Africa' in *African Affairs*, 1978.

8. See, for example, Chakela's interview with *The Vanguard*, National University of Lesotho, December 1980.

9. For detailed speculative discussion on the Peka talks, see *The Vanguard*, January/March 1981.

10. Jonathan Steele in *The Guardian*, 26 May 1986.

11. *The Herald*, Harare, 31 August 1984.

12. This was related to the editors by one of Jonathan's ministers a few hours after the *coup d'état* was announced. The former minister said that Jonathan had replied that if this was really the case the general should go on the radio and say so. No such announcement was forthcoming. The same minister, before the names of the Letsie brothers were made public, said they were behind the *coup d'état*.

13. *ARB*, Vol. 22, No. 6, p 7668-7669.

14. *A Profile of the Victims of the South African Raid on Gaborone, Botswana*, 23 June 1985, mimeo, Michael D. Appleby.

15. *Sunday Star*, Johannesburg, 16 June 1985. The remark was reported to have been made by a Crocker aide.

16. *South Africa in Southern Africa: The Intensifying Vortex of Violence* edited by Thomas M. Callaghy, Praeger Publishers, New York, 1983.

17. *ARB*, Vol. 16, No. 6, p 5154-5155.

18. *ARB*, Vol. 17, No. 3, p 5458-5459.

19. *AED*, 25 January 1986 and *African Business*, London July 1985.

20. It was reported to one of the authors in a private interview that there was only one week's supply of maize in the country in May 1985.

21. South African minister of agriculture, Hendrik Schoeman, in 1980.

22. *New York Times*, 13 April 1982.

23. *The Herald*, 1 January 1985.

24. News agency reports of Botha's speech to parliament on 9 May 1984 and *Republic of South Africa House of Assembly Debates (Hansard)*.

25. *FM*, 12 July 1985, interview with Festus Moagae, permanent secretary to President Masire and head of the Botswana civil service.

26. *Rand Daily Mail (RDM)*, 9 October 1985, citing 'Pik' Botha. In March 1985, the South Africans had claimed that 48 sabotage missions had been launched and/or planned by the ANC in Botswana. See *RDM*, 15 March 1985.

27. *The Herald*, 14 September 1986.

28. Patrick Laurence, 'Security Drive with Lesotho and Botswana speeds up' in *RDM*, 11 May 1984 (emphasis added).

29. *FM*, 28 June 1985. Williamson had some years earlier infiltrated the

International University Exchange Fund (IUEF) in Europe which provided scholarships to, among others, refugees from South Africa. Over a period of years, he provided Pretoria with invaluable information through his anti-*apartheid* contacts. Recently it was claimed that he had resigned from the security police and set up his own security company in South Africa, a claim treated with considerable scepticism.

30. *The Herald,* 30 January 1986.
31. *The Herald,* 14 February 1986.
32. Joint Swaziland–South African statement, Pretoria, 31 March 1984. for full text, see Appendix 4.
33. Letters in the possession of the editors and reproduced in Appendix 4.
34. 'Pik' Botha said that the matter of the land transfer 'was very close to [Sobhuza's] heart ... The king made it clear to me that he very much wanted. all his children together'. *RDM*, 29 June 1984.
35. In early March 1986, Enos Mabuza, representing the Inyandza National Movement, had three days of talks with the ANC in Lusaka. Mabuza was received by the Tanzanian High Commissioner and representatives of Botswana and Angola, and had a private meeting with President Kaunda of Zambia. *FM*, 7 March 1986.
36. For an analysis of Swaziland's dependence, see *The Times,* London, 5 September 1985. The SADCC *Macro-Economic Survey,* 1986, provides statistical details. *Business in Swaziland*, June 1983, provided economic information of the new Mpaka to Mananga rail link, which opened in February 1986.
37. *FM*, 29 June 1984.
38. *RDM*, 17 January 1985, and *AED*, 15 March 1985.
39. *Africa* , London February 1982, and *RDM*, 9 December 1981.
40. *Moto*, Harare, September 1984.
41. For campus unrest and expulsion of white radicals, see *AfricAsia*, Paris, April and June 1985. It was reported in the *RDM* of 10 December 1984 that Shibi's death might have been related to the power struggle within Swaziland. For other reports, see *RDM*, 22 December 1984, and 4 and 5 January, 1985.
42. For details of one such incident, see *AED*, 4 January 1986.
43. *Weekly Mail*, Johannesburg, 30 January 1986.
44. *FM*, 11 October 1985. The Swazis told the OAU that they opposed sanctions as 'they threaten our own survival'.
45. *The Herald*, 27 January 1986.

CHAPTER 6

1. The Freedom Charter contains the philosophy of the ANC.
2. For further details, see *South Africa's Defence Strategy* by Abdul S. Minty, published by Anti-Apartheid Movement, London, 1969.
3. *Rand Daily Mail (RDM),* Johannesburg, 29 September 1983.
4. *Business Day (BD),* Johannesburg, 11 December 1985.

5. *RDM,* 12 April 1984.

6. *The Times,* London, 19 September 1980.

7. *The Times,* 3 December 1983; *Financial Mail (FM),* Johannesburg, 6 August 1982.

8. *The Times,* 2 August 1984; *The Star,* Johannesburg, 17 September 1984.

9. *The Rise of the South African Security Establishment – An Essay on the Changing Locus of State Power* by Kenneth W. Grundy, The South African Institute of International Affairs, August 1983; see also 'South Africa's Evolving State Security System' by Deon Geldenhuys, Kenneth W. Grundy and John Seiler, paper presented to the Study Group on Armed Forces and Society of the International Political Science Association, West Berlin, 15 September 1984; various press reports including *FM,* 8 October 1982; *The Star,* 24 and 26 September 1983; *The Guardian,* London, 14 September 1983; especially Nicholas Ashford in *The Times,* 1 September 1980; *Africa News,* 10 October 1983; and *Press Trust of South Africa,* 24 August 1983.

10. *FM,* 15 January 1982.

11. *Cape Times,* Cape Town, 10 September 1964.

12. *International Defence Review (IDR),* Geneva, October 1984.

13. Ibid.

14. Abdul S. Minty, Statement to UN Security Council Committee, 9 April 1984, published by World Campaign against Military and Nuclear Collaboration with South Africa, Oslo, 1984.

15. Abdul S. Minty, Statement to UN Special Committee against Apartheid, 12 December 1977, Document A/AC. 115/L.485 dated 22 December 1977.

16. Report of the Security Council Committee Established by Resolution 421 (1977), Document S/14179, 19 September 1980.

17. For details of some cases see particularly statements by Abdul S. Minty to the Security Council's 421 Committee, 23 September 1983 and 9 April 1984.

18. *How Britain Arms Apartheid,* Anti-Apartheid Movement, London, July 1985.

19. Minty, Statement to 421 Committee, 23 September 1983, op. cit.

20. Report of the Security Council Committee Established by Resolution 421, Document S/13721, 31 December 1979.

21. The SC 421 Committee reported (19 September 1980, op. cit.) that '...more clarity was needed with regard to (i) the provision to the South African authorities of certain items of strategic importance under the contention that such items did not form part of a weapons systems and were, therefore, not covered by the embargo; (ii) the continued provision, directly to the South African military establishment, of certain items intended for and known in advance to be destined for their use, under the contention that such items were 'non-military' in nature, and therefore, not part of the embargo; (iii) the provision to various companies or civilian customers in South Africa of certain items of strategic and military importance, which later found their way, inexplicably, into the hands of the South African military authorities, and

which, either directly or indirectly, helped to strengthen the South African military or police forces.'

22. *Automating Apartheid,* published by NARMIC/American Friends Service Committee, 1982.

23. *Plessey Arms Apartheid*, report by the Anti-Apartheid Movement, published in co-operation with the World Campaign, London, 21 May 1981.

24. *The Guardian,* London 6, 9, and 10 December 1975.

25. Representations made to Britain by the heads of delegations of all the African states as well as the Group of Non-Aligned Countries, attending an international conference on Namibia in Paris on 29 April 1983, failed to prevent the equipment from being exported to South Africa. *Background Note on Marconi Radar to be Exported to South Africa by Britain,* World Campaign, Oslo, 20 May 1983.

26. For details about some of these see statement by Abdul S. Minty to UN Special Committee Against Apartheid, 12 December 1977, op. cit.

27. *Financial Times,* London, 14 September 1982.

28. *South Africa Digest (SAD),* Pretoria, 17 September 1982.

29. *Cape Times,* 10 June 1983.

30. *Newsweek,* New York, 29 November 1982.

31. *Sunday Express,* Johannesburg, 17 October 1982.

32. See, for example, *Jane's Defence Review,* Vol. 4 Nos. 1, 4, 6, and 7, 1983; as well as *IDR,* Vol. 16 No. 3, 1983.

33. See report in *Sunday Express,* Johannesburg, 12 September 1982.

34. *SAD,* 9 March 1984.

35. *RDM,* 8 December 1983.

36. *Jane's Defence Weekly,* London, 23 November 1985.

37. *The Star*, 12 April 1969.

38. *SAD,* 16 March 1973.

39. *Sunday Times,* Johannesburg, 21 October 1973.

40. See report in the *NATO Review,* Brussels, No. 4, 1973.

41. *Hansard,* London, 6 November 1974, col. 1042.

42. For detailed information about this aspect and the role of the Advokaat system, see *Apartheid, a Threat to Peace* by Abdul S. Minty, published by the Anti-Apartheid Movement, London, 1976.

43. *The Times,* 6 November 1975.

44. *The Guardian,* London, 19, 20 and 21 November 1980.

45. Letter to Anti-Apartheid Movement, London, 1 December 1980.

46. *The Mail on Sunday,* London, 20 November 1983; *Sunday Times,* London, 20 November 1983.

47. *Republic of South Africa, House of Assembly Debates (Hansard),* Cape Town, 24 September 1981, cols 4677 and 4678.

CHAPTER 8

1. The term 'capital' as employed in the text refers generically to that social

class which predominantly owns the major means of production – the capital assets of the economy – and is the main employer of labour. This does not necessarily imply a uniformity or unity among the different grouping or 'fractions' of capital. What is suggested is that in relation to the cheap labour system of *apartheid* there exist a wide measure of common interests within the class of capital operating in South Africa.

2. The historical roots and development of the colonialist base in South Africa are analysed extensively in H.J. and R.E. Simons, *Class and Colour in South Africa 1850 –1950*, Penguin 1969.

3. According to the estimates of Michael Savage of the University of Cape Town.

4. Lewis Carroll, *Alice's Adventures in Wonderland and Through the Looking-Glass,* first published 1865 and 1872. In *Through the Looking-Glass*, the Red Queen takes Alice by the hand and they run very fast for some time only to find they have not left the tree where they started. In the story, Alice is a pawn in a game of chess.

5. For a comprehensive contemporary analysis of the South African gold-mining industry, see Vella Pillay, *Apartheid Gold,* UN Centre Against Apartheid and British Anti-Apartheid Movement, 1981.

6. Jeremy Keenan, *South African Review* No. 2, 1984.

7. Cited in J. Keenan, op. cit. The Carnegie enquiry derives from the Carnegie Commission which held a conference in South Africa in 1985 at which academics and others presented papers on the social and economic situation in the country. The commission was sponsored by the US-based Carnegie Endowment for International Peace.

8. Fatima Meer, 'Indentured Labour and Group Formations in Apartheid Society' in *Race and Class,* Spring, 1985.

9. R. Horwitz, *The Political Economy of South Africa,* Wiedenfeld & Nicholson, 1967; W.H. Hutt, *The Economics of the Colour Bar,* Deutsch, 1964; and M.C. O'Dowd in Leftwich, *South Africa: Economic Growth and Political Change,* Allison & Busby, 1974.

10. *The Guardian,* London, 7 October 1985.

11. Herbert Blumer in Guy Hunter, *Industrialization and Race Relations,* Oxford University Press, 1965.

12. Merle Lipton, *Capitalism and Apartheid*, Temple Smith/Gower, 1985.

13. *The Guardian,* op. cit.

CHAPTER 9

1. Best shown in three studies by Deon Geldenhuys, South Africa's would-be Henry Kissinger. First, 'Some Strategic Implications of Regional Economic Relations for the Republic of South Africa', *ISSUP Review,* Institute of Strategic Studies, University of Pretoria, January 1981, was in fact a government study which played a seminal role in the evolution of economic destabilization and selective sabotage tactics. The second,

'Destabilization Controversy in Southern Africa', *South African Forum,* position paper, September 1982, is a further promotion for those destabilization tactics. The third, *The Diplomacy of Isolation: South African Foreign Policy Making,* Macmillan, Johannesburg, 1984, is an extremely thorough and authoritative study of all aspects of South African foreign affairs.

2. See E.L. McFarland, 'Benefits to the RSA of Her Exports to the BLS Countries' in *Botswana's Economy Since Independence,* M.A. Oommen (ed), Tata-McGraw-Hill, New Delhi, 1983.

3. See 'Economic Sanctions against South Africa' series, especially No. 5 (M. Bailey, Oil), No. 10 (R. Riddell, Agriculture), No. 11 (M. Fransman, Manufacturing), No. 12 (R. Murray, Mining). International University Exchange Fund, Geneva, 1980.

4. This point is emphasized in the founding declaration of the Southern African Development Coordination Conference (SADCC), *Southern Africa: Toward Economic Liberation,* SADCC, London/Gaborone, 1980. SADCC members are Angola, Botswana, Lesotho, Malawi, Mozambique, Swaziland, Tanzania, Zambia and Zimbabwe.

5. See Geldenhuys, *Diplomacy of Isolation,* pp 121–166 for a detailed exposition including transport, energy, agriculture, mining and private enterprise. The role of the railways as built up by the former general manager, J.G.H. Loubser, has been especially important. See Geldenhuys, pp 153–55; Loubser, 'The function of transport as a line of communication between states in Southern Africa', speech, South African Railways and Harbours (roneo), 1980, and 'Transport Diplomacy' lecture to Institute of Strategic Studies, University of Pretoria, 26 September 1979; G.H. Pirie, *Aspects of the Political Economy of Railways of Southern Africa,* Occasional Paper 24, Environmental Studies, Department of Geography, University of the Witwatersrand, Johannesburg, 1982.

6. See annual *SADCC (SATCC) Transport and Communications* sectoral papers to annual consultative conferences, SADCC, Gaborone (SATCC, Maputo), 1981–86. See also A. Nsekela (editor) for SADCC, *Southern Africa: Towards Economic Liberation,* Rex Collings, London, 1981, especially chapter on transport.

7. Lusaka Declaration, op. cit.; Geldenhuys, op. cit.; Loubser, op. cit.

8. Geldenhuys, 1981, op. cit., note 4.

9. Every SADCC annual conference except the first has had a 'calling card' in the form of a sabotage raid against a SADCC project. The blockade of Lesotho just prior to the January 1986 annual conference was a sharp retort against SADCC's pro-sanctions position. Geldenhuys, in *The Diplomacy of Isolation, passim,* clearly shows that Pretoria's perceived regional interests, including transport, are much more threatened by a body committed to economic liberation than by a trade promotion body. PTA comprises 15 states in eastern and southern Africa, such as Kenya, Uganda, Ethiopia, Djibouti. Three SADCC states (Angola, Botswana, Mozambique) are *not* members of PTA.

10. See *African Contemporary Record (ACR)*, C. Legum (ed), 1979–80; and Geldenhuys, *Diplomacy of Isolation*, op.cit. esp. pp 107–158 and sources cited for detailed discussion. Geldenhuys clearly views 'constellation' proposals as overambitious, and he deprecates 'communist bogey' thinking as inaccurate and misleading for analysts and politicians.

11. For a standard description of SACU see D. Hudson, 'Botswana's Membership in the SACU' in C. Harvey (ed), *Papers On The Economy of Botswana*, Heinemann, London, 1981. But c.f. sources at note 14 as at the time Hudson still believed membership to benefit Botswana.

12. J. Stephens, 'Rate Cutting And The Presentation Of Dependence: South Africa's Response To Transport Initiatives In SADCC', conference paper, December 1985, publication pending.

13. *Ibid.* However, if the rand continues to recover (from a low of US$ 0.35 in late 1985 to US$ 0.46 in late February 1986, according to foreign exchange quotations in the *International Herald Tribune* and *Financial Times*), further rand cuts will be needed to preserve this advantage.

14. Manuscript studies by P. Selwyn and R.H. Green (Swaziland) and P. Selwyn (Botswana) for 1966–1976. A Botswana study prepared for a 1981 SACU meeting ('Estimate of Duty Content of Botswana's Imports') arrives at a no gain–no loss estimate. J.S. Gray and S.G. Houhlo, 'The Direct Duty Content of Lesotho's Imports', Ford Research Project Paper No. 1, Roma, 1978, shows a tax gain but at the cost of an 8.5 per cent higher average import cost (so that world sourcing and constant tax revenue would still allow lower user prices).

15. See Loubser, op. cit; J. Stephens, op. cit.

16. See SADCC, *Overviews* (to annual consultative conference), 1981–1986 SADCC, Gaborone. See also *ACR*, 1981–82 and 1984–85, chapters on southern African economic co-operation by R.H. Green, Africana, London.

17. Personal communications to authors from enterprise, transport and government officials.

18. See 'Constellation, Association, Liberation: The Struggle for Southern African Development Coordination' by R.H. Green, *ACR*, 1979–80, op. cit.

19. SAFTO interview by D. Cammack, August 1984; *Financial Mail (FM)*, 12 April 1985.

20. See J. Stephens, op. cit.

21. Mozambique has since struck back. New special contract rates are being negotiated with Zimbabwe exporters. These are effectively to be payable in US$ but with a set rand/dollar conversion rate so as to remove the risk of currency fluctuation for the exporter. As of January 1986 this counter-attack appeared to be regaining ground lost as early as 1983.

22. See J. Stephens, op. cit; SADCC, *Macro-Economic Survey 1986*, Gaborone, 1986; A. Rusinga 'SA Firms "Thwarting Freighting In SADCC" ', *Business Herald*, 30 January 1986, and related leader, 31 January 1986.

23. *Ibid.*

24. Shown by trade and transport data from the Zambia Central Statistical

Office in *Monthly Digest of Statistics,* Lusaka. See also J. Stephens, op. cit. On transport see also Geldenhuys, *Diplomacy of Isolation*, pp 271–272 for a South African account of the background to Zambia's reversion to using SATS routes and ports.

25. For example, Mineworkers' Union chairman, Timothy Walamba, defended imports from South Africa, indeed called for more purchases, saying: 'Much as we have to help our brothers and sisters still under racist regimes, this should not be at the expense of our own people' (*Daily Mail*, 29 December 1983). This is a grimly ironic tribute to South Africa's public relations since its consumer goods are in general more expensive in Lusaka than local or Zimbabwean products.

26. Loubser, op. cit; Geldenhuys, op. cit.

27. J. Stephens, op. cit. Port Elizabeth in particular would be moribund without copper and other metals and concentrates from Zambia, Zaire, and to a lesser extent, Zimbabwe.

28. Loubser, op. cit.

29. See Merle Lipton, *Capitalism and Apartheid: South Africa 1910–84*, Temple Smith/Gower, London, 1985. Lipton may well overstate the degree of conflict between big business and *apartheid* but her case as to the weakness of high capitalism's political influence is compelling.

30. Carol B. Thompson, *Challenge to Imperialism, The Frontline States in the Liberation of Zimbabwe*, Harare, Zimbabwe Publishing House and Boulder, Westview Press, 1985, Chapter 4.

31. Samora Machel, closing speech at SADCC summit, in Gaborone, July 1984, quoted in *Agência de Informação de Moçambique (AIM)* Bulletin, No. 97, July 1984, p 12.

32. Among many others which document colonialism in southern Africa see Barry Munslow, *Mozambique: The Revolution and Its Origins*, London, Longman, 1983; Gerald Bender, *Angola under the Portuguese*, Los Angeles, University of California Press, 1978.

33. Ann Seidman, H. Ndoro, B. Zwizwai, G. Austin, J. Oforma, 'Transnational Corporations and the Sugar Trade: The Zimbabwe Case', (mimeo) Economics Department, University of Zimbabwe, November 1982, p 4.

34. Robin Palmer, *Land and Racial Domination in Rhodesia*, Berkeley, University of California Press, 1977; Roger Riddell, *From Rhodesia to Zimbabwe: The Land Question*, London, Catholic Institute for International Relations (CIIR), 1978; *The Herald* (Harare), 1 December 1984.

35. Ann Seidman, 'A Development Strategy for Zimbabwe', (mimeo), Economics Department, University of Zimbabwe, 1982, p 1.

36. Michael Sefali, speech at SADCC conference, Harare, 30 January 1986.

37. SADCC, *Overview*, Harare, 30–31 January 1986, p 12.

38. SADCC, *Transport and Communications*, Harare, 30–31 January 1986, pp 6, 10, 12.

39. SADCC, *Food and Agriculture*, Harare, 30–31 January, Appendices B under each section. Botswana, Lesotho, Malawi and Zimbabwe all co-

ordinate different sectors of agriculture. See note 42.

40. Reginald Herbold Green, 'Economic Liberation and Economic Survival, SADCC 1980–84', (mimeo), p 8.

41. SADCC, *Food and Agriculture,* Mbabane, 31 Jan – 1 Feb 1985, p 38.

42. The sectors assigned to each country are:

Angola – Energy

Botswana – Agricultural Research, Animal Disease Control

Lesotho – Soil and Water Conservation, Tourism

Malawi – Fisheries, Forestry, Wildlife

Mozambique – Transportation and Communication

Swaziland – Manpower Training

Tanzania – Industry

Zambia – Mining, Southern Africa Development Fund

Zimbabwe – Agriculture, Food Security

43. SADCC, *Industry,* Mbabane, 31 January – 1 February 1985.

44. Ibid, pp 20–21, 33.

45. *The Herald,* 28 November 1983.

46. Barry Munslow *et al,* 'Effects of World Recession and Crisis on SADCC', (mimeo), Review of African Political Economy Conference, University of Keele, September 1984, p 16.

47. Personal interview, SADCC Lusaka Conference, January 1984.

48. D.G. Clarke, 'Economic Linkages in Southern Africa', (mimeo), Geneva, April 1982, p 25.

49. SADCC, *Overview,* Mbabane, 31 January – 1 February 1985, p 4.

50 *African Business,* January 1985.

51. *The Herald,* 5 October 1984.

52. Food and Agricultural Organization, United Nations, *SADCC Agriculture toward 2000,* Rome 1984, pp 7, 8.

53. Interviews in Swaziland and in Mozambique with SADCC officials, March 1984.

54. Interview of Pedro Figueiredo, SATCC Technical Unit, Maputo, 28 March 1984.

55. SADCC, *Programme of Action, Annual Report 1984–1985, p 6.*

56. SADCC, *Industry,* op. cit , p 42.

57. Julius Nyerere, speech at Gaborone SADCC Summit, 6 July 1984, quoted in *Africa Research Bulletin–Economic, Financial, Technical,* Vol. 21, No. 6, 31 July 1984, p 7327.

58. SADCC Agricultural Ministers, 'Response to Policies in Agriculture and Rural Development, prepared by the Nordic Countries, February 1984', Maseru, September 1984.

59. Thandika Mkandawire, 'SADCC: Problems and Prospects', paper presented at conference on Regional Development in Canada and Southern Africa, University of Zimbabwe, 16 February 1984.

60. The value added requirement for goods to be considered from PTA country origin is 45 per cent. For 'goods of particular importance to the

economic development of members', the requirement is reduced to 25 per
cent; for 'goods currently in short supply', it is 30 per cent. Further, Clause (v)
(bb) states 'the goods must have been imported into the member states and
have not undergone a process of substantial transformation but in the opinion
of the Council shall nevertheless be deemed to have undergone a process of
substantial transformation and are contained in a list to be known as 'List B'.
Once a specific product is included in ...'List B', the exporter does not need to
do any calculation unless it is specifically required.' 'Protocol on the Rules of
Origin for products to be traded between the Member States of the PTA',
quoted in *CZI Industrial Review,* Harare, October 1984, pp 19–21.
61. Duncan Innes, *Anglo American and the Rise of Modern South Africa,*
London, Heinemann Educational Books' and New York, Monthly Review
Press, 1984.
62. Peter Mmusi, opening address at SADCC Council of Ministers, Mbabane,
31 January – 1 February 1985.
63. Reginald Green, op. cit., p 18; Joseph Hanlon, *Progress, Projects, Prospects,*
Special Report No. 182, London, Economist Intelligence Unit, 1984, p 20.
64. 'The costs of Destabilization of Member States of SADCC', reprinted as
Annex B, *Overview* (to Harare annual conference), SADCC, Gaborone, 1986.
65. Specifically endorsed by SADCC chairman, Peter Mmusi, in his opening
statement to Harare annual conference, 30 January 1986.
66. See 'Economic Sanctions against South Africa' series op. cit; *Sanctions
against South Africa,* CIIR, London, 1985; R.H. Green, 'Economic Sanctions
Against South Africa: Some Notes on Problematics and Potentialities'
UNA/Anti-Apartheid Conference, 'Frontline States and South Africa's
Policies of Aggression and Destabilisation', 29 February 1984, available from
CIIR.
67. By the Nordic states, Commonwealth states, European Economic
Community (EEC) and even the United States.
68. For example, in 1985, Alfa Romeo, Peugot and Renault shut down their
South African operations and Ford merged its subsidiary into an Anglo-
controlled firm retaining a minority interest. In August 1985, Apple decided
to cease selling computers in South Africa, while in 1986 Svenskt Sta ceased
buying South African manganese, citing governmental recommendations and
its own 'fairly strong opinion in favour of reducing ties with South Africa'.
69. No real agreement has been reached. The mediator – Swiss Banker, Fritz
Leutwiler – has proposed a compromise rolling foward of 95 per cent of the
$14 billion due in 1985 to 1 April 1987 at a one per cent interest penalty, with
renewal thereafter contingent on progress toward abolishing *apartheid* as well
as on financial balance. In the meantime, the improved current account
balance and halted debt service have raised the rand, leading Reserve Bank
governor, Gerhard De Kock, to quip 'Prepare to meet thy boom'. But with
both unemployment and inflation at record levels, there is little prospect of
significant recovery. See also note 2, MaFarland op. cit.
70. See sources cited at note 66, especially R. H. Green, *South Africa: The*

Impact of Sanctions on Southern African Economies and R.J. Davies, *Trade Sanctions and Regional Impact in Southern Africa*, No. 3 No. 9 IUEF series.

71. See press reports such as 'Human flotsam at Botha's mercy', *Sunday Times*, London, 4 August 1985; 'Unemployment in SA strengthens dismissal threats', *Zambia Daily Mail*, Lusaka, 6 June 1985.

72. *Record*, SADCC, Gaborone, 1986.

73. See chairman's opening statement, *Overview*, conference communique, Harare annual conference, 30–31 January, 1986.

74. As amply demonstrated by South Africa's January 1986 blockade.

CHAPTER 10

1. James A. Michener, *The Covenant*, New York, Fawcett Crest, 1980, pp 1203–1204.

2. Ibid., p 1227.

3. For more detail on the period 1960–1980, see chapters 5 to 8 in William Minter, *King Solomon's Mines Revisited*, New York, Basic Books, 1986. A useful brief summary, focused on South Africa, is Thomas Karis, 'United States Policy toward South Africa', in Gwendolen Carter and Patrick O'Meara, eds, *Southern Africa: The Continuing Crisis*, Bloomington, Indiana University Press, 1982.

4. See the text in Mohamed El-Khawas and Barry Cohen, eds, *The Kissinger Study of Southern Africa*, Westport, CT, Lawrence Hill, 1976.

5. National Archives, G Mennen Williams papers, 19 October 1964.

6. Study Commission on US Policy Toward Southern Africa, *Time Running Out,* Berkeley, University of California Press, 1981, p xxii.

7. William J. Foltz, *Elite Opinion on US Policy Toward Africa*, New York, Council on Foreign Relations, 1979, pp 20–21: *Africa News*, 25 May, 1979.

8. Laurence I. Barrett, *Gambling with History: Reagan in the White House*, Harmondsworth, Penguin, 1984, p 61.

9. Kevin Danaher, *The Political Economy of US Policy towards South Africa*, Ph D dissertation, University of California, Santa Cruz, 1982, p 5.

10. Donald de Kieffer, whose law firm had received as much as $2.5 million for lobbying for South Africa from 1974 to 1979, became special counsel in the office of the president's trade representative after the election, where he played a role in loosening restrictions on South African trade. Replacing de Kieffer's firm as the major lobbyist for South Africa was the law firm of former Reagan campaign manager John Sears, at a rate of $500 000 a year. Another former Reagan campaign manager, Stuart Spencer, picked up a $12 500-a-month contract to lobby for the South Africans on Namibian issues. Marion Smoak and Carl Shipley, who from 1980 ran the US-SWA Trade and Cultural Council, were also prominent in Republican Party circles.

By 1985 the panoply of South African agents, which also included the Democrat-connected law firm of Smathers, Hickey and Riley and right-wing black lobbyist William Keyes, had an annual budget of well over $2 million. And Christopher Lehmann, brother of the secretary of the navy, had left his post at the National Security Council to handle a $600 000 Unita account for Black, Manafort, Stone and Kelly, where partner Paul Manafort had served as national political director for Reagan's 1984 campaign. See *Africa News,* 16 December 1985 and 24 February, 1986.

11. The article is reprinted in Jeane J. Kirkpatrick, *Dictatorships and Double Standards,* New York, Simon and Schuster, 1982. On Kirkpatrick see also the article by Seymour Finger in *Foreign Affairs,* Winter 1983/84.

The neo-conservatives, who claimed a liberal heritage, were led by Norman Podhoretz, editor of *Commentary* magazine and author of the anti-communist manifesto, *The Present Danger.*

Kirkpatrick's mission was populated by ideological soul mates, such as Kenneth Adelman, who set out his right-wing views in a 1980 book *African Realities*, and Carl Gershman, head of the militantly anti-communist Social Democrats-USA and a long-time prominent backer of Jonas Savimbi in Angola. At the State Department, she could count on allies such as Norman Podhoretz's son-in-law Elliot Abrams, who started out as assistant secretary for international organization in 1981 and later moved to the State Department human rights post. Kirkpatrick and her colleagues at the UN mission showed little respect for UN majority views on African issues, and indeed hardly disguised their antagonism to the institution as such.

12. On Casey see Philip Taubman, 'Casey and his C.I.A. on the Rebound', in *The New York Times Magazine,* 16 January 1983 and Louis Wolf, 'The "Cyclone" Moves In at Langley', in *Covert Action Information Bulletin,* April 1981.

13. On Haig see Roger Morris, *Haig: The General's Progress,* New York, Playboy Press, 1982; Alexander M. Haig, Jr., *Caveat,* New York, Macmillan, 1984. The comment by Norman Podhoretz is from *The New York Times,* 23 December 1980.

14. The significance of the mineral resources of southern Africa and the area's strategic significance was a favourite propaganda theme of South Africa and of the far right. See the analysis by Larry W. Bowman, 'The Strategic' Significance of South Africa to the United States: An Appraisal and Policy Analysis' *African Affairs* 81, 1982: and my review of several publications on the subject in *Africa News,* 13 October 1980. The topic is to a large extent a red herring, however, since whatever the strategic importance of the region, the question remains whether US interests are best served by alliance with the South African regime.

15. Seymour M. Hersh, *The Price of Power : Kissinger in the Nixon White House,* New York, Summit Books, 1983, pp 38–39. One of Allen's tasks for Portugal was to deny the reports of the Wiriyamu massacres in Mozambique in 1972, which he termed a Czech disinformation scheme. See *Mother Jones,* November 1980 and the syndicated Jack Anderson column of 17 December 1981.

16. On Clark see Steven R. Weisman, 'The Influence of William Clark', in *The New York Times Magazine,* 14 August 1983.

17. Neither Shultz nor McFarlane were innocent of 'hard-line' views on the Middle East or Central America, for example. But on Africa policy the two were generally seen as more realistic and open to negotiations than their predecessors.

Haig's downfall, when it came, was not precipitated by policy differences so much as by his imperious manner and personal conflicts with others in the administration. Nevertheless, his replacement in June 1982 by George Shultz was generally taken as a gain for 'moderate' Establishment views. President of the multinational Bechtel Corporation and former secretary of the treasury, Shultz was a man with a conciliatory manner who was comfortable with 'pragmatic' solutions when necessary. The ideologists might balk at doing business with or negotiating with communists and revolutionaries while, fighting against them. But Shultz was a more sophisticated conservative open to a variety of tactics and even to compromise, when it seemed the most advantageous thing to do.

When Clark resigned in October 1983 to take over the Department of the Interior, he was replaced by his deputy, Robert McFarlane. McFarlane, a former Marine Corps officer, had a reputation as an effective administrator. In a *New York Times* profile of October 1982, he was described as a 'hard-liner' but 'also a realist'. The far right was not happy with his appointment.

On Shultz, see B. Gwertzman, 'The Shultz Method', in *The New York Times Magazine*, 2 January 1983, on McFarlane see Leslie H. Gelb, 'Taking Charge: The Rising Power of National Security Adviser McFarlane', in *New York Times Magazine*, 26 May 1985.

18. See Chester A. Crocker and William H. Lewis, 'Missing Opportunities in for the '80s' in *Freedom at Issue*, No-Dec, 1980; Chester Crocker, 'South point of view include Chester A. Crocker et al., 'Southern Africa: A U.S. Policy for the '80s', in *Freedom at Issue*, Nov-Dec, 1980; Chester Crocker, 'South Africa: Strategy for change', *Foreign Affairs*, Winter 1980 and Chester Crocker, 'African Policy in the 1980s', *Washington Quarterly*, Summer 1980. For Crocker's early views on Rhodesia see *From Rhodesia to Zimbabwe: The Fine Art of Transition*, Washington, CSIS Monograph, 1977.

19. Jeffrey Davidow, *A Peace in Southern Africa*, Boulder, Westview, 1984, provides an extended analysis of the negotiations along these lines, from the point of view of a State Department observer.

20. Crocker and Lewis, op. cit., pp 146–147.

21. Chester Crocker et al., 'United States Policy Towards Africa', in *Issue*, Fall–Winter 1982.

22. Merle Lipton, 'British Investment in South Africa: Is Constructive Engagement Possible', *South African Labour Bulletin*, October 1976; Samuel P. Huntington, 'Reform and Stability in a Modernizing, Multi-Ethnic Society', *Politikon*, December 1981.

23. Wisner had served as a key aid to both Kissinger and Cyrus Vance in southern African negotiations, and was appointed by President Carter as ambassador to Zambia in 1979.

He also derived some status in Washington from prominent family connections. His father, Allen Dulles's right-hand man in CIA covert operations, had co-ordinated the programme to bring ex-Nazis to the US after World War II. The senior Wisner's last post had been CIA station chief in London (1959–1962), before his retirement and suicide in 1965. Wisner's stepfather was the experienced Washington columnist Clayton Frichey. Frichey's son-in-law, *Fortune* editor Herman Nickel, was appointed US ambassador to South Africa in February 1982.

24. See documents in *TransAfrica News Report,* August 1981.

25. SABC, 5 March 1981.

26. Press conference, 28 August 1981.

27. Chester Crocker, 'Regional Strategy for Southern Africa', address before the American Legion in Honolulu, Hawaii, 29 August 1981.

28. *Wall Street Journal,* 6 May 1980.

29. *Guardian*, London, 26 March 1981.

30. *AfriqueAsie,* 1 February 1982.

31. *Washington Post,* 23 January 1982.

32. *Africa News,* 7 December 1981.

33. *Africa News,* 22 October 1984.

34. Ibid. On nuclear ties see *Washington Notes on Africa,* Summer 1982, Winter 1983; and *Africa News,* 27 September 1982; 26 September 1983 and 8 April 1985.

35. *Africa News,* 6 December 1982; 13 June 1983.

36. *Africa News,* 9 May 1983; 22 October 1984.

37. See *Africa News*, 8 April 1985; 20 May 1985.

38. Helen Kitchen, 'The Eagleburger Contribution', *CSIS Africa Notes,* 30. July 1983.

39. See, for example, William Minter, 'Major Themes in Mozambican Foreign Relations, 1975–1977', *Issue,* Spring, 1978, and 'Setting the Terms for Pretoria', *Africa News,* 17 March 1980.

40. See summary statistics maintained and updated by the American Committee on Africa (ACOA), and *ACOA Action News* issues during 1985.

41. See *Washington Notes on Africa* and other reports by the Washington Office on Africa during 1985.

42. Sanford Ungar and Peter Vale, 'Why Constructive Engagement Failed', *Foreign Affairs,* Winter 1985/86; and Michael Clough, 'Beyond Constructive Engagement', *Foreign Policy,* Winter 1985/1986.

43. A US State Department financed study in 1984, for example, introduced questions about divestment to factory workers by comments implying the workers would lose their jobs, and not surprisingly found they were generally opposed. See Michael O. Sutcliffe and Paul A. Wellings, 'Black Worker "Attitudes" and Disinvestment: A Critique of the Schlemmer Report', in *TransAfrica Forum,* Fall, 1985. A Gallup poll in 1985 (London *Sunday Times,* 1 September 1985) asked if 'other countries are right or wrong to impose economic sanctions unless South Africa agrees to get rid of the apartheid system'. Urban blacks, three to one, thought it was right.

44. See William Minter, 'The Cold War and the Winds of Change,' in *Christianity and Crisis,* 30 September 1985.